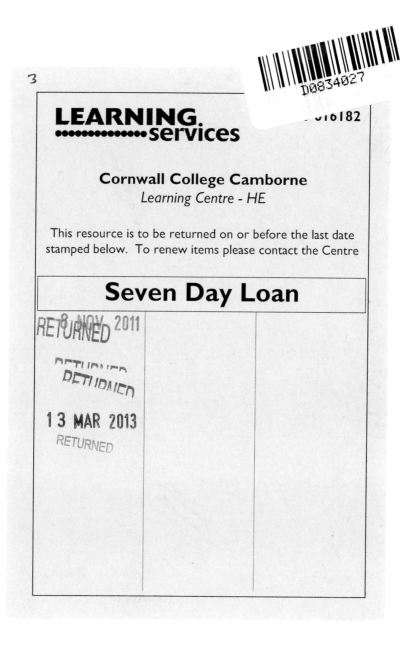

One for the Girls!

The Pleasures and Practices of Reading Women's Porn

Clarissa Smith

One for the Girls!

The Pleasures and Practices of Reading Women's Porn

Clarissa Smith

intellect Bristol, UK / Chicago, USA

First Published in the UK in 2007 by
Intellect Books, PO Box 862, Bristol BS99 1DE, UK

First published in the USA in 2007 by
Intellect Books, The University of Chicago Press, 1427 E. 60th Street, Chicago, IL 60637, USA

A catalogue record for this book is available from the British Library.

Cover Design: Gabriel Solomons
Copy Editor: Holly Spradling
Typesetting: Mac Style, Nafferton, E. Yorkshire

ISBN 978-1-84150-164-2

Printed and bound in Great Britain by The Cromwell Press.

Contents

List of Illustrations

ACKNOWLEDGEMENTS

Any book is a labour of love and the product of the generosity of friends, individuals and academic good Samaritans. First and foremost my thanks to all those who helped me with this project, especially Alison, Anne, Christine, David, Diane, Eve, Gill, James, Jane, Julie, Kate, Laura, Mia, Michele, Susan, Tessa who devoted considerable time talking or writing to me. I hope I have repaid your candour with a fair and honest account. Also, my thanks go to Liz Coldwell, Jane Collins, Ruth Corbett, Kitty Doherty, Zak Jane Keir and Jonathan Richards for responding so helpfully to my inquisitions about their work and *For Women* magazine.

My sincere thanks to Dr Martin Barker who was a fantastic supervisor of my DPhil research, a brilliant colleague and now true friend.

I have also had the help and support of friends and colleagues at University of West of England, University of Sussex, Falmouth College of Arts and University of Sunderland, in particular Jayne Armstrong, Jane Arthurs, Kate Brooks, Russell Clarke, Mark Douglas, Alex Goody, Sam Greasley, Jean Grimshaw, Michelle Henning, Jim Hall, Maria Magro, Val Reardon, Niall Richardson, Catherine Spooner, Angela Werndly and Jason Whittaker. Thank you for your kind interest, newspaper cuttings, references, cups of tea, reading and commenting on chapters and offering moral support. Thanks also to Manuel Alvarado, Luke Hockley and John Storey for pushing me into finally writing this book.

Special thanks to my mum, Enid, I wish you were here to see this in print, to my dad, John, for reading chapters and making lovely positive comments and suggestions and to my sister Helen for enduring the terminal embarrassment of the Special Collection at the British Library; Julia & Brian, Sean & Tracey, Yves, Julia, Eliane and Val for friendship and encouragement. To Shane, Hannah and Callula, for wreaking havoc and making sure I was constantly distracted, much love!

Thanks to *For Women* for permission to use images and quotations from the magazine.

Elements of chapters 2, 3, 4, 5 and 6 have previously been published as:

A Perfectly British Business: Stagnation, Change and Continuities on the Top Shelf in Lisa Z.Sigel (ed), *International Exposure: Perspectives on Modern European Pornography 1800–2000*, (New York: Rutgers University Press 2005)

Fellas in Fully Frontal Frolics: Naked Men in *For Women* Magazine in Judith Still (ed), *Men's Bodies* special issue of *Paragraph*, (Edinburgh: Edinburgh University Press 2003)

"They're Ordinary People, Not Aliens from the Planet Sex!" The Mundane Excitements of Pornography for Women, *Journal of Mundane Behavior*, (February 2002), available at http://www.mundanebehavior.org

Talking Dirty in For Women Magazine, in J.Arthurs & J.Grimshaw (eds), *Women's Bodies: Discipline and Transgression*, (London: Cassells, 1997)

Introduction

> In the movement's rhetoric pornography is a code word for vicious male lust. To the objection that some women get off on porn, the standard reply is that this only shows how thoroughly women have been brainwashed by male values. (Willis 1983: 463)

On a cold wet day in 1992 I took refuge in a newsagent and picked up a copy of a new magazine which claimed to speak to me as an intelligent woman with an interest in sex. So began my connection with *For Women* magazine; that encounter came at a time when I was studying for an MA in Women's Studies where pornography featured as a key area of debate for feminists and an area of concern for all women. The seeming contradiction of theorizations of pornography as a field of representation and consumption inimitable to women's experiences of sexuality with the existence of an expensively produced mainstream publication which intended to act as a spur to female sexual arousal was just too interesting to ignore. I was not alone in my purchase, the first issue of *For Women* was reprinted three times to meet demand, a demand fostered in part by the massive coverage of the launch of this 'new women's pornography'.

Throughout the spring of 1992, the press, radio and television debated *For Women* and its rivals. Chat shows invited the male models, editors and contributors to appear and justify the publication to studio audiences. Newspapers featured commentary on the contents and interviews with editors and potential readers. The tabloids were largely in favour: the *Daily Mirror* and the *Sun* both featured double-page spreads with photos of some of the models accompanied by editorial stressing the links between the magazines, dance groups such as the *Chippendales* and the tabloid's own Page 7 Fellas. For both the *Mirror* and the *Sun*, these magazines were 'fun' if a little disappointingly 'limp'. Nonetheless, they were a welcome addition to women's explorations of sexuality: 'At last... the dirty magazine for women' (*Mirror*, April 29 1992: 9).

What Was All the Fuss About?

During the previous twelve months a number of UK publishers investigated the possibility of launching a sexually explicit title for women. The reasons for this were twofold: firstly and probably most importantly, the soft-core market was experiencing hard times: sales were dropping and rival formats were squeezing the magazine sector, while legislation seriously curtailed any room for manoeuvre within the traditional formats of top-shelf publishing. Secondly, developments in popular culture suggested that the time might well be ripe for a movement out of the traditional customer base of men and into targeting women. This might be cited as more evidence of the continuing and unstoppable expansion of pornography into every sphere of UK culture and consumers' willing acceptance, but this book will show that the picture is somewhat more complicated than that. Pornography for women was not a new idea; two titles had previously been launched in the UK: during the 1970s *Playgirl* and *Viva* magazines had tried to emulate the successes of the adult 'lifestyle' magazines *Playboy* and *Penthouse*. Both were unsuccessful in attracting and maintaining the interest of sufficient readers and advertisers to guarantee longevity, and they have subsequently been used as evidence that a mass-produced pornography for women is doomed to failure.[1]

For Women was then a risky project but one that seemed to be worthwhile making. The magazine was launched alongside two sister publications, *Women On Top* and *Women Only*, and joined three rivals – the existing *Playgirl* and two newcomers, *Ludus* and *Bite*. Its publishers, Northern & Shell, were convinced there was a market for a soft-core magazine for women but they weren't sure what format would work, so they published three – covering what they saw as all the possible bases for women: sophisticated sex, cheeky sex and sex for couples. The sister publications and the rivals closed within the year, *For Women* is the only surviving title. Beginning with the hunch that women wanted more than *Cosmopolitan*, *For Women* was a text in search of a readership and it needed to discover exactly what would count as *more*. In searching for a readership it also needed to establish a form of community and continuity: like any other magazine, *FW* needed to keep readers returning. Novelty may have encouraged the initial purchase, but a magazine (even one with avowedly pornographic intentions) needs to also offer a sense of familiarity – *this is territory you know, understand and like*. *FW* began its career as a hybrid using the traditional formats of women's magazines as well as the more 'brazen' attributes of soft-core titles. In labelling itself *For Women*, in offering itself to women as more than *Cosmopolitan*, the magazine appeared to be inviting all women 'wanting more' to enjoy its contents. Of course, the editorial intention was not to speak to *all* women but to a profitable number prepared to take up its proposal to join discussions of sex and sexuality. In an interview with me, founding editor Jonathan Richards described the thinking behind the magazine:

> The whole *FW* concept is not just to take the clothes off the models, the other idea is to address sexual issues in a candid way. I look at *Cosmopolitan*, and it promises all kinds of things on its front cover, but then fails to deliver all of those things once you open it up. This is a good time for us to launch the magazine because

> other women's magazines have been successful with their sex supplements, but we aim to push the boundaries further than they've done, we're trying to demystify the whole sexual process, the whole interaction, and we try and do it in a way which has humour, we try and take away the fear of it. Other publishers tend to promise the earth and then fail to deliver. With *FW*, I think we do deliver because we can be very explicit – look at the guide to semen – it's all there. (Interview: 13.1.94)

Richards's comments suggest that the character of the magazine would appeal to a 'reader personality': women he described as 'bold, intelligent, tough, horny and not afraid of talking about their pleasure in sex.' A glossy, relatively 'up-market' magazine, each issue featured an editorial outlining that month's contents; Girls Talk (Plate 4) and product reviews offered gossip about celebrities, luxury consumer items, health reports, film, TV, music and book reviews; and a Hollywood interview. Fashion and beauty spreads, two further celebrity interviews and a two-page travel feature were also included. The inclusion of these standard features of glossy women's magazines in a publication attempting to sell itself on its sexually explicit content suggests recognition of the uneasiness some women might feel in buying a magazine whose content was entirely sexual. The instantly recognizable elements of more traditional women's magazines eased readers in and indicated to distributors, advertisers, readers and commentators that the magazine was *for* women. When launched, the magazine was accused of disguising its true target audience – gay men. These girlie items, while not necessarily excluding gay men, ensured a more easy fit with 'feminine' interests.

The limiting of these items to the front quarter of *FW* also indicated a desire to make the magazine itself 'safe' – these elements could be perused on the bus, so the magazine did not have to be hidden in a bag until safely home. This hiding of 'naughty' material behind an 'innocent' facade was further illustrated by the limited advertising in the magazine: pages of sex toys, phone-lines and contact ads were strictly confined to two sections in the back half of the magazine; the back cover occupied by a vitamin advertisement and the front cover featured the face of the male celebrity interviewed within.

These items proffered the magazine's invitation to join in a saucy, sexy world, to pamper yourself with 'safe' sexiness: sexy dresses, sexy chocolate, sexy make-up, sexy men. But fantasy and sexual allure were not just located in consumer products or the unobtainable Hollywood idol, feature articles contributed to the possibility of 'ordinary' women as sexual personae. Each issue included up to four feature articles focussing on sexual pleasures, practices and problems. These areas particularly marked *FW* as different to other magazines, not in terms of the subject matter but in the approach to subjects like oral and anal sex, S & M fantasies and realities. Alongside these were interviews with famous women about their sex lives and/or attitudes to sex. Of course, the two features setting the magazine apart from its mainstream rivals were the inclusion of male nudes and sexually explicit stories. These were the items that really caused a fuss! As the *Daily Mirror* put it, 'Not so hard porn', the magazine was assessed in terms of its explicitness and the *Sun* posed the inevitable question that underpins much of the discussion that follows here, 'Are naughty pics of men's bits a turn-on?'

Why Study *For Women*?

This book isn't simply an analysis of a single text. Rather it attempts to marry a number of seemingly incompatible ways of thinking about production, consumption and textual formations to facilitate an engagement in wider debates around pornography including its imputed harmful or liberating effects and notions of pornography as an inherently 'male' form. This book works through a number of perspectives – from the magazine's location within legal and regulatory frameworks to its marketing positioning, its textual format to moments of consumption. I draw on theories of dialogism, media consumption and audience research rather than the feminism, psychoanalysis and effects research which have tended to dominate questions of sexually explicit representations. I do this in order to open up debate regarding female sexuality and the production and consumption of 'pornography for women'. *For Women* is used as a case study to show that pornography is not simply a set of ideas operating on minds too weak to resist but that, as with any media text, it must establish a relationship between itself and its readers, in this case, to affirm their right to talk about sex, to share information and ideas about sex, to acknowledge the possibilities of pleasure and danger in sexual activities for women and perhaps most importantly to offer sexual stimulation. In this respect, *For Women* offers a sexual imaginary, a way of thinking about the social and lived place of sex.

In most studies of pornography it is usual to offer some definitions: what is 'pornography'?; how does it differ from 'erotica' and what is its relationship to the 'obscene'? The particular answers given by individual authors to these questions are intimately linked to the further development and substance of their thesis. A literature review often results in an extremely confusing array of different definitions that hardly seem to explicate any one instance of 'pornography' let alone the umbrella category 'the pornographic'. Jennifer Wicke has suggested that

> Pornography jumps many disciplinary boundaries and critical barriers in its translation into metapornography, a discourse for all seasons. Many of the implicit assumptions about pornography in feminist theory and criticism have affinities with debates further afield, especially with considerations of consumption and mass culture often unacknowledged in what seem to be much more pressing matters of sexual politics. The subterranean connections are there, however, in myriad guises, especially when pornography is set up as an objectifying and commodifying form of patriarchal expression and when more subtle differences between pornography and artistic practices are probed. (1993: 67)

Many accounts of pornography are then, accounts of other areas of concern, social, cultural, economic and political, but the detail gets lost in the need to make generalized claims about 'pornographic' cultures, imaginations and effects. Wicke argues that the study of pornography requires an understanding of it as a genre with

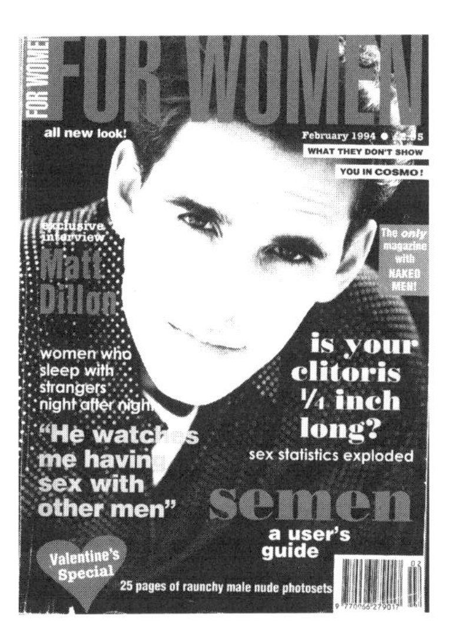

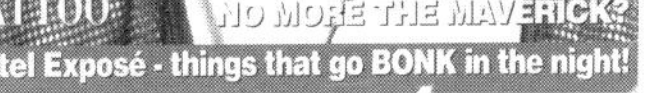

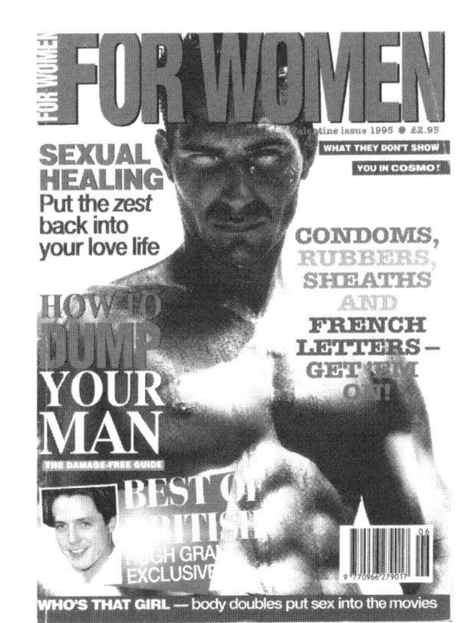

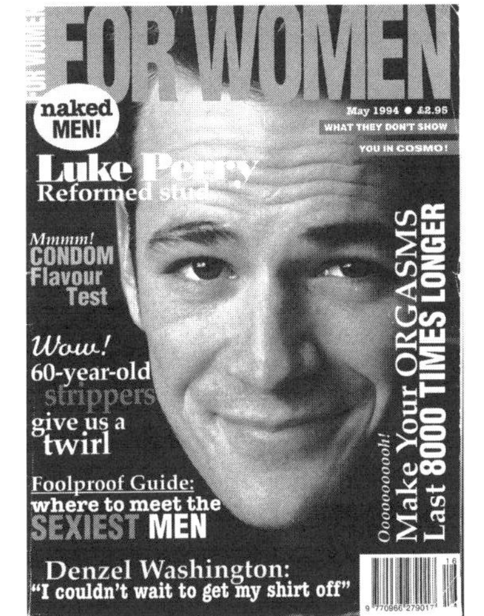

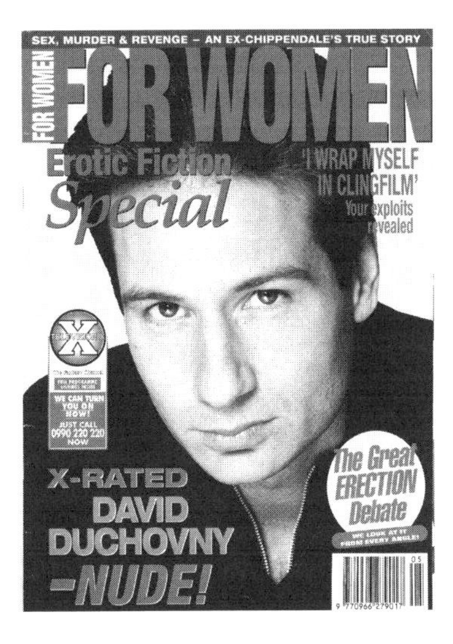

Plate 1. *For Women* covers.

All images by kind permission of *For Women* magazine and Fantasy Publishing.

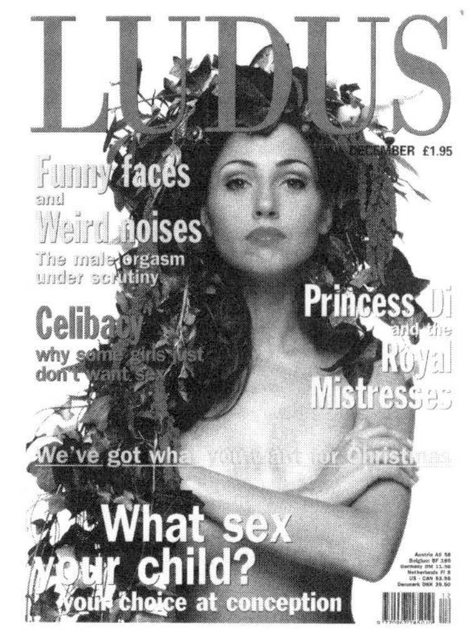

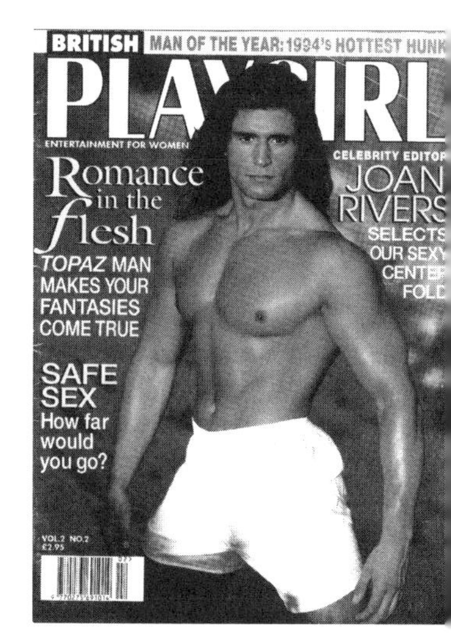

Plate 2. The rivals.

Plate 3. The sister publications.

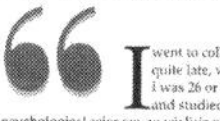

SM has become fashionable of late; designers are even creating fetish outfits for the catwalk. But as Niki Wolf, editor of *Fetish Times* says, SM is as old as the hills: "You can go back to the earliest literature and you'll find references to SM." Niki, at 32, has been into SM for a good many years, and she started *Fetish Times* 18 months ago; its motto is 'celebrating sexual diversity'. "We're interested in all forms of sexual expression," says Niki. She told me all about it

I went to college quite late, when I was 26 or 27, and studied psychological sciences, specialising in sexuality. When I finished, I started writing articles for magazines on the subject. I was writing a news column on the fetish scene and someone approached me and asked if I would edit a fetish mag. That was 18 months ago.

We cover all sorts of subjects — making and starring in your own sex videos, designing dungeons, SM gear for under a fiver, whips and where to get good ones and so on. A very important aspect of the mag is sexual politics — I've just been over to Strasbourg to report on the Spanner Appeal to Europe, which involved a group of men who were heavily into SM and imprisoned for abuse.

I think SM is becoming popular because it's basically really good fun. I like the freedom to explore different aspects of myself. If I'm topping, being dominant, I like the feeling of control and power. I get a buzz out of leading someone through an experience and giving them pleasure; if I'm submitting it's very liberating to hand over the responsibility to someone else. I swap roles, which is quite common.

Trust is incredibly important in SM; you have to be able to trust the person you're playing with. SM is consensually playing with power, power freely given, but because it can involve pain and humiliation it can look like violence. Intercourse without consent is rape, a kiss without consent is disgusting, and SM without consent is violence. But when consent is given, SM becomes a very beautiful sexual experience.

I'm a very active practitioner of everything I preach. I enjoy pain, quite extreme pain sometimes. I'm into humiliation and role play. I like thrashing people — I'm an all round bad girl really. I enjoy body piercing; I get very turned on by it. I don't have any permanent piercing, I do it as part of SM play. I've never pierced anyone's penis but I have had my clitoral hood pierced which was very intense.

> "I enjoy body piercing. I've never pierced anyones penis but I've had my clitoral hood pierced which was very intense"

Finding a partner can be very difficult, but I'm moving in a world in which sex is a major part; everyone is very up front about it and it's something that is talked about a lot. The line between friendship and someone you have sex with is quite blurred for me, as it is for a lot of the people I know, and so if you're talking to a friend about fantasies and you discover that there is something that you both really want to do, it seems fairly obvious to try it together.

The SM scene is not what people think it is; men who are into SM are not violent rapists or sex offenders, all they're looking for is a willing partner. Groups like 'Countdown on Spanner' are actually great places to pick up really nice, gentle, non sexist, enlightened men. There are also men who think they're submissive who can actually be a pain in

Plate 4. *For Women* contained many of the staple features of women's magazines from gossip, through celebrity interviews to problem pages and readers' letters.

GOSSIP

May

interviews

14 **cool hand luke** luke perry talks about sex, love, marriage, madonna and much more!

24 **behind closed doors** denzel washington's just an old-fashioned guy when it comes to sex in the movies

LOVE & SEX

20 **how to make your orgasms last 8000 times longer** our step-by-step guide to sheer bliss

36 **sexual signals** forget what he says, what he does in bed gives much more away

54 **suck it and see** the ultimate condom flavour test

68 **erogenous zones** our foolproof guide: where to hang out to meet the sexiest men

features

40 **sunset strippers** what an eyeful: 60-year-old american burlesque stars give us a twirl

46 **shock waifs** what men really think of small-breasted women — as if we cared

50 **tunnel of love** the grand tour: where to find europe's horniest males

FOR WOMEN May 1994

FASHION

72 **dirty weekend** sexy clothes for undressing

80 **denim revival** summer's best buys in blues

survey results

91 **sexual thoughts** you told us just how often you think sex thoughts

photo sets

28 **natural light** the boy next door — as you've never seen him before

57 **seaside postcards** nostalgic, sepia-tinted images

66 **free naked man!** this issue's man of the month could be yours

82 **aztec gold** a south american legend comes to life

fiction

94 **recovering** another winner in our erotic short story competition

REGULARS

7 **beauty parlour** health and beauty update

8 **girls' talk** news and gossip

93 **survey** tell us if you've been unfaithful

110 **the sexpert** dr andrew stanway on making your own sexy video

119 **this is your sex life** karen krizanovich, the sharon stone of agony aunts

120 **problem page** jan birks helps out

123 **mail shot** your letters to us

124 **travelogue** horny hotels and cheap deals

126 **horoscopes** martine delamere's astrological forecast for the month of may

128 **sexy star sign** this issue: taurus

130 **the last word on sex** novelist simon beckett succumbs to our charm

AIDS complacency

A new study of 12,600 people by condom makers Durex shows that over a third (34%) of heterosexuals believe they are not at risk from HIV, even if they have unprotected sex. A crazy one in 20 respondents (6%) had indulged in unprotected sex with a new partner in the past year. Dumb, or what?

Faking It

Smart girls cheat when it comes to early summer tans — try Bronzing Powder, £4.95, or the Gel Stick, £5.25, from Yardley's Easy Bronze range.

need a lift?

Feeling in need of a pick-me-up in time for a big date or your summer holiday? Try the *Perfector Program*, available now at beauty salons around the country. For face or body, Perfector uses a low frequency micro current to firm, lift and tone. Prices from £35 for a half hour session — phone 0628 532007 for your nearest salon. Our reporter tried a one-hour facial treatment — and promptly fell asleep! — and said she saw the best results two or three days later.

girls' talk

CAN YOU HELP?

MALE ESCORTS

Have you ever used the services of a male escort? Would you like to if you could find one? Touch Productions are currently researching a documentary on the world of male escorts and would like to speak, in the strictest confidence, to anyone who may be able to help with their research. Contact Jamie Simpson, Touch Productions, 14-18 Heddon Street, London W1R 8DP or call him on 071-287 5520.

If RUBBER's your thing, check out Tentacle's designs. Shown here rubber salopettes £77. Send £5 for catalogue and samples: Tentacle, PO Box 2[illegible] Grantham Lincs NG3[illegible] 5RB. Or call 0572 768156 for more in[illegible]

PHEROMONE FACTS

STOP PRESS • Men whose natural pheromones fail to turn on the girls will soon be able to buy a pack containing a human pheromone for sexual attraction. The product, Pheromone Factor, has been developed by Dr George Dodd of Warwick University, and will be available from Interactive Fragrance Technologies by mail order for £30. There's no mention of a money-back offer if the product fails to do the job.

KEEPING IT UP

by Kitty Doherty

You're looking across at your partner of many years. You think back on how you used to get so wound up about him leaving the top off the toothpaste. Nowadays you're grateful if he occasionally cleans his teeth. When was it, you ask yourself, that his fantasy stopped being Saturday night with the woman in the Flake advert and became Sunday lunch with the Oxo mum? When did his breasts get bigger than yours? Wasn't it about the same time that he stopped falling asleep before you came because you'd fall asleep before he started? Suddenly Neil and Babs are warbling on the radio, "you don't bring me flowers anymore..." ►

Plate 5. Humour and sharing...

Jay Kay's Problem page

Jay Kay has given sex advice to everyone from teenagers to grandmas. She studied Sexology at university and did her final year thesis on young men and sexuality. For a candid, honest answer to your problems, write to Jay today

mail shot

STAR LETTER

The sender of our star letter each month receives this suspender cami, worth £36, from Wild Designs.* Please state size (from 8-16) and colour (black or red) when you write!

TRUE confessions

Here's your chance to share your experiences of love and sex with FOR WOMEN!

Plate 6 (above). Readers' talk to *For Women*:
The problem page
Mail shot page
Invitation to contribute.

THE GREAT ERECTION DEBATE

who's throwing cold water on our enjoyment?

As Britain's only sex magazine for women we think it's only natural that we should be able to show you men looking sexually aroused and ready for action. But we can't. So what we want to know is who exactly is denying us this pleasure and why? In our six page special we take a look at erections from all angles - what the law says, what the newsagents say, what the politicians say, what we at For Women say what a stack of celebrities have to say... and then we want to know what you have to say...

Obscene Publications Act, 1959

CHAPTER 66

Obscene Publications Act, 1959

ARRANGEMENT OF SECTIONS

An Act to amend the law relating to the publication of obscene matter; to provide for the protection of literature; and to strengthen the law concerning pornography. [29th July, 1959]

BE it enacted by the Queen's most Excellent Majesty, by and with the advice and consent of the Lords Spiritual and Temporal, and Commons, in this present Parliament assembled, and by the authority of the same, as follows:—

Plate 7 (left). Campaigning – the general erection campaign.

FLYING HIGH

John Travolta's acting career was in grave danger of crashing and burning badly — until Quentin Tarantino stepped in, that is. *Pulp Fiction* single-handledly restored Travolta's credibility — the swarthy actor looks set to provoke a similarly fevered response with some sure-fire hit movies for 1996. *Brad Ritzer* caught up with the man whose career is staying alive

I've been lonely for too many years, now I know it's time to embrace life

Saturday Night Fever

Blow Out

Plate 8. The star interview.

its own strategies of production, distribution and consumption (1993: 68). She suggests that such recognition will prevent the attempts to subsume texts like Milton's *Paradise Lost* into the category pornography, a problematic assimilation which contributes to the 'reification of pornography into one singular phenomenon' (1993: 79).

Medium is Immaterial

All forms of media technology can be used to produce sexually explicit materials, and, in the drive to define 'pornography' as a category, the medium-specific differences between, for example, video film and the photograph have to be flattened out in order to make the generalized case. Similar slippage occurs across other divisions, for example, when arguments about heterosexual materials are transposed to gay and lesbian porn, or where 'kiddie porn' is used as the example of all pornography's potential as a record of actual abuse. As Corner (1991) comments in his discussion of television, too often researchers fail to recognize that television is a 'formal system and … a social process' (276) leading to a tendency to essentialize the medium. This tendency to unify can be found in many discussions of pornography: indeed often it is a deliberate strategy of analysis in order to expose the supposed uniformity of content as part of a more general theory of effects. For example, Cole suggests that it is the only way to look at the products of the sex industry:

> … pornographs [*sic*] should be seen in large numbers. As a group, they all tend to look the same. This fact challenges the wishful and sometimes willful [*sic*] thinking of observers who claim that pornography reveals an astonishing range of sexual possibilities. It's difficult to see any such range when pornography presents women many times more often than men; pornographs, on their face, don't even manage to take into account both genders, let alone the presumed range of sexual practices. If pornographers were as imaginative about sexuality as they are about how they can subordinate in new and different ways, the discussion might be quite different. (1989: 31)

Thus, differing grammars across forms of sexually explicit material become less important than the crude measure of whether or not one gender appears more often than the other. Differing levels of address, referentiality, intertextuality or discourse are not sufficient to complicate the analysis of 'pornography' whatever medium produces it, because 'gender' and 'gender inequalities' are the sole measurement of what counts as 'pornography'. (Dworkin 1981; Dworkin and MacKinnon 1988; Kappeler 1986). This 'concentration' or 'distillation' of the 'essence of pornography' distorts the ways in which we should or could understand the uses of individual forms of sexually explicit materials in all their specific contexts and possible meanings. The means by which one delineates this or that material as examples of the 'pornographic' are also obscured by the ways in which the generic term is used to express dismay at many different phenomena – as Gayle Rubin observes:

> Due to the stigma historically associated with sexually explicit materials, we already use the words 'obscene' and 'pornographic' to express many kinds of

> intense revulsion. For example, war may be 'obscene' and Reagan's policies 'pornographic'. However, neither is customarily found in adult bookstores. (1993: 37)

This tendency, found in theory as well as 'common sense' discourse, to produce 'pornography' as genre and form without boundaries has contributed to an avoidance of the material elements of its production and reception in favour of its social role as the repository for all things abhorrent. Nowhere is the level of political abhorrence so apparent as in feminist anti-pornography writings with their focus on the 'harms of pornography'. Williams has suggested that this 'rhetoric of abhorrence has impeded discussion of almost everything but the question of whether pornography deserves to exist at all.' (1990: 5) The category 'pornography' functions socially on a number of levels, but the tendency within radical or anti-pornography feminism has been to refuse distinctions between forms of sexually explicit materials.[2]

For writers such as Kappeler, drawing on Marxist theory as well as anti-pornography feminism, there are no distinctions between forms of 'pornography': it is produced within a system, capitalism, which privileges the powers of patriarchy. Thus all products, whether 'erotica' or 'pornography', are symbolic representations of that power and the means by which that power is maintained and reproduced. Others, like Kendrick (1987), argue that in a censored world, censorship being the prerogative of the powerful, all pornography is subject to that power and must conform to its dictates in similar ways leading to the expression of the forbidden and the transgressive characteristics of pornography. Thus the genre's homogeneity is either produced by the power it wishes to support/sustain or by the power imposed upon it.

It is this 'dialectic of power' which Williams argues has turned 'all histories of pornography into histories of the legal battles fought in the wake of relatively recent laws against obscenity.' (1990: 14) For this reason, she suggests,

> The very marginality of pornography within culture has led us to argue only about whether pornography, like sex, should be liberated or repressed. And the fact that, as with sex, we simultaneously take for granted its 'obvious' definition – assuming for example, that it is either a liberating pleasure or an abusive power – has only confused matters. (1990: 14)

The rehearsal of a 'history of pornography' is not my intention in this book: instead I focus upon one publication produced by one of the major UK publishers of soft core. This focus will, of course, require that I examine issues which relate to the current state of the marketplace in all its complexity: legal, economic and social, but it is not intended to offer a definitive study of UK (or wider) pornography. This position can be defended by noting Williams' comments on the scarcity of writing about 'actual texts' (1990: 29),[3] which has led to the polarization of the debates such that pornography is either totally divisible from other forms of cultural production or is entirely coterminous with other forms. Williams observes that 'Pornography may not be special, but it does have a specificity distinct from other genres' (1990: 29). That specificity lies in its representational intention to arouse its viewers/readers sexually, but within the umbrella category there are myriad differences in the forms of representation on offer. In the discussion which follows, I call *For Women* pornography, but it will become clear that the magazine belongs to 'soft core' rather than 'hard core': its photographic representations owe more to the traditions of male pin-up than explicit representations of actual sexual intercourse and yet within the legal and cultural frameworks of soft-core publishing in the UK, it is labelled and marketed as 'pornographic' because it speaks of sex and sexual fantasy.

It is this primary intention to sexually arouse its consumers that sets pornography apart from other cultural forms even as it might share some of the representational tropes or draw upon narrative structures and themes of, for example, mainstream Hollywood film or the photographic arts. Anne Barr Snitow (1984b) has argued persuasively that Harlequin (Mills & Boon in the UK) romances can be regarded as a form of pornography but their sexual potential is disguised: hidden beneath tales of exotic locales and romance told with a pace and rhythm that can facilitate erotic responses. Unlike pornography, however, the romance novel does not overtly state its intention to sexually arouse its readerships. Likewise, women's magazines have recently been considered, by more conservative observers, as bordering on the overly explicit, however, they still retain their educational/informational focus such that their sexual 'pleasure zones' remain undeclared.

The labelling of films like the *Death Wish* series, *Basic Instinct* and *Dressed to Kill* as pornographic ignores their membership of distinct filmic genres with codes and conventions of their own. While it is possible that these films may arouse some viewers, it has yet to be proven that most viewers approach them *as* pornography with the primary expectation of sexual arousal/release.[4] The anti-censorship position which attempts to contradict the 'special status' accorded to pornography by those opposed to its continued presence, traces links to other cultural products but actually contributes to a further obfuscation of the uses and various forms of 'pornography' proper as a genre. Commenting on Annette Kuhn's (1985) analysis of *Dressed to Kill*, Williams criticizes her tendency to swerve away from pornograph*y* to the pornograph*ic*. In ignoring the specificities of the pornography text: the specific elements of its production, content, codes and conventions – precisely those elements that make 'hard core' hard-core pornography rather than a slasher/horror film – remain unexamined.

Williams' history of the development of hard-core movies in the United States is a fascinating analysis of the form's evolution from early stag films to a more 'sophisticated' examination of sexual pleasures through narrative devices. The 'frenzy of the visible' made possible by the film camera's all-seeing eye allows for the examination of sexuality and pleasures in ways not necessarily possible in the magazine photograph or the telephone sex line. Therefore we need to be aware that the pornography industry (if it can be categorized as one industry) may well have a singular intention to arouse its viewers, readers, listeners for profit, but each medium it employs offers particular kinds of sexual arousal to its users and cannot help but offer some further exploration of the meanings and possibilities of sex.

Thus in her exploration of the academy's fascination for pornography, Wicke suggests that the refusal to engage with all the various specificities of pornography's different forms may be because some forms are more obviously pathological and therefore more interesting than others and fit more easily into models of consumption which stress 'satiety, passivity, absorption' (1993: 68); these pleasures being particularly problematic for observers of 'pornography'. Much of the literature regarding pornography is generated in the United States and quite properly takes the American experience as its subject matter. The problem arises when definitions that may be appropriate there are imported wholesale to the UK case.[5] As Thompson (1994) has indicated, the legally available products of the UK pornography market are no match for the explicit materials on sale in the US. There, soft core encompasses depictions of actual sexual activity between two or more people and hard core is reserved for more minority pleasures/'perversions' (1994: 2). Discussions of 'pornography' often conflate the very real differences between the types of material available here in the UK[6] with those in the States. These objections do not, however, address some of the more substantive claims of 'porn-theory', and they are not offered as a means of suggesting that the British case is less 'awful' than that abroad.[7] Rather, I draw attention to the differences between the legal systems of the UK and the US that have significant impacts upon the content and form of sexually explicit materials.

The expedient concentration of 'pornography' in theoretical/analytical frameworks is also reflected and constructed in the various legal restraints placed upon sexually explicit materials. Currently, the UK 'pornography' industry is primarily regulated under the provisions of five laws: the *1959 Obscene Publications Act* which prohibits depiction of actual sexual activity and any other images deemed obscene; the *1984 Video Recordings Act* which ensures all video films are subject to the classification procedures of the British Board of Film Certification – an 18R certificate can be given for depictions of simulated sex to be sold only in sex shops;[8] the *1876 Customs Consolidation Act* which focuses on and prohibits the importation of 'indecent' materials; the distribution of indecent or obscene materials via the post is prohibited by the *1953 Post Office Act* and the *1978 Child Protection Act* which makes it an offence to produce or possess any material featuring any sexual depiction of a child. The definitions underpinning these laws are notoriously slippery: [9] what constitutes the obscene and indecent are largely left to the discretion of the officials who oversee the enforcement of the statutes' provisions.[10] However, this legislation in large part designates and/or creates the category 'pornography' and helps to formulate the boundaries which impact on producers and their products.

The development of a legitimate UK pornography industry was curtailed by this legislation. Where both the US and Europe saw massive expansions from the early-eighties into new technologies from film/video production through to Internet sites, the UK market remained largely reliant on top-shelf magazines, a few video spin-offs and telephone chatlines. Some commentators have argued that it is not the legal limits placed upon pornography in the UK but the lack of competition that has allowed the industry to stagnate. Precisely because the laws are difficult and none of the agencies policing their provisions are willing or able to give precise guidelines to would-be producers of sexually explicit materials, a culture of self-censorship has emerged in the UK. This has given rise to a peculiarly British kind of product rather than the extreme examples cited by Dworkin et al.

In addition to tight controls on the content of 'pornography' in the UK, strict controls over its place of sale are also in existence: sales of sexually explicit magazines are limited to the hundred or so sex shops in the UK and/or the newsagents' top shelf.[11] Thus sexually explicit products are physically assembled together and, because of the difficulties getting started in the business, often produced by the same groups of companies. Again, this concentration distorts the ways in which we approach the materials for analysis; leading to claims such as Hardy's that

> In Britain ... the last refuge of pornography has been the top shelf of the newsagent's magazine stand, where the appearance of colourful diversity belies uniformity of content and quality and the fact that, like brands of washing powder, 'top shelf' magazines are almost all owned by the same two or three parties. (1998: 52)

Like washing powder and many other mass-produced commodities, 'pornography' suffers from a surfeit of contempt which manifests itself in characterizations of the category's homogeneity and following from that, the uniformity of possible responses to, or expectations of, its subsets. However much the products may appear alike on the shelves, this cannot be an indication of the ways they are used once removed from there. Then, although an individual magazine still retains its generic properties and its links to the larger category 'pornography', the expectations which lead to its selection will now achieve their fulfilment, or not. It is this level which needs to be addressed to understand the meanings of the individual sexually explicit product for its readers. I should make clear that in wishing to focus on the individual product and the individual reader it's not to merely offer the truism that different people like different things for different reasons. That seeming truism is a problematic to be acknowledged by research into the uses of sexually explicit materials. The investigation of an individual text and its readers necessitates understanding the specifics of one sexually explicit publication (in this research *For Women* magazine), and the ways it promises its readers it can 'carve out a space' for explicit sex and the possibilities of pleasure.

I Know it When I See it and I Know it Before I See it

Within cultural studies the difficulties presented by the tendency to 'know' the object before starting out on its investigation have been the subject of much discussion. Tudor cautions that genre studies often know the material before they set out to define the material,

> That is, we are caught in a circle which first requires that the films are isolated, for which purposes a criterion is necessary, but the criterion is, in turn, meant to emerge from the empirically established common characteristics of the films.' (1976: 121)

Nowhere is this tendency so marked as in the study and delineation of 'pornography' and follows from the notion of 'subordination' or the 'sexualized objectification of women' as the single most important convention of 'pornography'. 'Subordination' is, of course, a subjective term but more than that, as I show in my subsequent discussions, if researchers set out to find it, it can be 'discovered' everywhere by ignoring every other code and convention which marks the investigated text as a horror film or romantic novel. Setting out on my investigation of *For Women*, it became clear very early on that subordination of women or their objectification were useless as tools of analysis for this magazine. Moreover, to merely look for the role-reversed counterpart, the sexual subordination of men, would have been a fruitless and intellectually stultifying exercise. The most significant problem with subordination as a trait of porn is that it presupposes a stasis: pornography is assumed to be unchanging, but even as its focus remains steadfastly sex, its forms, styles and interests evolve, as even the most cursory historical analysis attests.

This book seeks to examine a particular moment of change, in the address by a soft-core publisher to female consumers and how and why those consumers chose to read *For Women* magazine. In spite of the received wisdom that women were not interested in pornography, a number of commercial enterprises thought a sizeable group could be interested and the evidence of sales figures suggested they were. This focus has required that I try to understand the relationships between women and the magazine as a textual imaginary, but I have also tried to understand how and why the producers and consumers of the magazine thought the time was right. So this book relies heavily on discussions with members of staff at Northern & Shell publishers and, more particularly, with readers. The turn to the moment of consumption within media and cultural studies has opened a rich field of investigation into the uses of certain forms of television, film, formulaic fiction and women's magazines.[12] These studies have raised questions about the theoretical and methodological problems of engaging with audiences' talk. While we must be aware of the dangers of simply 'letting people speak for themselves' we need also to ensure that our textual investigations reflect the kinds of relationships our interviewees describe as important to them. Thus, to search in the first instance for signs of objectification, subordination and degradation begins a process of investigation of 'ideological instruments' that precludes and overwrites the responses of readers. It is my contention that those accounts that have stressed the power of the text to determine responses to pornography have reduced the text to simply arousing desire for sex. That mono-purpose is regarded as a bad thing, there is nothing complex about the text: it simply requires arousal. Interestingly, rather than say directly 'that's a bad thing, don't masturbate', these accounts impute a generalized harm: by reducing response to sexual feeling, readers/viewers are supposedly encouraged to dehumanize all women through their use of photographs of women. Despite the move towards the study of readers/viewers of other cultural forms, pornography and its readerships within academic study remain locked in a 'closed' relationship, imprisoned by their monotony and monologic desperation for sexual release.

Encapsulated in those critiques of pornography as having 'no value besides the sexual' (Hardy, 1998: 49) is the linking of gender and genre. The characteristic mono-focus is, so Hardy argues in his analysis of *Men Only*, entirely 'lop-sided' – 'what lies behind this difference is the gender of the intended audience, and it is this which really distinguishes pornography as a genre' (1998: 49). Pornography addresses a male audience and does so through sexual styles generally understood as belonging to 'male sexuality': as Hardy explains it 'short, sharp exchanges and rapid, almost documentary switching of positions, partners and orifices – all of which gratifies a typically masculine obsessive eclecticism' (1998: 49). Such a definition may point to some of the representational tropes of pornography but again stresses homogeneity – its mode of address is always male orientated, its pace and style always the same. Hardy notes that the characterizations of male and female sexuality which underpin such a definition may be beginning to be outdated, but still claims that pornography's uniqueness lies in its exclusive focus 'on one [female] sex ... for the sole edification of the other [male]' (1998: 49).

Again the essentializing of 'pornography' and its text-reader relations leads to the reification of one kind of reception: at its most benign, a form of getting to know but at its most extreme, learning and practising the pleasures of the subordination of women.[13] In many accounts to talk of the meaning of 'pornography' is to immediately move to a level of response based on gender relations. This is then solidified around the 'realities' of gendered identity such that the male reader must have a 'male' response predicated upon the worst forms of social relations between men and women. This ignores the concerns raised by anti-censorship feminists regarding the totalizing equation of pornography with sexuality, specifically male sexuality and, in so doing, to confidently assert the representation of sex as the representation of gender.[14] Hardy's claim, 'As a genre mass market (heterosexual) pornography remains overwhelmingly of women but by men and for men' (1998: 49), is understandable but elides the slipperiness of sexual response and desire beneath an assumed gendered division within production and consumption. The consequential position is that no woman, with an appropriately female sexuality, could be turned on by 'the short, sharp exchanges' and that in masturbation, all women look for the same rhythms they might require in sexual activity with a partner. It assumes a particular usage of the product dictated by its production and thereby confirms the impossibility of other usage. Moreover it confirms the tendency found in other areas of media and cultural studies to celebrate female usage of mass media as 'open' and 'polysemic', while men's use is condemned as 'closed' and 'monologic'.[15]

Pornography may often be misogynist and reflective of wider gender inequalities: for example, Hugh Hefner's introduction of *Playboy* to its presumed readership appears to encapsulate gender attitudes of the time:

> If you're a man between 18 and 80, PLAYBOY is meant for you. If you like entertainment served up with humor, sophistication and spice, PLAYBOY will become a very special favourite.
>
> We want to make it very clear from the start, we aren't a 'family magazine'. If you're somebody's sister, wife or mother-in-law and picked us up by mistake, please pass us along to the man in your life and get back to the *Ladies Home Companion*. (Hugh Hefner, *Playboy*, quoted in Skordarki, 1991: 22)

That Hefner clearly makes a gendered appeal for his product is not, however, enough to suggest that women could not find some pleasurable elements in the magazine, or indeed, that all men stumbling upon or going out to buy the magazine, would find its contents entirely to their taste. The magazine might attempt to speak to gendered subjects but in doing so; it cannot prevent a pleasured[16] response in those it had attempted to place outside its constituency. Thus my point here is to argue, as Segal does, 'that the codes linking sexuality to hierarchical polarities of gender, though always present, are never fixed and immutable' (1994: 242). Sexuality must be uncoupled from physiological imperatives and biological reductionism. Segal goes on to argue that the conflation of biological sex and sexuality can be

> subverted by insisting upon the ease with which our fantasy life (and much of our reported experience of sexual pleasure) refuses to conform to conventional patterns of supposedly feminine or masculine ways of loving. Nothing is more common, in fantasy, than for us to be experiencing ourselves as the person we desire to possess, or to be – often someone of the 'opposite' sex. (1994: 159)

A definition of pornography which rests upon its intention to sexually arouse does not, in itself, preclude the possibility of female sexual arousal through the perusal of those cultural products produced by biological males; or, its supposed opposite, the possibility of male sexual arousal through cultural products produced by biological females.

Thus, in the discussion that follows I accept Kuhn's suggestion that pornography can and often does produce meanings 'pivoting on gender difference' (1985: 24), but not that those gender differences 'speak a truth' about a particular female or male sexuality (if indeed those can be talked of in the singular). Certainly Hefner's description of a particular kind of male subject who will enjoy *Playboy* proposes and facilitates a particular orientation to the product. But this needs to be understood as part of the process of marketing the text, the claim that this is not a 'family magazine' distinguishes the text and its readers and attempts to increase circulation through a definition of maleness in opposition to the 'family'. Indeed Ehrenreich (1983) has suggested that Hefner was opposed to 'wives': his *Playboy* philosophy was not just maleness in opposition to femaleness but to a particular form of respectable, self-censoring femaleness. The *Ladies Home Companion* was the safest and most conservative of women's magazines in the US at that time, and it is this historical locatedness of individual instances of the 'pornographic' that are lost or flattened by analyses which claim that porn is all the same.

Why make this distinction? I want to avoid the impasse reached by any number of commentators on *For Women's* launch and those theoretical accounts which have tried to offer alternative views of pornography as a 'resistant' media form. As I show in chapter three, the magazine's launch sparked debate about whether or not this was actually a female pornography, if it was, was it good for women? Those questions cannot be answered simply by looking at the text in isolation, moreover, they raise very problematic assumptions and suppositions about women and their use of media. Whether or not *For Women* told the 'truth' about female sexuality, it was positioned within the marketplace as *for women* and that served to open it up to women to read. Its title had a marketing function – delineating the magazine as for women, therefore, not for men. That labelling also makes a claim to be different from that 'awful stuff' men's porn does. What is interesting about the magazine is not how far it meets *my* idea of what constitutes female sexuality but what it perceived female sexuality to be and how that could be represented, how it offered to women the possibility of joining other women in discussing sex and imagining sex. Much of the criticism levelled at *FW* centred around its genesis within the portfolio of a publisher of male pornography, therefore its editorial team were supposedly incapable of articulating an 'authentic' female sexuality because of their masculinist 'taint'.

For Women was received as 'porn for women' on the basis of its perceived intention to arouse its readers sexually, and for some women it certainly worked as an occasion of sexual feelings. However, I don't want to foreclose my investigations of the magazine by suggesting that that response was purely one-dimensional. The magazine invited responses from readers clustered around sexual feeling but not limited to immediate sexual release. Indeed, the magazine only worked as an occasion of sexual arousal because it managed other concerns and interests that readers responded to. Thus, the main shift in this book begins from recognizing arousal and response to sexually explicit materials as more than a physiological response or the receipt of 'ideological meanings'. Rather than focus on whether a representation is good or bad, in terms of its 'truthfulness' about women or the opportunities I assume it opens up for readers or the potential harms I assume to be a feature of the production, reception and circulation of the magazine, I look at the magazine as a cultural product. That is, produced according to a range of institutional practices, offered to readers again within systems of distribution, reception and consumption regulated by institutions, examined in terms of the complex interrelationships the magazine has with its readers. Their relationship is conceived here as dialogic, thus I move away from those analyses which have tended to focus on the text as the purveyor of meaning and readers as simply decoders of those meanings. In stressing the dialogical (Barker 1989; Volosinov 1973) nature of the relationship, I suggest, in later chapters, that readers were engaged in more than simply decoding the magazine, their responses to *For Women* are indications of the ways in which the magazine proposed a *social* relationship between itself and readers and an invitation to them to participate in its discussions of sex.

To that end I have paid attention to the *specifics* of this magazine, its historical location, its production processes, its formal organization and repertoires, and its readers' uses, likes and disappointments. This has allowed me to ask different questions from those of previous analyses which have, as I have briefly outlined here and will discuss in more depth in the next chapter, proceeded by sidelining questions of production (which is presumed to be male, even by those who are willing to celebrate women's use of porn) and the nature of the pleasures that women may take in such materials. In looking in detail at the specifics of one publication, I have not been constrained by assumptions of the supposed power of pornographic texts to objectify and/or harm women. I have, therefore, gained access to concrete understandings, rather than theoretical stipulation, of the relationship between this text, *For Women*, and its readers.

Numerous books have appeared recently, from within academic and more lay research, which stress the increasing sexualization of culture – a term rarely explained but understood to be a truth universally acknowledged. In these accounts, American and UK culture are described as having come out of the dark shadows of 1950s prudery with an explosion of explicit sexual representations which assault our senses from every angle. Brian McNair calls this 'striptease culture', the 'pornographication of culture'. Ariel Levy describes it as 'Raunch culture' whose cheerleader is the 'empowered woman'; Pamela Paul decries the ways in which our world is 'pornified' and the role played by pornography in 'transforming our lives, our relationships and our families'. These accounts come from different ends of the spectrum, but, essentially, they trace the same phenomena: McNair sees this increasing explicitness as a form of liberalizing attitudes, Levy is more circumspect and wonders what has happened to feminist demands for women's freedom when the world seems only willing to allow women the freedom to flaunt their bodies, and, for Paul, the situation is dire with relationships collapsing under the weight of the emotional isolation, distrust and disgust caused by pornography's infiltration of our everyday lives. These authors share a common belief in the widespread acceptance of behaviours, attitudes and representations that until a couple of decades would have outraged public decency.

The claims that culture is becoming increasingly pornographic rest on measurement of media representations displaying an instinct for transgression – as McNair puts it, pornographication is a result of

> ... the collision of ideological shifts caused by decades of sex-political struggle with a postmodern intellectual climate in which the meaning of the pornographic can be remade, and its perverse pleasures recognized. (2002: 81)

He goes on to claim that we are witnessing a 'collective ease with the public exploration of sexual culture' (2002: 86). While I don't want to disagree that discourses about, and representations of, sex have proliferated in the past two decades, I think there are significant problems with the wholesale acceptance of the idea that 'sex sells' or that 'sex is everywhere'. In particular it tends towards the flattening of the particular ways in which 'sex sells' or is sold. Moreover, McNair's essentially positive take on this process – that we are becoming increasing comfortable with sexual representations – is too easily adapted to cries that we are witnessing a coarsening of culture or the increasing exploitation of sexualized bodies, especially those of women and children. As Slade has argued there is a significant problem in the bandying about of figures of increase – for example, the claim that the sex industries generate more profit than Hollywood and other cinematic industries put together has gained a credence that emphasizes the idea that this is an unstoppable force of capitalism and, given the overwhelming academic view of capitalism as a commodifying force, therefore must be exploitative. But Slade observes that 'the amount Americans spend on sexual expression each year is roughly twice what they spend on hot dogs, but only a third of what they spend on gardening supplies.' (1997: 3) The emphasis on quantity refuses to engage with the kinds of sexual products purchased and the meanings those products have for their purchasers.[17]

To illustrate this more concretely let me examine a few of the claims made by Brian McNair in his book *Striptease Culture*. His examination is a largely sanguine account of the media spaces which have adopted the representational tropes of pornography since the 1980s. Starting first with *Deep Throat* which brought hard core imagery to mainstream cinemagoers and developing through the use of 'explicit striptease' (67) in pop videos through to the rise in documentary and 'reality' genres focusing on the production of pornography, the pornographication of culture has grown exponentially. These instances of striptease culture are evidence of a 'less regulated, more commercialized, and more pluralistic sexual culture' where it is possible to play with the representation of sex while denying any affinity with the pornography industries – adopting a kind of 'porno-chic' (61) drawing on the aesthetics of pornography without being tarnished by accusations of exploitation and objectification. Moreover, the development of new technologies like home video and the Internet enables everyone the opportunity to produce their own sexual representations (Jacobs 2004). Thus, pornographication is represented as a supply and demand economy that has spread its tentacles through every feature of the mediascape.

Like McNair, Ariel Levy masses a range of examples of increasingly sexualized behaviours performed for the camera for broadcast on mainstream television and magazines as evidence of a new cultural phenonomen of 'Raunch':

> I first noticed it several years ago. I would turn on the television and find strippers in pasties explaining how best to lap dance a man to orgasm. I would flip the channel and see babes in tight, tiny uniforms bouncing up and down on trampolines. Britney Spears was becoming increasingly popular and increasingly unclothed, and her undulating body ultimately became so familiar to me I felt like we used to go out. (2005: 1)

Yet this analysis is an insistent flattening of the production and consumption of sexual images. Just as early analyses of pornography refused to acknowledge any distinction between the varieties and forms of the images, their place in cultures of production or their differential appeal to consumers, the claims of pornographication, whether positive or negative essentialize the meanings of sexual representations to either liberation or commodification. Kipnis' argument that pornography is always viewed as an uncomplicated regime of production, representation and consumption returns as appropriate to these supposedly new explorations of sexual imagery. Indeed, McNair's formulation of the pornoscape explicitly refuses the regulatory, political and economic conditions for the developments of individual instances of porno-representations. This seems particularly unsatisfactory as an analysis of UK sexual representational cultures given the fact that calls for regulation of sexually explicit materials remain insistent rather than diminishing and that Madonna's flirtations with porno-chic are enabled precisely because of the specific institutional boundaries that mark her work as *not* porn. Madonna's transgressive moments are only comprehensible via acknowledgement of the historical imposition of boundaries which form the complex topography of sexual production and reception. The logical end point of McNair's tracings of increasing explicitness would be the final breakdown of all boundaries and impediments to full exposure and yet, this can only occur if the organizational networks of regulation and the market refrain from reacting to these perceived changes. O'Toole's examination of the cosy cartels of soft-core publishing in the UK suggest this view is entirely naïve – regulation is a key component in the profitability of soft-core production. McNair's examples are largely drawn from images and productions that actively seek male audiences and while he attempts some discussion of feminist/feminine interventions in his pornoscape they are confined to those which simply confirm his claims that the sexual sphere is a continuously expanding force: for example, his suggestion that *Ann Summers* shops illustrate the ways in which women are joining in the sexual free-for-all completely misses the institutional dimensions in which *Ann Summers* exist – to read McNair is to imagine that local government, obscenity laws, morality campaigns and license fees don't exist or have no impact upon the forms and products of sexualized culture.

Furthermore, the claims that culture is becoming more liberal in attitudes towards sex and its various representations suggests a linear movement from fear to acceptance and then embrace, but, clearly, these processes are much more uneven than proponents suggest. For McNair, any evidence of dissent to striptease culture is a product of outdated attitudes and backward thinking and again his conclusions refuse to recognize the complexities of the current sexual landscapes of western culture. For example, Hekma has explored the ways in which the image of a liberal Dutch nation hides a very complex picture of quite conservative sexual practices and attitudes: 'explicit sexual imagery is pervasive in the media, and many people seem to enjoy this. But, in general, very few people ever do themselves what they see depicted in these images, according to national sex surveys.' (Hekma ud: 2)

More interesting to the work laid out here are the studies undertaken during the 1990s which attempted to redress the ways in which discussions have proceeded at an abstracted level: one such study (as yet unpublished), by Eleni Skordarki, examines the ways in which pornography is 'a product of human labour and human interaction' (1991: 7) produced within an often hostile (although legally sanctioned) social environment which contributes in significant ways to the content of the pornographic magazine. Laura Kipnis' (1992; 1996) analyses of *Hustler* magazine trace the socio-cultural location of an individual text to discover the particularly classed dimensions of the feminist antagonism to its 'inappropriate' sexual representations. It is *Hustler*'s particular fondness for the gross and the corporeal which indicates, for Kipnis, that the magazine is premised on class dissatisfaction rather than simply gender differences. Another recent intervention has focused on the voices of male consumers to show how 'any effects which pornography might be said to have are mediated through his [the Reader's] subjectivity' (Hardy 1998: 4). Jane Juffer (1998) has examined the ways in which pornography has become increasingly domesticated. By focussing on the 'everyday-ness' of the use of pornography, Juffer avoids the reiteration of those claims which focus on pornography's role in the intimidation of women within domestic spaces; she emphasizes women's increasing access to pornography and suggests that such access has real impacts upon the form and content of sexually explicit materials for women. Another study has taken this idea of the environs in which women might consume porn to examine the ways in which women's feelings for pornography are profoundly influenced by the feminist anti-porn stance – Karen Ciclitira found that women's use of pornography is directly negotiated with the arguments about harm and objectification. Finally, within the branches of feminism labelled I-, third wave- or post-feminism, there have been a number of first-hand accounts of the pleasures and pains of sexually explicit materials and their role in allowing individual women the opportunities for expressing elements of feminine sexual identity previously condemned as 'sluttish'.

These interventions are important because they attempt to move beyond the bad boy/good girl and Madonna/whore dichotomies dogging earlier debates. Their focus on the negotiations made by producers and users of sexually explicit texts with the discourses which circulate, both to limit and to produce pornography as texts, are timely reminders that pornography has no existence outside of the cultural sphere in which it is produced, circulated and consumed. It is this focus which informs my own research into the pleasures and uses of sexually explicit material for women and how those are made possible by a magazine produced within particular legal and social constraints in order to make a profit. That pornography makes a profit is indisputable (although the levels of profit are hotly disputed) and is 'frequently used as condemnation of it' (Carol 1994: 127). As my analysis will show, the decision to publish *For Women* magazine was dependent upon largely intuitive predictions that a potentially profitable market existed for a sexually explicit magazine targeted at a female readership and the spoiling tactics of its producers, Northern & Shell, who refused to allow other publishers to steal a march on a potentially lucrative new market sector. Thus chapter two explores the reasons for the magazine's launch and the ways in which the company's aim to move into more mainstream publishing informed the content and distribution of the magazine. I outline the development and production of *FW* magazine and its status as 'product' which indicates the editorial team's efforts to reconcile the contents of the magazine with the shifting concerns of potential readers. These attempts shaped the content of the magazine such that the finished project straddled two genres: *top-shelf pornography* and the *woman's magazine*, a strategy which generated a huge amount of public debate turning on the themes of female sexuality and sexual desire as significantly different from the forms and pleasures of male sexuality, and which were a response to the editorial positioning of *FW* and its attempt to manage the seeming incompatibility of sexual 'fantasy' and 'reality' for women as I discuss in chapter 4.

This straddling was a deliberate ploy to ensure the magazine's accessibility both commercially and textually with the intention of building upon the already burgeoning market in female erotica led by the 'shopping and fucking' novels as well as the increasingly sexualized content of women's mainstream magazine publishing. The publisher's attempts to position the magazine as oppositional and responsive to already existing market demands is important to an understanding of the ways in which the magazine attempted to delineate itself as new and different and therefore a publication specifically *for* women readers.

Chapter five begins the detailed analysis of readers' responses to the magazine. By examining readers' talk it became clear that anti-porn arguments about a woman's response to pornography are seriously flawed. It is ironic that some academics share the idea of an undifferentiated woman's response to porn with common-sense discourses. In chapter six, I discuss the magazine's photographic imagery. The production team saw themselves as at the forefront of the attempt to uncover a visual vocabulary of the male body that would work commercially and, perhaps more importantly for the readers, as sexually arousing. Chapter seven analyses the magazine's fiction. These chapters outline *FW*'s attempt to delineate a pleasurable sexual imaginary without ignoring the problems and difficulties associated with sex for women. Material gained through interviews with readers is examined in each of these chapters to illustrate how far the delineation of a female-space enabled women's responses. My investigation of the textual formation of the magazine is derived from the discernable patterns and themes within readers' talk. By approaching the magazine as multi-voiced, I offer an analysis of the magazine which focuses not on identification or persuasion[18] but on dialogue between text and reader, specifically a dialogue on, and of, female sexual desire.

My interview material suggests that the function of the magazine could be sexually arousing for these women in very immediate ways. However, it also enabled more long-term personal explorations of the individual's notion of their own sexual identity and the realities and meanings of sexual experience for women as an identifiable group. Such findings point to more than the problematic celebration of transgressive activity. As Juffer argues

> In some ways, we are no better off with transgression as a normative value than we were with the nuclear family or the missionary position. Avoiding prescriptive claims means that we must not read erotic texts as a gauge of the author's or

> presumed reader's ability to violate gendered and sexualised norms. Using transgression as the standard of interpretation, one could easily dismiss much ... erotica... as co-opted, reinforcing gendered norms and essentialist notions of female sexuality. (1998: 23)

Thus I attempt to draw together the themes emergent in readers' talk and the particular elements of the magazine which facilitated pleasures in the widest sense for these readers. In so doing, I draw attention to the ways in which the magazine can be characterized as failing to deliver some of its promises to its readers. These disappointments are as important as the pleasures to be found in the text and yet are curiously absent from much previous work on pornography. Where female disappointment in pornography has been discussed, it is almost entirely related to the notion that female sexuality is opposed to pornographic discourse and thus is linked to an innate dislike of the genre. Rather than see disappointment/dislike as a measure of appropriately female response to the magazine, I found that the disappointments experienced by readers, especially those who wanted to like *For Women*, enabled understanding of its attempts to speak to female experience. I show that disappointment or criticism does not necessarily mean that these readers were able to 'see through' the magazine or to reject it as oppressive. Disappointments and pleasures suggest particular orientations in coming to the magazine, a range of expectations to be met via engagement with, and interpretation of, the text; expectations shaped by the discourse and meanings circulating and producing that text.

This book is intended to explore the very particular dynamics of an instance of pornographic publishing, and I hope it is an accessible and critical examination of the role of a particular sexually explicit product in the lives of its female consumers. The recognition that western culture is increasingly sexualized poses particular problems for traditional arguments about women's lack of interest in pornography and so my intention here is to address the problem question – what can pornography offer women? With that question in mind, the following chapters will continually return to some of the key themes of the 'pornography debates' in order to show how discourses of pleasure and danger, entitlements and risk, fantasy and normality are fundamental to those arguments.

This book is about the assumptions and theoretical claims made about pornography, it examines the problems inherent in more than 30 years of intense debate about the meanings of pornography; it addresses the gaps and inconsistencies in those discussions – particularly the refusal to engage with the ways in which producers and consumers of pornography talk about sexually explicit materials and the social, cultural and legislative environments in which these texts and their audiences operate. It offers an alternative theorization and methodology for investigating women's use of sexually explicit materials and makes a proposal that such investigations need to be aware of the constructive force of theories of 'gender difference'. Thus, while the focus of this book is quite narrow – on one magazine, its production, consumption and textual formation – its implications and the research paradigm I employ here could be usefully extended to other instances of pornographic representation and uses.

Notes

1. As Braithwaite puts it, 'the British girl never took to such overt pictures and the magazine was but a passing, short-lived fancy.' (1995: 102) It should be noted, however, that *Playgirl* did survive for at least two decades. The magazine was printed in the UK under licence from its American owners and thus never seemed to reflect the particular concerns or interests of British women. It appears to have functioned as a 'if the boys can have theirs, I'll have mine' publication, purchased occasionally in order to strike a blow for women's lib. The demise of its specifically UK format in 1993/4 may well be attributable to competition from *For Women*. McKay notes that 'while it is correct to note that some magazines die because they probably should never have been born others die because they have reached the end of their natural life.' (2000: 206)
2. Gloria Steinem attempted to show that erotica and pornography could be separated from each other by recognizing erotica's focus on 'the idea of love and mutuality, positive choice, and the yearning for a particular person' (1995: 241). It should be noted, however, that many anti-pornography and anti-censorship writers agree that this 'clear and present difference' has no analytical value. For example, Dworkin sees no distinction between the two because erotica simply uses better props, better lighting, clothing etc., therefore it is merely high-class pornography. On the other side of the divide that point is reiterated by, among others, Bill Thompson, 'erotica is a convenient term to describe material which needs an "expert" to tell you where the sex is' (1994: 1).
3. As well as the lack of writing about actual texts there is also a scarcity of work that includes examples of the material being described, analysed and theorized. Diana E. H. Russell's *Against Pornography* (1993b) includes 'pornographic' images and analysis but conforms to the criticism of generalization from the most extreme examples and abstraction posing as analysis of specific texts and their use. The anti-censorship collection, *Caught Looking* (Ellis et al. 1986), also reprints a vast range of sexually explicit images but without commentary; the collective's intention being to allow readers to form their own judgements. Both Juffer (1998) and Williams (1991) have acknowledged the impulse to validate individual interpretations but have criticized the ways in which the collection may contribute to the decontextualization, ahistoricism and placelessness of pornographic images. It is also difficult to attempt to examine the validity of a theorist's reading of a text because pornographic materials are somewhat ephemeral: distribution can be haphazard and the contents of one sex shop may not be found in another part of the country. In the UK, there is a requirement that all publishers submit a copy of each issue of their publications to the collection at the British Library, making research into the mainstream UK magazines relatively easy (although gaining access to the Special Collection where these are housed is often fraught and embarrassing).
4. Annette Hill's (1997) *Shocking Entertainment* indicates the very complex motivations and responses experienced by viewers in watching 'violent' movies. The ascription 'pornographic' to films indicates a range of assumptions about viewers as well as the movies themselves. Research such as Hill's, Barker & Brooks (1998) and Clover (1992) demonstrate those assumptions are untenable.
5. Products of the American culture industries have long been regarded as problematic in the UK, thus the concerns regarding consumption, harmful influence and swamping of home-grown culture are concentrated in a generalized but often unacknowledged anti-Americanism. Materials from Europe are also regarded as a problem; see, for example, the newspaper and parliamentary debates about Red Hot Dutch, a cable porn channel. However, the British custom of laughing at our mainland European friends seems to prevent the same levels of hysteria permeating debate except where the material under consideration is child pornography.

6. Much anti-porn discourse promulgates the idea that the British Isles are awash with filth of the most obscene and violent kinds and that the situation will worsen if unhindered. Valverde (1985) has called this the 'domino theory of the passions' and the 'slippery slope' (150), where legal punishment and social stigma are the very last bastions which prevent culture sliding into the very worst excesses.
7. Although, of course, this has been a substantive claim of pro-censorship arguments – keep the filth at bay.
8. The recent appearance of educational videos such as the *Lovers Guides* series have blurred the lines somewhat, although the educational tag means that they have sidestepped the legislation as it is applied to, for example, the *Electric Blue* series.
9. In an article for the *Guardian* newspaper, Julian Petley has offered an excellent exposition of the vagaries of British censorship laws, the current mess of conflicting criteria and the attempts by Jack Straw and The Home Office to reinforce controls. An expanded version of the article is available on the MelonFarmers website: http: //www.melonfarmers.co.uk/brjp.htm.
10. The problems inherent in the provisions of these laws and the instability of the categories 'obscene' and 'indecent' have been examined by various commentators including Carol (1994), Thompson (1994), O'Toole (1998) for the anti-censorship position and for the anti-pornography position by Dworkin & MacKinnon (1988) and Itzin (1992). All agree that the subjective terms are problematic although the anti-pornography feminists would argue that the law could be used to decide on the acceptability of certain representations using the definitions of harm.
11. Items can also be purchased by mail order.
12. This research constitutes an exciting and burgeoning area including Ang, 1985; Barker & Brooks, 1999; Gauntlett & Hill, 1999; Gray, 1992; Hermes, 1995; Hill, 1997; Kehily, 1999; Radway, 1984.
13. Cole insists, '*Pornography is a practice of sexual subordination. Its producers present sexual subordination for their own sexual pleasure, and its consumers get sexual pleasure from the presentation of sexual subordination.* To understand pornography as a practice, it's necessary to dispense with the idea that pornography is a thing, a two-dimensional artifact, and consider it more a series of activities.'(original italics) (1989: 22)
14. Lynne Segal argues it is 'necessary to theorise sexuality *autonomously*, separately from gender – if only to see the possible diversity of their connections. Feminists have battled with each other over sexuality precisely because of the conceptual and practical difficulties of trying to separate sex and gender. Both the most traditional patriarchal thinking, and the most recent forms of radical feminist theory, equate male sexuality with male dominance.' (1994: 71)
15. See Barker (1996) and Gripsrud (1995) for discussion and review of some of the problems in studies of sci-fi fandom and soap opera viewers. See Fiske (1987) for an example of the tendency to celebrate uncritically.
16. For some readers an angry response to *Playboy* might well be pleasurable if the magazine confirms every assumption the reader has about sexual representations. I am suggesting that continuing to read a particular form or text does not necessarily require a positive response to it. As Ang showed in her work on *Dallas*, some people watch a TV programme because they hate it and their pleasure in watching is based on the confirmation of their superior feelings towards, for example, 'American junk'.
17. That there are massive amounts spent on gardening supplies does not mean that we have returned to an agrarian culture – what is being purchased and to what end is surely an element to be investigated before we can draw conclusions.
18. Studies of both women's magazines and pornography for men have tended to stress the function of these texts as instruments of ideological and sexual control effected via their encouragement of 'reader identification'. I discuss these problems throughout this book.

1

APPROACHES TO PORNOGRAPHY

The last thirty years have seen much debate within (but not limited to) feminism about pornography: its meanings, pleasures, pains and effects. Over this period the arguments have appeared increasingly polarized and seemingly unresolvable, and, yet, alongside this debate has been the increase in 'erotic' publishing for women. But there are significant problems in theorizing women's pleasure in sexually explicit representations: many cultural theorists have posited that pornography for women is different, locating a possible source in romantic fictions published by Harlequin/Mills & Boon (Radway 1986; Snitow 1984b). At the same time, some studies have located women's sexuality in touch rather than the gaze (Irigary 1985) and, drawing upon a notion of female sexuality as emotionally, psychically and physically different from the sexual experiences of men, that pornography is thus unable to fit with women's erotic potentialities (Faust 1980). In some accounts this non-fit is seen as actively produced with the intention to distort, even to destroy female sexual desire in the service of institutionalized heterosexuality (Griffin 1981; Dworkin 1981; Jeffreys 1990; Levy 2005; Paul 2005). Others, however, have suggested that pornography can and does hold particular pleasures for female subjects and that its use can be best understood as transgressive of heterosexist norms rather than supportive of them (Rubin 1984, 1992; Carol 1994; Vance 1992a; Lumby 1997; Albury 2005).

These accounts (identified as feminist despite their significant differences) join a vast array of discussions of pornography from writers within legal, philosophical, sociological, aesthetic and moral traditions. O'Toole has described the ways in which porn, its contents and regulation are intensely political matters. It is also a continuously expanding phenomenon, constantly able to 'reinvent' itself (although the extent to which its favourite representational tropes are reinvented is the subject of some dispute) utilizing new technologies such as CD-ROM, video and the Internet in order to reach more and more consumers. Its exploitation of new technology is matched by its ability to cater to ever more specialist markets witnessed, for example, in the rise of materials addressed to gay and lesbian consumers and the growth of S/M materials. These expansions have seen pornography move from a very narrow availability to, what at times, seems like a very mainstream acceptability.[1] Perhaps most important to pornography's continued presence in academic and theoretical work, is its central place within discussions of representations and specifically how those contribute to understandings around gender and sexuality and their connections to inequalities in the wider social, political and economic spheres. The continuing debates – how might the real character of pornography be revealed, how does it work, what are its effects and how can they be examined? – making pornography a topic of concern for academics whatever their discipline.

The Study of Pornography

Often writings 'about' pornography are more interested in the question 'should pornography exist?' than the specifics of its textual formations. Some commentators are so incensed by their response to porn that they call for the total banning of the object of their investigation. Indeed, in the 1980s the opposing sides were sufficiently antagonistic to be described as 'at war'.[2] Numerous accounts of these 'sex wars' have been published (O'Toole 1998; Carol 1994; Segal & McIntosh 1992; Strossen 2000; McElroy 1995; Tong 1998; Thompson 1994; Chancer 1998) making a further rehearsal here somewhat superfluous. With that acknowledgement of superfluity in mind, I offer a very brief overview of the histories and main arguments of the debates, focusing on studies which could be considered 'emblematic' of particular positions, sufficient only to put my own discussion into context.

Defining Pornography and Creating Orthodoxy

The history of pornography is perhaps most easily recognized as a history of regulation and repression. Kendrick (1987), O'Toole (1998) and others have described the ways in which materials deemed pornographic because of their sexual explicitness have been hidden from wider attention: only those who would not be 'corrupted' being allowed to see it. Hunt has shown that pornography had no existence, as we understand it today, until the early nineteenth century when technological innovation made widespread dissemination of printed materials profitable. Prior to that time, sexually explicit pamphlets and illustrations had been the vehicle for attacks on political and religious authorities (1993b: 10). Thus Hunt argues that pornography was 'linked to free-thinking and heresy, to science and natural philosophy, and to attacks on absolutist political authority' (1993b: 11). Early attacks on pornography centred on the corruption of morals and the identification of obscenity both suggestive of the ability of sexually explicit materials to offend 'authority' and as Hunt argues 'pornography as regulatory category was invented in response to the perceived menace of the democratisation of culture' (1993b: 12–13).[3]

Thus porn's early history is one of proliferation and suppression on political grounds, reaching its zenith in the works of the Marquis de Sade and the French Revolution. With the move to mass production and mass literacy in the nineteenth century, O'Toole and Kendrick both argue that pornography was less of a political problem than a moral one. Histories of pornography have been difficult but have indicated that there are 'major bursts' (Hunt 1993a) of sexual imagery coincidental with radical political and philosophical movements. Hunt has drawn attention to the ways in which the political and the moral were inseparable in the response to pornographic representations of women. 'As new biological and moral standards for sexual difference evolved, pornography seemed to become even more exotic and dangerous. It had to be stamped out. Much ... of our modern concern with pornography follows from that conviction.' (1993b: 45) In similar vein, Sigel has shown how the menace was more particularly thought in reference to the poor – if the lower orders had access to photographs of naked bodies then they were obscene images: 'the judgement passed on pornography changed based on where, when, and by whom it was viewed.' (2002: 4)

With the patchy move towards sexual liberation in the 1960s, 'corruption of morals' was a less easily accommodated category of reproach in an increasingly secular society. Once again, the behaviours of upright citizens were satirized in political magazines and the Left used sexual innuendo as a form of radical political critique (Segal 1994; Hunt 1998). Although the effectiveness of 'sex as subversive' (Segal 1994: 1) was, and is, debated, the designation of sexual representations as 'obscene' played into the subversive court. Alongside the diminishing of the power of the accusation 'obscene' went a rise in sexually explicit material whether printed, filmic or live shows (O'Toole 1998; Thompson 1994). The 1970s saw a boom in pornographic publishing and the development of a sex industry in the UK (Hunt 1998; O'Toole 1998; Skordarki 1991).

Right-wingers and moralists viewed these developments with some horror, exclaiming at the growth of the 'promiscuous society' and the concomitant social breakdown (Hunt 1998; Petley 2000). The floodgates appeared to be open for increasingly explicit material, but the voices against pornography were given a major fillip in the late 1970s by radical feminist analyses of sexualized representations that moved discussion from moral to political outrage. Against the backdrop of sexual liberation, this outrage arose from the feminist axiom that the 'personal is political' making the connections between sexual representations and male violence in the claim 'Pornography is the Theory, Rape is the Practice'. Central to these accounts are the American radical feminists Robin Morgan, Susan Griffin and Andrea Dworkin, whose works systematically attempted to critique and deconstruct the twin edifices of patriarchy and heterosexuality. In achieving those aims, these writers trace historical continuities that place sexuality, specifically heterosexuality, at the centre of women's oppression.

In three works Griffin (1978, 1979, 1981) emphasizes the links between women and nature to argue that the male institutions of Church and Science mobilized 'the pornographic imagination' in order to destroy women through rape and the use and production of pornography. Rape and imperialism are linked to the development of regimes of representation which seek to 'silence eros' and the authentic and natural sexuality of women. Griffin's emphasis that male fear drives violence against women differs somewhat from Dworkin's (1981) assertions that violence is endemic to male sexuality, however, both are able to discern links between the state and the pornographer which go back centuries if not millennia. Morgan (1980) also finds a similar and ancient lineage: Neanderthal man offers the origins of men's terrorization of women through the strategic deployment of sexual violence. For Brownmiller rape is 'nothing more or less than a conscious process of intimidation by which *all* men keep *all* women in a state of fear' (1976: 15). These analyses did not start with pornographic texts *per se*; rather they derive from theorizations that sought to account for the institutional role of heterosexuality in the cultural subordination of women.

A key claim of anti-pornography feminism is that pornography tells lies about women's sexuality, specifically that it shows female sexuality as taking voracious pleasure in subordination, degradation and a generalized and all-pervasive oppression of women through violence. The critique of pornography is arrived at through a focus on the power dynamics of rape: that dynamic ensures that each individual act of rape contributes to the climate of fear experienced by all women and causes them to submit to patriarchal control via marriage (Brownmiller 1976). Women have no freedom to choose heterosexuality or marriage because they have no right to refuse it: their freedoms are always only provisional. Moreover, because rape within marriage is rarely recognized as rape, women are understood to have no right to control their own bodies.[4] Thus radical feminism theorizes sexual activity/relationships between men and women as inherently and always embodying an unequal power dynamic, as MacKinnon claims, sexuality is seen as 'the primary social sphere of male power' (1982: 516). Developed from that conceptualization is the assertion that pornography is a document of sexual activity and, as sexual activity is based upon the paradigm of rape, its representations are documents of the terrorization of women.

Pornography has an ideological function[5] able to encompass very different forms. For instance, the inequalities of the power dynamic are not always best represented through depictions of violent 'doing', by employing discourses of liberation and sexual pleasure, pornography is able to mask its relationship to violence against women. By presenting women with the appearance of their enjoyment and embrace of sexual activity, pornography convinces men that this is actually what women want and persuades women of the naturalness and positive benefits of the system. Looking back on the 1960s, a period when women supposedly experienced sexual freedom, Sheila Jeffreys claims

> Behind the baloney of liberation, the naked power politics of male supremacy were being acted out. The high priests of sexologic, helped by the pornographers, progressive novelists and sex radicals continued to orchestrate woman's joyful embrace of her oppression through the creation of her sexual response. Sexologists have for a hundred years dedicated their lives to eliciting orgasms from women in order to prevent our liberation. The 1960s was a period when greater opportunities were open to women and the 'sexual revolution', rather than being liberating, helped to defuse the potential threat to male power. (1990: 2)

The power dynamic is not, therefore, simply forced onto women but is actively constructed as a state of being to be embraced by women: the ideological development of 'femininity' which embraces the power dynamic as natural, healthy, sexy and, crucially, liberating for women (Dworkin & MacKinnon 1988; MacKinnon 1982). The answer, for US radical feminism, lay in recourse to legal restriction of pornography under those statutes which would remove First Amendment rights from pornography and would enable individual women to sue the producers for harms suffered as a result of their products' availability. A central premise of this legislative turn was that no woman freely chooses to appear in, or to read/watch/enjoy pornography.

The focus of this book is women readers and their relationships with a sexual explicit magazine; thus, I contend that anti-pornography critique is of little practical use to my discussion. Quite apart from the array of conceptual and other problems that other critics have drawn attention to in this approach (Carol 1994; Kipnis 1996; Rubin 1993; Segal 1990, 1993, 1994; Vance 1992a), without exception anti-porn accounts offer no means of understanding the motivations of women readers of sexually explicit materials except in terms of their victimization. Furthermore, their supposed analyses of pornography actively prevent understanding of the materials themselves, as I argue in subsequent chapters.

Being an Enlightened Woman is Method Enough

Any examination of pornography must acknowledge the influence of Andrea Dworkin and Catherine A. MacKinnon: Dworkin's *Pornography: Men Possessing Women* was published in 1981 and is the most prominent text of the radical feminist position. Her claims about pornography have been enduring and, despite the many criticisms of her work, the central themes of her analysis resurface time and again in discussions of sexually explicit material whether identified as a product of the so-called pornographic industry or of more mainstream and 'respectable' media. During the past twenty years, Dworkin's analysis has provided a blueprint for neatly packaging pornography as a transhistorical and instantly knowable category of cultural production and consumption (see, for example, articles in Itzin 1992). Linking photographs in *Hustler* to the literary works of Miller and Lawrence via the developments of medical science, Dworkin has set the tone for the kinds of analysis that will count. The framing of pornography as a representational regime which harms women through its documentation of 'actual' harms, its pernicious lying about women's sexuality and its active creation of more 'whores', has led to a retreat from individual texts.

Dworkin claims to have uncovered the true meaning of pornography: 'it is a book about the meaning of what is being shown.' (Preface) Her analysis finds that pornography and its representations are timeless and recognizable but *only* if we know how to look.

> I had to study the photographs to write about them. I stared at them to analyse them. It took me a long time to see what was in them because I never expected

> to see what was there and expectation is essential to accurate perception. I had to learn. (1981: 303)

This process of learning is directly related to gender. As a woman, Dworkin has to learn to see as a man, she has to learn to recognize that the image is of torture and that torture is sexually exciting:

> I developed a new visual vocabulary, one that few women have at all, one that male consumers of pornography carry with them all the time: any mundane object can be turned into an eroticised object – an object that can be used to hurt women in a sexual context with a sexual purpose and a sexual meaning. (1981: 303)

Thompson (1994) calls this the Hezikial factor, the need to point out to everyone else what one can see. It is an evangelical desire to educate others; a blowing of the trumpet of doom and in paraphrasing her work it is difficult to convey the powerful sense of unmasking which permeates her writing. But this style has another function: it effectively masks the ways in which Dworkin's examples are a mishmash assembled only in order to prove her claims about male sexuality and the symbiotic relationship between the 'pornographer' and the consumer. Employing long descriptive lists of the materials under 'analysis' and insisting on the links between various kinds of sexual representations elides the distinctions in the materials offered for discussion.[6]

Sliding between images in *Playboy*, through more specialized bondage and S & M imagery, to the works of de Sade, via women's experiences of rape and torture, to the genocides of the twentieth and preceding centuries and then back to the realms of representation in 'Snuff' movies, Dworkin ignores a whole range of differences – not least media forms, textual structures and narrative strategies,[7] in favour of a focus on male power:

> The strains of male power are embodied in pornography's form and content, in economic control of and distribution of wealth within the industry, in the picture or story as thing, in the photographer or writer as aggressor, in the critic or intellectual who through naming assigns value, in the actual use of models, in the application of the material in what is called real life (which women are commanded to regard as distinct from fantasy). (1981: 24–5)

As well as effacing the differences between materials, Dworkin also refuses the differences between reality and fiction. These images are *documents* of harm: they are physical documents of the real state of male/female relationships. The use of real women in the images shows that pornography is not just implicated in the mistreatment of women but in fact *is* the mistreatment of women.[8] It also offers a very direct relationship to readers, they do not mistake this element of pornography: they recognize it and use it. Thus the relationship Dworkin envisages is a mono-dimensional one. She is not alone: [9] this idea has become steadfastly a feature of anti-pornography critique. In *The Pornography of Representation*, Susanne Kappler claims that the pornographer 'is in direct communication with another subject, the spectator or reader' (1986: 52).

Delving into the Mucky Stuff

Making claims about the content of pornography necessarily involves making suppositions about the nature of audience responses. In Dworkin's claims that pornography is not just a result of the power struggle between male and female there is a conception of the reader/viewer of pornography. If pornography is a driving force behind the continuing inequality of women (sexually, economically, politically and socially) and defines women as less human than men, then its readers must be taking its messages and using them in their real lives. This *is* Dworkin's claim; the male viewer relates to and understands pornography via his identification with, and approval of its power to render women as objects. Identification is made possible via the male protagonist of the narrative/image, his substitute (any object used to penetrate the model) or the look of the camera. It is part of a circuit of effects:

> In fantasy, the male can experiment with the consequences as he imagines them of loss of power over women. He can expect that what he has done to women will be done to him. He can view his own devastation in his imagination, experience it as self-induced, self-contained, masturbatory sexual reality and, when the book is closed, as a result of having read it, be armed more thoroughly against any vulnerability that might imperil him. He will be convinced that male power can only be maintained by an absolutely cruel and ruthless subjugation of women. (1981: 35)

Different from that of the right-wing Christian movement (or most researchers in the effects tradition[10]), Dworkin's version of effects is not one which might operate on viewers without their knowledge, subconsciously operating, or via a process of desensitization: these are effects which men actively seek. Men read pornography precisely because it will affect them, precisely because it will make them insensitive to women's pain, it offers them a manual for rape and understanding the world. Pornography acts to stop men slipping out of the power role; it reminds them that power is a sensual, marvellous thing. The system constantly replenishes and reinforces itself through the production, distribution and consumption of its own image. In an example, citing a set of photographs in German *Playboy*, Dworkin offers the following description:

> A second photograph shows the woman's naked ass and legs. The top border of the photograph is cropped just below the woman's waist. She is standing. Her legs are spread.... The woman's skin is brown. Several laser beams appear to penetrate her vagina from behind. The rays of laser light converge from below at what appears to be the point of entry into the woman. It is as if the woman were hoisted on laser beams going into her vagina. The text explains ... *Playboy* editors in Munich 'have a slightly different approach to eroticism, one that is a refreshing break from the homegrown variety. As you can see from these pictures, their taste runs to the technological'. The woman is called 'an exquisite volunteer'. (1981: 139)

Using scientific and military sources, Dworkin explains at length the dangers of lasers and the links between the *Playboy* images and the genocidal history of Germany. A history linked to male sexuality:

> The importance of the two specifics – Jew and woman – resides in the resonating power of sexual memory. It is her image – hiding, running, captive, dead – that evokes the sexual triumph of the sadist. She is his sexual memory and he lives in all men. But this memory is not recognised as a sexual fact, nor is it acknowledged as male desire: it is too horrible. Instead, she wants it, they all do. The Jews went voluntarily to the ovens. (1981: 146)

Dworkin's exploration of the links from the images to history to male sexuality is extremely long and, like a rollercoaster ride, leaves her readers shaken. For the described viewer to recognize the full import of these images he must go through the following stages. To register, at least, that the woman is not white, that lasers have military uses and can be extremely dangerous, that the images are of German origin and that the technological element is significant as an instrument of death. Connections then need to be made across time, acquiring cumulative evidence of historical and racist/sexist ideologies, in order to produce a sadistic pleasure in this particular form of sexual torture. The process is still not complete. The pleasure needs to be accompanied by the disavowal of man's natural sadism and the transference of this fantasy on to the woman in the image and all women such that her/their victim status is effaced. Particularly interesting is Dworkin's apparent faith in men's willingness to recognize and join in the narrative of a set of photographs – a response already conditioned by the producer. It appears nothing will prevent a reader responding accordingly. There is no space for a reader's boredom or revulsion or just unwillingness to spend the time looking at those particular images. Instead committed engagement is assured in order that the viewer makes the connections thereby unlocking the full import of the images and producing his sexual arousal. The evidence for such commitment ought to be available; engagement of this kind could surely be tested. There is, of course, no evidence available.

Anti-porn feminism has never claimed a methodology as such, indeed Dworkin explicitly states that science or enquiry based on scientific models are inappropriate to understanding the ways in which pornography functions because they are directly implicated in the work of silencing and harming women. The pornographic imagination is at the root of every branch of male endeavour so that female pain is unrecognizable whatever methodology is employed. The answer is analysis of pornography tracing the connections between proliferations of porn (especially so-called violent pornography) and actual increases in violent crimes against women. Despite criticism of this approach, the refusal to employ any form of systematic mode of enquiry into the production, reception and contexts of pornographic media texts still enjoys status. Pornography *is* harm against women and there is no need to argue the case – anyone who thinks otherwise is blind to women's pain or is in the pay of the pornographers (or both).[11]

The radical feminist theorization of pornography thus establishes the boundaries of 'pornography' as entirely arbitrary – any image of women can be classed as porn (and therefore bad) if to Dworkin's 'nose' it smells like porn. Her conclusions therefore make quite irrelevant any examination of why or how men like different kinds of sexually explicit materials, or why they may choose one kind over another. Perhaps more important, her conclusions make irrelevant any examination of why men might refuse her analysis.

Turning to Psychoanalysis

A central claim contra Dworkin's position is that her account offers no way of understanding the waywardness of desire. Dworkin has no truck with Freud (ironically much of her analysis shows his influence), but for some feminists psychoanalysis appears to hold out the promise of getting closer to the slippery meanings of pornography. Segal (1994) suggests that a psychoanalytic approach might enable the uncovering of the problematic and often unexpected workings of the pornographic image for its readers,[12] specifically some of the male 'castration anxieties' which she suggests pornography seems determined to disavow. Wilson has suggested that 'Far from being the celebration of male power, pornography sometimes seems to reassure men and allay fears of impotence' (1983: 166). In a similar vein, Pajaczkowska (1994) suggests that male identification may not follow gender lines but instead, the reader/viewer identifies with the female of the image in order to experience the pleasures of a traditionally feminine passivity. Indeed Kuhn has noted that such moments of 'pleasure and unease' may offer the possibilities of disrupting 'the spectator's masculinity' (1985: 35). Each of these depend upon claims of what *may* happen: despite the optimism, psychoanalysis singularly fails to deliver an account of porn reading that is not merely suggestive of possibilities. To illustrate this failure more concretely I draw on a recent study that sought to reposition the psychoanalytic account of men's use of pornography through a focus on pornography's textual strategies to efface sexual difference.

Kaite's *Pornography and Difference* traces 'the dominant themes in pornography's regime of representation' (1995: 19). Using a variety of pornographic images: soft and hard core, straight, TV/Transsexual and gay, Kaite looks to the ways in which the masculine subject is addressed and to the kinds of identification made possible by pornographic texts. Contra Dworkin and others, Kaite proposes that the 'masculine moment' of pornography is actually unstable and capable of different readings:

> Pornography is indeed a radical play on difference and 'otherness', to the extent, however, that normative boundaries of masculinity and femininity are transgressed rather than reinforced. ...The pornographic engages in the systematic transgression of codes of sexual difference so that sexual difference is a strategic deployment of signs and subject to renegotiation(s). ... [A] preoccupation with certain images and narratives is a return to the sites of reassurance and an indication that identities, cultural and psychic, are characterised by slippage. Hence one reason for the obsessive and repetitive fascination with pornographic tedium. (1995: vii)

Whereas Dworkin argues the display of female genitals is indication that men find women's bodies hateful, Kaite suggests that such representations transgress bourgeois notions of the body enabling 'seduction'. These transgressions are facilitated by the phallic significations of the accoutrements of the porn model: the pearl necklace, stiletto heel, lace and leather. The image is constructed to suggest 'indifference' as much as difference, that is, images of women are sexually arousing because they articulate a female body which is phallicized, transgressing the boundary of difference and enabling the seductive moment that 'writes' the viewer as desiring subject. The phallus is a 'sign' rather than inherent feature of those bodies designated biologically male:

> ... difference (castration) does not reside with women and female 'lack'. Phallic desire may look like the prerogative of men, not because they are or have the phallus but because it embodies singularity, the principle of one, and because it is modelled on the organ with which it is synonymous. (1995: 28)

Women in pornography are accorded a phallic (powerful) status obscuring difference and subverting the concept of the fully realized masculine subject/viewer. 'The pornographic model ... carries the signs of his phallic masculinity: it is this play of differences, this erotic theft, and the indifference to difference involved, that seduces.' (1995: 29) Furthermore, this approach inverts the traditional questions raised by pornography, 'Rather than "What does pornography reveal?" the question here is, "What does it conceal?"' (1995: 11). Kaite claims the traditional question suggests that in revealing the true meaning of pornography we can see that our response to it is already formulated within the text whereas the second approach posits a more complex relationship between the pornographic text, the imaginary and the reader. Unfortunately this more complex relationship remains no more than an abstract premise, her analysis of images only points to the possibilities of complexity, with the addition of a heavy layer of theorization that is only convincing if you are already convinced.

The difficulties of psychoanalytic readings of contemporary media texts are outlined elsewhere (Bordwell 1989; Hardy 1998; Jackson 2000; Prince 1996) and Kaite's analysis, while opening up some interesting questions, is actually as bad an account of pornography as could be imagined. The circuitous and tortuous routes her analysis takes are, one suspects, designed to flatter others operating within the psychoanalytic tradition. Observing that 'tracing the history of something – a practice, the circulation of a fashionable object – does not explain how it works.' (1995: 13) Kaite goes on to claim that she 'offers a synchronic reading of the systematic and conventional coding of the image, and an investigation into how (and why) elaborations of sexual (in)difference, simulated gratification, and machinations of the fetish conspire to seduce.' (1995: 13) A great deal of word play, etymologies, selective description and generalized claims follow: 'typically in soft-core' (1995: 40) and 'the most common representation' (1995: 37). Lacanian interpretations are then imputed to both text and reader. In a discussion of a set entitled *Anal Fantasy* Kaite claims:

> The penis, while perhaps 'stiff and sharp' itself, is partially obliterated/castrated in visual terms, by the vaginal enclosure. The juxtaposing of this representation with the doubled performance of the anus – i.e., it is poised to project, expel (it must be 'stowed'), defile, and penetrate, and at the same time is an organ set to contain, seize, and capture – is an incitement to castration. The 'pungent' anus, 'sharply painful' threatening to become unplugged, is the metonymic twin of the phallic projectile. And the fetishized penis, visually a part-object engulfed by the vagina, is 'cut' to reveal more of the testicles than the penis itself. Both representations set up the reader to be absorbed, engulfed, unmanned, hence partially feminised. (1995: 51)

Bordwell's (1989) complaint that psychoanalytic accounts need only novelty to prove their worth seems apposite to the gymnastic wordplay offered here. Circuitous elements of psychoanalytic theory are rehearsed alongside images underpinning her assertion that in/difference is located in the phallic signifier. Her claim to illuminate what pornography would conceal is merely a reassertion that pornography's appeal lies in the unconscious. It is simply a matter of rehearsing the articles of psychoanalytic faith: 'symbolic castration', 'phallic hyperinscription', 'voyeurism' and their effects: the engulfing of the viewer.

Women viewers are mentioned only once, to claim, 'If straight women "use" or are aroused or seduced by mainstream pornography, that is not to say that the text works the same way for both men and women.' (1995: 15). Kaite's reader is male and an 'ideal'. His suffering is great: although she makes no overt claims for ideological effects, underlying her accounts are alienation, crises of instability in subjectivity and then ultimately dissatisfaction. Images are seductive and threatening, 'The sexual choreography in front of the reader is more indifferent than different; and the reader, too, "spends himself" on the bodies beyond the keyhole, lost in the fabrications before him.' (1995: 129). The images work on the viewer without his conscious participation, however, all of these claims are suppositions, perhaps just her own responses 'Castration anxiety, yes, but I think the porn reader *does* want to step into her boots.' (1995: 104).

Where Dworkin and others draw links across a number of historical periods to show a lineage of male violence against women, Kaite divorces pornography from any empirical connections to its modes of production or consumption. The metonymic associations filling her work are drawn from Partridge's *Historical Slang*, so that history becomes a quaint and arcane explanation for the workings of pornography and insulate Kaite from difficult questions. Her account offers no way of understanding the production of pornographic texts, the medium specific nature of their representations, nor the responses of anything other than an ideal reader deeply immured in oedipal and castration anxieties.

Her account is an account of effects. Porn is instantly recognizable; its effects are irresistible and only by phallicizing the female body is its terror and disgust disguised. The concept of identification is disguised as recognition of in/difference: in desiring, the phallic woman and the male viewer become the same. This analysis, supposedly a major challenge to MacDworkinite thinking, actually reinforces the notion that pornography tells lies about women's sexuality. Psychoanalysis evacuates conscious participation or engagements on the part of pornography's viewers. Not only is such participation removed from the textual interface, but also there is no sense that it would have connections to the production and distribution of those texts, their histories and their roles in cultural life. Kaite's claims about pornography's offensiveness stress transgressive possibilities but transgressive of what and to what end? The faceless spectator and the equally faceless producer are locked in an unending circle of erotic theft and signification oblivious to the world outside.

***Hustler* and the Disgust Machine**

A less esoteric account of the reader and the pleasures of pornography are discussed in Kipnis' analysis of *Hustler* magazine. In a book-length study of US pornography, *Bound and Gagged* (1996) and an earlier essay, '(Male) Desire and (Female) Disgust: Reading *Hustler*' (1992), Kipnis claims that pornography offers a discourse about social class as well as gender and that acknowledgement, coupled with a psychoanalytic focus, reveals the particularly unruly relationship between pornographic text and reader. These relationships are opened up via the mobilization of bourgeois disgust. Drawing on Freud's observations on jokes, Kipnis argues that *Hustler* is obscene to some women and not to others because of 'the degree to which a certain version of female sexuality is hypostatised as natural, versus a sense of mobility of sexuality, at least at the level of fantasy.' (1992: 381) Female disgust is employed by *Hustler* in order to provoke male laughter and arguments that *Hustler* is misogynistic, simply disguise their classed dimensions.

> Pornography isn't viewed as having complexity, because its audience isn't viewed as having complexity, and this propensity for oversimplification gets reproduced in every discussion about pornography. (1996: 177)

Focusing on *Hustler*'s body typology, Kipnis argues that this signals the magazine's distinctiveness from its mainstream rivals, *Playboy* and *Penthouse*.

> The *Hustler* body is an unromanticised body – no vaselined lenses or soft focus... it's a body, not a surface or a suntan: insistently material, defiantly vulgar, corporeal. In fact, the *Hustler* body is often a gaseous, fluid-emitting, embarrassing body, one continually defying the strictures of bourgeois manners and mores... *Hustler*'s favourite joke is someone accidentally defecating in church. (1992: 375)

Kipnis argues powerfully for the magazine's address to its readers' 'blue-collar urge' (1992: 391) which responds to 'the strategic uses of nudity ... as an offensive against the rich and powerful' (1992: 387). Hence she finds that *Hustler's* detractors are members of the middle classes or powerful elites: these same people are also found in the magazine as its target. Examining these representations Kipnis finds that the magazine's primary target is not gender but the wealth and privilege enjoyed by educated and cultured elites, often at the expense of the 'ordinary American citizen'. Any account not engaging with the classed discourse of the magazine is thus bound to align itself with bourgeois hegemonic values – precisely the very values that a class-less feminism and *Hustler* have in their sights. It is this political element of the magazine which receives her focus, therefore Kipnis stresses the shifting relationships between 'high' and 'low' culture and suggests that pornography is 'a repository for those threatening, problematic materials and imagery banished from the culture at large.' (1996: 94) Pornography *is* the return of the repressed – a 'social service' (1996: 12), a Rabelaisian assertion of the lower bodily stratum and its functions. Reading *Hustler* has status as an act of political resistance.

Kipnis explains that obsessive relationships are a key feature of the engagement with pornography, for user and anti-porn campaigner alike. The language of addiction she uses posits a particular power residing in the text over which we have no real control – its effects may be different for different viewers but its modes of affects are the same. Thus her claim that the chicken plucker's delight and Robin Morgan's tears are caused by the same textual elements (1992: 373): the anti-pornography account is exposed as the unspoken and subjective discourse of shame engendered by the sight of the naked female body.[13] Identification is a central theme of Kipnis' analysis – readers have choices: in so far as the subconscious allows choice, they can identify with the shame of the sexualized body or they can revel in its unleashing of the 'contents of the unconscious'. (1992: 377)

The historical antecedents of pornography vindicate this encounter with the political nature of *Hustler*. However, Kipnis is less convincing in showing the relations between the political elements (anti-bourgeois) and the sexual pleasures offered by *Hustler*. In rejecting the 'compensatory fantasy life mobilised by *Playboy* and *Penthouse*' (1992: 383) Kipnis argues that in *Hustler* power, money, and prestige are disparaged at the same time as they are acknowledged as central to sexual attractiveness, thus 'identification with these sorts of class attributes [are countered] on every other front. The intersections of sex, gender, class and power here are complex, contradictory, and political.' (1992: 383). Although the statement about the contradictory nature of the magazine is important – it reminds us that there is more to pornography than the purely physiological – it is only through the authentic expression of class-based discontents that *Hustler* is seen as 'better' than its mainstream counterparts. Her account stresses contradictory relationships of class irritation, a sense of disenfranchisement driving readers' sexual thrills: the irredeemably vulgar content of *Hustler* is isolated from its other elements and celebrated as the quintessential textual feature. But this returns us to hierarchical discriminations: inverse perhaps – *Hustler* comes out tops in the transgression stakes – leaving *Playboy* readers wallowing in the pap of upwardly mobile bourgeois mores.

Kipnis acknowledges audience research is necessary to test her hypothesis, however, there are real difficulties in her account that might make such research impossible. Defending pornography as an 'expressive medium in the positive sense' her account limits its expressiveness to a binary antagonism accounting for only two personalities, the ideal reader (male and working class) and the ideal figure of fun (the middle-class feminist academic). She is, in effect, defending *Hustler* by making it into 'not-porn'. The analysis of class-based distinctions is important and needs to be retained in any detailed exploration of responses to pornography[14]: on this I must agree with Kipnis, but I would add that this cannot occur at the expense of the specifically sexual dimensions of these magazines. Her claims that the 'softer' modes of porn offer 'compensatory fantasies' is too similar to the moral objections to all pornography, that fantasy is a bad and degraded waste of time which somehow cuts its 'victims' off from the 'realities' of life.

The Disembodied Spectator

Furthermore, the fluidity of responses to pornography which form a part of her account are seriously compromised by Kipnis' observation that

> Pornography grabs us and doesn't let go. Whether you're revolted or enticed, shocked or titillated, these are flip sides of the same response: an intense, visceral engagement with what pornography has to say. (1996: 161)

Endemic to psychoanalytic approaches is the problematic theorization of viewing as driven and reactive, beyond the control of the spectator. The impulse to view pornography is conceived as entirely sexual and voyeuristic – the 'scopic' drive, a product of unconscious desires and expression of their repression. Consequently one turns to pornography because it meets hidden needs which have no solace elsewhere. No distinctions are made regarding the age, emotions, or stage of physical/sexual development of the viewer. Essentially removing any agency whatsoever from the production and consumption of the pornographic text, these are imperatives that cannot be ignored and which explain everything. As Kipnis argues:

> Pornography's allegories of transgression reveal, in the most visceral ways, not only our culture's edges, but how intricately our own identities are bound up in all of these quite unspoken, but quite relentless, cultural dictates. And what the furore over pornography also reveals is just how deeply attached to the most pervasive feelings of shame and desire all these unspoken dictates are. Pornography's ultimate desire is exactly to engage our deepest embarrassments, to mock us for the anxious psychic balancing acts we daily perform, straddling between the anarchy of sexual desires and the straitjacket of social responsibilities. (1996: 167)

Focusing on the unconscious nature of pornographic discourses and responses leads to the conception of response to pornography that is almost a contradiction of her earlier descriptions of complex classed responses. Discrimination between images cannot be accounted for at a cognitive level, nor can the possible expression of not just disgust but pleasure or boredom or incomprehension. The problem lies in the conception of the spectator within psychoanalytic theory. As Stephen Prince has observed:

> To the extent that the scopophilic drive is activated by visual imagery, psychoanalytic film theory tends to see all spectators as being positioned by perceptual stimuli and has remained silent about how viewers process that imagery by constructing rational analogies with their real-life experiences, values and precepts. (1996: 82)

The process of *using* a magazine or a film becomes lost in such accounts. The process of becoming aroused is ignored in favour of deeply buried needs. Pornography meets those needs through its use of cues: the phallic signifier; excessive elements (spurting come, extreme practices, taboo activities, large bodies, bulging breasts etc.); the use of close-ups and fetishized imagery. The image conjured by theory and by descriptions of pornographic texts and their effects upon readers suggest a fixated gaze at the image: a visual attentiveness that is oblivious to everything except the image.

It may well be true that the viewer of pornography stares at an image but because these magazines (and films) are understood only in terms of their capacity for sexual arousal (in the vernacular as 'one-hand mags' – a description which references one particular mode of use), theorists have avoided thinking about the range of embodied practices also associated with viewing a pornographic magazine (or film). The response envisaged wipes out the processes of acquiring the textual material, of the spatial and temporal enjoyment of it, the anticipatory pleasures of opening the magazine or switching on the video. It assumes that the intention in opening a porn magazine is to be aroused sexually and, that once aroused, the reader will want and attempt sexual release. Only academic, radical feminist or moralist viewers seem able to experience responses other than the 'purely' sexual: they can talk of their boredom! 'Ordinary' porn users are never disappointed, embarrassed, put off, worried or appalled and their pleasures can only be understood as singular and masturbatory.

Focus on 'the gaze' also suggests that this is the only sensory experience invited by the pornographic image, however, as I show later, readers describe more than visual pleasure: photographs and written text are capable of engaging a range of sensory responses. Significantly, readers' talk indicates that they employ a range of evaluative and cognitive interpretations of the text, judging at the very least the credibility of the image or narrative. It is through those responses that the potentials of the magazine are made available to readers. The study of readers' explanations of their relationships with a specific magazine indicates that physiological arousal is only possible if other interests, pleasures and activities have been acknowledged, invited and addressed. Even where theorists have discussed the ways in which, for example, *Playboy* attempts to do more than provide the material for onanistic activity, other affective processes are overlooked. The implications of additional levels of response have been ignored in favour of the articulation of a generalized male response in terms of the 'subordination of women' or the transgression of taboos.

This approach to pornography is rooted in the belief that pornography has no purpose and value over the sexual. Some theorists may acknowledge the complexity of the material – as Kipnis does (even, implicitly, Dworkin), but the implications of that complexity are never fully explored. Psychoanalytic accounts stress the fluidity of possible identifications and yet the cues that allow these diffuse responses are represented as timeless and entirely knowable for the academic. If the cues are so well known then they operate as constants, as anchors. To paraphrase Freud: there is no need to ask readers of pornography for their story, we know it already. This criticism can also be levelled at any number of accounts that don't take psychoanalysis as their basic unit of theorization. For example, Stephen Marcus' observation that pornography is little more than propaganda because it has a 'singleness of intention ...to move us in the direction of action... and away from language.' (Cited in Ross 1989: 182)

Challenging the 'True' Feminist Position

Despite the attempt to present the anti-pornography position as *the* feminist perspective on pornography, there were and are significant challenges to the claim that all pornography harms all women. These arguments are often intimately connected to the guiding principles of the feminist movement and its purpose, thus the critique centres on the inappropriateness of radical feminism's attempts to blame pornography for all women's ills and its reduction of women's experiences of inequality to the printed page. As one collection made clear, at stake was the 'challenge to reclaim feminism' (Assister & Carol 1993).

Many feminists have argued cogently and passionately against the 'premature orthodoxy' (Rubin 1984) of radical feminism and its claim that all women agree on the need for, and form of, restrictions on pornography. Refuting the specific claims that violence[15] and women's degradation are key features of all pornography and drawing out the complexity of sexual pleasures and responses (Vance 1992c; Webster 1984), these arguments are important analyses of the *construction of pornography as an object of study*. They illustrate the ways in which researchers' orientations to the object have determining effects upon outcomes and conclusions. Thus these accounts have highlighted the subjectiveness of claims of women's degradation (Carol 1994; Hollibaugh 1984) and the dangerous assertions of appropriate femininity. Elizabeth Wilson's (1992) critique labels anti-porn campaigns 'feminist fundamentalism' accusing them of attempting to lay down rules and prohibitions for ways of living which curtail the possibilities for individual women and their explorations of sexuality and selfhood:

> Women in the anti-pornography discourse have no lust and desire at all. Ironically, therefore, this way of discussing the issue actually objectifies women, who are positioned as passive objects of male lust – precisely the aspect of pornography about which feminists feel so unhappy. The campaigners, in fact, re-create the fantasy world of porn, where men are always ready to perform, erections are repeatable and ejaculation is never premature. Thus the campaigns reinforce all

> the misinformation about sexuality which porn itself is accused of purveying. (1992: 27)

Rubin (1993) in particular has highlighted the ways in which 'sexual value systems' underpin all arguments regarding pornography. Drawing on Foucauldian insights, Rubin observes that discursive conceptions of 'normality' and 'healthy' are especially mobilized in discussions of sexuality, establishing hierarchies of 'good' and 'bad' sex which enable the construction of appropriate sexual activity for men and women. Ironically, the sex value systems of moralists, traditionalists and radical feminists appear remarkably similar, especially where women are concerned. In her discussion of female passivity and Spanking stories, Albury observes that a key claim against pornography relies on the assertion that women only engage in 'bad sex' because they are driven by male desire and thus porn must be condemned because it insists on 'depicting and/or describing heterosexual women *as if they actually desired* bad sex'.(1998: 52)

The criticism of pornography as showing women as desirous of sexual activity indicates the deeply embedded conception of 'normal', 'healthy' female sexuality as passive and receptive within much anti-porn analysis. This is one of a number of inconsistencies to be found in MacDworkinite argumentation alongside, as Pollard (1994) argues, flawed conceptions of ideological power leading to claims of causative effects. Segal (1994) has pointed to the assumption of cognitive slippages in claims that readers of pornography too easily conflate fantasy and reality. McElroy (1995) and Strossen (2000) have indicated the dangers of any strategic alliances with the legal system in order to 'protect' women. Although I do not wish to negate the importance of these accounts, they are antitheses of the anti-pornography arguments: they rely on the existence of those arguments in order to offer their own insights. The anti-porn position is a pre-requisite. One side blames sexual representations for the promulgation of sexism and the continuing oppression of women, while the other emphasizes the positive possibilities of those same representations to inspire and contribute to women's increasing freedom to express their sexual desires. The same object is responsible for markedly different outcomes. Neither side engages with the textual object: radical feminism generalizes from a range of unnamed and unattributed sources and, for their opposition, pornography figures as a range of texts whose possible complexity and consequent vulnerability to unhappy legislation must be acknowledged and defended. The focus on the rights and wrongs of pornography has largely been conducted at a level that does not deal with the individual and perhaps very ordinary details of a 'pornographic' text.

The complexities of the relationships offered by a pornographic text are rarely acknowledged and the roles of the reader and producer of that text have been subject to assertion and generalization. Although writers claim to be dealing with the concrete representational strategies of pornography, it is representation in the abstract, where theoretical assertion replaces investigation, description and analysis. Nevertheless, these assertions have been used as if they constitute method or logically grounded conclusions.

Recent years have witnessed what one author has termed a 'paradigm shift' (Attwood 2002) in discussions of pornography. Attwood traces this shift to the pioneering work of Linda Williams which takes a close analytic focus on the actual texts of filmic porn and to Walter Kendrick's historical account of the classifications of pornography. Furthermore, she outlines a number of moves away from the 'tired binary' oppositions of anti- or pro-porn arguments towards a 'contextualisation of pornography' (Attwood 2002: 93). Attwood is right to suggest that there have been moves away from the focus on the moralities of sexual representations, through the gender politics of those representations and their supposed imbrications in the mess of male sexual fantasies of violence and degradation to sometimes more nuanced accounts of pornography's place in everyday life (Juffer, 1998).

This book adds to the continually growing corpus of debate but differs from other analyses of pornography in that it seeks to address the absence of women readers of sexually explicit materials in most discussions. An earlier evaluation of the field argued that pornography is traditionally discussed in terms of its relationship to male sexuality and that female sexuality as addressed by pornographic texts rarely surfaces even in feminist work (Brewer 1986). That absence has begun to be addressed in recent years (see, for example, Albury 2005; Lumby 1997; Vance 1992a; Ellis et al. 1986; Segal 1994), but has tended to focus on the rather generalized claims of an expanding textual field for women and by celebrating the possibility of transgressive use by women. My research seeks to understand the pleasures of reading the British magazine *For Women*; it examines under what conditions women participate in the publication's sexual world and how *For Women* was accommodated to their own sexual world-view.

Traditionally, discussions of pornography have failed to directly engage with either the producers of pornography, except as the vilified and shadowy figure of the 'pornographer' (Itzin 1992; Dworkin 1981) or with readers of such material except where those readers 'confess' to the ways in which pornography has contributed to their corruption (Itzin 1992; Russell 1993a). Where women's voices have featured in accounts of the pornography industry, it has generally been as victims either of its production processes or of its use in social or personal situations (Itzin 1992; Russell 1993b; Dines et al. 1998). These accounts, with their attendant focus on the 'harms' of pornography, have also tended to sediment the gender divisions of 'male perpetrator' and 'female victim' so that pornography has achieved dubious status as *the* subordinating representational regime underpinning patriarchy. The central characters in the pornography drama have not, of course, gone unchallenged. For example, Avedon Carol (1994), Lynne Segal (1994), and the various authors in Assister and Carol (1993), Segal and McIntosh (1992) and Vance (1992a) have all raised important questions about porn's monolithic status within academic, legal and social discussion. However, these interventions are not problem free: again, their focus tends towards the valorisation of certain 'transgressive' practices of producing and using pornography which can contribute to a further hierarchizing of desire with 'radical' or politicized porn at the top and the more mundane and widespread use of mass market porn at the bottom. The fundamental premise of the anti-pornography position that men, as producers and consumers, use porn to victimize women is not seriously challenged by the assertion that there are some people able to critique heterosexist norms through their production/use of taboo materials. The pitting of Annie Sprinkle against Larry Flynt or the lesbian sado-masochist against the heterosexual man merely complicates the picture drawn by Dworkin and others but speaks to a readership which, like the theorist who proposes the oppositions, rarely wishes to get their hands dirty in order to understand 'ordinary' porn and its 'ordinary' producers and readers. So let me begin my alternative approach – getting dirty – by examining some of the contextual issues relating to the production of *For Women*.

Notes

1. One of the central tenets of moralistic and radical feminist discourses on pornography, is that pornography proliferates faster than any other media form and that the content is increasingly violent – such claims are rarely substantiated with any evidence but this lack of measurement seems not to matter – any sighting of pornographic materials makes it an object of concern.
2. Pornography was not the only area of dispute in the 'sex wars', but it was a key issue which threatened to split the feminist movement (Snitow et al. (eds.) 1984).
3. Although it is important to note the satirical purpose of some forms of pornography, we should not lose sight of the fact that still more, for example, Cleland's *Fanny Hill* had a straightforwardly sexual intent.
4. The right to choose is a central demand of all branches of feminism, but some conceive that choice as less constrained than radical feminism does, for example, Segal (1992, 1994) and Carol (1994).
5. The nature of that function is developed further in those accounts which claim that pornography has so pervaded women's lives that they are afraid to walk home at night and that in those areas where pornography is sold the incidence of rape has increased (Itzin 1992; Lederer 1980).
6. Rubin (1992) offers a similar critique of the anti-pornography slide shows and their tendencies to lump together all kinds of images and texts as if context and production were unimportant.
7. Rick Altman (1999) has noted this tendency in film theory regarding genre: 'Because genre is conceived as a conduit down which are poured textual structures linking production, exhibition and reception, genre study produces satisfactory results only when it has the right type of material to work with, i.e., texts that clearly and simultaneously support all aspects of the standard generic trajectory: blueprint, structure, label and contract. Only when the label and the structure provide a clear blueprint for production and a demonstrable basis for reception can this particular approach to genre operate properly.' (17) Thus, in Dworkin's account, the primary consideration marking pornography as pornographic is its 'male-ness'.
8. Photography occupies a special place in Dworkin's theorizing because it appears as a 'representation of the real'; her arguments about mistreatment would seem to be stretched by, for example, drawn/cartoon or computer-generated imagery. However, in drawing on and expanding Dworkin's ideas, MacKinnon has suggested that representational modes make no difference to the harms to women. Indeed her polemic *Only Words* (1994) expands at length on the ways in which words, drawings and sexual taunts are rooted in the culture of hard-core porn and are therefore to be redefined as deeds and thus offences against women.
9. It is not limited to anti-pornography feminism, in 1972 art historian Kenneth Clark commented to the Longford Parliamentary Commission on Pornography 'To my mind art

exists in the realm of contemplation, and is bound by some sort of imaginative transposition. The moment art becomes an incentive to action it loses its true character. This is my objection to painting with a communist programme, and it would also apply to pornography.' Quoted in Jill Bennet (1996: 245).

10. There is a whole tradition of work which seeks to trace links between pornography and violent actions: I do not deal with this material here because it seeks to examine responses within laboratory situations and its flawed methodologies and findings have been discussed at length elsewhere (Pally 1994).
11. There is an obvious analogy with creationists here: those who adduce evidence of evolution are in the pay of Satan.
12. Segal (1994) mounts a vigorous critique of various forms of psychoanalytic writing, claiming that most accounts fail to move beyond the limitations of Freudian psychoanalysis, to build upon its strengths. 'When Freud suggested from his findings that "libidinal attachments to persons of the same sex play no less a part as factors in normal mental life ... than do similar attachments to the opposite sex", he laid the seeds for something altogether more ambitious: reclaiming not just what we now call "transgressive" sexualities, but "normal" heterosexualities as well, as problematic exchanges which can and do challenge the existing ideological binaries masculinity/femininity, activity/passivity, dominance/subordination. But to sprout these seeds we will have to move well beyond the circular pathways traversed by psychoanalysis, as it liberates sexuality from gender, only to chain it the more securely later.' (164). A subsidiary of the pornography debates pondered women's fantasies and the possibility and/or necessity of 'decolonising' the female imagination (Bartky 1990 and Grimshaw 1993).
13. The subjective nature of anti-porn critiques are inextricably linked to their analyses of gender, thus, Kipnis goes on to argue that women are not best equipped to carry out the analysis of pornography:

    > Western feminism has often been accused of wearing blinders, of formulating itself strictly in relation to the experiences of white, upper class women. Insofar as the feminist anti-porn movement devotes itself to rehearsing the experience of disgust and attempting to regulate sexual imagery, the class issue will continue to be one of its formative blind spots. One might want to interpret feminist disgust as expressing *symbolically* the very real dangers that exist for women in the world. But the net effect is to displace those dangers onto a generalised disgust with sex and the body (or more specifically, onto heterosexual sex and the male body). Andrea Dworkin, for example, writes extensively about her disgust at semen, a lower bodily production which, she tells us, she regards as a form of 'pollution'. Her disgust is her prerogative...but even as mobilised against a perception of violation to the female body, it's more than problematic in a political movement devoted to achieving liberation and social equity. (1996: 140–1)

14. Similar arguments have been made in relation to other forms of denigrated popular culture texts, see, for instance, Thomas Boyle's (1989) *Black Swine in the Sewers of Hampstead*, New York: Viking Press which draws out the ways in which 'sensationalism' was produced as a concept in the 1820 to 1860s. Amongst his examples is the case of Dr William Palmer, a murderous surgeon – the resulting press assault on doctors (a body-related profession) was, claims Boyle, a class-based form of rejection of middle-class norms and hypocrisies.
15. Much of response has been about myth debunking; for example, Carol (1994) exposes the tendencies of anti-porn writing to present 'snuff' movies as fact and then to claim that all porn involves violent sex.

2

Sex Sells

As I noted in my introduction, a number of academics and cultural commentators have observed the ways in which sex has become a favoured representational trope of mainstream popular media having moved from a 'private affair' to a celebration of consumer culture, fun and 'calculated hedonism'. The elements they trace, of celebrity bodies increasingly shown in sexual display, more explicit discussion of sexual positions, activities and feelings, and the formulation of women as sexually desiring and active, were all a backdrop to the decision to publish *For Women*. What is left out of these accounts is a more thorough analysis of the ways in which these changes were implicated or created out of changing economic, practical and business environments. The proliferation of sexual representations is read in these accounts as emblems of liberation, self-pleasure and fun and, of course, I don't want to deny those aspects but it is also important to recognize the institutional contexts in which it became possible to offer these representations of 'sexual desire'. These are the elements I want to explore in this chapter.

In chapter 1, I indicated the difficulties of defining pornography, indeed in exploring some of the attempts to define the object 'pornography' I claimed that 'pornography' operates as a point *outside* discourses (that is, unconstrained by particular media and ignoring historical location) but constraining them. My point is that there is no coherent 'pornography' to be defined, instead we must look to the historical and social locatedness of all particular instances of sexually explicit materials. I therefore trace the magazine's origins in this chapter and argue that its launch and continued presence cannot be viewed in isolation but must be seen in the light of the changes to the periodical markets, both mainstream and soft core. In addition, I show that developments in wider popular culture made it possible for Northern & Shell to envisage the possibility of a successful sexually explicit title aimed at female readers. That account, though of necessity rather truncated, touches on the social, economic and cultural changes central to the emergence of the magazine but there is also a political dimension to its inception. This politics is of a personal kind but no less important for that. Subsequent chapters will show how those politics were reflected in *FW*'s letters pages, in the attitudes of *FW*'s editorial team and the comments by readers. Despite changes in personnel,[1] the magazine still retains a sense of attempting to foster and develop sexual possibilities for women. Traditional accounts of women's magazines and of pornography stress the collusion of editorial staff in the promotion of limited and/or false ideas about women and their lives. For example, Marjorie Ferguson, an ex-magazine journalist, suggests that the role of editor

> ...has a social significance. It involves the making of decisions about the current definitions of the cult of femininity – as a social institution to which all females can belong, and as a set of practices and beliefs which define the female gender role. In making such choices, the women's magazine editor's personal attributes, her perceptions of others, and her own beliefs play a major part. (1983: 119)

That overstates the editor's room for manoeuvre and ignores the very real practical considerations of achieving sales targets. While an editor will surely stamp her own authority on a magazine, the need to maintain readers and to build advertising revenue act as constraining factors. Gough-Yates' sees the role of editor as a complex juggling:

> Magazine producers face ethical dilemmas in relation to the conflict of the interests of the reader with commercial interests on a day to day basis ... They negotiate a path that must be attractive for advertisers, inoffensive for distributors, profitable and prestigious for their employers, and appealing and informative for readers. (2000a: 242)

With that complex juggling in mind, this chapter examines the 'history' of the magazine. Received as 'porn for women' on the basis of its perceived intention to arouse its readers sexually, the magazine was subject to a range of institutional conditions; how those conditions emerged in the forms of the text will be discussed in later chapters. But first, an overview of its market contexts.

I have written elsewhere on the recent history of the UK soft-core market and argued that any such history is hampered by lack of access to specific and detailed information about soft-core publishing (Smith 2005). The major players supplying the legal top-shelf market in Britain have been ignored in general histories of British media, for example, the many books published by academic presses with titles like *The Media in Question*, *Media Culture* and *The Media Reader* fail to mention sexually explicit publications. Where pornography does enter such works as in Briggs & Cobley's *The Media: An Introduction*, the focus remains on the efforts to regulate productions rather than any detailed analysis of the business conditions under which soft core is made available in the UK. This failure to deal with porn may be because the divisions between mainstream media production and top-shelf practices were strictly maintained, not least by the soft-core producers themselves. This situation has changed significantly in the past decade since publishers such as Richard Desmond

(Northern & Shell) and David Sullivan (Gold Star and Conegate) have attempted to move into those markets considered respectable. Both Desmond and Sullivan are now owners of national newspapers and alongside their moves to the mainstream has been a major increase in the attention their business activities have drawn.

The more specialized histories of regulation and censorship have described how the latter half of the 1970s had seen growth of the porn industries in Britain with the expansion within Soho and into the provinces[2] and how sexually explicit materials also became more commonplace and mainstream (Hunt 1998; Killick 1994; Thompson 1994). The expansion of sexually explicit materials during this time seems at odds with the facts of British censorship laws which are generally held to be the most restrictive in Europe (Petley 2000; Thompson 1994) but Hunt suggests that success was due to 'the Pornocrats work[ing] *with* capitalism' (1998: 23) and that the law was on the side of the publishers in that its inconsistencies and loopholes meant prosecution was difficult and its results uncertain. The law (in particular the *1959 OPA*) was, of course, open to interpretation and constant challenge.[3] Not least from entrepreneurs like David Sullivan who sought to ensure that his products remained on the cusp of what was permissible (Smith 2005). And yet, such material remained determinedly on the fringes of the mainstream, Barnard claims this is because 'their brief was always titillation, not anthropology' (2005: 9) so that their forays into discussions of sexual behaviours or practices remained hidebound by a peculiarly British morality.

> The British mindset always saw the sexual revolution as something sordid. A sign of moral standards slipping ever further into the abysss. The only way you could even write about unusual sexual behaviour was to adopt a stern voice that warned the reader of the physical symptoms of decay they would experience if they dared enter the squalid world of fucking without guilt. (Barnard 2005: 10)

Hence, he suggests that UK soft core kept its focus on saucy fun rather than explorations of changing mores. That argument maintains the narrative of repression and moral condemnation which is a feature of most discussion of British soft core; there is no doubt that the voices raised against top-shelf magazines have been vociferous in their condemnation of sexual representations for their own sake but does little to really explicate the impact of this British mindset on the practices and products of top-shelf publishing. For example, it is possible to see the traces of the public debates about appropriate depictions of sexuality in their 'seizure' and reworking by David Sullivan who piggybacked *Festival of Light* campaigns against his plans to open branches of his company's *Private* sex shops in towns throughout the UK, as publicity for those shops. He and other publishers defended their publications on the terms allowed by the OPA of 'public good' and, by naming one of his publications *Whitehouse* after Mrs Mary Whitehouse (leading figure in the *Festival of Light* and *National Viewers and Listeners Association*), ensured that magazine staked its claim to be anti-authoritarian, cheeky and fun.

Thus I want to argue that regulation and calls for censorship have not been simply repressive but have also been productive and an essential part of the material conditions in which pornography has developed in the UK. O'Toole has argued that soft-core publishing in the UK may well have been subject to the inconsistent provisions of the law but that this has actually served to *protect* home-grown publications from competition from those originating in less censorious national environments. O'Toole suggests that there is a cosy cartel operating in the UK which benefits from the *OPA*'s restrictions on the importation of material from abroad: 'the first thing wrong with British porn magazines is that they're not very good ... the publishers aren't trying hard enough. They don't have to' (1999: 138). This critique stresses the *benefits* to top-shelf publishers and highlights questions of quality but does not address the practices that follow from meeting the requirements of the law. The cosy arrangement O'Toole highlights forms a set of production imperatives with significant effects on the *content* of magazines but not only in terms of quality or explicitness.

Mainstream availability was crucial to the success of titles like *Men Only*, *Rustler*, *Whitehouse* and *UK Penthouse*: nationwide distribution allows for high-volume sales and that is a business relationship. Under the terms of the Act it is not only the publisher who can be prosecuted but the distributors and wholesalers can also face legal action. As companies operating on the right side of the law, porn publishers have had to be circumspect; breaking the law (or even being suspected of it) is an expensive business. The reward for self-restraint has been a place on the top shelf of the nation's newsagents, revenue from mainstream advertisers and wholesale deals with market leaders WH Smiths and John Menzies who still account for more than 70 per cent of wholesale trade in the UK. Menzies and Smiths have to meet the requirements of the law but they are also a filtering component in the production chain and therefore play a significant role in limiting the widespread availability of printed sexual materials. All publishers wishing to distribute their materials via these companies must submit proofs for vetting by the head offices of Menzies and Smiths in advance of printing. The publications are therefore subject to those companies' understanding and implementation of 'community standards': this vetting has very real consequences for the narrative motifs of British soft core.

In a fascinating account of working and researching at three men's soft-core magazines, Eleni Skordarki (1991) describes how letters sent to the magazines by readers were amended to ensure that they stayed within wholesaler guidelines. Readers' letters formed a significant part of the written elements of the magazine and often detailed readers' real or imagined sexual experiences: many of them 'copycat', replicating the narratives of previously published letters (1991: 170). Despite the copycatting, the letters required substantial revision or refining in order not to break the rules set by distributors. As well as ensuring that the style of letter was interesting and well written, members of staff had to pay attention to the theme of the letter to excise any mention of prohibited activities (for example, incest, sodomy and under-age sex). Likewise, significant changes were made to letters containing references to alcohol or forms of persuasion in the pursuit of a woman's sexual favours (1991: 184ff). The removal of any 'questionable' justification for a woman's participation in sex was necessary in order to get past, first, the company lawyers and then the distributors, but this significantly changes the nature and motivation of the stories. Thus women in these narratives have to be presented as 'up for sex'. She gives the example of a letter where the sexual action in the original is largely driven by the fact that the two protagonists are cousins attracted to each other but unaware of the other's feelings. Because the magazine's lawyer was afraid that this story might constitute an 'incest' story for the distributors that 'feeling-generating' fact was removed (1991: 188). Skordarki observes

> ...distributors' policies can dictate what can or cannot appear in a men's magazine in a way that the *Obscene Publications Act* could never do. Unlike the 1959 Act, distributors adopt concrete criteria of the unacceptable rather than the acceptable. They define what should not appear rather than what should, and can check every issue with that negative checklist in mind – if something is ticked as present, the magazine is penalised. (1991: 181)

Thus some of the supposed tropes of soft core – for example, the nympho-woman who can't get enough – are actually produced by the interpretations of the law: 'Censorship ... is not only unable to curb the pornographic reduction of sex into mere body movements, noises and secretions, but instead, encourages it *further* by removing any references to feelings that there might be.' (1991: 188) Most importantly, for Skordarki,

> These letters, especially in their edited form, also illustrate that censorship which is based on technical criteria of what is an unacceptable act, must necessary [*sic*] ignore intentions and feelings. Mental and emotional conditions cannot be ticked as present or missing with the same ease that a censor can tick whether a feature contains, for example, 'bondage', 'sodomy', 'bestiality'. (1991: 199)

This highly suggestive account indicates the ways in which the content of pornography is subject not simply to authorial intentions but to a range of filtering practices.[4] Thus the representational regimes of soft core don't operate in isolation, they respond to the conditions in which they are produced.

Kipnis's argument, introduced in chapter 1, that reading *Hustler* has status as an act of political resistance also illuminates the ways in which the textual formation arises from the interaction between the producers of the magazine, its cultural place and the social positioning of its readers. Leon Hunt has argued that a similar element was a feature of British soft core which articulated a collective sense of irritation and disenfranchisement from the supposed gains of 1960s sexual liberation. Donnelly has suggested that there is a mythology about 1960s liberation in Britain and that far from benefiting everyone, 'permissiveness ...was handed down from above rather than taken from below.' (2005: 117) Hunt suggests that porn's march into the suburbs during the mid-1970s offered a 'vulgar hedonism' which sought to claim sexual liberation for the ordinary John on the street, in particular, 'Sullivan's magazines hinted at the upward mobility of the aspiring pornocrat, but solicited an impatient working class "punter" who wanted the goods delivered at an aggressively lower price. The "Readers' Wives" – Sullivan's invention – grew out of this ethos.' (1998: 130) This has formed an authenticating discourse around sexual representations in the UK whereby publications claim to be offering what the customer wants in spite of and in defiance of the authorities and religious, moral campaigners. As Hunt shows, this authentication was explicitly employed as a marketing technique by John Lindsay following his unsuccessful prosecutions; his films began with the boast

> I, John Lindsay, was prosecuted at Birmingham Crown Court in 1974, and at the Old Bailey, London, in 1977, under the Obscene Publications Act 1959 and 64. I was acquitted in both cases and the jury found my films not to be obscene under the aforementioned Act. (Quoted in Hunt 1998: 23)

Even so, the claim to an expanding field of sexual representation during the latter half of the century was fairly hollow: once legal publications achieved the depiction of total female nudity, there was very little scope for trying something new within the limits of the Obscene Publications Act. Thus the legitimate porno magazine market of the late 1980s and early 1990s can be characterized by its relative stagnation and reliance on a rather pathetic anti-authoritarian stance. Various legal instruments were introduced during the 1980s which further limited the ability to expand the market – legislation at local level – the 1983 Local Government Miscellaneous Provisions – and at national level with the 1981 Indecent Displays Act and 1984 Video Recordings Act created further restraints on production and distribution of pornographic materials.

During the 1990s the market was estimated at perhaps 10–15 per cent of all journal revenue, with a value of £100–£150m. Despite that value, regular readers were estimated to account for no more than 6–8 per cent of the UK male population (Spillius 1996). Although soft-core/adult magazines for men performed well during the 1980s, unit sales for individual titles plummeted since their 1970s heyday: in 1971, *Playboy* sold 90,000 per month in the UK, it barely managed half that during the 1990s. The fall in circulation may have been a result of *Playboy's* increasingly outmoded personality and its American style, but UK publications also had to contend with falling circulation figures. For example, sales of *Fiesta* dropped from 238,000 in 1991 to 162,000 in 1996 (Spillius 1996). While the total number of magazines had increased to 150 titles, individual titles were no longer the cash cows they once were.[5] There are a number of reasons for this which need some explanation.

In the early 1970s, when *Penthouse* sold up to 300,000 per month, men's interests were inadequately catered for by the mainstream magazine industry. Hobby publications existed but for those men who wanted 'variety', perhaps a mix of celebrity interviews, car reviews and some sort of social/cultural commentary, there was little or no choice available. *Penthouse* and *Playboy* with their mix of the 'erotic' and 'hard-hitting editorial' were able to appeal to a wide range of male readers and a whole host of mainstream advertisers. The advent in the late 1980s of men's magazines offering a very diverse mix of journalism, celebrity, consumer goods, relationships and some sexual content without the attendant 'dirty mac' label, dealt the most decisive blow to the adult market. By 1989 *Penthouse*'s circulation dropped to 45,000; in 1996 it had risen again to around 120,000. In its heyday *Penthouse* had appealed to an ABC1 readership; in 1996 that readership was much more likely to be constituted by CDE males[6] – their more affluent counterparts having moved to titles like *Esquire*. Men's lifestyle magazines were successful in persuading celebrity women to bare, if not all, then certainly get pretty skimpy within their pages, and readers seemed to prefer the respectable centrefold. Advertisers followed and found in titles like *Esquire, GQ, FHM* etc. the perfect vehicle for reaching high-earning male consumers.[7]

Soft-core publishers responded to the drop in circulation with titles targeted at particular tastes: 'niche' magazines such as *Big Ones*, *Asian Babes*, *Black & Blue*, *Big & Fat* and *40+* were the publishers' successful response to the pressures of increasing competition from other media. In particular, Richard Desmond's Northern & Shell was a leader in this area of publishing. Titles such as *New Talent* and *Real Wives* had a novelty value and required much lower circulation figures for profitability because they were run on shoestring budgets and had a longer shelf life[8] than the more prestige titles. Clearly, the 1990s saw increasing pressure on publishers to move into other market sectors. Of the four main players in the UK, N & S was the most willing to attempt new market sectors, prepared to move in where ever it spotted an opportunity: gay men, football fans, children and older women have all been on the receiving end of the company's niche publications. N & S have aggressively pursued more mainstream ventures and have been able to recognize and respond to gaps in the existing markets which could be exploited without huge investment.[9] Towards the end of the decade only 10 per cent of the company's earnings derived from pornography.[10]

Targeting Women Readers

In the early 1990s Northern & Shell still saw a profitable future in soft-core publishing, particularly with the move into niche publications, and one niche they believed worth entering was the female market. Figures for the popular soft-core letters magazine, *Forum*, suggested that 40 per cent of its readership was female, and mainstream magazine publishing seemed to provide overwhelming evidence that women wanted sexual representations specifically geared to them. Despite the earlier lack of success for an expressly titled 'pornography for women' in the 1970s, women's access to sexually explicit materials had begun to rise by the end of the 1980s. Discussions of women's sexuality appeared across a range of media in confessional and novel formats (*My Secret Garden* by Nancy Friday and Shirley Conran's *Lace* through Julie Burchill's *Ambition*). Even the romances of Mills & Boon had begun to feature sex. Newspaper reports suggested that the increasingly popular *Anne Summer's* parties and rocketing sales of 'saucy' and sexy underwear were evidence that women were embracing a more aggressive and visible female sexuality. Early 1980s advertising images of men's bodies had begun a process of education of consumers to see men's bodies as sexually appealing (Carter, 1985: 111). Advertisers utilized the conventions and codes available in music video and film, using, for example, 1950s iconography and musical accompaniment in order to sell Levis 501s. Levis advertising seemed to encapsulate a changing mood: 'The male body displayed for enjoyment allows women to look actively and powerfully at these private rituals. For a change they are responsible for their own voyeurism and their own desire.' (Moore 1988: 54–5).

The developments in advertising were the continuance of the trends begun in pop music. Beatlemania in the 1960s had begun the targeting of women. At least it was significant in actually acknowledging and encouraging women's response: 'The Beatles were sexy; the girls were the ones who perceived them as sexy and acknowledged the force of an ungovernable, if somewhat disembodied, lust.'(Ehrenreich et al. 1997: 19) Traditions of looking at men (usually limited to their faces and naked torsos) had been well established within pop music by the late 1980s. Teeny-boppers had screamed at and forgotten Elvis Presley, Cliff Richard, David Cassidy, the Osmonds, David Essex, *Bay City Rollers*, Leif Garrett, *Wham!* and others before the rise of the 1990s boy band, perhaps best typified by *Take That*.

The crossover appeal of the male body between music and advertising was made most explicit in the use of white rap artist Marky Mark as the body that filled Calvin Klein underpants. Some observers (Simpson 1994; Moore 1988) attribute the success of these advertisements to the mobilization of a gay erotic gaze and its incorporation into mainstream culture. From the mid-1980s women's art collectives produced exhibitions which sought to establish a female erotic gaze through 'funny and tender' images of men (*What She Wants* 1992; *Women's Images of Men* 1988). High-street shops such as Athena sold posters of men in varying stages of undress to men and women alike signalling the popular crossover of art and its enquiry into the possibility of men as sexual objects, into the mainstream. TV programmes also dealt with sex both as a 'dispassionate' subject of documentaries (*Sauce for the Goose* 1993) and as the titillating factor in programmes like *Good Sex Guide*.

Developments in popular culture were beginning to legitimize the idea of a 'porn for women' – a 'domesticated pornography' – that is, sexually explicit materials which have been 'tamed' of their specifically 'male' elements in order 'to carve out spaces for its consumption and for fantasy within … daily routines' (Juffer 1998: 5). It is in the context of these different media phenomena that *For Women* and its rivals emerge. To the publishers, women appeared ripe for exploitation as a new market and reachable on the discursive territory of 'liberation' and anti-repression that they had exploited so successfully in earlier decades for male consumers.

Perhaps the most significant contribution to the evolution of women's porno magazines was the increasingly sexual content in mainstream women's magazines. In his history of women's periodicals, Braithwaite observes that by the early 1990s editors had thrown caution to the wind, 'No sexual holds have been barred, no byway unexplored.' (1994: 157) Women's magazines have always had an element of sexual content and the fears about the effects on readers of their irresponsible promotion of amoral activities have also had a long tradition (Beetham 1996). What seemed to be changing towards the turn of the 1980s was the nature of their discussions about sex. The late 1980s were particularly turbulent for the UK's mainstream women's magazine market (Braithwaite 1994). According to *Marketing* magazine, the advertising/marketing commentator, there were 120 women's magazines in 1986 generating £190m on cover price and approximately £160m in advertising revenue, but overall circulation was dropping and the share of advertising spend was in decline.[11] Publishers responded with 'narrowcasting': the segmentation of the market targeting niche areas with specialist titles (a parallel with the specialization in soft-core magazines). Where once a woman's magazine might have 'spoken' to all adult women, the 1980s saw a massive growth in the numbers of magazines which targeted narrower and segmented age groups. Offering individual titles to those in the 19–25, 24–35, 35–45 age groups with further titles aimed at the over-50s, and those with interests in crafts and home-making etc. The trend towards segmentation can be traced back to the 1960s with the launch of titles like *Honey* and *19* for the younger end of the female market. Industry analysts have identified three factors responsible for the acceleration of that trend from the 1970s: 'advertisers wish for more tightly targeted media; the reader's desire for more specialised information; and the publishers' instincts to expand' (Davidson, *Marketing*: 3 July 1986).

During the 1980s, UK publishers were under attack from invaders from Europe with German companies like Bauer and G & J hitting the weeklies' market hard, and the French company Hachette entering the monthly glossies market. Although the magazine market as a whole was expanding, individual titles were performing badly. Some titles seemed to do phenomenally well, especially those published by European companies which had been able to identify lucrative niche markets (for example, *Elle* was launched for the young woman with a primary interest in fashion, *Hello!* for those women who wanted celebrity gossip). Established UK publishers were feeling the pinch of foreign competition and even the flagship publications like *Cosmopolitan* suffered (Winship 1993; McRobbie 1996a). The point to note, of course, was that the right idea could make its own market.

Established magazines found that increased sexual content met the necessity of proclaiming their distinctiveness from rivals (McRobbie 1996a). This strategy was not without its own set of problems.[12] The resulting outcry from parent groups, teachers, MPs and others caused the temporary removal of certain titles from some supermarket shelves and calls for many titles to be moved to the top shelf.[13] The particular problem for many critics was that it no longer appeared to be enough to answer women's questions about sexual matters, magazines were all too ready to celebrate sexual activity outside the narrow perimeters of 'procreative sex'.[14] The magazines hit back at their critics by focussing on the 'information' they offered and the ways in which young women need different forms of information relevant to the changing sexual climate of the UK and the effects of sexually transmitted diseases, especially AIDs.

Industry commentators were not convinced by this argument; the increased sexual content was seen as a drive to maximize profits at all costs. A 'cynical camouflage' of sex boosted circulation without a care for the effects on women and girls. For academic commentators there also appeared to be a very close link between this content and wider developments in the industry and increasing competition (McRobbie 1996a, 1997b). However, as Gough-Yates has suggested this has 'failed to contextualise the issue of sexual content in women's magazines within shifts in the moral cultures of contemporary Britain and in relation to broader debates about morality, femininity, youth and media regulation.' (2000a: 230) Her argument, that a focus on these shifts opens up questions regarding readers' relationships to, and investments in, discussions of sexual matters rather than simply limiting discussion to the imposition of those topics on anaesthetized readers by circulation and profit-hungry publishers, is persuasive.

The targeting of women happened much earlier in the States where Ehrenreich et al. (1987) observed that female sexuality became a matter of consumption rather than reproduction or monogamy – 'The pursuit of pleasure – at a reasonable price.' (1987: 105) The decades from the 1970s saw considerable bending of sexual codes: contraception became a matter of good parenting or personal life-planning rather than selfishness on part of women, and the rise of consumerism opened up opportunities to exploit the interests of affluent teenage and young adult spenders. For example, McLaren claims that 'The success of *Playboy* magazine dramatically demonstrated to corporate America that producing pornography was not a subversive undertaking, but a sound business venture.' (164) And that this enabled 'the emergence of a variety of new sexual scripts' (166). Some of these took their cue from Kinsey's 1953 report which highlighted the particular difficulties attendant on repressed sexual desires – especially for women who were understood to have limited opportunities for experimentation outside of marriage and were, therefore, less likely to enjoy sex once married – thus sexual experimentation was presented as important to self-knowledge and thereby articulated to liberation.

Hence the development of porn for women can be linked to the increasing discussion of sexual practices encouraging women to question and explore their own sexual interests separated from earlier models of heterosexual monogamy. Sex manuals addressed women as 'liberated' urging them to move beyond passive receptivity and feelings of shame to a more active and pleasure-seeking involvement in physical relations. Texts, ranging from feminist theory through how-to manuals to erotic novels, emphasize female orgasm through clitoral stimulation alongside a focus on the routines of women's everyday lives in a move towards the 'mainstreaming of masturbation' (Juffer 1998: 69). Feminist discourses and masturbation projects of second-wave feminism constructed the pursuit of orgasm as a question of sexual liberation, freedom of choice within a project of personal knowledge – *Our Bodies, Ourselves* being the bible of this movement.

Some feminists viewed this expanding exploration of female sexual pleasures with some suspicion, at least in terms of the political status of such exploration. The 'sex wars' of the 1980s cast various shadows over the conceptualizations and understandings of the possible pleasures of sex for women whether heterosexual or not. As Williams notes

> If phallic sexuality is contaminated by power, ... if it is essentially violent and perverse, then female sexuality shall be defined as its opposite: as non-violent and not-perverse – a pure and natural pleasure uncontaminated by power. (Williams 1990: 20)

Shifts across a range of publishing, legislative and cultural sites did, however, make the possibility of sexually explicit publications for women more attractive to publishers. Attractive does not simply mean that a target audience had been identified as ready for the publication; publishers (especially those given the title pornographer) prefer to carry on their business without intervention from the state or arousing too much controversy from moral groups. Therefore, it is not simply that a profitable group of women seemed ready for sexually explicit publications but that wider culture appeared accommodating although, as I have suggested, that accommodation was not without its limits.

What They Don't Show You in *Cosmo*!

For Women was launched into this divergent market in 1992, taking its cue from the 'sexcess' of titles like *Cosmopolitan* and *Company*. As I have already noted, Northern & Shell was on the lookout for new areas to develop, and the women's magazine market was one they were keen to enter. *FW* would combine that ambition with their experience of erotic publishing. Managing Editor Jonathan Richards had proposed and successfully launched a variety of sports titles and had ideas for two lifestyle titles for women and gay men. Originally conceived as a one-off *Penthouse For Women*, further discussions convinced the editorial team that the time was right to launch a magazine proper rather than a supplement to a men's title. A member of that original team, Zak Jane Keir, explained:

> The social climate had seemed to be changing for a year or so before we started: it was the time of huge publicity and popularity for the Dreamboys and the Chippendales – though the whole 'ladette' thing was another two or three years off. (E-mail: 10.10.2000)

Jonathan Richards claims a conversation at a dinner party had convinced him that women wanted more than *Cosmo*, 'I look at *Cosmo* and it promises everything and then fails to deliver' (interview 13.1.94). That sounds as if the launch was based entirely on intuition but that would be doing N & S a disservice: their business is publishing and recognizing opportunities. Despite the problems outlined earlier, N & S were convinced the magazine market was sufficiently mature and dynamic that they could enter it without having to do the very expensive groundwork of establishing a niche. The production of *FW* actually stands out as anomalous in Northern & Shell's operations. Within the company's portfolio, specialization and 'narrow casting' had led to the paring down of magazines to minimal editorial and lots of pictures – these are much cheaper to produce and pictures can be recycled and used in sister publications. The magazines are laid out on Apple Mac with minimal editorial input required and a spread of personnel across a range of titles. *FW* was launched with a variety of expensive editorial elements: problem pages, expert advice, fiction, in-depth articles as well as photographs. Although produced by a very small team (especially by *Cosmo* standards) it had quite expensive production values and intentions to breach the mainstream. Thus the cover line 'What they don't show you in Cosmo!' was designed to do a lot of work! It was, first and foremost, a 'placing of tanks on *Cosmo*'s lawns', an indication that *FW* intended to usurp *Cosmo*'s crown as the most s-explicit of women's magazines. It made clear the magazine's intention to be more than *just* a sex magazine and meant that the challenge was recognized by cultural commentators in the media – arousing their interest and generating pages of copy detailing the nature of the challenge. Perhaps most importantly, it also meant that readers would know what they might be in for within the pages of the magazine. It set a tone by drawing upon the already existing and well-known persona of *Cosmopolitan*.

But the market for female erotic was, and still is, in its infancy. Despite *Cosmo*'s increasingly sexual content there was never any overt intention to *sexually arouse* the reader in that magazine. Its articles and features were about the cerebral aspects of sexual activity or the acquisition of techniques rather than the possibilities of fantasy and actual bodily activity. This distinction is crucial, not just because it means that the 'pleasure zone' of *Cosmo* was sufficiently disguised that it could defend itself against censure from watchdogs but also because there may be less expectation of a magazine which *analyses* rather than attempts to *produce* sexual feeling. *FW* began with few market precedents to draw on, and its editorial team had to feel its way around 'female sexuality' and what might be possible; this required a responsiveness that erred on the side of caution. Such caution does not make for a confident editorial stance, and I will argue later that *FW* was only ever briefly confident of its message and its appeal.

As we've already seen, anti-pornography feminists argued that any representations of female sexual desire had the potential to degrade women and were also at risk of misappropriation by patriarchal forces. The editorial team were very aware of this tension, most of them worked on other publications within the N & S portfolio, on titles which addressed male purchasers with representations of 'girl-on-girl action' and 'sluts on parade'. Thus the arguments about, for example, representations of lesbian sexuality as a playing up to male desire were a part of the backdrop to their everyday work practices. In interviews with me, the team acknowledged the conflicts, tensions and complexities of sexual experimentation and its representation in terms not unlike those employed by academics, but they felt it was possible to produce and consume sexually explicit materials without surrendering female sexual autonomy. If anti-porn arguments completely refused the idea of women's autonomous desires under patriarchy, '...although theoretically acknowledged as possible in a utopian future, [female desire] remained an ethereal and remote presence' (Vance 1992: xix), Keir and Richards felt it was possible to make this ghostly presence felt in the pages of a magazine. Moreover, they were keen to reject the key requirement of a properly 'feminist' sexual practice which insisted on the removal of all eroticization of power, not just in heterosexual relations where men were seen as wielding pleasure in order to ensure their grip on power over women, but also in lesbian relationships where gender equality was expected to 'undermine (or magically "destabilize") power imbalance' (Gaines 1995: 392).

There were editorial disagreements: many about the nature and function of a female erotic magazine. Keir told me that

> What went into the magazine was arrived at by putting questions to as many women as we could get our hands on and distilling their answers (or, as I seem to recall, ignoring the ones that some people didn't think were normal or appropriate). All other decisions were arrived at depending on what was available, affordable, and didn't have us rowing with each other too vigorously. (E-mail 10.10.2000)

For Keir, not all writings about female sexuality were in women's interests and certainly not in the interests of enabling women's sexual explorations. The difficulties of addressing women's sexual needs did not go away; I discuss the nature of the magazine's negotiation of sexual dangers and pleasures later in this chapter. The editorial team felt that they were doing something significant and that the magazine was more than 'just another product'. Some members of the editorial team had a radical, perhaps even evangelical, approach to the magazine – through *FW* they hoped to put discussions of female sexuality and sexual pleasure firmly on the agenda. At the very least it would challenge any lingering remnants of sexual repression. The address to readers was to be as much about commitment to equal sexual rights as a pleasurable leisure activity. Taking seriously its straddling of two genres, the woman's and the soft-core magazine, *FW* was to be a heady mix of froth and provocation that your mother wouldn't like. Richards intended it to 'break the tyranny of the top-shelf' and Koprowski thought 'it [would] meet ... the needs of modern women... they want full nudity and feel cheated without it' (quoted in Sullivan 1992). Unfortunately, even within the editorial team, too much was expected of the magazine. While some in the team placed profit above politics, Keir, deputy launch editor, hoped for better things, 'I did have a political viewpoint at that time (still do). I was very sure that sexual pleasure for women, sexual freedom for women, mattered a lot (and wasn't based on buying the right lipstick).' (E-mail 20.10.2000)

These expectations were linked to the delineation of *FW* as different from other publications in N & S's portfolio. That difference was not to be expressed in terms of 'men's magazines are sleazy and ours won't be' but a woman's magazine was seen to offer the possibility of opening up, of accessing, a level of discussion and exploration of sexuality which might lead to change. *FW* was oriented to the future possibilities of sexual freedom (those aspirations were to be tested by readers and critics). That *FW* had a difficult juggling task is evident: advertisers stayed away, after an initial high, sales dropped, costs were cut, affecting content and leading to further drops in sales. Had the magazine been published by anyone other than N & S it is almost certain to have been closed. Commercially, it is only N & S's business practice of specialization on pared-down budgets that makes the magazine's continued presence possible. For a niche publisher the magazine has sufficient readers. But the failure to keep women's interests was reflected in a loss of managerial confidence. Up until mid-1995, *FW* operated with relative autonomy alongside its limited budget. From mid-1995 onwards the magazine was beleaguered, its content seemed less assured and parts of the magazine were being set aside because they were expensive. A number of disastrous direction changes were made, dictated by N & S's advertising department.

From the very start the magazine had failed to draw in major advertisers and had relied on the bulk purchase advertisers who pay a flat rate for inclusion in six N & S publications. This posed a real dilemma for the magazine, some of those advertisers were considered entirely unsuitable for a woman's magazine, especially those for telephone sex-lines but their money was absolutely vital to the continuance of the publication. Mainstream advertisers did not seem convinced of the magazine's ability to deliver substantial numbers of target women, nor did they like the possibility of their glossy ad being placed next to male genitalia. In an attempt to appeal to those advertisers, the advertising department insisted on a cover-up.

The folly of this was blindingly apparent to then editor Ruth Corbett: in a magazine which claims its unique selling proposition is the courage to show what is not on show anywhere else it was absolute suicide to dispense with the genitals. The trial run ran for six months precipitating a real decline in sales: to add insult to injury, the magazine was not moved from the top to middle shelves in newsagents (as had been hoped) and advertisers stayed away. The 'Willies are back!' edition appeared in January 1996 but there was a price: a 10 per cent reduction in content. This was the first of many setbacks: an attempt to relaunch with a lower cover price and the injection of more humour in late 1996 also failed to halt the downward trend. WH Smiths removed the magazine from its stores to make way for more profitable sandwiches. The return of the General Erection campaign called for change in the law but just seemed to trade on cheap innuendo when considered alongside the lack of substance in the magazine. The slide continued. *FW* is still published nine times a year but in reduced circumstances with a current budget of £2500 per issue and a part-time editorial team of three.

Confined, as *For Women* is, to the top shelf its importance as the only sexually explicit publication targeting women has diminished radically. This book isn't about predictions but it seems very unlikely that *For Women* will ever achieve a mass readership. In an effort to rid himself of the title 'Dirty Desmond', Northern & Shell's owner put his X-rated publications up for sale, and the new owners are content to let the magazine continue on its limited budget but make no effort to increase its circulation. Other rivals have arrived – *Scarlet* is the most recent and benefits from a prominent position on the middle shelf in many urban centres[15] – reflecting a newer moral economy which sees the equality argument as already won and disputes with distributors and regulators as a waste of money. Ironically, the battles the team at *For Women* thought were worth fighting – for full nudity in their photo spreads, explicit fictions and sexual content with an implicitly politicised edge – appear to have been lost in our age of pornographication. The tyranny of the top shelf has not been broken, it remains dominated by publications aimed at male readers: we could claim that this is an indication of women's continuing refusal to be seduced by porn, however, the regulatory and economic structures of the industry play their part in the marginalization of magazine soft core for women, a marginalization which really can only be understood in the context of the contraction of the soft-core magazine trade.

The major players in the UK no longer view the top shelf as a cash cow, Sullivan, Desmond, Raymond and the Gold Brothers have all moved into other areas of commercial interest. The top shelf has been seriously wounded by the advent of *FHM* and *Loaded* and by the development of new technologies which offer more 'exciting' representations of sexual activity. While the law still protects British soft core by forbidding the high street availability of hard core, most licensed sex shops now sell continental and US porn featuring couples and actual penetration. The surfeit of contempt which has always characterized the consumption of one-hand mags is still a peculiar feature of any exploration of the contents of newsagents' top shelves, an attitude fostered by the willingness of the publishers to allow their products to settle ever further down market.

This history of *For Women* offers a perspective on the political, economic and social forces that circulated the textual formation, distribution and reception of this particular instance of pornographic publishing in the UK. The magazine emerges at a particular historical moment and, as I'll show, refracted a developing manifestation of female sexuality within popular culture. The organizational constraints which operated on the magazine: the commercial interests, legal frameworks and media markets all took their toll on content – not just to restrain the discussion/representation of sexuality it could offer but to produce particular ways of justifying and expressing 'female sexual desire'. This regulatory and market landscape has undergone significant changes in the decade and a half of *For Women's* existence, as there has been a loosening of the constraints on representing sex – with the relaxation of R18 certifications, the explosion of Internet pornography, the development of retail environments targeting women as sexual actors and the evolution of a range of mainstream publications focused on the female body (the lads' mags) – the top shelf has become more and more a symbol of outdated and generally lacklustre representations. But in its early incarnation, *For Women* appeared to offer something new and exciting and it's that promise I want to return to now.

Notes

1. Jonathan Richards maintained his connection with the magazine throughout 1992 to 1994, first as editor and then managing editor alongside Helen Williams. Ruth Corbett

replaced Williams in July 1994. Liz Coldwell who had been fiction editor then took over in 1997 and remains editor. Jane (J. K.) Collins, one-time agony aunt, was also editor for a period during 1996.

2. Soho had 54 sex shops; 39 sex cinemas and cinema clubs; 16 strip and peep shows; 11 sex-orientated clubs; and 12 licensed massage parlours' (Thompson 1994: 44). David Sullivan opened the first of his Private Shops in 1978 (Hunt 1998: 24).
3. A central line of defence offered by the 1959 Act was the claim that far from being pornographic, a book, magazine or film was a work of art and therefore open to the protection of the law. Pornography could be recuperated in the courtroom, '...the defence of "public good" – artistic, scientific or some other kind of merit which distinguished the meritorious from the exploitative...pornography ... could be interpreted as being for the "public good" by an astute counsel, as a series of therapeutic masturbation defences proved.' (Hunt 1998: 21)
4. Skordarki also emphasizes the 'interfering' role of the magazine owner; the costs of production and the limitations that places on content; the need to provide novelty as well as continuity.
5. In 1996 Northern & Shell claimed a circulation figure of 1.5 million magazines per month but their magazine profits have also dropped significantly (Company Report 1996).
6. *Penthouse* attempted a relaunch in 2001 under the editorship of Jonathan Richards for Paul Raymond Publications. In order to win readers, a strategy was devised of inviting celebrity couples to feature in interviews and photosets – it wasn't terribly successful.
7. Sean Nixon (1996) details the 'search for the holy grail', the high-spending male consumer, a quest which united manufacturers, advertising agencies and magazine publishers in the early 1980s.
8. Where other magazines have a limited lifespan of a month indicated by the date on the front cover, *Real Wives*, for example, gives only a volume number so that it can remain on display for months, if not years.
9. N & S could be described as a 'me too' publisher, a term Braithwaite (1994) uses to describe how some publishers jump on the tailcoats of successful new formats. Certainly N & S moved into gossip publications only after *Hello!* had done the groundwork; the same could be argued for its foray into gay magazines.
10. Since the purchase of *Express* Newspapers, the company has sold off its soft-core titles (only retaining its X-rated television channels).
11. In 1981 the consumer magazine industry (some 2,434 titles) as a whole accounted for 7.8 per cent of advertising spend, this figure dropped to 6.9 per cent in 1991 (*Marketing* Feb 25 1993).
12. For *Company* the strategy proved successful but others continued to experience rapidly declining sales, for example, *Cosmopolitan*'s sales were still falling by 12.7 per cent in 1993 and 1994. According to the *KeyNote Report*, 1995, many titles were believed to be running at a loss in 1991.
13. Interestingly, at the same time as magazines at the younger end of the market were focusing on sex as their USP, the major success stories of the period were those titles aimed at more housewifely pursuits and rather traditional values. This sharpening divergence in the women's magazine market indicates that some magazines found audiences that increasingly wanted to *avoid* explicit sexual content while others found women increasingly seeking and delighting in discussions of sex. This divergence is further confirmed by the upsurge in the market in 1993, which was fuelled not by more sexually explicit magazines but by health and fitness, parenting and in-store titles. Subsequent growth has been on the back of men's magazines and home-and-garden titles.

14. The fears of groups like the Social Affairs Unit, which published its *British Woman Today* in 1997 amid a media fanfare, are perfect examples of this tendency to regard the state of women's magazines as an indication of the progressive decline in standards of morality. The central theme of the twelve essays was that magazines like *Company*, *Cosmopolitan* and *Elle* provided readers with 'a depressing portrait of the modern British woman' (1997: 18) and fostered individualist pursuit of aggressive sexual pleasures and material indulgences to the exclusion of responsibilities and care for others.
15. This may well be because it advertises itself as 'The only women's mag featuring erotic fiction', its status as a 'rival' is very similar to *Cosmo* explicit but not too much so.

What Turns Women On?

I outlined a number of emblematic accounts of pornography in chapter 1 and argued each of them made suppositions and claims drawing on the 'figure(s)' of the audience for pornography: what are readers like, what are they doing, how do they do it, what do they take from their reading. At no point, do any of them actually engage with the responses of individual readers; rather, they construct an abstract reader whose responses can be known by textual analysis or reference to theoretical patterns. This book seeks to do something different and, I'd claim, something better. Audience studies are a burgeoning branch of Cultural Studies although they have yet to stretch very far in examining readers or viewers of sexually explicit materials. It has, however, become a commonplace of audience research to offer justifications for turning to 'ordinary' viewers and readers. I'm afraid I don't think this is necessary. Researching women readers is not new and no longer needs to be justified, the insights offered by, for example, Radway, Gray and Hermes have significantly expanded our understandings of the ways in which women relate to their chosen media forms and have definitively shown that if it is worth investigating the textual formation of any media, it is also worth inquiring into the relationships readers/viewers establish with them. There are of course, methodological and theoretical issues which arise from the claims and evidence of audience research (and I briefly discuss these in appendix 1) but the requirement for investigation of audience responses no longer needs to be defended. If you still need a defence, Laurence O'Toole's remark that , 'it has never occurred to anyone to ask porn users what's going on... [F]olks think they already know all there is to know about porn users: they look at dirty images, they become aroused, they're sad' (1999, 284) will stand in for it. By turning to actual readers I propose other ways for thinking about pornography moving beyond examining *ideas* about readers to examining readers' *experiences* of a sexually explicit text. The audience research which forms the backbone of this book is small scale, is self-selecting (how could it be otherwise?) and, like all other researches, it has its limitations but it attempts to intervene in debates which have become polarized and particularly characterized by their stasis.

The success of my methods, evidence and arguments can be judged at the end of this book. But to delay your gratification a little longer, before I turn to readers of *For Women*, I want to examine the buzz and commentary which greeted the magazine's launch. Given the tenure of porn debates which constantly stress how unlikely it is that women would be interested in a magazine like *For* Women it was not surprising that a small controversy in the British press greeted the first issue and this, of course, contributed to the ways in which readers made sense of and responded to the magazine.

At Last! The Dirty Magazine for Women

Although labelled dirty by the tabloids, *FW* was positioned as not as dirty as men's magazines: this was best exemplified by a tiny piece in the *Sun* regarding the release from prison of one-time *Penthouse* editor Linzi Drew. Ironically, a former Page 3 girl, Drew was described as the disgraced pornographer of sordid men's magazines on the same day as two pages of celebration of women's 'saucy' magazines. How to account for this? Of course, the *Sun* is about 'sex' and 'fun', add women who like sex and fun and it's the perfect recipe: Page 3 being the case in point, as Holland has argued, 'it is part of the *Sun*'s discourse on female sexuality which invites sexual enjoyment, sexual freedom and active participation in heterosexual activity' (1983: 111). However, the perfect recipe stands in opposition to that other: exploitation. The *Sun* patrols the borders of the acceptable and, possibly, to 'protect' Page 3, espouses many of the arguments about sexual exploitation in male pornography.[1] *FW* managed to achieve a level of 'respectability' because of its avowedly female angle.

Over a period of two weeks, the *Sun* devoted five full pages to *FW*[2] and subsequent weeks saw a variety of smaller snippets: this was the most sustained coverage the magazine obtained. The tone of the *Sun's* coverage was largely positive: under the headline, 'Penthouse Petts', Page Seven fella, Kevin Petts explained how and why he posed nude for *FW*. Throughout the article the 'upmarket' credentials of the enterprise are stressed: Jeff Kaine is a 'top photographer' (Kaine also snaps for the *Sun*'s page 3) – 'he would make them [the photos] look classy – not cheap'. This was Kevin's first-time full frontal and it was something 'he really wanted to do'. His girlfriend also approved and accompanied him to provide 'a woman's viewpoint'; she 'told us what women would go for. She wasn't upset at the photos. Like me, she felt it was an up-market product.' Just to ensure that there were no vestiges of homoeroticism, Kaine 'looked everywhere but in the direction of my groin'. Interestingly, Petts is also at some pains to convince readers he was not excited by the process of posing. That avowal, which surely undermines the 'truthfulness' of the images, is represented as a sign of the higher standards to which *FW* aspired. 'To be honest it was the most unsexy thing I have ever done ... Showing a man excited would drag the mag down to hardcore levels. I'm sure most women have the imagination to work out for themselves what it would look like anyway.' Just in case that idea of women and imagination should be threatening, Petts assures male readers that 'I also hope no boyfriends get jealous if their girlfriend buys *FW* to have a look. After all, men buy girlie mags for a turn on. If girls have a mag to turn them on too, it's only their boyfriend who's going to benefit. He's there in the flesh, I'm only a photo!' (*Sun*, May 6 1992: 5)

A number of ideas are mobilized in Petts' story. Women's right to look is normalized via references to high art but the main anchoring device is the use of his girlfriend: a woman's viewpoint was offered, thus the photo shoot is legitimized and made safe. Moreover, Petts offers his body without anticipation of sexual pleasure for himself, he is not exploiting female sexuality, merely offering a pleasurable experience for women – a one-off – he hopes they will enjoy: 'I hope they don't giggle. I'd like them to get excited by it, not embarrassed.' The photographs are offered as 'classy', non-threatening, fun, inviting imagination and, perhaps most importantly, not intended as a replacement for real men (boyfriends), rather the pictures may well act in men's best interests as incitements to sexual activity.

The *Sun*'s focus on *FW* was more extensive than the other popular newspapers but it was not alone in offering an angle on the definitions of 'woman', 'women's interests in pornography' and 'what women find sexually exciting/arousing'. The debate found expression in the responses to the nude images in *FW*, its sister publications and *Ludus*. Arguably the naked men were the defining element of these magazines: to the casual observer, these were the things that made these publications different from other women's magazines and from other top-shelf magazines already available at UK newsagents. Of course what really interested the columnists was the penis, thus the range of headlines focussed on the revelation of the male member and its limitations:

'A load of new cobblers' *Sunday Telegraph*
'Turning over a blue leaf' *Today*
'Full Frontal Attacks' *Evening Standard*

Alongside the double entendres ran the major theme, as the *Independent* posed in its headline: 'Do women like looking at pictures of naked men?' The question was largely rhetorical: most of the writers clearly believed they did not and that, at best, the magazines were only partly getting to grips with what women want sexually. The answers were known before the questions had been posed suggesting that, whatever the editor of *FW* might think, the newspapers still believed in the differences between men's and women's responses to visual stimuli, especially sexually explicit images. As Jessica Davies asserted:

> The whole idea of the magazine is alien to the female psyche. You simply cannot role reverse the centrefold concept, put it on the news-stands and expect women to buy it. (*Daily Mail*, 5 May 1992)

For Jenny Rees, this alien-ness was down to women's focus on the very personal features of an individual man rather than the abstract physical attributes of Man:

> Women, and even New Women, tend to do what they have always done, dream and wait – or read a good book. They do not tend to sit and dream about big biceps, or whatever. Men notice breasts and bottoms and legs; women like a man's voice, his sense of humour, the way he smiles. (*Sunday Telegraph*, 19 April 1992: vii)

For others the problem lies in the male body itself – it is not attractive, at least not if represented 'realistically':

> According to some, the reason nude men in *FW* look so ridiculous is because they are shown in an unexcited state.
>
> But I don't believe that if they were shown with full passion they would be any more erotic.
>
> A completely naked man's body is not attractive. He looks ridiculous. (Antonella Lazzeri, *Sun*, 8 May 1992)

This last is an almost perfect example of what Ros Coward (1984) calls the failure at the heart of heterosexual desire – women are not encouraged to find men physically attractive. Even where commentators allowed that women like the pin-up male, their responses were still regarded as different from men's – the naked form was not sexually exciting to women: they might like to see men's bodies but only for a laugh.

> It's a fallacy to say women don't like male pin-ups ... For years women have been having fun like this at hen parties. They like to see bulging crotches and bulging biceps. Women won't be panting over this. They'll buy it for a giggle. (Proops, *Daily Mirror*)

A further obstacle to the magazine's success was also seen to lie in the problems of the dynamics of pornography:

> Male pornography kindles images of woman as sexual vessel: the whole point is the model's sexual readiness, her supposed invitation to you, the male reader, to do something to her.
>
> I don't think women's fantasies run on the same lines. For one thing, their physiologies demand a less blunt, to the point approach.
>
> But the real factor against the venture [*FW*] is this: women require a different kind of pornography which, itself, purveys a less generalised image.
>
> I can't see what sexual pull there can be about a picture that has so unimaginatively and unsubtly been produced to fit the stereotype of what is deigned pornographic.

> You can never be too obvious for a man, that we know: but I do believe you can be too obvious for a woman. (Nigella Lawson, *Evening Standard*, 23 April 1992: 11)

One assumption was repeated again and again: patterns of response are limited to 'men's' and 'women's'. That some men might have a less obvious response or that some women might like the generalized is not admitted. Barely hidden was the assumption that all male viewing is bad and women are just incapable of replicating that activity. The delineation of differences between male and female sexual response was married to the more general theme of 'pornography as the quintessential mass product': routine and standardized and producing standardized and passive consumers via unimaginative, unsubtle and obvious imagery. Men's physical make-up might make them prone to the generalized pleasures of pornography but women, both physically and aesthetically, are able to rise above the sexual pull – whatever the attempt of the producers, the general will not suffice for women. The media's idea of appropriate responses to the magazine is thus limited to rejection, revulsion or just plain amusement.

These differentiated needs of men and women were also at play in the *Sun*'s interview with photographer Nikki Downey. An ex-*Penthouse* model turned photographer, Downey explained that her previous experience gave her a unique insight into both the practices of soft core and women's sexual needs.

> The people who give us what are supposed to be sexy pictures in magazines don't realise what turns women on.
>
> We're palmed off with shots of guys with their equipment dangling on show – what most of us want is something more subtle, where there's a bit left to the imagination.
>
> I know all about the difference just a bit of subtlety makes. I spent years striking poses that weren't exactly the most subtle in the world. (*Sun*, 5 May 1992)

There were some who saw the magazine as potentially interesting. Molly Parkin and Sally Brockway both emphasized the idea that the magazine was breaking taboos and that *FW* was long overdue as a measure of women's equality:

> I read in the ever prurient Press crusty old comments being wheeled out by killjoys about the new, fun, *FW*, magazine due to be launched this month, which is packed to the gills with full-frontal male nudes and everything else to inform and enlighten those females with sensual appetites and an interest in the opposite sex … meaning every one of us. When the hell are we going to drop this appalling view of coy womanhood, imposed on us in the first place by males? They would have us toeing the line and tripping around the kitchen in a pinny, being sunny and sweet with never a thought of what is in anyone else's trousers. (Parkin, *Mail on Sunday*, 19 April 1992)

Tessa Cunningham, writing in the *Sun*, (22 April 1992) also viewed the appearance of the magazine as a matter of equality:

> Britain's first porn magazine for women hits the shops next week – with a firm promise to expose the parts other publications have never reached.
>
> Men have been ogling pictures of naked women for years in a huge range of top-shelf mags.
>
> Now the girls are getting their chance with *FW*, out next Tuesday at £2.95.

Sally Brockway, also in the *Sun*, (8 May 1992), suggested the magazine was only the start of the revolution:

> I look forward to the day when there are as many male nudes on the top shelves as female – full frontals.
>
> A man can walk into the newsagents and gaze at the female form in all its glory. Why don't I have the right to do the same? I'm sick of the male mentality – you show me yours but I won't show you mine.

For some, however, the search to find a particular female aesthetic, a particular brand of male to appeal to all women was a significant problem:

> *FW* magazine is viewed by some as a thrusting projectile of modernity. Its first issue boasted a circulation of 400,000. There are others, however, who resent being informed that the *Dreamboys*, a glistening loin-clothed dance troupe featured there, are their 'idols of erotic fantasy'. There are many things left to do with one's life, but paying 48p a minute to ring up *Dreamboy* Trevor ('my private striptease will drive you wild') is not one of them. Centrefolds displaying pouting Tonys and Kevins who have spilt a pint of milk over their bottoms prove that *FW* has not appreciated that too much time spent in the gym, too much hair-brushing and too much ortho-dentistry are not the agents of stimulation. (Berens, *Arena*, September 1992)

These commentaries emphasize a number of motifs: taste, common sense, equality, gender and sexual differences: evidence of the interchange between what might be termed general and the more specialized critical discourses drawing on the concerns raised by academics – feminist and conservative. The constant focus on the natural order of representation – women's bodies made for looking at, men's bodies inappropriate for viewing – draws on a number of cherished theorizations of the visual field, for example, Dyer, MacKinnon, Mulvey (discussed in chapter 7). In addition there was an absolute refusal to state just what it was that *FW* intended to do: a coyness which is part of the same syndrome which refuses to admit male nudes, as in themselves, attractive/arousing.

In the 'war of words' it wasn't enough to focus on the inabilities/banalities of the pin-ups: evidence of the deviousness of the opposing side was found in the 'maleness' of the production of the magazine. Thus stories focused on the fact that the editor was male and that he also worked for *Penthouse*: 'Despite the fact that the editorship is in the hands of a man, Jonathan Richards (ex-*Forum*, ex-*Video World*), Isabel Koprowski will have a heavy influence. This is useful, as she has an impressive sexual cv.' (*Sunday Telegraph*, 12 April 1992). The big scoop came with photographer Nikki Downey's story of her mistreatment at the hands of the magazine. In an article in *Today* (11 June 1992) newspaper, Downey claimed that her commission was merely a ploy to suggest that women produced the magazine and that she had been paid less than her male counterparts. The attempt to fool the readers was, in Downey's view, an indication of the stranglehold of male values within the industry:

> The editor is a man and many of the staff are male. They are imposing their values about what is sexy on to women. My pictures are not just blatant full-frontals, they are very tasteful. But they tried to insist that women just wanted full-frontal dangly-bits. Far from being a revolution for women, the magazine is just the old story of a male dominated porn industry simply trying to bring in more readers by targeting women. (Whitcroft, *Today*, 11 June 1992)

The interesting paradox, that women don't want this material but men still target them, is never explained. The limitations of the male imagination were stressed in these accounts: male imagery focuses on stereotypical bimbos whereas women have a more diffuse and varying appreciation of the body. Indeed, many commentators claimed that women's desire was beyond definition, an important theme which finds its echoes in readers' responses, as I will go on to discuss. The gendered identity of the production team was especially interesting to the broadsheets; there, the claims for 'classy women's entertainment based on equality' were tested fully. The magazine was declared 'like *Jackie* with spunk' (*Guardian*, 10 July 1993: 61) and if there was little point in making it, the only point in buying it was to confirm how silly it all is: our response ought to be superior:

> Miss Koprowski, a precocious child, read *Fanny Hill* at 11, and sadly had to give up her PhD thesis on Latin erotic poetry because *Forum*, another pseudo-serious sex magazine in the *Penthouse* stable, was anxious to secure her talents. These people in what can only be described as sex journalism are so intellectually sophisticated. That's because it isn't pornography they are peddling. Of course not; it is something much more high class. (Rees, 19 April 1992: vii)

Scepticism of the educated Ms Koprowski is allied to Rees' notions of appropriate female sexuality: only feminists and pornographers have it wrong. Feminism has led to *FW* through its 'banging on' about pornography and its claims that women and men are subject to the same sexual longings (the conflation of two very different strands of feminism is obvious). The common-sense knowledges of the marketing men and 'boyfriends', on the other hand, are correct: 'The girls may go out in their hen parties to see male strippers and the naughty but nice *Chippendales*, who keep their G-strings on; but it's just a laugh, and their boyfriends know it.' (Rees 1992: vii). Because the magazine so clearly has women wrong, there can be only one explanation: 'Could *FW* turn out to be for gays?'

The final assessment of the magazine emphasized the commercial attempt to package female sexuality through the tainted media of popular culture and photography. In failing to grasp the complexity of female sexual response the magazine is doomed to failure. These accounts are linked by their refusal to explicitly state *FW*'s purpose – it is categorized on the basis of its genesis in Northern & Shell's portfolio; it is measured against other sexually explicit popular culture forms; assessed against a range of questions which arise out of differing conceptions of womanliness and female sexuality; and classified on the basis of classed conceptions of value, although those conceptions are never spelt out. For example, Lawson's account differs from Proops' even as they share some similarities. Both see a 'woman's' response as undifferentiated: for one, women will hate the magazine, the other, that they will think it a giggle. The difference lies in the mobilization of categorizations of aesthetic value: the reproduction of cultural distinctions. Interestingly, while one set of comments suggests that women will be 'missing out' if they do not get a copy of the magazine, the other makes it clear that there is absolutely no point in bothering with this particular product.

Why Buy It?

Newspapers and their columns are produced under particular social and historical conditions: the above newspaper responses are evidence of a range of debates about women's sexuality, its purpose, its appropriateness, its defining features. The responses to *FW* are indications of wider debates and arguments, they are part of a struggle to define what will count as women's media and as authentically female expressions of women's experiences.[3] This is as much a struggle for the right to define women as it is about *FW*. The press coverage created a buzz around the magazine, contributing to the success of the first issue and also to the ways in which readers felt able to discuss the magazine. The following replies are examples of the ways in which readers acknowledged motivations and ways of knowing about the publication.

> Oh my friend reads, um my friend sometimes reads er this kind of thing and er she ... we were shopping... and she got it and er she said... I said 'why do you buy that?'.. I'd heard about it but I'd never seen it before and she had copies so I looked at them... out of interest really... interest... because they were there... at her house. I wouldn't buy it ... I would never buy it myself. (Michele)

> I bought the first one, I can't remember if it was FOR WOMEN, whatever, it was about two years ago and I bought one of those. And I think my mum found one or bought one and she gave it to me to look at.... I bought it because I was interested, I thought it would be funny... it was quite interesting to see what they were trying to do... (Susan)

> I bought one near the beginning but not the first one I don't think. I um bought it cos it was there really... I um just thought why not? I did buy it for a while cos I thought it was a bit different. (Gill)

> I don't buy them at all [....] I bought some of the ... they had a phase of bringing out men for women but they're just too tame really... (Christine)

> A guy I know showed it to me, he thought it was really interesting, quite sexy um.. some nice pictures ... he thought I might like to look at it... that I might find it interesting. (James)

> Y'know, I wasn't really interested ... when I bought the first magazine, I was basically interested because they were everywhere...on telly and ...conventional wisdom tells you that no woman wants to see this kind of magazine and then I thought it was quite an interesting magazine and I quite liked the ways the articles were written...(Mia)

> I work in an office and everyone was talking about it and ... then ... someone, the receptionist I think... she had it ... not *For Women*... but one of those, so we all had a look ... and a laugh... because it was ...different really...y'know? (Alison)

The question about buying the magazine came about five minutes into the interviews and by that point it was unlikely that anyone was sufficiently relaxed or trusting of me to start talking openly of a desire to be sexually aroused. However, it would be reasonable to suppose even if their avowed motivation for buying was 'interest' there was also some expectation of being aroused. These answers point to an implicit acknowledgement of the inappropriateness of women reading a magazine for its purely sexual content (it became clear later in interviews that some of them certainly did find *For Women* facilitated masturbation). Many women were intrigued by the notion of a 'woman's pornography': what would it look like? The use of the word 'interest' suggests a quasi-intellectual response to the magazine – one woman, Laura, made this very explicit:

> I think I bought the first copy, maybe another copy after that. I bought it for curious, for curiosity, just to see what it was like... Um, I bought it because I thought it was an innovation, to actually make something and target it at women.

Later she says:

> ... it sounds very aloof but I bought it out of intellectual curiosity and um to see if it had a kind of sensuous impact on the, or erotic, arousing impact ... Yeah, I think I did buy it to see if it would turn me on but I think I'm just too cerebral and I wouldn't let it put the bullet, whereas other things have worked in that sense. (Laura)

Thus her purchase was an experiment to see if the magazine *could* turn her on but without much expectation of it actually doing so. Indeed, she refuses to allow it to 'put the bullet'. 'Interest' lies in seeing how the magazine will handle sexually explicit material for women and to measure it against her own intellectual criteria. Many of the respondents were careful to distance themselves from the purchase of the magazine (a friend bought it or a colleague actually paid money for it), Laura distances herself through intellectual curiosity – an intention to assess its ability to arouse. Implicit in her talk is the assessment of the magazine on the basis of *how well does it offer a woman's sense of the sensuous, the erotic, the arousing*. Moreover, she expects it to be innovative (being measurably different from men's porn): she approaches the magazine with a desire to be impressed with its ability to 'actually make something and target it at women'.

That expectation actually conditions Laura's orientation to the magazine and is productive of her response to *For Women*. I discuss her responses further in chapter 5; in this chapter, I want to begin to identify another orientation to the magazine that offers a contrasting view. Some women did suggest that they might have the expectation of sexual thrills from the magazine, however even these deflect a purely masturbatory dynamic:

> I first bought *For Women* in May 1994 and I bought it because my marriage … um, there was no sexual aspect to it and I felt … very frustrated, pissed off … um I just wanted to read what other people had to say about things like that and … other issues like that. So I wasn't happy in my non-sexual relationship … um and I don't buy it regularly, not now. I did. (Jane)

This response moves from an acknowledgement of Jane's sexual frustration through anger to a search within the magazine for community with other people, not that she expected to use the magazine as a replacement for the sexual inactivity of her marriage although this obviously forms the subtext of her response. Another response does point to wanting to use the magazine in a particularly sexual way:

> I bought it to be turned on in some way. (Tessa)

Tessa was incredibly open about her use of, and pleasure in, hard-core materials featuring images of anal, oral and vaginal penetration but the way she phrases this suggests that the 'turn on' would not necessarily lead to masturbation or orgasm. So what expectations were brought to the magazine? Some approach it as a 'peculiar' object, a curiosity and this in itself offers a measure of satisfaction:

> … it was quite interesting to see what they were trying to do. Y'know, why they had done it in those sorts of ways. I think it outlined that in the first one. (Sian)

> I liked the idea but I think they could have done a lot more with it so I was disappointed in what they'd done with it. I thought it was potentially a good idea and they wasted it really. (Emma)

However, this view of the magazine as an experiment also causes some disquiet: exactly what is it trying to achieve, how should it be measured as sexually explicit? The following response is the most clear about a sense of disorientation experienced in encounters with the magazine, but the frequency of 'it was weird' or 'I don't know who they were aimed at' and 'maybe it's just me but I thought it was a bit strange' in the transcripts suggests that many of my respondents were unsure how they should evaluate the magazine and turned to other discursive repertoires for explanations.

> Oh well, I dunno really ... it's difficult to say because it's a long time ago but I think I was just a bit confused really ... like what is this? All the time, y'know, you think that this stuff is just for men ... that it's only men who have stuff that is obviously there for a turn on and women .... Er just have to think ... sort of ... sideways with other stuff and get off on that. Like reading Mills & Boon... there are some of those ... that are really sexy ... y'know, no sex but ... like you can take them further than they go. So yeah... it was like 'hells bells, what have we here kind of thing'. I don't think I thought it would be very erotic or anything and in a way it really wasn't actually. I don't know why not really, just like, ... um the men, they weren't really all that sexy but they were but... (Gill)

This inarticulateness is resolved by a turn to the more familiar female genres of romance novels and mainstream magazines as frameworks for judgement:

> It was like ... it's just ... yeah ... it's just like *Cosmo* with men with no clothes on. (James)

> I don't really like it... It seems to have ... there's not enough men in it... I don't know, there seems to be something odd about it ... the next one I bought there seemed to be some weird sort of fashion spread and there was one particular article about breast size and it didn't seem to me to be catering for women... So to have these kinda articles and fashion spreads, I didn't like that – that isn't why I buy the magazine and I don't find even in *Playgirl* the articles are good enough to buy them for any other reason than naked men. Or the erotic stories ... and I have found the erotic stories in there something strange and that might have something to do with censorship as well cos they seem kinda soft ... Again, like they've confused the purpose of the magazine... It doesn't seem to be geared towards a turn-on kinda thing, it's sort of geared towards these other girly interests with the men sort of thrown in and a few sleazy sex toy adverts. (Tessa)

> I quite liked the way the articles were written because I think there is a big difference between them and the ones that appear in like ... other women's magazines ... er like *Cosmo* ... it seems to be a different attitude towards sex in those articles. (Mia)

This turn to the more familiar territory of traditionally 'female' sites of cultural activity throw up a number of rather contradictory responses to the magazine: for some the similarity to *Cosmopolitan* is a good thing.

> Um... my first impressions of *For Women* were ABSOLUTELY EXCELLENT, I thought my god I've found a magazine at long last .... I've found a magazine at long last that speaks about the real things that happen in life. Not a lot of old nonsense, oh er, so many things about *For Women* made sense and it made me feel like I was with one of the girlies so I thought it was excellent. (Jane)

For this woman then, the magazine does manage to offer that companionship, that sense of being where the 'girlies' are which women's magazines are conventionally thought to offer. Significantly, Jane's search for 'girlie-dom' had been frustrated in other magazines and it is through its talk of 'real life' that *For Women* avoids 'a lot of old nonsense' and can claim to speak to and for a community of women.

> Yes, I think it is written especially for women in the way that it talks to us about all the men's little idiosyncrasies and only as a woman you'd know what its about. Um also about the silly little things that only women worry about. Um and it's not about childcare or cooking or knitting its about... how good is your sex life, is one boob bigger than the other, do you get it often enough, what attracts men, oh just so many things that are just really good to read about and they don't just dilly dally about they get to the point and they really discuss things. Um... it's different from material aimed at men because it treats us as intelligent human beings.... (Jane)

For this woman it must speak directly to her experience as a woman about those things 'only women worry about'. Again this draws on the notion of women as significantly different from men, not only that, but men are incapable of understanding the 'silly little things'. That acknowledgement of the silliness of some of women's concerns self-consciously draws attention to the 'constructions' and performance of women's experiences.

Evident in respondents' talk is the desire to see something 'different', offering a particularly female perspective on sexual matters. This does not, unfortunately for me, lead to consensus on the magazine: for some the magazine is brilliant, for others it fails. One of my questions asked 'Is this magazine for women?' and received mixed responses that often seemed to diverge around 'well, I'm a woman and I liked it, therefore it is for women' or 'well, I'm a woman and I didn't like it much, therefore it isn't for women'. In part, orientations to the magazine are dependent upon an assessment of its doing something out of the ordinary. How far had the editorial team moved away from the standard features of an ordinary woman's magazine and moved beyond male definitions of female sexuality. Laura and Jane draw on ideas of female sexuality as different from men's, however, for one the magazine does not work and for the other it does. For Laura, the magazine simply confirms what she knew all along – that a pornography for women is nothing more than a distant and unobtainable vision. For Jane something else happens. There is an association of two things in her account, a sense that she could be different from men and not have to worry if that made her inferior/superior, it is just a 'girlie' domain. Following from that, is her willingness to get excited over *For Women*. I return to Jane's account in order to explore her responses more fully in chapter 5.

Tastes and Classifications

It is, however, important to recognize that as Ang (1989) observes 'what is at stake is not an understanding of "audience activity" as such as an isolated and isolable phenomenon and object of research, but the embeddedness of audience activity in a network of ongoing cultural practices and relationships.' (101) Women's responses are not to be understood as simply arising out of biological difference, a close investigation is necessary of the ways in which cultural tastes come into play in their uses and reception of texts. As Bourdieu (1984) has shown, these tastes, which inform the judgement of and the subsequent use of texts (including *For Women*), differ across groups occupying different 'habitus' and having access to different cultural competencies. The preferences expressed regarding cultural forms are the result of education and social origin and that 'the manner in which culture has been acquired lives on in the manner of using ... as a marker of "class".' (Bourdieu 1984: 2). Thus, 'habitus' is an indication of origins and a 'structuring structure' found in a person's choices, ways of living and

> ...in the practices in which they manifest their distinction, sports, games, entertainments ... Taste, the propensity and capacity to appropriate (materially and symbolically) a given class of classified, classifying objects or practices is the generative formula of lifestyle. (Bourdieu 1984: 170–3)

Bourdieu's difficult but suggestive proposition is that modes of aesthetic appreciation or 'reading formations' of cultural forms are governed by an individual's habitus and can be differentiated as the 'pure gaze' and the 'popular aesthetic'. Bennett acknowledges the criticisms of Bourdieu's tendency to polarize the distinctions too much but regards the argument as effective in

> ...underlining the fact that works of popular fiction may be differently received and interpreted according to the principles of taste and criteria of value which inform the judgements and preferences of different communities of readers. (Bennett 1990: 398)

The popular aesthetic is characterized by the 'continuity between art and life' whereas the 'pure gaze' looks to form rather than content, to contemplation rather than involvement, to distance and critical appreciation of 'art for art's sake' rather than functionality. In order to explain this more fully and to understand in more detail the nature of these different appreciations, I want to turn to the text and the status it sought to establish for itself. To do this, I draw on Juffer's recent study of sexually explicit materials for women in the US in which she argues that rather than stress women's problems with, or subversive pleasures in, pornography, we should examine the conditions of their access to such material. She suggests that the increased spending power enjoyed by women in the latter half of the twentieth century has had some influence on the production of pornography in that a 'domesticated pornography' has emerged which is clearly differentiated from demonized male porn through various marketing and distribution strategies. Her examination begins from two key observations. First, that arguments for and against pornography and its potentials for women, good or bad, fail to consider the mundane aspects of its use: the ways in which pornography is brought into the domestic sphere and becomes a part of everyday routines. And second, that an examination of the processes by which pornography has been 'tamed' or domesticated highlights the utilization of a range of legitimizing aesthetic judgements and criteria in order to facilitate women's access to sexually explicit materials. Juffer's position rejects the idea that pornography is a 'coherent category of texts' (1998: 28) in favour of analysis of pornography as a 'field of regulated dispersion' (1998: 28) which acknowledges that 'texts themselves are participants in setting the rules for access' (1998: 24). The classification and marketing of certain texts as 'erotica' rather than 'pornography' has allowed those texts to enter the mainstream and become acceptable to a female audience.

Thus a central claim is that cultural studies' tendency to condemn assertions of aesthetic quality as inherently elitist is incorrect in that 'it is precisely the erotica's claims to aesthetic status in relation to subjectivity that legitimates it in a manner that guarantees accessibility in a very material way.' (1998: 29) This status is claimed as an important marketing tool, delineating certain forms of sexually explicit materials as worthy of their place on the shelves of high-street booksellers and, crucially, as palatable and justifiable texts for women's consumption. Juffer's principal claims about aesthetics and accessibility are linked to the emergence of a specifically female branch of erotic publishing which attempts the rewriting of the codes and conventions of the 'erotic' novel in order to encompass a 'women's way of writing' (1998: 105). This rewriting contributes to the establishment of 'women's writing' as different from the masturbatory impulses of men's 'pornography', although those differences are not to be located in terms of explicitness,

> women's erotica often relies on traditionally upheld literary qualities, such as the development of plot and complex character portrayal, in order to create a story in which women's everyday concerns are represented as part of the same world in which explicit sexual desires and fantasies occur… Because women's erotica deploys these literary features in the interest of making erotica relevant to women in the contexts of their everyday lives, it produces a much more *located* sense of sexual practice than does most pornography. (Original emphasis 1998: 107)

In producing this located sense of sexual practice, women's erotica achieves a measure of balance between fantasy and everyday 'realities' which sufficiently confirms a sense of female 'identity' through sexual explorations for its female consumers. In other words, women's erotica is constructed as authentically female and expressive of women's true sexual selves in and through its claims to quality. These truth claims are assembled and established by the editors of collections of women's erotica in order to set up the 'correct' way of reading the stories therein.

Juffer quotes the following introduction from *Pleasure in the Word: Erotic Writings by Latin American Women*:

> Pornography is the negation of literature because it is the negation of metaphor and nuance, of ambiguity. It seeks a material reaction in the reader, a direct sexual excitement; eroticism, on the other hand, although it can be tremendously brazen and strong, goes through the filter of metaphor and poetic language. Pornography does not enter into literary disquisition. I think that as women, we have to rescue erotic language because in the final analysis it is dominated by male fantasies. Every one of us must tell one's own truth, trying to express the other's desire, because the last thing that wants to be expressed is desire. (1998: 113)

Thus editors draw on women's status as moral arbiters and a collective sense of female disenfranchisement from the 'discourses of lies' found in pornography in order to 'shape' 'but ... not exclusively determine the conditions under which women consume ... erotic stories.' (1998: 114)[4] Aesthetic judgement is a constituent part of the ways in which sexually explicit materials circulate and are organized. To the extent that Juffer recognizes the constraints and conditions under which women gain access to sexually explicit materials her account is particularly suggestive; her conclusions about the nature of the pleasures and affirmations women obtain once they have access to such material are not, unfortunately, as insightful returning, as they do, to notions of 'identification' and 'structuring' of responses rather than an examination of the interactions and pleasures made available to women. These are elements I will address in later chapters and my discussions of women's responses to *FW*. Nonetheless, for my purposes her ideas about the creation of accessibility to women are important, not least because her notion of access moves beyond simply complaining about 'commodification' of female sexual desire.[5]

For Juffer, the importance is access, so her analysis stops short at the point of 'domestication'. I am particularly interested in the ways in which the shaping of that access is the result of social dialogue and socially specific struggles over sexuality. The attempt to draw on aesthetic criteria and the linking women's pleasure with complexity are both indications of the ways in which these ideas are marked by their encounters with other meanings and attempts to limit the contexts in which it is possible to articulate a 'female pornography'. The earlier section of this chapter examined the labelling of *FW* by commentators in the press to show how the magazine was framed externally; similar issues arose in my reader's responses and found their way into *For Women*'s readers' letters page. Questions about the effects of sexually explicit materials have inhibited analysis of the setting and availability of these materials. Juffer's approach requires the acknowledgement of 'the conditions of access, which are determined not only by textual content but also through the publication, distribution, circulation, and reception of texts' (1998: 5) and their importance to the meanings and pleasures of the sexually explicit for women. Thus, I'm arguing that an analysis of *FW* must examine its distribution/circulation as a 'woman's pornography', 'a good read' and as an object of classification. Moreover, the ways *FW* must participate in dialogue, not just with its readers, but with the range of 'classifiers' – reviewers and critics – the cultural 'authorities' whose interpretations and evaluations of the magazine appeared in the press has to be acknowledged. *FW* drew on certain aspects of feminism's claims to equality for women: equality was a central theme of the editorial right from the launch issue:

> Welcome ... You are holding the first issue of *For Women* magazine. We thought an intelligent, adventurous women's magazine WITH, yes, pictures of naked men, was long overdue.
>
> In it, we've assembled a heady, sensual cocktail with you in mind. Yes, you. You told us how you wanted a magazine that went further than the mainstream women's glossies. You resented the fact that men can ogle women in dozens of publications, but that when it came to turning the tables, all bets were off. Well, we've found some men that aren't shy, including Page Seven fella of the year, Kevin Petts. You can enjoy him on page 44.
>
> There's loads more, of course. We're all for froth – our celebrity nudes testify to that – and we have our serious side, too. Robin Warshaw on date rape is essential reading for every woman; the article on Tao sex will revolutionise your sex life and as for our no-holds barred look at sex aids – well, what can we say? Everything you could want to know is there. *For Women* is dedicated with respect to women the world over. It's racy, provocative and bold. Rather, we would guess, like you. Although we're pretty sure your mother won't like it. – *The For Women Team* (Spring Special 1992)

If men can look, so can women; if men can be aroused by sexually explicit materials, so can women. The utilization of female emancipation in order to sell magazines may be characterized as little more than advertising-speak, nevertheless it is part of the meanings that circulate the magazine and, as such, formed part of its reception. It also provided a benchmark by which its commentators and detractors could measure the magazine. The problem for many commentators seemed to lie in the overt commercialization of the role reversal; it was the profitability of sexually explicit materials that detracted from their possibilities as 'authentically' woman-led or offering a measure of transgression.[5] The male body is clearly subject to the same conditions of commodification as the female body – the desire to maximize profits meaning that <u>any</u> body is up for grabs if it will shift a product or products. Therefore, for these critics, the appearance of naked or near-naked men (whether for women or men) cannot be understood as offering oppositional or taboo-breaking identities for the viewer as their display is always at the service of capitalism and its profiteers. These ideas featured in the populist discourses of newspapers and other media but come from feminist theorization and Marxist analysis. They are evidence of Volosinov's observations that

> Countless ideological threads running through all areas of social intercourse register effect in the word. It stands to reason, then, that the word is the most

> sensitive *index of social changes*, and what is more, of changes still in the process of growth, still without definitive shape and not as yet accommodated into already regularised and fully defined ideological systems. The word is the medium in which occur the slow quantitative accretions of those changes which have not yet achieved the status of a new ideological quality, not yet produced a new and fully-fledged ideological form. The word has the capacity to register all the transitory, delicate, momentary phases of social change. (Original emphasis 1973: 19)

This quotation would seem to invite the laying out of those words I think are most disputed in the discussions of *FW*: certainly there is a 'struggle' within those discussions to define women's sexuality and what might be appropriate to arouse desire in women. However, the most significant deployment of language in the newspaper columns was the refusal to name what it was that *FW* was doing. In almost every account coy euphemisms are used for the supposed defining feature of the magazine – its full-frontal nude males – and for the responses those might be designed to elicit. In fact, the dispute could be understood as centring on what *could not be spoken* rather than what was. The penis remained cloaked in mystery, masturbation remained the secret possibility and sexual activity, from mutual ecstasy to violent rape, the unspoken. In the 'disputes' over *FW*'s right to claim that it offers a truly female pornography, we see social dialogue in action: the back and forth over whether or not women could be turned on by a magazine is an illustration of the conflict over what will count as authentically female sexuality and, drawing on the ideas of Bourdieu, a matter of taste. The claims and counterclaims about women, sexuality, erotica, pornography, the right to look, the desire to look are examples of the ways in which meaning is constantly in conflict. Volosinov has much to say about the conflicts over meanings and how these contribute to an 'atmosphere ... of speech performances' (1973: 19), the ways in which language is shared and must be struggled over, as he comments:

> Each word, ...is a little arena for the clash and criss-crossing of differently orientated social accents. A word in the mouth of a particular individual person is a product of the living interaction of social forces. (1973: 41)

FW takes its part in that clash and criss-crossing; indeed, it printed selections from the newspaper commentaries I discuss here: offering them to readers to decide for themselves how accurately their magazine was reflected in the comments.

> Not that we're ones to blow our own trumpet, but we do seem to have created a bit of a fuss with the launch of *FOR WOMEN*. If we're talking column inches – and let's face it, everyone else has been! – few stories could measure up against it. Here we've picked out just a few choice comments, both for and against, from people who think they know whether or not *FOR WOMEN* is for you. (Summer 92: 14–15)

More than simply offering its own justifications in the light of criticism, the magazine was attempting to manufacture a space in which women could join in explicit sexual conversations. In its modelling on the woman's magazine, it straddled the line between the authentically female and the commercial.[6] Rather than dismiss *FW* as a commercial enterprise which co-opts female sexuality in the causes of capitalism and patriarchy, let's examine the ways in which the magazine was made available to women.[7] The magazine's first editorial page stressed *FW*'s intention to speak to, and for, women with a certain attitude to sex. The appeal was to like-minded women, a popular call to appreciate the values of the magazine that serves to mask a very complexly constituted audience of women. This can be seen as wishful thinking on the part of the editorial team – while acknowledging that women are not a homogeneous group, they clearly hoped to appeal to a 'state of mind' which recognized female sexuality as a source of possibilities to be addressed via articles, letters, fiction and general editorial. The magazine attempted a debunking of all those who would seek to limit female sexuality to the dangers, problems and constraints. Those 'protective' elements are not omitted from the magazine, rather they produce a kind of boundary which demarcates the 'female-ness' of the magazine.

The right to be taken seriously as *women's* porn was established through a number of textual features: the link to *Cosmopolitan* and typical features of women's magazines; references to women's equal rights (you wanted this and you should have this); the acknowledgement of and attempts to deal with the 'realities' of women's experiences of sex through messages of safety. These were joined by a range of legitimizing elements, for example, experts were used to endorse the claims to 'know' about sex both as problematic and as a territory for exploration. Early issues of the magazine featured extracts from already established erotic writers – Anais Nin, Alina Reyes etc. The credentials of these authors are already established outside of the 'porn industry'; in fact they belong to the ranks of (reclaimed) feminist writers. The use of celebrity women (and men) added an air of respectability and a sense of the magazine as up-to-date: *FW* was presented as at the heart of activity in popular culture, refusing to exist on the fringes as most porn has been condemned to do.[8]

These textual elements speak to a female identity: it is an identity made possible by feminist activism and debates about the social and cultural construction of women and sexuality. Further it is an identity which emerges from the political and theoretical challenges of the 1980s to the previous decade's feminist politics[9]. The 'woman' envisaged by *FW* could be described as 'post-feminist' in that she has moved beyond 'the impulses and images' (Brunsdon 2000) of early feminism and is 'permissive and even enthusiastic about consumption. Wearing lipstick is no longer wicked, and notions of identity have moved away from a rational/moral axis and are much more profoundly informed by ideas of performance, style and desire.' (2000: 291) *FW* was not attempting a political definition of a particular collective identity, nor was it a backlash against the gains of feminist activism. The important point, as Brunsdon has noted, is that 'the post-feminist woman has a different relation to femininity than either the pre-feminist or the feminist woman...she is neither trapped in femininity (pre-feminist), nor rejecting of it (feminist). She can use it.' (2000: 292). That femininity is expressed in the magazine as a range of desires and expectations. Of course, that version of femininities and 'woman-ness' has some relation to 'difference feminism' which would stress that women have very different ways of talking and feeling than men (Gilligan, 1982). That idea of difference feeds into the 'aesthetic' claims and counterclaims of the magazine and the popular commentaries.

The complaint that the magazine failed to grasp complexity or the mystery of female sexual response is an echo of much feminist discourse regarding the 'erotic'. The search for an authentically female orientated sexually explicit form is not to be found in the products associated with men and profits. The magazine is a product made to con women, our response therefore should be condemnation – at least that would be the sophisticated response. Central to the dismissal is the perceived attempt by the magazine to be 'tasteful'. *FW* was classified as an obvious attempt to distract women from the acquisition of certain forms of 'proper' knowledge which can only come via those cultural forms which offer 'satirical acuteness' (Lawson) or 'wit and irreverence' (*Guardian* 10.6.93): the oppositions are made and the magazine is judged as lacking imagination. Kipnis (1996) has argued that critiques of pornography often rest on the rejection of 'lower class' sexual tastes and certainly that attitude is at play in the dismissals of *FW* by amongst others Berens, Lawson and Rees. While I agree with Kipnis' identification of taste formations as an unacknowledged element of critique, her validation of 'lower class' tastes as a repudiation of and resistance to bourgeois norms is problematic. The tendency to separate the 'transgressive' from the 'ordinary' is also a feature of Sontag's famous essay 'On Pornography' in which certain kinds of pornography bordering on Art, such as *Histoire d'O* and the works of Bataille, are celebrated. Carter's suggestion of the 'moral pornographer', a figure based loosely on de Sade, also argues for a pornography which transgresses the bourgeois boundaries of culture and offers a critique of sexuality with only a supposed secondary purpose of arousal.

> When pornography abandons its quality of existential solitude and moves out of the kitsch area of timeless, placeless fantasy and into the real world, then it loses its function of safety valve. It begins to comment on real relations in the real world. Therefore, the more pornographic writing acquires the techniques of real literature, of real art, the more deeply subversive it is likely to be in that the more likely it is to affect the reader's perceptions of the world. The text that had heretofore opened up creamily to him, in a dream, will gather itself together and harshly expel him into the anguish of actuality. (Carter 1978: 17–19)

The focus on transgressive sexualities is also found in the irritated dismissal by many anti-censorship feminists of 'vanilla sex'. Uniting each of these are the assumptions that 'ordinary' pornography is dull, repetitive and unable to move its readers beyond the immediate sexual satisfaction of masturbation. Good or transgressive pornography will make us think by unsettling us and it will use the techniques of the avant-garde in order to transgress the 'tasteful'. As Wicke (1993) has shown, buried within the distinction transgressive/ordinary is the assumption that the mass media have a 'stranglehold' on *real* sexual desire and feeling: if only we could let it out. Drawing on Juffer's account, I attempt to avoid that delineation of materials into good/transgressive and bad/bourgeois because it returns study to the 'judgement of desires' (1998: 28). Furthermore, it fails to account for the ways in which women liked and/or disliked *FW*, favouring instead the celebration of the 'transgressive' reader against less 'adventurous' readers. My textual analysis in succeeding chapters will show that to designate *FW* as not transgressive is surely mistaken – by speaking out about the practicalities and pleasures of 'perverse' sexual activities like anal, non-monogamous and multiple-partnered sex, the magazine certainly undermines traditional sexual values. Indeed, some of its production team saw themselves as precisely attempting to debunk and demystify certain 'repressed' sexual attitudes. And, yet, it is also intensely 'ordinary', the magazine does not offer the 'specific and sharpest inflection of the themes of lust, "the obscene"' (Sontag 1982: 60). The delineation of transgressive pornography, the kind with value as a critique of social mores, against ordinary porn with little or no cultural value is another line of classification. It enables the elision of questions of content and refuses to deal with readers and their pleasures. As Juffer states,

> The problem with this emphasis on the violation of norms, or transgression, is not with transgression itself; rather it is that transgression seemingly exists in the aesthetic form itself and awaits the critic, who will make the transgressive meaning available for (appropriately trained) readers. (1998: 19)

This section has specifically addressed questions of aesthetic value and access in order to argue that the magazine cannot be understood without reference to the conditions of access and forms of classification which contribute to its reception as 'pornography for women'. Let's turn now to the readers' letters page and see what they had to say.

The Sexual World of *For Women*

So eventually, we turn to the text – the analysis here begins by trying to identify the ways in which *FW* created a woman's world of sex. In attempting to produce a space for the discussion of sex as a fun and pleasurable activity *FW* pushed against the boundaries of the acceptable and challenges the normative rejection of women's pleasure and agency in heterosexual sex: a conceptualization shared by bourgeois ideology and, ironically, radical feminist theorization. The rejection of 'good girl' behaviour is the most clearly delineated expectation of the magazine, expressed in letters to the readers' letters page, 'Mailshot'. The letters page is a standard feature of most women's magazines and an extremely important element of *FW*. This is a space where readers were given their say, although commentators on women's magazines often doubt their provenance (McKay 2000). Their authenticity[10] is, I think, less important than the work they do.[11] It is quite true that letters are written in response to articles in the magazine and in that sense the magazine sets the agenda, but these letters also indicate relationships between reader and magazine. Zak Jane Keir (a member of the original editorial team) told me that when she had a major dispute with Jonathan Richards about the printing of the *Janus Report*, she was offered a right to reply via *FW*'s letters' page. This indicates a particular dimension of the readers' letters page important to understanding its function within the magazine. The question is not are these letters genuine but how does the letters' page indicate the nature of the contract between magazine and reader? The letters are presented as the genuine outpourings of readers in response to the magazine and its agenda, it allows for a right to reply, a space in which readers are encouraged to voice their concerns. The letters' page is presented as a contractual element of the magazine: you can write to us and we will listen to your requests. Hence the early issues would print the picture of the celebrity requested by the letter writer – *your wish is our command, we do what you want.* In early editions there was no advertised 'reward' for writing to the magazine, readers were simply asked to contribute ideas,

> Who is it that turns you on the most? Write in and let us know who you want to see posters of ... John Fashanu? Ian McShane? Richard Gere? Remember, we want to print the pictures you want to see, so write to us... (Vol. 1 no.11: 13)

Rewards of £20 for each letter printed and a sexy garment for the star letter were later offered. Letters often featured the 'sex lives' of readers, their experiences, comments and opinions. Sharing feelings and views about partners and good or bad sexual experiences. Replies to other readers' letters often featured giving the appearance of a dialogue between readers. The editorial team contributed to this dialogue with their replies to readers. The common interest on the page is, of course, women's relationships to sex, including problems in letters on 'serious issues' such as women who murder their violent husbands and date rape. Readers were given space to outline a fairly detailed argument and received an *it's an important topic – what do other readers think?* reply from the magazine. The Mailshot page was given between one and three pages; letters were sometimes as little as a couple of lines long, probably edited from larger wholes, to one or two column lengths. The majority of writers were female; men were not excluded, although I found they only featured in two ways: to celebrate the magazine or to demonstrate attitudes the magazine opposed. For example, the summer 92 issue included this strange letter:

> The Gloves Are Off
>
> I am a professional boxer. I love my wife with great strength. You are saying to her and me that she should become a whore, always ready to do things with men.
>
> You are tempting her with your magazine. No one shall take my wife away from me.
>
> Who is reading this? You are coming in the ring with me. I'll see you have the gloves, it'll be the same for both of us. I take good care of my people.
>
> You will stop your words to my beloved wife. Put up or shut up!

> Tell me your names; all of you. I'm not afraid of the ring. Come in singly or all together. Even if you left me for dead, I'd come and find you. I know where you are. Do you think I'd let worthless whores and women who lust after their own kind take away my wife?
>
> I will never forget this time.
>
> *This correspondent did give us his name and address, but we have chosen not to print it, because we're sure his friends and neighbours would point and laugh at him in the street. If this man's wife is reading the magazine, she has our utmost sympathy and we suggest she consults a psychiatrist on his behalf or a good divorce lawyer for herself.* (Summer 92: 9)

That letter was an extreme; men usually wrote how much they agreed with the principle of the magazine, a few comments about their own liberated attitudes to female sexuality and their appreciation of the magazine's particularly female take on sexual questions. These letters may or may not be real but they are to be found in other women's magazines and perhaps offer a reminder that there may be some men out there who do understand, offering the possibility of hope! They are also indications of one of the clear purposes of the letters' page: the 'we/they' distinction – the 'club' inside the magazine and those outside. The distinction can be between women and men, but does not have to be; if men are prepared to respond – to be a part of the magazine with all that that entails – they can be. Crucially, these letters also indicate the precariousness of some women's sexual explorations: the boxer's letter makes clear that some people would violently object to *FW*'s proposals about sex. Importantly, the magazine refuses to be cowed. The delineation of who is and isn't a *FW* reader can be seen in this letter from vol. 1 no 2:

> Jealous Husbands
>
> I have a tale to tell about your last issue. I searched for two days, visiting seven newsagents before I found one that stocked FW. The girls at work and I all 'oohed' and 'aahed' over the dishy pictorials. At home, my boyfriend saw that I'd bought a copy and refused to speak to me for two hours, despite the fact that he reads girlie magazines (I found them hidden in his football kit bag). I lent my copy of the magazine to my sister and she returned it to me a few days later, totally ripped to shreds by her husband.
>
> My question is: what the bloody hell is wrong with men? They openly ogle women in the street, on television, in magazines and I've even known a few who masturbate over the underwear section of clothes catalogues. So why can't we have the pleasure of buying and reading a magazine for women? Maybe we ought to start staring at men's crotches in public and wolf whistling at them, not to mention all the other indignities men put us through. This way maybe men will learn to accept, as we do, the fact that we get pleasure from seeing pictures of naked men.
>
> Joanna Skeivys, Bristol

> *Ah yes. The battle of the sexes continues unabated. We are all thrilled that your brother-in-law acted in a manner he did. It suggests we're getting things very right on FOR WOMEN.* (Vol.1 no.2: 12)

This letter does a lot of work: it references the practical difficulties of obtaining a magazine of this kind but then details the much more significant problems encountered in the bringing of the magazine into the private sphere. The magazine becomes a negotiation of personal relationships that, of course, have their echo in more macro political debates (the battle of the sexes). The magazine's printing of, and response to, this letter confirms the right to read and to have a public expression of female sexuality. The resulting upset at home operates in the editor's reply as a measure of *FW*'s transformative potential. What does this point to? These letters are indications of the ways in which the magazine proposes particular uses of itself. For women attempting to work out a more expressive sexual sphere for themselves, the magazine acknowledges their room for manoeuvre is often limited by sulking or violent boyfriends, or by friends and relatives expressing their disgust; but even so, women's sexual explorations will be encouraged by *FW* and the letters' page acts as the space where those explorations can be shared with other 'ordinary' readers.

For example, the following letter includes commentary on the magazine as an idea, as an expression of female emancipation; it also comments on the contents of the magazine and makes suggestions for future issues.

> Football Fantasy
>
> I buy your magazine every month. I think it's brilliant and thoroughly enjoy the babe-liscious men (shame about the lack of erections!) I also read the articles with avid interest. I particularly loved the November issue with the pictures of John Alford of London's Burning. He certainly set me on fire!!
>
> I have a request: my friends and I are in serious lust with a certain football player called Jamie Redknapp who plays for Liverpool FC and we would love to see him minus his kit in your magazine. We are really hoping you can persuade him to do a photo session, we would love to see him in all his wonderful glory! Please, please, please, please try.
>
> We will be buying every edition from now on with hope of seeing Jamie – he's lush.
>
> H. L. Rawling (May 1996: 65)

The letter addresses itself to the magazine: I like your magazine and could you do this for me? This tone is a feature of many letters and indicates the nature of the ongoing relationship: in the use of 'your', the expression of 'ownership' of the magazine and its version of female sexuality is not as strong as others which take a more proprietorial approach to the magazine.

Power Lust

Did I imagine it or was *FW* supposed to be for independent, modern women with a sex drive (and mind) of their own? Pulling Power (October issue) amazed me with its dated talk of feminine wiles, the little woman behind the great man, and the brainy woman who has made the mistake of achieving something in her own right. Is this 1993 or 1923?

What does the author, Fran Last, want? Women to fade back submissively into little wifey roles and let the chaps in suits swagger all over us? As a matter of fact, I know several 'powerful' women who do very nicely indeed, crumpet-wise. Men often find successful women a turn-on too, you know.

Perhaps Fran Last should try it sometime?!

Chris Hobrook, London

We've had a word with Fran and she'll be doing just that! We like our FW journalists to do their research thoroughly! (December 1993: 11)

This letter indicates the kind of contract expected by some readers: *FW* is supposed to be above silly feminine tricks. The letters' page acts as a forum where the parts of *FW* which 'work' can be praised/discussed and the others admonished. These letters indicate the parameters of the codes and conventions, the contract being set up between *FW* and its readers. The letter from the boxer *is* strange but indicates that the magazine is on the receiving end of threats because it 'dares' to speak about women's sexuality. The magazine is shown to be pushing boundaries, it is going further than some men would like women to go in their explorations of sexual activity and feeling. The boxer, the feminine wiles complainer and the editor's responses to both letters contribute in different ways to the establishment of a particular standard of sex talk that can be expected in *FW*. Only certain kinds of people will understand, like it and join in. The following letter appeared on the same page as the boxer's,

Liberated Lady

Firstly, let me be among what must be many discerning women to congratulate you on your magazine.

I have listened to angry comments, read letters in the papers and can only assume that these people who make such rash comments must have closed or small minds, not open to freedom of speech, etc. Perhaps they haven't even bothered to read or see these things for themselves, but just taken others' word for it.

I don't particularly find the naked male body – especially the wedding tackle – appealing, but it does have its uses

I have never really appreciated being told what I should do. I always managed to do it quietly, my own way, whenever possible. I've made my comments above about the nudes, but otherwise I like them.

I chose to buy your magazine, I chose to read it through ... I will be getting the next issue too.

P. B., Oxford

What can we say ... except that Issue Three will be out on July 30. (Summer 92: 9)

Again, this letter is indicative of the contract between magazine and readers; indeed it is a demonstration of the take-up of the proposed orientation to the magazine as a symbol of women's rights to sexual exploration. This form of letter became a kind of convention in the magazine: the 'would-you-believe-it-*I*-love-*FW*' letter:

Thoroughly Modern Granny

Greetings from a very liberated 80 year old grandmother. What can I say about your second edition? There were so many items of interest to me: HIV, condoms, sex education, safer sex and gorgeous centrefold Tony Pacino. I bought your first edition and shared it with my daughter. Why should all you young girls have all the fun?

My three children are all married and I have five grandchildren to educate about safer sex. This nanny is not going to be left out of this modern, fast-moving world.

As you can see, I'm not the stereotype mother and grandmother. I'm a very open-minded wife; your magazine helps keep me that way.

Liz Hinks, Maidstone

Sounds like you don't need much help from us Liz. What's that they say about grannies and egg-sucking? (Vol. 1.no.2)

Many of the letters suggest a participatory readership: readers have a part to play in the magazine's development and the themes it should explore. For example, letters regarding articles on S & M praise the relevant article because it handled the issue sensitively without moralizing and didn't prescribe; the letter-writers ask for more of the same. The magazine is also conceived as a space and possible beginning of a movement to a new kind of sexual world: for example, the emancipation/liberation arguments of letters regarding the lack of erections – *why can't we see them, in the late twentieth century we should be able to do what we want.* Linked to those and to the 'I-love-*FW*' letters are examples that exclaim enthusiastically about how fantastic the magazine is: 'At long last, what I've been waiting for; *you* really speak to *me*'. These letters don't suggest that the magazine allows women to 'escape' for a couple of hours, rather it seems that they are able to address their own personal issues and difficulties with personal relationships through the magazine, its articles, stories, photos and letters. In which case, inappropriate features are to be criticized:

> Recipe for Disaster
>
> As one of your most avid readers, I felt I had to write in to register my disappointment with your September issue. If I wanted advice on which type of lipstick to buy (*The Perfect Pout*, September 1994) and which hair styles to have (*Head Hunters*, August 1994), I would have bought *Woman's Own*. Will it be recipes next?
>
> Please, please keep up to your usual standard.
>
> Jill Marshall, Worcestershire
>
> *Never let it be said that we won't accept criticism – your suggestions are part of what keeps FOR WOMEN fresh and exciting (we hope). But you can't please all the people all the time, as Jill's PS proves. She goes on to ask for 'some older models' – just what Diana from Lancashire* doesn't *want. Similarly some of you have written* praising *our new look beauty and health pages. However, we can assure you, Jill, that unless we discover a recipe for a meal that guarantees to make you better in the sack, we won't be having a cookery slot in FOR WOMEN!* (December 1994: 124)

The letters' page is constructed as a space in which readers can have their say and perhaps alter the content of the magazine. Whether the majority of letters were authentic, the editorial team used it as a means of testing readers' reactions. Another regular theme was the proposal for a Readers' Husband page, the counterpart of men's magazines' Readers' Wives. In men's magazines these amateur photographs of 'ordinary' women fulfil a novelty function but when I spoke to Richards and Corbett in 1994, the idea of readers' husbands was viewed with some distaste as tacky and downmarket. They also presented a set of logistical problems: some magazines offer prizes for Readers' Wives pictures and by that means ensure a steady supply of fairly good quality images. Other magazines are less concerned about quality, it's the authenticity of the 'at home' *mise-en-scène* that matters (Whittaker 1997: 88). Neither of which sat particularly well with the aspirational intentions of *FW*'s editorial team. During 1994 the theme resurfaces again and again, offering a justification for the inclusion of a readers' husbands page as well as encouraging readers to send in their photographs. The feature was 'debated' and agreed via the Mailshot page although clearly this was an orchestrated campaign benefiting *FW* financially – the chubby hubbys are a cheap and cheerful feature – and promoting it as responsive to readers. Recognition of that orchestration does not detract from the importance of the page in giving a sense of collective discussion of ideas and experiences driven by readers' interests.

This chapter has outlined how the magazine offered an area in which women could express their rights to sexual pleasure and to propose that such expression was also a demonstration of personal freedom. I've also shown how newspaper commentary on the magazine stressed its lack of sophistication and failure to meet the aesthetic demands considered appropriate to women readers or emphasized the idea of 'fun', a means of defusing any potentially political significance in reading the magazine. These fairly damning complaints/faint praise are indications of the sanctimonious contexts in which use of sexually explicit materials is seen as evidence of arrested development and infantile sensibilities. The focus on 'quality', social and educational 'value' in the critiques of *FW* are part of the conditions of access to the magazine but how are those related to its consumption? I want to conclude this chapter by introducing a reader of *For Women*, whose responses to the magazine are often paradoxical but which illustrate that these commentaries I've outlined are part of the conditions under which readers meet the magazine and join with the status the magazine claims for itself.

Anne

Anne bought the magazine because she had been watching *Kilroy* when the editorial team were interviewed; the discussion spurred her to go out and buy *For Women* and her account of reading the magazine is full of the questions and ambivalences that formed a basis of press commentaries and the dialogues of *For Women's* letters page. Anne was intensely aware of the contemporaneous categorizations of the magazine but she also comes to it with her own understandings of 'pornography', 'sexism', women's sexuality etc.

Every month for four years, Anne went out on publication day to buy *FW*, she would read it and then invariably throw it in the bin in anger – on occasion she was so enraged by it that she tore it up. Anne first wrote to me in response to my letter in *For Women* in 1994, like Julie, she continued to write until December 1997 and we exchanged some 30 letters. Anne had much to say about pornography as a genre and her responses to it could be described as a 'classic female' response – she finds considerable displeasure in sexually explicit imagery:

> I'm always being upset by explicit sexual images. I find them sexist and unfairly pressurising to us girls to look good. It provides too much competition like a rival in a love triangle. Men don't have the same pressure and it's about time they did. I hate sexually explicit stuff which contains violence towards women. I hate seeing rape scenes and seeing women being chased and beaten and punched by men. I hate all those *Hammer Horror* films that always show naked women being offered as sacrifices to the devil, they always get stabbed to death by a man. Why do people make films like that? Do they really hate women that much? I saw that Jodie Foster film *The Accused* and that was awful. Not the sort of film you'd want to watch over and over again... unless you were some sort of woman hating

> pervert. I always check the film reviews in the *Radio Times* and if there's any rape scenes in a film I won't watch it. If there's any sex scenes in a film I usually try not to watch it but sometimes I do. Then I feel terribly depressed afterwards and feel angry about it for days. Its probably because I've got nothing better to do at the moment as I'm in my fourth year of unemployment and my whole life depresses me. I did watch *Basic Instinct* and thought it was a good film, good plot and storyline and characters, but, of course, sexist cos Michael Douglas didn't give us a full frontal. Though I don't know what all the fuss was about Sharon Stone crossing and uncrossing her legs. She only revealed the top of her pubic hairs. The way people carried on about it I thought she was going to open her legs wide open so we could see her tonsils. What a load of fuss over nothing, men eh?? One pubic hair and they're away with the cuckoos!!' (Questionnaire)

In part, this demonstrates a level of moral response to sexual imagery, should we be seeing images of this kind and are they good for us? The existence of rape narratives and the possible pleasures they may give indicates a level of the depths to which men can sink and this makes Anne very angry, perhaps because she has no in-depth resource to religious or philosophical moral objections. Anne experienced her anger as impotent, even sometimes quite self-destructive, and one of her ways of dealing with this was to write letters, to the *Radio Times*, to the television companies, to publishers and to her local newsagents. As well as the anger, Anne experienced incomprehension; she could not understand why people read pornography. Therein lies one of *For Women*'s attractions to her – she can legitimately purchase the magazine – it's for women – and through it she can try to understand. Anne's use of the magazine is not characterized by sexual use so an account which seeks evidence of physiological arousal would simply say it did not work for her. And it is on that basis that Anne claimed not to be a reader of *FW* despite buying every issue of the magazine from launch. She declines the label 'reader' on the basis that she understands 'readers of pornography' as people who take sexual pleasure from sexual representations, thus her response to the magazine is not simply a case of rejection, instead it is a negotiation between her prior knowledges of what pornography is for and her measurement of *For Women* as meeting or failing to meet those purposes.

In her numerous letters to me, Anne claimed to dislike almost every element of the magazine, her first letter made her dislikes clear.

> I have been buying *For Women* since it first came out and am sorry to say that it has not impressed me at all. I thought the idea was to provide a PORNO mag for us girls but alas and to my horror there are more tits in this mag, than dicks. And I hate reading reports about prostitutes, strippers and sex show stars, mistresses and famous actresses who take their clothes off. That sort of stuff is for men to read about in the *Daily Sport*. I want to read about *heterosexual* male prostitutes and strippers etc. I also hate the fashion pages that *For Women* have deemed necessary to give us. We get all that rubbish in *Woman's Own*, *Elle*, *Cosmo* and all the other twee glossies. Obviously *FW* are having a few problems

> in selling their mag so they need the extra financial support. I also hate the photosets that they have been using. They should get rid of them and provide us with more pages of different men, more choice, different ages, colours and physical builds, and no more naked women. I just want a mag that is 100% tit free. Are we not allowed to get away from other women's breasts and arses? Is there some sort of secret law that says every mag *must* have tits in them. I think there must be.

The themes and critiques offered in both press commentary and the readers' letters page are reproduced here – Anne measures the magazine for its difference from 'male pornography', she comes to it wanting to find material about men as sexual objects (male prostitutes and strippers) and for it to be '100% tit free'. That comment about percentages is very interesting and is a common thread in Anne's letters – my impressions of her over the years of correspondence were that she trawled the magazine counting and assessing each feature, image, story etc. for its depiction of sex. What is particularly interesting about the statement above is that nowhere does it offer any reasons for reading *For Women*, there is very little in the magazine which Anne actually likes, so why does she continue to buy it? Clearly, Anne's relationship to *FW* was a contradictory one. She can also be characterized as the most proprietorial of the readers I interviewed, writing to the magazine frequently and being exceptionally pleased when her letters were published (in the interests of confidentiality, I have not reproduced any of those letters here as they were printed with her real name). This indicates the level at which her relationship with the magazine operated – it is not in the meanings of the individual textual features of the magazine that Anne finds pleasure, the meaning of *For Women* lies in her responses to it, her processes of engaging with the magazine. What drives her interest is her dislike of 'sexism', she can enjoy the magazine when it shows itself to be challenging 'sexism' but there are also pleasures to be gained from seeing that the magazine is less 'political' than she is in its rejection of sexism. Central to her relationship with the magazine and her primary or only stated reason for buying it was that it offered a measure of equality to women and thereby operated as a kind of antidote to the plethora of male orientated titles on the shelves of the newsagents: women should have the same 'rights' as men.

> I think there should be more proper porno mags for us girls and they should be available in newsagents just like men's porno mags are. We shouldn't have to send up for them by post to some dodgy address to whom we send our cheques and postal orders and receive nothing in return.

Anne was sure that women liked to look at men: 'Girls do like to look at the naked male form just as much as men like looking at the female form but we are never given the chance' (letter 1). At the same time she also expressed real difficulty in understanding why they would want to look. Her own reaction to looking at nude pictures is interesting: I asked, 'Does looking at naked men ever make you feel uncomfortable?' her reply was 'Embarrassed more like!' Sexual representations depress Anne, and she is unable to talk about images she finds erotic in any way.

At one level this is because she is constantly searching for evidence of men and women being treated 'equally', for example, her problem with the film *Basic Instinct* is that it fails her measurement of equality – its star, Michael Douglas doesn't give us a full frontal. But this measuring of 'sexist' elements is also a distancing technique: she adopts a measuring attitude towards the photography and the physical attractiveness of individual photosets:

> Most of the photographs are taken by other men which I'm not too sure about. There's too many black and white pictures and too many badly taken pictures. The photographers just don't seem to think about the composition of the pictures at all. If you look through the Jan 95 issue of *FW* you will see (that's if you agree with me ha ha!) that the sexiest most seductive pictures are of women … And to be quite honest with you I have not seen one sexy picture of a naked man in this mag since it started. The men just stand there with everything dangling away. The photographers just don't know how to get these men posing sexily and seductively, either that or the men can't be bothered making an effort. The sexiest man in *FW* up to now has been Walter, 50 years old Nov 94 issue, at least he knows how to look into the camera and give us that come on look! still no chest hair though. Hmm I think *FW* have got something against hairy chested men. (letter 1)

This assessment of the photographs enables Anne to take an appraising eye to the magazine as suggested by all those commentaries that men's bits aren't very attractive but it is also part of the very individual response she has: by adopting the dispassionate position of the aesthetic gaze she can manage those areas of the magazine that are problematic to her. Consider Anne's statement that she is a virgin: 'I myself am a virgin who's never had a boyfriend' (letter 1). Her status as virgin was very important to her and she described it as simultaneously an advantage and a problem: it is a kind of marker of superiority, setting her apart from other women readers of the magazine; it ensured her a level of objectivity but also naivety. Her relationship to the magazine is in part defined by its offering a learning experience to her: what is sex like? what is all the fuss about? what will it be like for the first time? what are men's bodies like? what does a penis look like? These are the questions Anne wants *For Women* to answer. But she hasn't got any real experience (as she sees it) to measure the magazine against – that is something other women have. Another interesting dimension of her relationship with the magazine lies in her sharing *For Women* with her friend and then her sister. Together they'd look at it and talk about it. Both the friend and the sister were sexually experienced, therefore they had the practical knowledge to tell Anne whether or not the magazine had got the female experience right. But these visits also allowed Anne to show her superiority to them in that she could challenge their views of her as uptight: for all their experience, *she* is the one brave enough to buy the magazine. In this sense and in her objections to the magazine she feels herself importantly atypical of other women:

> Other girls have sex with boys and they like it, so I presume they like boys and their genitals, so why don't they demand more equality in the porno industry. They just don't seem bothered by the enormous lack of male pornography. … I bet that

> the results [of an *FW* survey on pornography] will show that most women accept pornography as it is and that they never thinking that it should change in any way whatsoever. If magazines like FW want to do well there has to be a more of them, we have to be told that they exist and they have to be rammed down our throats constantly (gulp) so that we can get used to them and not be afraid of them, cos let's face it (yes really) men's naughty bits are a bit scary aren't they?! (letter 2)

Evidently, Anne situates herself within a community of women who are looking for sexual representations, representations different from those available to men but her interest in the magazine is not just in it for 'sake of sex' but of knowing about sex.

> The thought of first time sex being not very good for the female puts me off having first time sex (questionnaire)

She fears the 'first time' but by reading *For Women*, she imaginatively prepares herself for it – explicitness is a pre-requisite for Anne, her preparations are only possible if the magazine's stories are truly explicit and if it shows men's bodies, 'pricks and all'. Throughout her letters Anne returns to one theme, the magazine is not showing her enough that is new and different; it is not explicit enough and it is not disgusting enough. Anne absolutely loathed the magazine's Sex Directory and its adverts for sex toys.

> And that's another thing I hate about *FW*. The sex directory. It's all so ugly to me.

But when that section was sealed (as part of the attempt to move to the middle shelf), she was livid that she had to get a pair of scissors to open it. I could claim that disgust was a key response for Anne, which she sought out, trawling through each issue, getting cross, and pleased by turns. Up to a point I think that claim is valid but Anne loved and hated the magazine; fascinated by it, her primary use lay in coming to terms with the male body, her rights to look and the affirmation of her difference from other women. Its stories are not explicit enough, Xavier Hollander's are better and Anne thinks she could write more explicit stories herself but *here* are stories that she can get angry about. The magazine is also a focal point for her irritations about the inequalities of sexual representations, she can write to it and berate it for not being explicit enough. It also provides her with the space for communicating with other women who may be more like her than her friend and her sister – she was delighted when her letters received responses from other readers via the Mailshot page. This is the key element to Anne's involvement with the magazine: it is a space which may allow her to intervene. Like Jane, she recognizes it as a space where the 'girlies' are, but Anne wants that space to be different, so she writes in order to intervene in its delineation of sexy and sexually explicit stories, pictures and articles.

The above relation of Anne's use and relationship with *For Women* is shorter and less detailed than some of the other accounts I will offer, and her responses may seem considerably at odds with those others. I have used Anne as an example of what might be termed an oppositional reading position to *For Women* but such a position is *not* a rejection of the magazine. There is no doubt that she was (and may still be) a reader of *FW* even though she would refuse that label and her commentary was overwhelmingly negative. But therein lies her importance to my research. Anne indicates most clearly to me that understanding readers' interactions with their chosen media forms cannot be conducted at the level of acceptance, negotiation or rejection of the text's messages. Such accounts could not explain why Anne continued to eagerly await publication day, go to the newsagents, collect the magazine and read it from cover to cover. Nor why she should seek to spread its 'influence' by taking it to other people, or why she should write to the magazine often enough that her name was well known to the editorial team. Her mixed responses to *For Women*, of fascination and revulsion, confirm for her the need to be prepared for sex and the relation of sex to wider cultural considerations such as sexism and inequality. As we'll see for other readers, *FW* is a means by which Anne can take risks in a controlled way. The magazine is a resource for this woman, not as a spur to masturbation but because it enables her to give voice to her 'ideals': although it constantly fails to match her ideal she can point to *FW* and say, *I want more than this*. Thus her relationship to the magazine is characterized by paradox.

I started this chapter with discussion of newspaper commentaries which showed that the magazine was classified in particular ways, suggesting 'appropriate' modes of understanding the magazine and its intentions to arouse readers. Whilst these commentaries can be seen as part of the conditions under which *For Women* was received, they cannot fully articulate or produce responses, they are part of the shared knowledges about what will count as a female pornography and consequently are to be found as criteria for judgement in readers' responses. My brief outline of the various reasons women came across *For Women*, suggested an awareness of the categorizations of the magazine generated by the 'hype' it received but also an awareness of the wider cultural categorization of a woman's porn as an unlikely product. Thus, readers' first response is to 'check it out', to see what all the fuss is about, to see 'if it will put the bullet', and this conditions the ways in which they approach the magazine, it is an object of curiosity to be measured against a variety of criteria – how different is this text, how pornographic, how sexist or not, how womanly is it? Their subsequent relationship with the magazine, dismissive, intrigued, fascinated or disgusted is determined by their measurement of *For Women's* ability to offer what they considered a genuine representation of sex to women through its articulation of the hopes, fears and interests of their particular social locale. It is not that this is a truly female pornography, it does not replicate some basic female tendencies whether mental, emotional, physical or purely sexual (as anti-porn campaigners have claimed about pornography and its relationship to the male psyche) nor is it the imposition of a set of alien ideas of female sexuality – ideological false consciousness (as again, anti-porn feminists would claim). Hence, in Anne's account, there are indications of a number of factors at work in her responses to *FW*: 1) a sense of the moral dimensions of sexual representations; 2) the unfairness of sexual representations which focus mainly on women and therefore an acknowledgement of particularly feminist arguments; 3) her own sense of her lack of sexual knowledge and the difference this makes her feel from other women;

4) that there is the possibility of finding pleasure in sexual representations, that getting turned on is a response we can watch for and 5) that the magazine has a wider significance than her own response to it. Her taking part in my research enables a further exploration of her feelings about the magazine and other readers and illustrates the ways in which those responses are related to the characterization of the magazine by its critics as a 'peripheral' appraising discourse and by its readers as a more involved 'members-only' dialogue. Thus her account acknowledges other reactions to the magazine, ones which might be more 'positive' and gratified by *For Women*; Anne is aware she could take up those responses but she chooses not to. In subsequent chapters I'll examine these more positive orientations.

Notes

1. During the latter half of the 1980s, British tabloids began to reflect many of the concerns of feminist anti-pornography activists. The tracing of that movement is beyond the scope of this book but alongside their espousal of 'effects' research and *NVLA* condemnation of certain Hollywood films because of their violence went a growing concern with the activities of pornographers. These concerns are articulated precisely to demarcate the *Sun*'s own activities vis-à-vis Page 3. The campaign by Clare Short directed at the heart of the *Sun* had rocked its confidence. A tabloid with a large female readership could not afford to alienate female readers by attracting the label 'pornography'. In order to deflect such criticisms the *Sun* focuses positively on happy couples' use of sexually explicit materials within the very limited parameters of a loving and longish term relationship and on women's pleasures in sex games, sexy underwear, sexy performances. Negative commentary is reserved for 'sex fiends' and 'vice girls', those whose activities fall outside its construction of 'fun'. (Patricia Holland's 'The Page 3 Girl Speaks to Women Too', *Screen*, vol.24, no. 3, 1983; Mark Pursehouse, Looking at The *Sun*: Into the Nineties with a Tabloid and its Readers, *Cultural Studies from Birmingham*, Univ. of Birmingham, 1991). A detailed history of the tabloid's discussions of sexuality would also need to recognize the growing panic around AIDS during the 1980s, as Weeks (2000) has shown, the 'crisis' provoked increasing hostility to homosexualities in the press and 'popular' opinion. The sexual value systems that Rubin (1992) describes delineating particular hierarchies of 'appropriate' sexual activity were being reinvoked: 'Any sex that violates these rules is "bad", "abnormal" or "unnatural". Bad sex may be homosexual, unmarried, promiscuous, non-procreative or commercial. It may be masturbatory or take place at orgies, may be casual, may cross generational lines, and may take place in "public", or at least in the bushes or in the baths. It may involve the use of pornography, fetish objects, sex toys, or unusual roles.' (1992: 282).
2. These included interviews with photographer Nikki Downey; Isabel Koprowski and male model. A 'debate' between two *Sun* journalists – is it a turn-on for women? featuring a *you the jury* telephone poll followed up by *Sun* readers' comments (22 April – 8 May 1992).
3. Voracious female sexual appetites seemed to be on the agenda everywhere during the late 1980s and early 1990s: Madonna released her *Sex* book with its images of Sado/Masochism in summer 1992; myriad discussions of sex appeared on television, in magazines and newspapers; AIDS was still on the increase and heterosexuals appeared to be ignoring the risks (Haste 1992; Weeks, 2000). Popular culture's address to 'women's sexuality' and 'women's desires' was acknowledged with some reservations: for some, it leads to more promiscuity, single mothers and unwanted pregnancies; for others, it marks the beginning, however uneven, of women's emancipation.

4. Juffer argues that '... commodification is a necessary component of domestication; the process of domesticating a volume of erotica, a vibrator, a garter belt, or an adult video depends on the item's availability as a commodity. Its meaning, however, is not inevitably contaminated by its status as a commodity; a commodity is defined not by a set of internal properties but rather by the nature of the exchange process. As the commodity enters the home, thus, its meaning is redefined... Although some erotica tries to define itself as a purer, less commodified form than the big industry of pornography, its success as a genre that is now marketed widely in mainstream bookstores depends, clearly, on its commodification, a process that promises to multiply women's uses of sexually explicit materials.' (1998: 25)
5. This interpretation is not limited to discussions in the press, sociologists Peterson and Dressel see this use of equality as a deliberate disguise of the true purpose of sexually explicit displays for women. In their discussion of male striptease they comment:

    > From our observations of numerous male strip clubs, we would argue that the show functions to provide women access to opportunities for commercialised sex-related entertainment that men commonly have had. In this way it can be argued that participation by women who attend the show represents one aspect of liberation – egalitarianism...
    >
    > However, the fabricated nature of these comments [of the announcer at the show] emerges insofar as they persuade the audience to 'disattend' the basic channel of club activity which is commercialisation of sex as entertainment. Indeed, such fabrications appear successful, as evidenced by the customers' responses of yelling, whistling, drinking and collectively disparaging their men at home. Such dynamics contribute to the success of the show for its constituents: the management, support staff, and the dancers, all of whom benefit from the expenditure of money by an enthusiastic crowd, and the women in the audience, whose evening is made interesting, and perhaps exciting, by such collective rowdiness. Thus, the value of impersonal, commercialised male-female relationships is not called into question, but is extended and perpetuated by male strip clubs. (Petersen and Dressel 1982: 191–2).

    Thus pleasure operates as a disguise of the real intentions which are firstly to make money and secondly to promote the continuance of male-defined (hetero)sexualities. The conclusion is simply that women are duped: my research attempts to refute that simplistic equation.
6. Feminist criticism of women's magazines illustrates this straddling perfectly. On the one hand, women's magazines are acknowledged as providing affirmation of 'women's worlds' that is not found elsewhere. At the same time, magazines are 'reactionary' in their creation and reinforcing of an oppressive femininity through the constant examination of romance, the domestic and the 'trivial' concerns of beauty and fashion.
7. As Juffer notes, it is important to recognize 'that all forms of sexual representation are commodified to varying degrees, from hard-core porn to Annie Sprinkle's performances. If we don't acknowledge this omnipresent albeit un-even process, we run the risk of invoking, once again, the high art/low art distinction, in which the "good" form of sexually explicit material is available only to an elite few, while the masses wallow in their low-brow porn. A more instructive approach is to inquire into the relationships between making a product palatable for relatively widespread marketing, the content necessary for that commodification to occur, and the possible uses that result....' (1998: 26)

8. Linda Williams has argued the obscenity issue is to do with keeping porn out of sight, away from the public eye; it is the refusal to be hidden that seems to most offend moralist critics.
9. Barrett and Phillips offer a periodization of feminism in their collection of essays *Destablising Theory*, 1992, suggesting that 1970s feminism can be characterized by its agreement on the possibility of identifying the causes of women's 'oppression' within the social structures of patriarchy and/or capitalism (2–3). To considerably truncate their argument, the attacks on this largely white and middle-class feminist formation leads to a 1990s version of feminism which is much more aware of the differences between women such that it no longer becomes possible to talk in terms of 'woman' and 'women's rights' as if those are not contested by women themselves on the basis of sexuality, race, class etc.
10. The editorial team at *FW* assured me that letters were real although subject to editing. I have my own evidence of the authenticity of the letters' page: when my letter appeared in Mailshot, I received a response from two students at a northern university. They declined to be interviewed or to complete a tape but sent me a copy of their angry letter to the magazine, which *FW* had printed without amendment. Anne, who is introduced later in this chapter, also wrote to the magazine fairly frequently and had her letters printed (she told me, without amendment).
11. Jackie Stacey has argued readers' letters pose important methodological limitations. In her research into fans of Hollywood cinema, Stacey's first problem lay in the letters being written in response to articles in film magazines thereby limited by the processes of production and evidence only of 'audiences' responses to the discourses of stardom produced by the industry at the time. (1993: 55) A second problem lies in that the letters could not be representative of all spectators: only those who read the mainstream publications and felt they had something to say. Their letters were then processed by editors, so they are 'only a partial representation of audiences' feelings and opinions more generally.' (1993: 55) She concludes that

    > These letters cannot be analysed outside a consideration of how the discourses of the cinema and of stardom are organised within the specific magazines. In addition, the generic conventions of letter-writing for publication would need to be taken into account. Particular types of letters, such as complaints, criticism, appreciation, humorous anecdotes and so on, are recognisable forms for readers and editors, and knowledge of such forms will shape the kinds of letters written and selected for publication. Indeed, I found that the formulae for letters pages in the 1940s differed little from those published in the Birmingham local paper in the 1980s. (1993: 56)

    Stacey acknowledges that the form is an important one and that all data has its problematic constructions. Her provisos are useful in that they draw our attention to the construction of a magazine, but I take issue with her conclusions that letters must be treated with suspicion.

Creating a Woman's World of Sex

This chapter is going to examine the ways in which *For Women* was in dialogue with its readers, and I'm paying attention to the levels of talk within the magazine. This will require more than a purely formalist textual analysis and so I turn now to the work of Martin Barker on, of all things, children's comics which uses a dialogical approach to ideology based on the ideas of Valentin Volosinov. In his *Comics: Power, Ideology and the Critics*, Barker reviews theories of ideology which underpin critiques of comics and finds that all of them conceive of comics as offering 'flawed' knowledge of the world to their readers. Thus he criticizes, for example, McRobbie's (1978) study of *Jackie* and Edward's[1] study of *Beano* and *Dandy* on the basis that they presume to know what will count for readers and their tendency to view all elements of the magazine/comic as cohering around a central ideological theme – in the case of *Jackie*, the ideology of romance, in the case of the *Beano*, the values of greed and violence. In their place Barker proposes Volosinov's dialogics which stresses the socially situated nature of language in use. This is fundamentally different from those analyses drawing on Saussurian linguistics because it conceives of language as living and breathing in the act of communication and, crucially, response. Thus it is not enough to simply acknowledge that there are rules which govern every speech situation, we must take seriously the ways in which those rules often embody conflict. According to Volosinov, speech is divided into themes, speech genres and evaluative accents. Themes are meanings with 'social purposes' (Barker: 267) often accepted or 'sedimented' as a kind of common sense although this acceptance is only provisional: they are at risk every time they are invoked in the talk of social beings. Such talk occurs in speech genres or ways of talking to each other, these are the 'rules, conventions, procedures for progress and so on that reflect [shared] purposes' (1989: 267). The rules are dependent upon the ways in which our world is divided up socially, economically and politically: there are different kinds of talk for different kinds of spaces and purposes. Thus every time we speak we do so within a framework of known rules, obligations and possibilities: these divisions may be 'traditional', for example, the divisions between public and private spaces, but they are also capable of challenge and change. The important element to note here is that speech genres can be investigated as responses to material and ideological situations and/or conditions. The third element is evaluative accent; here Volosinov stresses the ways in which each act of speaking involves an attempt to persuade and at the same time invites a response. In speaking we draw upon past themes and previous talk and, crucially, we comment upon it:

> Thus the printed verbal performance engages, as it were, in ideological colloquy of large scale: it responds to something, objects to something, affirms something, anticipates possible responses and objections, seeks support, and so on. (Volosinov 1973: 95)

In speaking, the speaker invites the listeners to orient themselves to the communication and to respond. Barker suggests that this can be used to understand the material and ideological histories embodied in the rules of individual communications.

> In each case, we can ask: what views, what social circumstances, what gender, etc are assumed as the basis for orienting to and understanding the rules of a speech genre? Also, what are the boundaries of the speech genre? (Barker 1989: 270)

In order to take part in this communication what do I need to be prepared to do, how am I expected to join in and what boundaries are placed on my taking part? As Barker shows this has implications wider than merely acknowledging that speech is patterned or subject to 'controls': it means that to understand 'power in communication' we need to investigate the ways in which 'a particular unification of themes, speech genre and evaluative accent ... is able to persuade a particular group or groups to reorient themselves to become the "natural audience" of this kind of talk.' (1989: 272)[2]

Applying the Ideas to *For Women*

Barker's account stresses the usefulness of Volosinov's ideas to the analysis of stories. I think it can also be usefully applied to the full range of textual elements in a magazine like *FW*. Barker draws attention to the various kinds of stories which children learn to distinguish from an early age, from moral fables to adventurous stories and which appear in different forms and contexts, for example, books at school. He writes

> All acts of communication involve proposals. But a fictional story's proposal has two distinctive features. First, the proposal is in the form 'What if...'. It invites imaginative projection. A world is offered whose relation to our own lived world is problematic. Second, stories embody change and development. The commonplace that stories move from beginning to end turns out not to be so commonplace. *To read a story therefore, is to agree to orient oneself to its*

> *imaginative progression. It is to follow its proposal for kinds of sequence, unfolding, and resolution.* (Original italics 1989: 273)

All stories require that readers must manage a range of complex and crosscutting distinctions. The story offers an invitation to orient oneself in order to understand it and to respond to it. It is this complexity that leads Barker to Propp and to that part of his analysis of 'form' that focuses on the social relations offered by stories. An approach which combines Volosinov's emphasis on the historical, material and social production of a 'text' and Propp's patterning of the structures and transformations within stories would be able to uncover the 'socially typified' responses of 'natural readerships' (1989: 275). Thus rather than argue, as McRobbie does, that *Jackie* magazine limits girls to narratives of romance and love, Barker shows that *Jackie*'s stories are based on questions to which there are no spoken answers ('What is love like? How will I know and how should I get it?'): these questions of possibilities in the *future* are directly related to the life experiences of its readers, specifically teenage girls. In identifying this theme he also finds that *Jackie*'s confidence in 'true love' wanes in its latter years; a phenomenon linked to the production history of the magazine and developments and competition in the teen magazine market which contributed to the decline in status of the story-editor at *Jackie* magazine. Thus it is not simply enough to look for 'messages' in the text instead our accounts of a particular text will take account of its historical location and the material and social conditions which impact and inform it.

There has been a too easy conflation of all pornography as if it constituted a concrete and identifiable genre. Sexually explicit publications differ across the top shelf: with different proportions of written and photographic materials, fictions, 'serious' articles, letters, readers' fantasies, polemic etc. In looking at an individual title, these must be analysed together as separate features and as parts of the whole, if then the analyst believes that certain features are less important than others the reasons for that should be clear and defendable. Thus I'm not searching for those elements which confirm my pre-existing expectations of the magazine, my discussion here is guided by readers' assertions that particular elements were especially interesting to them and by an understanding of the ways in which the production team saw themselves as offering a significant intervention in sexual politics. That requires recognition of the magazine's conversations, not just with its readers but with those 'outside': to see the magazine in a range of struggles to define itself against other publics who have their own assessments and evaluations (as my discussion in chapter 3 made clear) and which extends to the range of industrial classifiers like WH Smiths and the authorities.

One criticism which can be levelled at this theorization of a 'pornographic' text is that porn has been defined as monologic or propagandist, precisely the kind of material which does not offer complexity and multi-layered narratives. My answer to that lies in the following chapters. At the risk of sounding defensive, *FW* is as complex as any novel and as deserving of understanding and analysis as any other text, because knowledge should not be limited to that which we assume we already know.

A dialogic account opens up the possibilities of discovery. This is not the first time that these ideas have been applied to pornography: Kipnis' Bakhtinian assessment of *Hustler* magazine is just one example. Robert Stam has also seen the value of a dialogic approach, although his conclusions actually close down the investigation of a text like *FW*. Stam employs a dialogic account drawn from Bakhtin and Volosinov[3] alongside Bakhtin's theory of carnival: a combination which leads him away from an acknowledgement of the dialogic nature of all communications to an ascription of value to certain forms of sexual communication. As usual the form assigned the lowest place is pornography:

> Bakhtin's comprehensive vision [of carnival] illuminates, if only by contrast, what is so oppressive about most pornography – its relentless single-mindedness, its humorlessness, its obsessive sexualist teleology manifested cinematically by the inexorable zoom-ins to the fuck, the cock, the cunt, its endless repetition of what Luce Iragaray [*sic*] calls 'the law of the same'. And it is this single-mindedness which generates porn's inevitable loss of aura and mystery. Although sex is autotelic and self-justifying, when it is focused on exclusively it seems to lose its quality and to implode. (1989: 177–8)

The contrast between Stam's use of carnival and that employed by Kipnis could not be more different. Where Kipnis uses carnival to proclaim the anti-establishment values of *Hustler*, Stam uses the same conceptions of sexual practices and textual formations to claim that pornography's obsession with the body is a form of monologic. Stam goes on to argue that a Bakhtinian theorization of language would enable the possibility of an erotic cinema with 'multitrack' possibilities: 'a communicative utopia, a micro-carnival characterised by "free and familiar contact" and transindividual fusion' (1989: 182). Thereby re-establishing the dichotomy: bad porn/good erotica. Drawing upon the films of the intellectual new wave film directors Godard and Mieville, Stam argues that 'appropriately' dialogic and carnivalesque erotic films are possible and would challenge the monologic patriarchal aggression of pornography. He is entitled to his claims about the lack of quality in pornographic films but his distinctions between monologic and dialogic forms of sexually explicit cinema cannot be sustained if we take seriously the central impulse of dialogic theory. All speech is dialogic, offered to a respondent: the proposals of a text are therefore not to be understood in simply stressing repetition or lack of quality. Pornographic films are not an exception to this 'rule', nor are pornographic magazines.

This section examines the magazine's attempts to articulate itself as new, different and specifically *for* women readers to experience the pleasures of explicit sexual transactions. A brief outline of the magazine's contents will offer some insight into the various kinds of 'conversation' offered within its pages. I have focused on the magazine from late 1993 through 1994 to 1995 because readers told me that despite their criticisms they liked the magazine best at this time. Furthermore, the magazine featured a high proportion of written material at this time: it had a lot to say about sex and therefore appears at its most confident. Budget cuts in 1995 led to many of its more mainstream features, the problem page, the 'expert' page and lengthy articles being dropped in an effort to streamline the magazine, thus 1993 through to the end of 1994 can be characterized as a period of relative stability. The textual analysis that follows is, then, a historical one.

Lengthy articles, usually at least three pages long were a regular feature and, in contrast to the short snappy pieces of Girls Talk, these articles were to be lingered over. Interestingly, these articles mixed scientific studies of sexuality; the problems of sexual activities – for physical and emotional health; discussion of attitudes, fear and repression alongside explorations of particular sexual practices as 'liberating', pleasurable and downright strange. This mixture signals one of the clearest ways in which *For Women* did not meet the standard benchmark of 'pornography' – the exclusion of problems. While sexuality was presented as a lifestyle option and a project of self-improvement, it was also discussed as an area of ambivalence and dilemmas, highlighting the ways in which sexual identities could be constrained by structural demands and in particular the limitations imposed by conceptions of heterosex as natural, companionate and centring on the eroticization of gender difference. Adopting the format used in mainstream women's magazines, articles focused in depth on issues of some importance to women: contraception, safety, sexual politics, restraints and desires. Thus the assumptions that follow from the delineation of pornography as a 'fantastic' realm are not appropriate to the textual formations of this magazine. Those assumptions insist that pornography is the representation of an unreal world of unlimited possibilities from which it follows that the material must be either liberating or oppressive, but in acknowledging the problems of sex, *For Women* offered a more complex articulation of possibilities which straddled the utopian/dystopian line. I have divided *FW*'s features into four themes called *techniques*, *peeping-in*, *conversations* and *problem-sharing*.[4] The features of these themes are not exclusive and often one article included elements of more than one theme.

Techniques

Sexual techniques were largely covered in the 'How to do...' articles: how to give good head, make your orgasms last longer, get your man to perform oral sex etc. The articles suggest ways of being happier, sexually and emotionally, and were written by various contributors including Tuppy Owens and Diane Poitras (a well-known fantasy fiction writer). *FW*'s role as 'adviser' was stressed in the instructional tone but there were tensions too. These techniques often involve practice and the magazine recognizes the tedium of this, so while it suggested readers try them out it also mocked the need for working at getting them right. For example: 'With these sort of claims, the ESO programme can't fail to get everyone's attention – that is, until you take a gander at what they want you to do.' (May 1994: 21) And, from the same article, 'Of course, if the thought of making like a Buddha mid-clinch is a little off-putting you could always concentrate on telling yourself you're having a good time.' (22)

Many 'how to ...' articles stressed that any problems experienced are often universal:

> Sound familiar? I thought so, it's happened to the best of us, and those who have escaped such a scenario will undoubtedly have witnessed and/or helped someone else through it. (Vol.1 no. 9: 41)

And used personal testimonies as a back-up for the efficiency of the sexual technique outlined. Testimonies also serve as a way of ensuring that the article was not prescriptive – with for and against verdicts given allowing readers space to accept or reject the practice discussed.

Peeping-in

Articles in this theme focused on the activities of other people, typical topics included: people who swing, practise S&M, sleep with their friends (male, female, gay, lesbian, bisexual) etc. The experiences of ordinary women, 'women like us' were made prominent through testimonies with at least two positive and two negative experiences of the practice under discussion. *FW* asks *'what is going on here?'* offering readers the opportunity to peep-in on other women's lives and understand what pleasures women found in experimentation. I found no evidence that these features insist a practice must be a part of everyone's sexual repertoire, rather the focus remained on seeing what other women are doing and why might it be good or bad for them.

Both the 'how to…' and peeping-in articles offered multi-narratives suggesting an expectation of readers to appraise the subject under discussion for themselves. This is particularly true of those articles dealing with the more contentious issues of anal sex and 'three-in-a-bed sessions'. In fact, much of this material encourages readers to reject certain practices as not for them. *FW* offers a chance to expand horizons without making those horizons compulsory. This doctrine is sometimes made explicit:

> We're not trying to force you into one pattern of sexual behaviour; if you want to experiment with the idea of multiple orgasms, feel free. But if you really don't want to get into the anal sex play which is usually involved, or if you find that prostate caresses don't give you any kind of pleasure, then don't worry. Sex should never be some kind of contest, but a place where physical enjoyment can be both given and shared. (Vol.1 no.6: 46)

Aided and guided by more knowledgeable contributors, readers are invited to take part in explorations of sexual matters. However, there are other kinds of relationships available to readers, where readers are asked to participate as equals. These are the articles I would label 'conversations'.

Conversations

One regular contributor often took a tongue-in-cheek look at a specific area of sexual manners: in the February 1994 issue, Kitty Doherty's 'Semen – a user's guide' examined the question whether to 'swallow' or not.

> What is it about semen? All of my friends have healthy, nay excessively healthy, sexual appetites. Why do they spend so much time doing it when they view the obvious outcome with the same distaste as something you brought in on your shoe? (48)

Inviting readers to puzzle about this question with her, we join a group of friends in a restaurant discussing the pros and cons. A call for agreement is made when Doherty offers all the reasons for not swallowing semen and then dismisses them 'Most of my friends describe the taste as "salty". Is salty enough reason for disgust? How do they manage crisps?' (49) Such questions invite readers to laugh at 'the friends' and perhaps question their own hang-ups.

This is a topic which may well be of interest to readers but would be difficult to approach from a 'how to do ...' standpoint. Here readers are invited to eavesdrop on a private conversation and, while the overall tone seems to suggest that dislike of semen is really rather silly, the article is written throughout as a round-the-table discussion enabling readers to position themselves anywhere on the issue. The use of first-person testimonies allows readers to get in close to the subject, to marvel at the sexual freedom of some women and to laugh at the inhibitions of others. The primary concern of this article seems to lie, not in the question of whether to swallow or not, but in having the space to discuss an intensely private issue without fear of recrimination.

Sharing Problems

The problem-sharing theme included the problem page and resident 'sexpert' Dr Andrew Stanway's page and features almost the entire spectrum of sexual positions, methods and problems, from how to use your tongue, make your own video, choose a vibrator, have safe anal sex, to female ejaculation. Stanway's articles often reflect male concerns, offering insight into the 'complicated male psyche'. In both these sections *FW* is anxious to outline the credentials of their experts:

> Jan Birks is Deputy Editor of Forum magazine and has been giving advice professionally on sexual matters for the last five years. (No. 1: 9: 104)

and

> Andrew Stanway MB MRCP is the author of more than fifty books, many on his specialist subject, sex and relationships. Dr Stanway has a thriving psychosexual and relationship practice and is the creator of the pioneering *Lover's Guide* video series. He lives in Surrey with his wife and three children. (Aug 1994: 114)

It is important that readers recognize the legitimacy of these contributors' claims to pronounce upon specific problems. Although these pages also offer multiple narratives it is unlikely that readers are given the same opportunities for appraisal as in the previous sections as both these items reflected a more authoritative voice within the magazine. For example, Stanway uses terms like 'From where I sit as a therapist all this is quite important' and 'A common question I'm asked by couples is ..' so that his expertise is always prominent but as his title 'sexpert' suggests, his is supposed to be a non-threatening expertise and one it might be safe to trust. I will address the problem page in particular in the next section.

These themes reflect the intimacy that *FW* wished to create and share with its readers, giving a sense of a direct communication between women. The magazine offered a variety of 'conversations' to its readers, all focusing on sex, sexuality and sexual behaviour. Labelling the magazine's address as conversational moves away from those accounts of women's magazines that stress the one-sidedness of the relationship between text and reader. It is through the format of informal conversations between women that *FW* offered ways of joining in a specifically female form of sexual dialogue.

FW is an odd mixture of the 'erotic' and the everyday. Unlike UK magazines for men (some of which are published by the same company as *FW*), the sexual explicitness of the magazine is related as real-life experience rather than fantasy. By that I mean that topics which would be used in, for example, *Men Only* as a basis for a narration which owes much to fiction genres and having a laugh, is here confined to relatively serious articles. The reader of *FW* is not given an extended narrative which runs from a meeting, through recognition of mutual desire, to sexual activity, to orgasm; instead we have small snippets of dialogue arranged in much the same ways as a discussion of work experiences might be laid out in *Cosmopolitan*. Thus the magazine is not predicated, as one might expect, on the relation of fantasy for the *sole* purpose of masturbation, but on information and sharing experiences which might then tap into fantasy and masturbation. This points to the ways in which the magazine is located at a very precarious site between sexual pleasure and sexual danger for women.

The Problems of Sex

Problem pages are perhaps *the* defining feature of women's magazines: no magazine seems complete without one. Where the feature articles stress communities of women, the problem page constructs an intimate space occupied by individual women, their problem and the sympathetic agony aunt or uncle. Alongside its how-to and problem-solving articles *FW* also provided answers to readers' intimate questions. The agony aunts at *FW* changed fairly frequently: Isabel Koprowski, Tuppy Owens, Jan Birks, Jay Kay and an ex-Chippendale all took their turn and each offered advice in their own way. Koprowski, Owens and Birks were probably more serious in their approach than Kay who often took the 'examine yourself'[5] line to new extremes with quite tart answers:

> Come on now, you're a grown woman, and you have control over how you live your life. If this was a one-off and you were in a dilemma about finding yourself in a relationship with a man who was already in a relationship I'd probably say 'these things happen. Prepare for someone to get hurt – but it might all work out in the end.' In your case though, this has become a habit... I wouldn't condone

this sort of behaviour in a man so why should I condone it in you? (Dec 1994: 121)

During 1996 the problem page was dropped as too expensive and then reinstated with the ex-Chippendale Murray Grant, whose advice was offered from a male perspective: 'Murray's the man with the sexpertise'.[6]

Researchers have emphasized the importance of the problem page to readers, for example, McRobbie has observed that the 'advice columns exist because of so much that cannot be said, or cannot be discussed elsewhere. They occupy a particularly important place in teen magazines because it is in adolescence that this knowledge takes on an urgency' (1991: 157). Thus the problem page has a social role which taps into the roles available to girls, their relative powerlessness, their lack of knowledge, their vulnerabilities and their duty of care to others (1991: 158 ff.). Frequently that aspect of importance has been used to suggest that problem pages renege on their duty to their readers – the problem page is a space in which women are misled. For Winship (1987) this occurs because the magazines reinforce women's oppression as personally experienced rather than shared – the particular form that the problem page takes actually contributes to that sense, especially when it encourages readers' pleasures through the spectacles of other lives being worse than the reader's own. McCracken (1993) suggests that, particularly in those advice pages where beauty and fashion feature, the intimate discourse serves to disguise the fostering of specific insecurities which only the products/actions recommended can solve. In other words, the problem page is a form of covert advertising for a set of established standards of beauty and feminine behaviour. These standard accounts of disguise and coercion are incompatible with the approach I have tried to develop here.

In her research into Canadian teenage girls' use of teenzines, Currie (1999) finds that girls read problem pages together and assess the problems in terms of their 'realism' – how far they are able to match girls' own experiences. Currie is particularly interested in readers' indications that the form of the problem page is important to their reading pleasures. In other words that the question and answer format is more pleasurable than a simple information format. Alongside the pleasure, Currie finds behavioural and normative messages offering 'goals and values which orient the reader towards traditional pursuits of beauty and heterosexual romance.' (1999: 170) These messages are conveyed via the specific 'knowledge' formations of the question and answer format – the questions indicate that this is 'something you need to know' (1999: 173) and the answers, the advice, are the responses of more knowledgeable individuals. Thus the format itself contributes to the imposition of certain ways of thinking because it doesn't simply present information to be assessed by readers; it offers answers as knowledge which actively shape the needs and interests of readers (1999: 174). Teenage girls' problems are 'depoliticized', the social aspects of adolescence are 'mystified' and the specifically female experience of life under patriarchy is 'obscured' via the attractiveness of the 'lure' of individualized promises of 'getting boys to like you'.

Although Currie aims to analyse magazines alongside reader definitions and understandings of the text, her analysis is limited by constant reiteration of the patriarchal nature of the texts. Any girl indicating that she 'recognizes' herself in the text must automatically be subject to the control and manipulations of patriarchy:

> ... textual power operates in local sites; if readers recognise themselves within the text, they have been positioned, as embodied female Subjects, by patriarchal definitions of both femininity and the social... this power [is not attributed] to the text but rather to the ability of commercial texts to colonise social life. (1999: 309)

Magazines work through their 'objectified knowledge' distinguished by its separation from other forms of more experiential and appropriate forms of knowledge. I argue differently. The suggestion that girls assess the page for 'realism' is very striking but rather than then blame the magazines for their promotion of limited messages, we could regard realism as an indication of the specific nature of the contract offered to readers; girls respond to their magazines because they *find affirmation that their problems are important enough to be in print.*

This suggestion is supported by the work of another researcher: Mary Kehily's account of British teenagers and their magazines reaches different conclusions from Currie's. Again, problem pages are read and discussed collectively, but they are also not taken 'seriously'. Her readers indicate that the answers are not very important to them: 'the "fascination" of the problem page lies primarily in reading about a problem where the "information" to be gleaned is contained within the problem as the reader expresses it rather than in advice given by the experienced agony aunt' (1999: 73). There is an exception to this: when the problem connects with their own lives in some way. Kehily finds that academics' analyses of the problem page, that they are ideologically constraining or that they expect self-examination, are not as important as simply '*the problem itself*, which may be read in friendship groups and discussed critically in terms of pleasure, humour, empathy and disbelief.' (1999: 73) Problems are assessed in terms of their appropriateness to the age of the reader, for example, she finds that '"the too in depth" and "over the top" features of *More!* transgress the boundaries of legitimacy defined by these young women as suitable for their age group and feminine identities.' (1999: 76)

This rejection of the problems in *More!* is not a refusal of 'messages' but shows that the magazine must address the social positioning of its readers. If the details of sexual activity are beyond their own personal knowledge, then the magazine fails to connect with them. Thus Currie's claims of 'luring' girls into patriarchal definitions of femininity through the question and answer format fundamentally misreads the relationship offered to readers in the teenage problem page and, by extension, all problem pages. The relationship offered *is* a pseudo-personalized one but it is also an *acknowledging* one in that readers' problems, however naïve or bizarre, will receive an appropriate answer (what constitutes appropriate is dependent upon the magazine's particular contract with its readers). McRobbie's statement that problems are aired here because there are no other spaces is important to recognize as a convention of the problem page. Readers can bring their issues here without fear of their being identified and other readers can read all about it: but the most important element of the problem page is surely that the agony aunt does not say 'why are you fussing about this – this isn't a problem'. So, for instance, in teenage magazines where girls have difficulties fitting in at school because of the codes of dressing etc., the agony aunt acknowledges the difficulties of being a teenager simply by answering the question asked. If, as Currie and Winship required, the agony aunt answered a question regarding applying mascara correctly with a discussion of the patriarchal beauty myth, this would not just bore the reader but it would deny the experience of the letter writer. Kehily's observation that the answer is not as important as the question alerts us to the proposal of the problem page 'we take your problems seriously'.

This opens up a variety of other possibilities within the page – readers can look at the problem and assess it themselves for its level of seriousness, difficulty, embarrassment or likelihood, *could it ever happen to me?* That allows a further proposition, if it was happening to you, what would be your response and has the agony aunt answered appropriately? Does the magazine get this answer right for me, for itself, for the magazine it claims to be? In *FW* the problem page needed to reference the specific issues of sexual pleasure, activity and experimentation. The standard features of the agony aunt, acknowledgement of the problem, acceptance of the individual and appropriate advice are all to be found in *FW*'s problem page. The specific orientation lies in the sexual focus and the need to 'tell it like it is'. This is probably best illustrated by examples:

> Fantasy Fright
>
> I am a happily married woman, but I am sure that I am bisexual. I have discussed my feelings with my husband, as we have a very open relationship and I know I can talk to him about anything. My husband says that he does not mind me indulging my fantasies as long as he is present and can participate.
>
> I am a little frustrated that he has given me an ultimatum, but I value our relationship too highly to sacrifice it.
>
> What is confusing me is that when I masturbate, I fantasise about sex with women, and also about my husband making love with me and the other women. This turns me on tremendously.
>
> A few months ago, we had the opportunity to act this out, and I just couldn't handle it. I feel like a hypocrite.
>
> I am disturbed by the fact that I am jealous, yet turned on by the thought of my husband having sex with another woman in front of me. I am also beginning to wonder if I really am a lesbian at heart.

> *You face the dilemma that many people have faced – the desire to have a novel experience with a new partner, coupled with the fear that the price of such an experience would be too high. You certainly are not abnormal because you have such fantasies. It does seem that you are happier keeping extra marital activities in the realms of fantasy, and there is nothing hypocritical in that – your admission is very honest. Relax, and stop being so hard on yourself. Your fantasies are doing no one any harm.* (Summer 92: 90)

The above answer refuses to pass judgement, acknowledging that the writer has a 'problem' but recasting it in terms of her 'honesty' in admitting her fears and fantasies. Sex may be problematic even dangerous (physically, mentally and emotionally) as well as pleasurable, for women and men. *FW* cannot ignore this, but it can attempt to construct a space within the magazine in which women can express their fears and pleasures. In seeking to construct a space in which women can experience sexual agency, *FW* cannot simply insist on a woman's right to pleasure, the nature of its contract with its readers lies in its 'honesty'. Being honest is not simply about asserting a woman's right to the control of her body, it also has to engage with the ways in which those rights may be circumscribed by double standards, fear, lack of knowledge and practical considerations.

Thus, letters to the problem page are answered with practical advice that does not moralize or cover up by the use of euphemisms:

> *... The anal canal is a delicate structure and it's a good idea for anyone considering penetration to take things easy ... [A]ny abrasion of the mucosa anywhere in the body will allow easy access to the HIV virus, and the anal canal is particularly delicate – so it is essential to use a condom...* (May 1994: 121)

Detailed descriptions of the physiological effects of sexual practices are a regular feature of the problem page, as well as advice on how to practice a particular kind of sex safely or simply to remove pubic hair safely. These practices are rarely commented upon, the reader asks for information and it is duly given: the establishment of boundaries of acceptable/non-acceptable are limited here to issues of choice – given the information women can make the choices they need to explore their own sexual pleasures and boundaries. Other kinds of question receive answers that do stress boundaries: some practices are not to be considered worth choosing, for example, the Bonk Account letter in June 1994's problem page. A reader asked for information on 'reputable escort agencies' she could join in order to finance her way through college. Jan Birks' refusal to provide the information was accompanied by a list of the dangers to be expected and the eminently sensible suggestion that the reader visit her bank manager.

The safer sex message in the magazine is firmly linked to the autonomy of the female body and female sexual desire: knowing what you want sexually includes knowing how to protect yourself. If the issue of safer sex is ignored then that amounts to a refusal to acknowledge the embodiment of sexuality. Sex for *FW* includes bodily fluids: for example, semen and vaginal lubrication. These are not revolting in the magazine, they are what makes sex sexy, but recognizing their sexiness means remembering their danger. It does seem to be the case that women are expected to take responsibility for safety – on one level, this seems eminently sensible but on another it places women back in the role of gatekeeper of men's less responsible desires. However, this is not simply about reaffirming women's roles, it is also an indication of the magazine's contractual obligations to its readers: the magazine will not pretend that women do not have to take responsibility.

For a magazine which advertises itself as a publication for the sensual woman and labels its contents as sexually explicit, *FW* does, in fact, devote a lot of space to the 'problems' of 'ordinary' sex lives. On one level this establishes sexual activity as something experienced by 'all' women and therefore 'normal' (even at its most perverse). For this reason, it is actually quite expected that the question of male sexual coercion or violence should figure within the magazine, despite being the antithesis of a 'fun' sexuality. As well as featuring regularly on the problem page there have been articles on date rape, stranger rape, women's reactions to male pornography and women's disastrous experiences of sex (funny or depressing as well as violent). The inclusion of these subjects demonstrates *FW*'s attempts to manufacture a space in which women can enjoy imaginative explorations of sex. For example, a four-page article on date rape and tactics for avoiding it featured in the first issue of the magazine as if to say, *'This is part of the reality for women, we know it, we have seen it, we want something done about it but what this magazine is about, is being naughty. If it was not like this, what kinds of fun could we have?'* Thus male violence is part of the real world but inside the magazine there is a space to discuss sex without having to keep one eye open for it.

As a sexually explicit enterprise *FW* cannot be seen as a space where everything goes. The differences between what might be considered possible for men and for women are obvious within its pages. The magazine is not about wild, frantic couplings between faceless strangers, or sexual conquests running into thousands and this reflects an awareness of the dangers of sexual activity for women. Fantasy is not a separate sphere from lived experience, separate from 'reality'. Fantasy and reality are not separated within the text but are linked in a complex formation. The serious articles and the problem pages are absolutely fundamental to the expression of *FW*'s ethos: *this magazine understands the difficulties and in sharing those with you, we can also begin to imagine having fun and playing with the possibilities of fantasy.* For that reason, the magazine must also be critical of those women who jeopardize their health/physical and emotional well-being by not taking seriously the responsibilities that go alongside the possibilities of fantasy. *FW* offers information about sex and protecting oneself, but it also opens up a space for discussion of sex as an object of pleasurable conversation in and of itself. In other words, the pleasures of fantasy are made available through the acknowledgement that sexual activities and relationships are not easy and require a level of autonomous self-reflexivity if they are to move beyond the rhetoric of sexual liberation.

This was made particularly clear in the regular feature 'This is your sex life' – an interview with a celebrity woman focusing on her sexual history. A variety of women featured, including Cynthia Payne (February 1994)[7], Karen Krizanovich (May 1994)[8], Marjory Proops (August 1994)[9], Arabella Melville (February 1995)[10], Ky Howles (June 1995)[11], Niki Wolf (July 1995)[12], and Juliet Hastings (January 1996)[13]. Each of these women detail their sexual philosophy and their experiences of sex (good and bad) in a narrative which stresses their interests in sexual explorations. The accounts often focus on the humorous problems of youthful sex – that is, fairly inexperienced sexual encounters,

> As a teenager I was really boring, really ugly – and *really* horny. And nobody wanted to sleep with me. I finally got this boy and said "Right James, I'm sick of this, we're going to do *it*!" We had penetrative sex for all of one minute, after which I immediately jumped off and looked in the mirror – but I didn't look any different! You expect suddenly to be this mature adult or at least have bigger boobs. (Krizanovich, May 1994: 119)

Some of the interviews emphasized the distress of bad sex – not just in terms of inability to orgasm but also focused on the associated problems of sexual relationships and the lack of power to say no or to articulate other needs.

> The next two years were torture. Sex was terrible – I am able to relate to people who write to me with similar problems because I know what its like to lie there with your hands clenched and praying for it to be over. I had a few brief relationships – little flings that had very little significance other than to make me realise that I could respond to [other] men – I didn't need to sleep with them necessarily, I've never been a promiscuous woman and I had many years when I had no sex at all. (Proops, August 1994: 79)

These more negative elements mostly featured in those interviews with women in their sixties, looking back on their pasts and on a collective past which had made it difficult for women to express their sexual needs or desires. Even so, these stories usually had an upbeat element, even if sexual fulfilment was a long time coming, it did eventually come as did better relationships and more pleasurable encounters.

> I got in the family way at 18, and then had several abortions, so sex was nothing but problems. It was just about babies all the time. I never learnt to enjoy it. Terry would say to me when we'd finished "Well, did you?" and I would say "Did I what?" I didn't know what he meant until my thirties. Then I met Omar in Tangiers, and it was wonderful. I used to go over there two or three times a year – just for the sex. (Payne, February 1994: 19)

In these narratives, it is not just that time passing or another lover enables better experiences. Rather, there is an implied critique of 'outdated' modes of thinking about masculine and feminine heterosexuality: a rejection of, in particular, feminine passivity as a failure to take control of sexual experiences, needs and desires. In the younger interviewees these pleasures may also include quite extreme practices:

> I'm a very active practitioner of everything I preach. I enjoy pain, quite extreme pain sometimes. I'm into humiliation and role play; I like thrashing people – I'm an all round bad girl really. I enjoy body piercing; I get very turned on by it. I don't have any permanent piercing, I do it as part of SM play. I've never pierced anyone's penis but I have had my clitoral hood pierced which was very intense. (Wolf, July 1995: 72)

What each of the narratives share is a belief in the possibilities of sexual fulfilment despite the problems posed by fear and/or repression. In descriptions of SM cultures, the sadness of mismatched libidos and stories of sexual health, the narratives explore the necessity of admitting to particular feelings and desires however 'odd' they might appear to others. An element of intervention in sexual culture is also implicit; Proops and Krizanovich suggest their interest in helping women deal with the emotions of sexuality; Payne talks about the need for sex workers in a culture which refuses to accept 'perverse' desires and Wolf and Hoyles talk about the possibilities of expanding sexual scripts and sexual knowledge – as Hoyles put it, 'I'm a woman on a mission now. For example, I hear women in the shop saying they don't bother with a lubricant ... and I'm alarmed that none of the messages about oils and jellies ... have got through.' (June 1995: 84) In their movement from the perils of first-time coitus through to more accepting acknowledgement of their own desires, these narratives suggest sex is a means of learning: experiences to be embraced for their pleasure and for what they can teach. All the interviews end on an upbeat note:

> Although I live on my own now, I definitely feel that I'm a sexual person. I think I always will feel like that – but sex for me now is just banter. I have flirty relationships with quite a lot of men; ... But if I was lucky enough to meet a man this afternoon who said to me, "Let's go out tomorrow", I'd say "Oh yes, let's!" (Proops ibid.)

These narratives serve to highlight the ways in which women's experiences of sex are neither wholly good nor wholly bad. The confusion that is a part of growing up, the problems of finding out what it is you want from partners, lovers and relationships are referenced in narratives of survival and optimism. They borrow explicitly from the 'permissive' discourse of liberating sexuality, that women should have equal rights to pleasure but, of course, in the explanations of being used by men for sex, money, emotional support, they also can't help but highlight the structural inequalities of gender relationships. However, the optimism lies in the recognition of those problems alongside the implicit refusal to give up on the idea of mutual desire and fulfilment.

I have focused on the ways in which 'serious' elements of the magazine stressed the need for safety, the recognition of the embodiment of sexual practices and their impact on sexual pleasure. Through that emphasis the magazine attempts a re-evaluation of sexual exploration as a source of interest, fun and self-knowledge for women. This bridging and re-evaluation was and is a response to the sometimes fraught and contradictory nature of women's relationship to sex. As Vance (1992b; 1992c) has argued in relation to the development of a feminist politics of sexuality, the emphasis on 'danger' must not be at the expense of women's pleasures in sex.[14] Although *FW* was not a 'feminist' project, it did attempt to balance 'pleasure' and 'danger' for its readers, using the familiar format of the woman's magazine, mixing elements of celebration and critique. Can we call it a political project? I'd hesitate to suggest an overtly political intention in the magazine and certainly Northern & Shell were publishers seeking commercial success, but individual members of the editorial team did see themselves as politically motivated. As I've already discussed, Zak Jane Keir, in particular, had specific aims: a longstanding member of Feminists Against Censorship, she hoped the magazine might become a platform for attacking normative sexual standards and promoting new possibilities for women through sexuality. Ruth Corbett was more circumspect in her expectations of what the magazine could achieve but based her editorial decisions on an ethic of responsibility.

> Our articles are more personalised … they're about how to find out about your own body and what you want, not what your boyfriend wants.… But they're not pretending that things are lovely and fluffy in the world out there, because in fact its not … you know it's a minefield. And we try to get across that you've got to come to terms with yourself as a sexual being and not to be guilty about that or to feel ashamed because its only been in the last few years that women have been able to say yes I have desires … its sort of Victorian attitudes that are slowly, slowly being eroded.

So the team saw themselves as providing a kind of antidote to antiquated ways of thinking about women and sex and that women had decisions to make about their sexual activities that recognized their needs but also the responsibilities these brought. In this sense then, the articles and discussion of problems offer women a means of gathering sexual experiences and knowledge which could enable effective embrace of desire. *FW* invited women to respond to its articles, letters, stories and photographs 'as women'. How far women took up that invitation is the subject of the next chapter.

Notes

1. Owen D. Edwards, 1977, 'Cow pie and all that' in *DC Thomson Bumper Fun Book*, Paul Harris Publishing.
2. The example Barker cites is the take-up of Enoch Powell's racist agenda on immigration. He draws attention to the ideas of different cultures which underpin Powell's speeches but also indicates that listeners did not simply 'hear' these arguments; they were encouraged to respond in particular ways 'as British' and emotionally attached to a 'British way of life' (1989: 272–3). The validation of 'natural' 'emotional' and 'common sense' responses embedded in Powellite racist ideas enables its take-up in those spaces (speech genres) where overtly political talk would usually be ruled out. Thus racist ideas and politics penetrated even the most relaxed and comfortable arenas of 'private time'.

3. There is some dispute over Volosinov's existence and, for some, Bakhtin and Volosinov are one and the same author.
4. I examine some of these features in an earlier article in Arthurs & Grimshaw (eds), 1997.
5. A common feature of problem pages seems to be the 'look at yourself and understand your motivations' kind of advice: see, for example, discussions in Barker 1989; Currie 1999; McRobbie 1991; McCracken 1993; Winship 1987.
6. Currie suggests that male advice is particularly problematic: 'Despite their value-free appearance, these texts legitimise patriarchal standards because men are advanced as authorities on what it means to be a woman' (1999: 187). Her claim derives from the seeming inappropriateness of men to comment on women's problems, it would need more detailed analysis of Grant's problem page and answers than is possible here to make a sustainable argument either for or against 'patriarchal authority' in his definitions of women, sex and problems.
7. One-time suburban madam famous for her Luncheon Voucher parties.
8. Agony columnist – 'the Sharon Stone of Agony Aunts'.
9. One of the UK's longest serving agony aunts and well-loved journalist.
10. Founder of the sex magazine 'The Libertine' a short-lived publication for men and women.
11. Owner of Sh! First of new breed of sex shops in UK catering for women.
12. Editor of *Fetish Times*.
13. Erotic writer.
14. In her introduction to the collection of essays arising out of the Barnard Sexuality Conference, Vance writes 'At the level of the theory, the concept [of pleasure and danger] most powerfully speaks to the necessary feminist strategy on sexual matters: simultaneously to reduce the danger women face and to expand the possibilities, opportunities and permissions for pleasure. Any strategy that focuses exclusively or predominately on one goal while ignoring the other will fail.' (Vance 1992b: xv)

Women, Sex and the Possibilities of Pleasure

The debates around the use of pornography have tended to cluster around the identification of active/passive, transgressive/accepting responses to the text or, as in the encoding/decoding model (Hall 1987), to find the preferred reading and then instances of its acceptance, negotiation or refusal (Hardy, 1998). The responses to *For Women* magazine I obtained were sufficiently contradictory to suggest that when it comes to sexually explicit materials there is no easy fit between textual analysis and audience responses – how does one text generate different responses and different levels of liking and disliking in individual readers? Positions that operate from the identification of ideologies in the text are only interested in readers' critical talk as a mark of refusal or resistance but I found that readers were critical of the magazine at the same time as some of them really liked it. These critical responses were not evidence of preferred, negotiated or oppositional readings, rather they are patterned and sophisticated accounts of why and how the magazine worked or did not work for individual readers. The interview material shows that readers' approbation and/or criticisms are not to be understood via measurement of the efficacy or failure of ideological messages.

So, how do we answer the question 'why do some women like porn when theory claims they not only don't, but can't, like it?' In stressing the need to take account of the different levels and conventions of particular speech events, a dialogic account remains sensitive to the ways in which most contemporary magazines are made up of many elements. These may well be formulaic or common to other magazines (indeed this commonality is important to understanding them) but each element invites and makes its own proposals to readers who, in turn, know and understand the terms and conditions of those invitations and proposals. For example, as we've seen, problem pages offer proposals to readers: problems are presented in the first person as the genuine cry for help from another reader and answered again as if in conversation by the agony aunt. The intimate personalized talk replicates a private conversation, and yet this is a public dialogue which invites readers to imagine how it might be to be this reader, to evaluate her problem for themselves and then to assess the answers given.

In taking up these invitations to join in, Barker suggests readers agree to a 'contract' with magazines and their contents.

> A contract involves an agreement that a text will talk to us in ways we recognise. It will enter into a dialogue with us. And that dialogue with its dependable elements and form, will relate to some aspect of our lives in our society. (1989: 261)

In order to understand what a comic/magazine is offering its readers, we need, according to Barker, to locate the 'natural readers' of a text.[1] In so doing the analyst is not looking for 'ideology', frequency of reading or for signs of 'critical' judgements but rather must search for a proposed social relationship between text and reader: an invitation to orient oneself to the magazine and participate in its discourse in particular ways. Thus when it comes to analysing respondents' talk, we are not seeking to identify symptoms of 'susceptibility' to the 'messages of the text' but for a 'willingness to participate' in its conversations.

> Readers learn what to expect, and what is expected of them. This is how they can recognise when their expectations are being disappointed. And perhaps these disappointments can be our best evidence of what those typified expectations were. If readers... reject one kind of story, and demand another kind of ... story, maybe they are distinguishing 'contract-fulfilling' stories from those which fail to meet their expectations. (1989: 258)

Barker is expressly talking of formulaic fictions but his suggestions can be applied elsewhere, offering ways of understanding the different kinds of experiences of pleasure, involvement and disappointment in *FW* expressed by my respondents (I address a specific instance of 'contract-fulfilling' in chapter 6.) His proposal is that we can investigate the ways in which 'typified social experiences' are offered by a magazine to its readers. Those readers can then be investigated paying attention both to the ways in which they do or do not take up those invitations to join in the typified social experiences offered. This moves away from the idea that young girls are dupes of their magazines because it acknowledges that other responses are not 'better' or 'worse' than those of the 'natural' reader, they are evidence of other social positions characterized by other kinds of response. This is crucial because it becomes a means by which we could start to investigate why and how some women responded enthusiastically to *FW* and others did not. It also allows for ways of accounting for changing relationships to magazines: an issue fundamental here, where readers moved from enthusiasm to disaffection. My understanding of Barker's 'natural' reader is that she agrees in this time and this place, with these particular social and cultural knowledges that she will join in the 'what if' proposal of a magazine. That relationship may well be temporary. Barker's proposal to academics is to abandon the search for evidence of 'harm' to readers or for ways of inoculating readers against less progressive ideas and attitudes and to begin to ask the questions why and how people enjoy particular media forms.[2]

Although the number of participants in this research was relatively small a mass of material for analysis was produced in the interviews. Even the shortest interview conducted resulted in eighteen pages of typed transcript and a great deal of detail which has had to be substantially edited in order to begin to offer some conclusions. This book is not about 'sampling' or drawing pictures of 'average' readers and so I focus on the in-depth exploration of the responses and interests of individual. In the broad field of audience research, criticism has been levelled at those accounts concentrating on the 'spectacular' participant: those people who have a particularly enthusiastic engagement with a media form. For example, discussion has centred on the tendency to celebrate 'fandoms' as examples of particularly 'active' users of media forms. The purpose of much audience research has been to challenge the notion of the passive audience: studies of fans have focused on groups of readers/viewers who are characterized by their resistance to textual/dominant ideologies through their appropriation of media texts (see, for example, Jenkins 1993; Lewis 1992). This particular conceptualization of the active reader is far from unproblematic in its celebration of the idea of 'resistance'. Too often resistance is simply measured by the extent of fan activity uncovered and the gender of the participants in that particular 'fandom'. In many cases the most 'aberrant' (not passive) readers are identified as female and are perceived to operate in collective ways, supposedly indicative of a more democratic and oppositional culture than that usually found in mainstream audience 'activity' (Fiske 1987).

The emphasis on activity/passivity is a remnant of the legacy of critical approaches seeking 'determinant moments' in people's media use. More recently, audience studies have attempted to undercover the complexities of the pleasures for viewers, in particular women, made available by formulaic mass media: the romantic novel, soap operas, fan fictions, B-movies and magazines. To a large extent the motivations for this work have centred on recuperation, the celebration of elements of women's textual pleasures, while still searching for the evidence of incorporation to the needs of patriarchy and/or capitalism. Thus in Ballaster et al.' study of women's magazines, audience responses are used to observe the creative and critical pleasures of women's use of magazines alongside the reiteration of feminist concerns about harmful constructions of femininity: 'this pleasure is by no means pure, unambiguous or unproblematic' (1991: 1). The uneasy acknowledgement of contradiction in media use is given as evidence that it might be possible to inoculate viewers against bad or reactionary messages via more liberating forms of knowledge.

Another tendency comes out of this particular ambivalence: that those who are critical of a media product are unlikely to be influenced by it. While it is tempting to celebrate the use of *For Women* as an instance of resistance to the common-sense proposition that 'nice girls just aren't interested in sexually explicit material', to do so, just because the readers I happened to talk with were women, would be false. The fact of them being female and using a sexually explicit magazine *is* interesting, perhaps because it appears to fly in the face of many discourses about women's sexuality, but my purpose in interviewing these women was not to recuperate their use of pornographic materials as resistant reading. Theoretical frameworks that stress the ideological determinism or unconscious processes of pornographic materials are fundamentally flawed, based as they are in suppositions and assumptions about the audience and its passivity (even about its activity). They no way of understanding the use of *For Women* as it is experienced by individual readers. A celebratory account of reader activity as resistance is an equally obfuscating tool.

Instead I have attempted to look at the ways in which women were invited to join in *For Women*'s explorations of sex. Barker's notion of the 'natural' reader proposes that some readers are likely to be able to illuminate more clearly the relationships, expectations and disappointments involved in engaging with a particular media form. This is not to suggest that we should only look to those readers as the single group worth studying, but we should be aware that there are some readers who are likely to be more enthusiastic than others and that their enthusiasms are indications of the relation between the individual and the social. To this end, I have focused on the interviews with those readers who expressed a particular enthusiasm for the discussion of *For Women*. In other words, I have separated out interviews on the basis that some responses could tell me more than others about *For Women*. This does not mean, however, that I have focused only on those women who liked the magazine or just on positive responses to individual elements of the magazine.

Other interviewees certainly had plenty to say about, for example, women and sexuality; the difficulties of coming to terms with the work of radical feminists and maintaining a commitment to the use of pornography as a means of validating gay lifestyles; the use of bondage and S/M imagery. Their exclusion might seem rather perverse given the difficulties obtaining participants for audience research, however, delineating between different interviewees' talk is absolutely necessary. As Hermes (1995) found in her study of readers of popular magazines, many people have little to say about their media use – their comments are often very general and refuse to accord individual titles or kinds of texts any personal significance. For Hermes, the disappointing nature of the responses she obtained could be accommodated by acknowledging the 'everydayness' of certain kinds of media use: magazines are 'easily put down' and therein lies their significance to many women (and men). I certainly found there were interviewees for whom *FW* was eminently 'put down-able'. Although they had been interested enough to buy or pick up the magazine 'to see what they were doing', for those readers, that interest was quickly dissipated. In those accounts which claim that women have no interest in pornography, this lack of interest would be confirmation of women's resistance to pornography's ideological messages and, from that point, no doubt, we could dismiss those interviewees who claimed to like the magazine as evidencing 'false consciousness'. However, my approach has assumed that *FW* is not simply a body of contents in search of converts;

the magazine is not merely a form of knowledge that can be accepted or rejected. Thus the selection of interviews is based on indications of the ways in which a participant accorded *For Women* a place in their understanding of themselves, their experiences of sexuality, the social 'place' of sexuality, pornography and relations between men and women, and the level of commitment and conviction they gave to those ideas.

I have selected five interviews to look at in depth in this chapter offering the possibility of examining the patterning of responses to the magazine. I'm not suggesting I can simply map 'readings' or 'decodings' onto individual women, or that these are somehow the only 'authentic' responses to pornography. Gender certainly is an issue in responses to the magazine – many of the women talked at length about the ways in which women needed something different from men in order to be sexually aroused, however, their conception of what women needed was not uniform. And certainly, their conceptions are at considerable odds with the ideas of Dworkin, Itzin and other un-enthusiastic viewers of sexually explicit materials. For some women, the magazine got it right, thus they are enthusiastic about its ability to speak about sex; but for others the response is less embracing – the magazine failed in significant respects. I should make clear that they are not simply *individual* responses – this chapter will show that they are socially and culturally located ways of understanding and participating in a specific cultural form. I am certain that there are other orientations to *For Women* that I have not been able to access, but someone else will have to do that work!

Jane

Jane was briefly introduced earlier and had begun reading the magazine shortly after the birth of her child. She continued to read the magazine for about a year up to the point at which her marriage began breaking down. In coming to the magazine, Jane had looked for evidence of a particularly new and female slant on sex and found *FW* spoke directly and very well to women. Her relationship to *FW* had two phases: a very positive connection with the magazine in its early incarnation and a highly critical appraisal of it post-May 1995:

> Whenever I speak positively it's about the magazine as it was up until... um, well the last one I bought that made any sense to me whatsoever was May 1995. So for about a year, I don't know what happened after that um... I think ... I can't remember why I didn't buy it anymore but for that year it was absolutely excellent. However, yes it is different from material aimed at men because ... it speaks to us as intelligent human beings and it doesn't ...um portray men ... um... you know like in er em... men's magazines, women are all legs akimbo, they all look like slags to be honest with you, pouting lips, oh yeah both types as well. But y'know. The way they portray men photographically in *FW* is just brilliant, they look beautiful, um, it's just not smutty or slutty. So I think they treat us as intelligent people.

Thus for her what signifies a direct appeal to her position as a woman is *FW*'s capacity to do something different to that which appears in men's pornography. Jane's conception of female-ness is defined by what it is not and was most clearly stated in her critical assessment of the magazine post-May 1995.

> In the magazine currently I don't like the way the journalists write, they write like children. um… Not really comfortable with sex, they just debase it, talk about it like it was silly, dirty, childish act not… um… not … um…not an enjoyable… um… not an enjoyable, mature… sexy thing… y'know, it's debased. I don't like the way they do that now. I don't enjoy reading things like here you go… Fantasy Bank: no problem with the actual article itself, it's very interesting to read about… um… women with women, group sex, two men together, professional sex, anonymous sex, yeah that's fine but… when they've got under the heading group sex, 'when one cop just isn't enough' it makes it sound debased again. Y'know, it's just um… the way they're putting it… I don't know, I just don't like the way they write anymore. I used to think they wrote in a really interesting way, that was informative, intelligent, sexy but not crude.

Clearly then, Jane wants to see articles written in a way which does not 'debase' sex or the person reading the magazine. She has no problem with explicitness, as such, so long as it is not 'silly, dirty and childish'. Certainly this could be taken as evidence that she invests heavily in the notion of women's sexuality being 'cleaner' and more 'sensitive' than men's, of women's sexuality embodied in a romantic ideal. However, Jane wants more than that:

> I think what shouldn't be banned is male erections, why can't we see hard ons? I don't think there's any reason why we shouldn't see hard ons what are we all gonna do? Faint? Oh my god, there's a big dick and it's hard! That's ridiculous, I think that should not be banned.

In statements such as these Jane rejects the normative notion of women as frail sexual creatures unable to deal with the overt representation of men's sexual arousal. Thus her conception of 'debased' sex is not the same as that enshrined in the current Obscenity Laws, nor is it so inchoate that there is no explanation of it. The coy and 'furtive' relation with sex which refuses to admit what sexual activity entails, is exactly part of what would make the magazine 'dirty' for her. Her comments on just what *FW* did do for her during the unhappy period of her marriage suggests that she is very personally aware of the use of double standards and the spectre of an ideal 'womanhood' to repress women's sexual feelings:

> You asked how it [*FW*] affected me and my relationship… well it's… at the time I was going through a very bad relationship… um… and the sexual aspect of it was a great big problem and… so it affected me but it gave me strength… I didn't feel like um… I didn't feel like my husband was the norm thank god… Y'know he wasn't the norm… there were blokes out there that did enjoy making love and did think it was okay to make love to their wives and things like that so it affected

> me by giving me strength. Um... it also affected me to realise that I didn't really have to put up with this and we are now separated and I can't say that's all *FW* that's separated me and finished my marriage – that's a bit ridiculous actually! But it did help me realise that I that I wasn't abnormal wanting to have sexual relationships with my husband, all the things that I wanted to do, they weren't abnormal. So it helped me realise that I was normal and er that I was just in a very difficult relationship.... So it was important to me at the time, it really was important because it helped me escape and it just helped me realise that it's okay to be a strong independent person, a woman rather, urm and that it's okay to have sexual wants and needs y'know that's basic human need really... I think magazines like *FW* help you realise that ... that you can break away and you can make a good life for yourself. You don't have to put up with the ... or conform to what's supposed to be socially accepted as long as you can accept it yourself.

Her involvement with the magazine helped Jane see that she needed to break away from a damaging relationship, a marriage that served to repress her sexual desires and her sense of herself as a strong, independent person. Her use of the word 'escape' is not based on a notion of fantasy through which she can forget for a while her real life; escape here means literally release from an oppressive domestic situation. She needed to feel that she was not abnormal and this is connected to her category 'debase'. In order for the magazine to offer her the resources to acquire the confidence to handle a bad situation, she needs to feel that the magazine confirms and affirms her sexual desires as normal, healthy, fun and valued. Her use of *FW* does not then contribute to a 'false consciousness' for her; it has made no contribution to a 'schooling' in oppression. Implicit within the above extract is a notion of 'media effects' but these are less about ideological than transformative effects. It did affect her; it helped her question her relationship with her husband through its affirmation of her sexual needs. These 'effects' were realizable because of the complex nature of her engagement with *FW*:

> What I used to get out of it was um... a sharing of comradeship with other women, that kind of thing... it was a good laugh it y'know broke up, y'know it was something different to do during the day... um... when, y'know, you've finished work, just wanted to relax or something like that, y'know, take your mind off work that type of thing. Um... sometimes I found it arousing some of the stories, some of the pictures. So it depends really what sort of mood I was in at the time what I wanted to get out of it but in short... companionship... um... excitement sometimes, arousal, escapism... um... a sense of belonging with other women. Um... like the problem page as was used to be really good and used to kind of make you think... um... I'm not the only one who's got these type of problems or this has happened to or whatever. Also it was informative er... it used to give me a feeling of um... how can I put it er... information is power that type of thing.

Evidently the nature of her encounters with *FW* was subject to variation: it can be merely a relaxing conclusion to the working day offering a laugh or excitement or even escapist fantasy in the company of women, but at other times it allows her to learn from others, finding a more nurturing companionship in the sharing of problems and information. The magazine's 'power' lies in its being able to speak to Jane in a number of ways. Before marriage she had had a very fulfilling sexual relationship where her sexual needs were met and received with pleasure and equal passion. She can allow herself to enjoy the magazine because it is prepared to acknowledge women's problems in sexual relationships but at the same time it is expressive of a fun and pleasurable female sexuality. It confirms that she is normal and therefore she gives herself permission to imagine herself as deserving of exciting and mutually rewarding sex.

For Jane it is perfectly feasible to talk of women's sexuality as real and representable in gratifying and involving ways. We can only understand *FW* if we pay attention to the ways in which it fits with aspects of its readers' lives. For Jane, the magazine allows her to play games with it and with herself: the imaginative projection of herself into her past where she knows she was desirable and desired and forwards to her future where she can be again. That this was only a temporary relationship – at least only good for a while – does not negate my conclusions, indeed, I think it confirms them. Jane makes demands of the magazine: she invested in it (month after month) and it must pay her back with a vision of her possibilities. She requires that it should not 'debase' her or sex: she should not feel guilty, embarrassed or ashamed of her sexual feelings and so, when the magazine moved to a more 'laddette' style in 1996 using euphemisms like 'when one cop is not enough', Jane was angered by its failure to deliver its promises.

Tessa

One woman does not a pattern make. But Jane begins to illustrate the ways in which the magazine speaks to women via its creation of a specifically female space for sex. Jane was not alone in looking for this space: other women recognized that this was what the magazine was attempting or should attempt in order to produce sexual pleasures for women. For them, the magazine was less successful in its management of the dilemmas of female sexuality. An American living in London, Tessa liked sexually explicit materials and had bought *FW* in the expectation that it would turn her on. Her response to the magazine was not entirely negative but *FW* presented her with a set of dilemmas. Sold on the top shelf and promising naked men and sexually explicit stories, the magazine puzzled Tessa because of its similarities to *Hello!* and *Cosmopolitan*. This was in large part because she was used to American materials that are much more explicit than legally available materials in the UK. Nevertheless, she was hoping for a sexual experience through the magazine and was quite clear in our interview that for her pornography was an aid to sexual pleasure albeit a second choice after sex with a partner. For her, the magazine is too coy; it is not explicit enough,

> ... like they've confused the purpose of the magazine... It doesn't seem to be geared towards a turn on kinda thing... it's sort of geared towards these other girly interests with the men sort of thrown in and a few sleazy sex toy adverts...

The girlie elements that pleased Jane are a problem to Tessa using the magazine for sexual pleasures. In fact, Tessa singles out the article on breasts which Jane expressed interest in as precisely one of the elements which irritates her most about the magazine.

> It just didn't work in these two issues ... I mean others might ...here I'll show you ... one of the problems was... like this sort of stuff that has a theme [Aztec photoset] – I hate this sort of stuff ...it just seems really contrived.... and I..er.. guess some of my problem. This stuff is all right, we've got a little bit of aesthetic values but when its too obvious and artificial ... like men in cowboy outfits it seems too kind of male, like we need some kind of fetish. So I guess .... so like these kinds of articles ... [breast feature] ... again, I think ... men would be more interested in this kind of breast size comparison... either you like your breasts or you don't .. I like mine...I really don't want this kind of comparison in a magazine for women. It just gets me upset because men don't read men's magazines and compare their penis sizes! Y'know they'll get a magazine that caters to their taste and I get this sort of strange thing ... I like interactive shots, y'know couple shots – they're sort of in here but not really. They're not really in *Playgirl* either.

The reasons for Tessa's dislike of the breast feature, which she named six times in the interview as a problem, is not particularly clear. In fact, it is only properly explicable through the patching together of other elements of her account of reading *FW* and use of pornography, romance and attending strip shows. I asked Tessa about her response to the magazine's serious articles.

> Again, I think they're er just trying to do the same job as women's magazines, like in *Cosmo*. I guess they're trying a little more for women getting pleasure than they are in *Cosmo*. I mean... most of those mags do a kinda ...kind of 100 ways to give – they're still lessons in giving head, in giving pleasure to men and these seem to be how to get your mate to please you except for this breast evaluation thing which I thought was really strange. So in that way they seem to be for women but I wouldn't say that I read them with great interest. So I mean as far as cutting edge sexual education goes I wouldn't say they'd got it. ...I guess my impression now that we're talking about these ... magazines is that they're ... er sort of embarrassed by their sexual content and they've ... sort of .... disguised it with their fashion spreads and Hollywood gossip interviews. I er ...don't know ....I just didn't find the articles very interesting. I guess... I guess... I want a woman's magazine that gives me nice visuals ... maybe a mix of GQ type men's shots and a few naked ones .... and some in-depth articles that don't cater to make-up and clothes. Y'know .... there just doesn't seem to be one.... and maybe... there just isn't that kinda ...kind of ... maybe... if women want that then they buy the *Economist* and this. I mean ... there just doesn't seem to be ... you just seem to get more in men's magazines.... more of a mix. All the articles just seem to be ... kinda... talking down and they just seem to be not very .... in-depth, er...a kinda kind of filler.... Just like other women's magazines. I would not buy this magazine if it didn't have naked men, not even at half price.

Tessa is American and that feeling of embarrassment she dislikes is allied to her recognition of this magazine's British antecedents. The elements of the magazine which make it good for Jane are problematic to Tessa precisely because they are evidence of censorship and a peculiarly British attitude to sex. This problem is allied to explicitness, in comparison to American materials, *FW* is too soft; but it is also very similar to Jane's requirements of the magazine. In order to begin to tease that out, Tessa's views on a number of topics need to be examined. First, her comments on naked men and strip shows followed by her discussion of erotic novels:

> CS: Do you think the men who pose are enjoying themselves?
>
> No, maybe that's what's missing. I get the idea from the pictures that they're uncomfortable, they don't know what to do, they don't know where to put their hands. It's kinda like speaking in public; they don't know what to do with their hands, or where to look. Maybe that's what's wrong. Maybe it's just being there for women. Maybe it's getting used to being looked at and men aren't that comfortable knowing that they're going to be looked at in such a way. Looked at as a sexual fantasy and for masturbating. And I guess that's what I find problematic about say Sharon Stone in *Basic Instinct*. Why would she want to do that? She may think she's acting but everyone else knows that all the guys are masturbating over her. And I guess that's what I feel about the sanitised kind of image in *Playboy*, what the centrefold represents for guys, they don't buy it to read, they buy it to masturbate and I just feel I wouldn't want my picture in there – not that it would be. But even if it were in the fat and 40s I would feel the same way. I wouldn't want that reaction. I mean a good or bad image used for masturbation.
>
> CS: Do you think men are more aware of that ... of what the image will be used for and that that's why they look so uncomfortable?
>
> I think they might be, just because they are so used to being the voyeur.... They are.... And ... and... and I found this true in a lot of my relationships... they're just really used to looking at some woman and if... you're looking... you're just too interested.

For Tessa, pleasure in a sexually explicit magazine would come from a number of elements being right for her. Her ideal viewing situation would be one in which the models look comfortable, but that is almost an impossibility on her own criteria because in being there for women they would need to show that they accept their role as spurs to masturbation. And that is a problematic role for Tessa whether the model is male or female. She launches into a mini-diatribe about Sharon Stone, a powerful female actress who *thinks* she's in charge but is really being used for masturbation. This, coupled with comments Tessa made earlier in the interview, is an indication that sexual representations are problematic to Tessa in terms of control.

This is not, however, control as in who produces the image but control as a shared experience. Throughout the tape, Tessa talks of women's desire for interaction and their propensity to look for individual men rather than types of men; she talks of women as more 'subjective' and 'interactive': 'I do look for something more interactive than just that man has a great ass and I'm attracted to him. It's just ... sort of ... isolated....' This is, of course, a fairly commonly expressed difference between men and women, but Tessa wants to make clear that it is more than simply needing to know who the man is (indeed in another part of the tape, knowing who he is, is actually unimportant to her). She complained about a 'bachelorette' party where the male strippers made it very clear that they were in charge.

> I had to leave because I was physically ill, sort of the same reaction I had to a lot of male gay porn... Um... you're being chatted up in the same sort of way and then ...you're expected to pay for it... Which I don't think is any addition to female sexuality... Even though there appears to be ... a great number of men advertising as escorts I er ... I don't think the choice for a lot of women is to just call a number and have someone show up and... just give him a 100 bucks. I don't know, maybe that's very ... maybe I'm wrong and there is a good market for that.... The same way in a strip club and I'm being harassed in the same sort of sleazy way. Instead of giving me the power back like men have in ... well, that's not entirely true either ... I hear it's different in Japan as well ... but men in clubs seem to be the one's with all the power. They're the one's who are paying, ordering table dancers and that seems to be the theory behind women's nights which are always either one night a week or two nights a week... It's it's not like they can fill the place seven nights a week with two shows ... It's ... The power still belongs to the men and they're still making the money. I find that awful [Pause]. That's a bit reactive ...y'know, it's, it's saying, same way as wanting to see all these naked men exposed when you go to the magazine rack as well, just to get even, but that's just how it is. I don't really like that unfair power exchange and I guess it's got something to do with being interactive as well. But it just isn't. [Pause] Yeah, it's like in the sense that men aren't allowed to show erections; they're still in control of their reactions whereas with women they're there, doing all sorts of things... inserting things. And just because there isn't that kind of evidence really that this person is sexually aroused ... a woman can look sexually aroused even if she is not ... even if she is bored... Don't tell them that! What I was going back to ... I guess I just don't really want ... to ... to be sold sex. It's just that sleazy element ... If I want to be sold sex, I can go to any corner pub and pick up a sleazy guy. I... I... I really think I could if that's what I wanted to do. With some of the bios, y'know they're always 'I'm a dancer' and then you have to question about what kind of men are going to pose nude anyway. And then you've got this kind of dilemma where I think I'm looking at a load of naked gay men anyway which doesn't turn me on either. I think I may have this problem where I'm too theoretical, and I'm too academic and I have too many gay friends so I can look at these pictures and I'm sort of thinking well he's ...kinda... kinda cute... but I'm picking up these gay vibes here and it's not working for me. Cos there's either this sleaze element where I'm here to just sell sex or because the guy's gay. Which

is what I get with a lot of strippers or dancers. So it isn't really interactive y'know... they have no interest in heterosexual exchange or maybe they have some interest in bisexual exchange but it seems a bit artificial. Which is interesting because I'd much rather have a magazine than be in a strip club. And I think it has a lot to do with that distance ... I'm allowed to sort of subjectify them in a magazine, sort of, but if they're there stripping then it's about what they want to offer rather than what I want to take. Especially y'know when they're wearing neon G-strings, glo-in-the-dark G-strings and they come out in Officer and a Gentleman uniforms and do all this. Oh one particular scenario was Oreo cookies – they had these two big black men and one white woman and I couldn't even deal with the racist elements ... I'm like, I don't really like this. So that's probably what it is, they're sort of channelling what I want or what I need and I don't really like that.

This complaint about women's fantasies being decided for them is also a part of feminist criticisms of sexually explicit media. It is interesting that Tessa can't actually articulate this fully in her discussion of *FW* without going outside of the magazine to live events for the explanation of her difficulties with the male nude. She recognizes that there are some differences between the nude photograph and the live show, for a start, she can 'subjectify' the model – by this she means she can imagine who he is and why he might want to pose. That can, in itself, be a source of pleasure allowing the opening up of the image if the photo is able to deflect 'gay vibes'. Tessa measures models against men she knows, she has too many gay friends to allow her to pretend that the model is not gay. The alternative position she can allow the model is not, however, more conducive to her pleasures – this is the sleaze element where he is simply there to sell his body. In other words, Tessa measures the image for an indication of actual sexual feeling. In order for this to offer her an ideal viewing experience the model needs to be attractive to her, to be 'kinda cute' but also she needs to believe that he would actually want to engage in a sexual interaction with a woman. She needs the distance between the image and an imaginable sexual interaction to be as narrow as possible. In order for a sexual representation to work for her, it must replicate the conditions that make actual sexual interactions conceivable to Tessa. This element of viewing images is discussed in detail in chapter 6. As I show in that chapter, the model being or appearing 'gay' would not necessarily negate for enthusiastic viewers the possibility of finding the image arousing. For Tessa, it is not enough that the image represents a man on the point of arousal: she also needs to know that this is a genuine heterosexual interaction, that this model wants to engage in an 'interaction' – he must appear responsive to women. This requirement is also articulated in Tessa's comments on erotic stories and novels.

I like them [erotic stories]. I ... I don't really like romantic stories... I find them irritating which just blows my theory [that women's sexuality includes a strong element of romantic longing]. They still serve the purpose of men all having the action... they're strong and save the heroine and I don't like that. I guess, I guess, I guess... I get into these problems where it's – what is reality? What you like it to be. So I have problems with it not being really realistic and I have problems if it's too realistic. I mean... I mean ... if the men are the way that men have always been... then I'm unhappy with that but then... er if the men are all... romantic then I'm not happy with that because I don't know any men like that. Where do you want reality to go – maybe a little bit of reality and maybe a little bit of changing things? Y'know... my thing of romance being dangerous.... well that's a part of... what women want and then they say that's dangerous.

CS: With erotic stories, what is it about them that you like?

The sexual element. I guess that's my biggest complaint with romantic novels which er maybe... deal with sex... Um... when they get to the sex acts then they're really flowery and short, they're flowery and very short and they're not based on reality again. I can't bear that. Again it just seems to me... like making sex harder to deal with for women. Y'know?

It's like when you go to see a strip show, the visual isn't really there er... the reality. You don't get... to see the penis which I find ... is really very problematic for me. Cos why go? I don't go to see them gyrate ... Again it's just... I just ... I just don't see reality. I wouldn't necessarily go to see a penis... I like to see men... in well cut pants but... still it's like... it's like they still have the power and even though it's supposed to be my night, my sexuality tripping, it's still under their control. [long pause] It's cheating.

There are two facets to Tessa's conception of reality: one is measured against the state of play between men and women currently, this is the macro-political relationship of heterosexuality where men appear to have all the power – cultural, economic, political and sexual. Thus the hero or male protagonist in an erotic story must not replicate the romance hero who is powerful physically and removes any necessity for the heroine to think for herself. This requirement is linked to but differs from her later statement that the 'romantic' hero is unrealistic. This is the second facet of 'reality' for Tessa: the hero is measured against men she knows personally – he must be real in terms of her experience of men. But there is a clear sense of a utopian ideal of reality here: it is a balance 'a little bit of reality and maybe a little bit of changing things' and, in this possibility, Tessa's orientation is very similar to Jane's. Both want to feel that sexual representations offer them a vision of possibility. For Jane, it is a very personal set of possibilities; for Tessa, the utopian ideal is more outwardly focused, it is the possibility that men might change and women might benefit. Although this ideal is utopian, it also offers measurable possibilities for Tessa's personal gain. When sexually explicit materials/entertainments get it right for Tessa, they confirm her sense of female sexuality and her own sexuality as a source of pleasure and not embarrassment. Her emotional and sexual needs should not be expropriated by coy attitudes to sex. Thus the use of props in strip shows – the dayglo G-string and the Officer and a Gentlemen uniforms – contribute to the sense of women's sexuality as a source of humour and/or discomfort:

> [Pause] I tend to be very honest about things and... I... I want everyone else to be too. I think if you don't make things explicit then people automatically assume its embarrassing.... So I find I'm embarrassed about my sexuality when I'm not ... y'know? That's why I don't get a bag for my magazine when I buy it. [Laughs] I was in a store and there's a *Playboy* open for the men to leaf through, but the *Playgirl* was still in the plastic wrapper and the guy at the counter, he was gay. He said 'Darling, I'll open one for you, if the guys can leaf through before they buy then you can too!' I said, 'Oh that's okay, I'll take my chances' – if I stand there and leaf through it then I'm certainly not gonna need to take it home. [Laughs]

The rejection of this level of embarrassment, the need to feel okay about one's sexuality is, of course, an element in Jane's interaction with the magazine. But Tessa finds it difficult to discover the opposite of embarrassment in *FW* because in straddling the mainstream and the pornographic, the magazine fails to live up to the degree of sexual explicitness that Tessa, as an American, is used to. Where *FW* gets it right for Jane because it talks about all the silly little things that women worry about, it gets it wrong for Tessa. Those silly little things are the elements that Tessa feels society attempts to make women feel are embarrassing about female sexuality or female bodies. Simply put, by 'channelling' the discussions into foci on women's bodies or problems, the magazine becomes a puzzle for her rather than a pleasure. *FW* does not achieve the necessary balance between 'reality' and 'changing things'. Even so, Tessa and Jane evidence the same orientation to the magazine – they both require explicitness, a refusal to regard women's sexuality as 'problem' and the possibility of transformation. The substance of these two interviews was echoed in interviews with other women: Susan, Gill, Mia and Alison expressed a similar interest in a female pornography characterized by an emphasis on the possibilities of pleasure. These pleasures can be separated out as follows:

- sharing with other women; sharing enjoyment, curiosity and/or laughter about sex. Sharing information and 'being serious' about sex can also be fun.
- confirmation of one's sexual experiences as shared by others and recognition of women's sexual attractiveness and capacity for sexual feeling.
- testing oneself and one's possible sexual interests: would I do that? Even if the answer is no, there is a pleasure to be gained from understanding other women's likes and dislikes and their motivations.
- finding out about other people, having a 'good old nose' into other people's private lives.
- acquisition of knowledge: new techniques, ideas and means of achieving orgasm.
- imagining sex – other people having sex rather than imagining self engaged in sexual activity.
- taking risks imaginatively: what might I like if I let myself go; trying out sexual fantasies in a 'safe' environment.
- looking at men's bodies and knowing that this activity is shared.
- reading for a turn-on, just to get excited.
- being turned on, physical sensations and/or satisfaction.

- participation in liberating women's sexual feelings; being there with other women and engaging in exploration.

Although Tessa and Jane had negative comments to make about *FW*'s representations of sex, their criticisms arose out of their belief that women's sexuality *ought* to be represented in print and that it *could be*. Moreover, that women have a right to forms of pornography which directly address their sexual feelings and that these are possible here and now. Even though Tessa had plenty to say about the ways in which many sexual entertainments failed her as a woman, she had not given up on the possibility of finding the ideal, indeed, in the States, her expectations had often been fulfilled. Thus this reading orientation can be characterized by its optimism and its belief in a 'woman's pornography', that belief might be disappointed at times but even in disappointment there is the glimpse of the possibility. I turn now to less favourable accounts to think about how those suggest other ways of engaging with the magazine.

Michele
During our interview, Michele constantly referred to classed and educated reading positions. Michele came to *FW* through a friend and described her interest in reading the magazine as simply an interest in any new woman's magazine. Her friend had a number of issues of *For Women*, *Women On Top*, and *Women Only*, and Michele had borrowed and read some of them. Because of the way she kept picking bits out of the magazines she brought with her to the interview, I believe she had gone through them beforehand almost as a research exercise, trying to understand them. Michele talked explicitly about readers' class positions and the various features in the magazines in terms of their appeal to those positions. Michele's orientation to *FW* arises from the complex compromise she makes between her perception of herself as simultaneously working *and* middle class and her attendant difficulties in reconciling explicit representations of sex with her own class ambivalence.

Her primary judgement of the magazine evaluates the information and education it offers readers. At the start of the interview Michele signalled her detachment from the magazines: she just happened to pick them up because she reads a lot of women's magazines. That distance was further evidenced by her mode of assessment of *FW*: she expressed no particular interest in the magazine itself but how far it was similar or dissimilar to *Cosmopolitan*. Her sense of herself as 'not the kind of woman' who reads these magazines was clear when she answered my question, 'What kind of women do you think read *FW*?' with the following:

> Well, who might go out of their way to buy them sort of thing? Well.. for ...those who might want a little bit of voyeurism type thing in their lives... The people who might read them? Well... the... before I read them, the sort of people I thought to myself, might buy them would be completely sort of complete strange people, weirdos all the rest of it. But when I read them... I thought no, they're not aimed at that kind of people, they're aimed at people, *Cosmopolitan* readers, who want more detailed information about sexual matters. But then again, they might still

> not be the kind of people who are going out to buy them because um… I buy *Cosmopolitan* but I wouldn't go out and buy that… so they might be quite different. I would have thought they would be quite middle-class, teachers… frustrated teachers and things. Middle-class people… you wouldn't get your average working-class person who was out of work reading one of these.
>
> CS: Why not?
>
> Because they don't think about… they don't think about… they don't have a lot of anxiety about things like this… they just go out and do it… They just go out and have sex and whatever… they wouldn't be reading up to see if it was right to do it… they're just going out and doing it.

Clearly, Michele came to the magazines with a very clear sense of who the readers might be and that they were significantly different from herself – 'complete weirdos'. However, her own reading of the magazines suggest they do not cater for an easily identified weirdo and so she modifies her sense of the reader, through a recognition of the magazine's *Cosmo*-qualities, to 'frustrated teachers' (less pejorative but still hardly flattering). Even though her reading of the magazines changes her perception of the reader 'they' are still not like her but now it is their class position which signals their difference. As I knew Michele prior to this interview, I know that she saw herself as straddling the classes: working class in origin and also middle class through education. This self-perception is evident in the dialogue above. When she moves to discuss the reasons why working-class women might not read the magazine, she calls them your 'average working-class person' and suggests that they are less anxious about sex than middle-class women. Michele is positioning herself between these two sites: she is not average working class 'who don't think' and she is not a 'frustrated teacher'. Embedded in this is a conception of particular class-based experiences of sexuality: middle-class sexuality is characterized by its anxiety and frustration and its requirements for information (detailed) and confirmation that an activity is sanctioned and respectable. In contrast, working-class sexuality is just there, 'they just go out and do it', it is spontaneous and not given to contemplation or worrying. These differences in attitudes to sex are mirrored for Michele in the different titles:

> I think the women who buy *Women on Top* might be more… your traditional working-class people… it comes across in how the articles are shorter, if at all, it's more pictorial, the whole set up of the magazines is all, mainly pictures, pictures of naked men, whereas the … *FW*, the first one I read of that it took a while before you got to the naked men and I was thinking 'All right, where are they?' all these pictures y'know. It took a few articles first before you got to them. But before… the *Women on Top* it was just all pictures before you got to the few articles. There is a difference in what they're appealing to.

Thus Michele also characterizes working-class sexuality in terms of its response to the visual, that working-class people don't want long articles and that their sexuality is much more 'in your face' than their middle-class counterparts:

> ... from the articles, not the articles... the photographs. There... a lot of the photographs there are from women who've sent in pictures of their husbands and things like that and it gives you the impression that it's women out there who are saying 'Look at my husband, he's a stud'. Y'know 'we're from the working class and my husband's gorgeous' and there's a section that says... There's a whole area up towards the end of the magazine that's all about women sending in photographs of their husbands and it's in the sort of the sex part and the explicit part, it's like the sex is the main thing in their lives and so therefore this something they can show off to the rest of the world. A bit like ... it is like readers' wives in um... *Playboy* magazine or whichever one it is which has readers wives in it. Because it's readers' husbands ... it's the opposite of that... so for me, *Playboy* and that style of magazine is very tacky and very sort of promoting, sort of blatant sexuality without any information or anything else linked to it. And this magazine is along that sort of line without any of the pictures being sort of well done or well presented, they're very poor quality.

To begin with, this input suggests a quite positive reading of some women's relationship with the magazine: it gives them the chance to 'show off', however, this is also problematic for Michele. So long as there is the very personal 'showing off', the spontaneous exuberance of sexuality, then the magazine's sexual content is okay but where it is too obviously similar to men's magazines, it becomes 'blatant sexuality without any information or anything else linked to it'. In later sections of the interview, Michele complained about the ways in which *Women on Top* seemed to be selling sex with its use of phone lines and adverts for escort services. She does not like the overt commercialization of sex. In this section of her tape, the 'missing' anything else is obviously a matter of taste, aesthetics and production values, because these pictures also fail in terms of quality. This evidently compares unfavourably with *FW*:

> Well, they're [*FW*] appealing to the sort of professional classes who maybe want some sort of confirmation that what they do is sort of all right and that there are other people out there, similar to yourself, doing these sorts of things so... And as well as that the articles are written in a style that um... educational, it's not like patronizing and saying...and talking down to people. It's written in a ... it's an assumption, a lot of the times, that you've already got basic knowledge of what like Freud's on about so... for somebody in the working class who's never heard of Freud, they would have difficulty grasping what the articles were about. Some of the language in the articles is very hard to understand.

Michele's judgements of the various magazines are in terms of cultural competencies: for *FW* the reader needs to be able to wade through lengthy articles, tackle difficult language and have some knowledge of Freud. *Women on Top* is basically just a lot of badly taken dirty pictures. What particularly offends Michele is the sense in which *Women On Top* is unashamedly about sex and sexual activity:

> Well, *FW* I liked *FW*, that was good... The *Women On Top* didn't give any information ...I didn't like the *Women on Top*, it didn't give any information about

> anything, it's just all sex.... It's just aiming at one area of sex, it's just titillating people, it's not giving them advice or looking at any problems they might have and then when it showed pictures of men with no clothes on or anything like that it had little phone numbers underneath for 0898 numbers which sort of made me think well, it's giving these pictures to make you feel sort of titillated and then you're going to do something about it by phoning these phone numbers. Instead of looking at your own personal problems and lives and going and sorting them out. It's sort of saying once you've done this and looked at this, you've got to ring these numbers to get any more.

Sexual representations for Michele should be about more than just titillation; they should offer a means of understanding yourself and your own problems. The pictures and phone numbers in *Women On Top* suggest that masturbation is the sole intent in reading that particular title and Michele's conception of masturbation is not a process of learning about yourself, its just a means to an end, orgasm, without any transformative possibilities. The criteria by which Michele appears to be judging these magazines owes much to the justifications often given of women's magazine reading in general: that they offer their women readers solutions to problems.

> ... they do educate, they do make you think well there are other things that are possible that you weren't aware of.
>
> CS: When you say educate, do you mean it in terms of health, health risks or something different?
>
> Not partic... some of the articles, especially the one about anal sex was health risk ...always wear a condom, things like that. There wasn't as much about wearing a condom in a lot of the other articles, more emotional... like some of the articles were looking at problems you might have um, certain types of men and how to avoid them... which you would find in any *Cosmopolitan* magazine. It seems to me that the message in them is like... opening people's options to all the different various kinds of sex out there and maybe letting them see that there's nothing wrong with it, sort of thing if you see what I mean. It's not a judgmental type of approach. [Pause] There was one article about anal sex, I didn't like that... Because it was saying that 92 per cent of people thought that it wouldn't be a problem in a normal relationship...
>
> CS: But you feel it is?
>
> Yes, I wouldn't want to do it.
>
> CS: Did you feel that the article was telling you that you ought to have anal sex?
>
> Well, it was sort of... no it wasn't saying that you ought to have it... it was saying that because 92 per cent of the people who answered this survey in this magazine ... and therefore they're more aware and liberated and all the rest of it. That it

> said it wasn't a problem within the confines of a relationship or whatever, then ... therefore, I should be feeling like that because I'm part of this... grouping. Y'know that this magazine's marketed towards... I didn't think ... I don't know ... I didn't like the way it made me feel that 'oh crikey, I'm such a prude'.... I don't like... I don't agree with something like that. It made me like oh, maybe I should be changing my views but then I thought, no, maybe I shouldn't... It did [offer the opposite point of view], it did but obviously it was more involved in talking about anal sex maybe as an issue so obviously people have that, do come across it in their lives and they need to... they need to talk about it anyway... I can understand that but it did make me feel uncomfortable.

Women's magazines are a resource for their women readers, a last resort for information which may be too sensitive to obtain elsewhere, and where *FW* gets it right is in offering this kind of resource to its readers. Furthermore this focus on information is a measure of how different from top-shelf men's magazines, *FW* is. Indeed for Michele the magazine must ensure that even its stories have a secondary educational role:

> The stories were good, they started off as just normal stories and then eventually they had a little bit of titillation and then they came back to being just normal stories so they weren't like explicitly like and then he took her clothes and shoved his dick up and all that sort of business. It was leading into it and they were written very well... [In men's magazines] they're a bit more graphically explicit. Giving men the idea that all they have to do is grab it and then they're away sort of thing. Without explaining... in one of the stories the woman is with her boyfriend and she hasn't been with him very long and she's trying to tell him what sexually, she does get to tell him and the problems with the relationship and the story's over a gradual few weeks and that's the sort of thing people would come across in their actual real life and that they'd want to get around that issue and it explains it in the story how to do that.

Thus, for Michele, titillation is not the primary orientation to the magazine, it must be a resource for sorting out problems, offering strategies for coping in life. However, Michele does not suggest that the magazine offered any ways of coping in her own life; the stories offer ways for other people to deal with their recognizable problems. Indeed her irritation at the anal sex article, which brought her right up against her own boundaries, suggests that Michele does not want the magazine to touch her. By that, I mean, she does not want her views on sex to be challenged by this kind of magazine. Thus, I believe her conception of *FW*'s obligations to educating its readers is actually quite a truncated learning experience. Although she wants people to have solutions, they must be solutions that are not challenging to sexuality as she perceives it.

> I don't think it should be giving people this idea that out there, people are living lives that are totally problem free and that all you have to do is go out and get laid to get rid of your problems. I don't think you should have that, I don't think

> that magazines should give you that idea because it'll just put forward even further all these negative views of sexuality and all the problems related to it and people won't be able to resolve their problems. It's probably a prudish point of view but... it had... it might not... it had these like date-line numbers and on it people had written their preferences for someone and things like, um, executive guy wants to meet slim black girl for fun and things like that. As if you could order up any kind of sex goddess you wanted on the end of it and I thought that's something I didn't like.... It was just like the magazine wasn't just informing you, it was selling sex ... it was a bit like prostitution.

What is most striking about this is the fact that sex is conceived here as problematic, always fraught with problems which must be solved. There is no sense here of reading *FW* in order to escape problems, it must not offer a utopian ideal of sex, it has to recognize problems and then resolve those. It must be realistic but, to be a good magazine, *FW* has to offer more than a physical effect. It is almost as if it must *not* offer a physical effect. Even where Michele was prepared to accede that some models could be erotic this is only to appreciate his body and its potentials as a kind of artistic contemplation. Michele's use of class, her delineation of the magazine titles and readers into average working class and middle class is evidence of her personal struggle to bridge the gap between her working-class roots and her present educated, middle-class, self. This bridging requires that women's magazines must be assessed for their use value, what good they can do for women. So Michele looked at *FW* first, in order to find her 'complete weirdos' and then on realizing that these were not weirdo texts, for its reaffirmation of her beliefs about women and sex. So long as the magazine offered information and appeared to be showing people who were engaged in sex not predicated on any commercial interest, then it is a reasonable magazine. But note she has no intention of it being sexually arousing. Sexual arousal, in itself, is not a good enough reason for reading the magazine, it must do more and that more does include boundary setting according to moral and aesthetic criteria. In coming to magazines like *FW* and *Women On Top*, Michele experienced a number of problems: focus on sex as physical activity without a sufficiently emotional dimension is worrying; the stimulus to sexual activity is also worrying and the commodification of sex, through, for example, the proposal to ring this number for more excitement, also makes her uncomfortable.

Laura

Another reading orientation comes out of an assessment of the prospects of representing female sexuality. On her self-recorded tape, Laura identifies herself as an academic researcher and a very occasional reader of *FW*. Throughout her tape it was clear that she had some very thought-out and intellectually rigorous orientations to sexually explicit material and that she was comfortable in discussing these matters with me as academic equals (we had met at an academic conference). At the end of her answers to the questionnaire she goes on to explore a number of issues which she felt she had covered inadequately:

> ... one issue is exclusion. I think that things I feel exclude me as a viewer don't arouse me at all and I think ... By exclusion I mean things that are framed by the male gaze as it were or male conceptions of what female desire should be and is and all the rest of it... um. And I think that works with male pornography and female pornography, that male pornography... pornography for males is obviously full of women and directed at the male gaze but what I think ...there's an element of even where, the conception of female desire as it is manifest in the way that pornography for females is created, still seems to me, mediated through a male consciousness of what female desire is and female eroticism is. Even despite the fact, whether it's women journalists working on a magazine or it's got a woman editor or whatever, I think culturally still what we take to be female desire is most often articulated through er male framing of what female desire is.

Laura's fundamental orientation to pornography is one of distrust: firstly she does not believe it tries to include her but she is also unable to conceive of a 'woman's' pornography which could: which is able to speak to a female consciousness whether or not a woman creates that material. This is in contradiction of her earlier expressed belief that *FW* could have done better, for now she clearly states that representing a truly female desire is culturally impossible.

> Um... another issue was agency and control, um... it's often, it's related to the last point which is... um... again who's the agent in this kind of exchange of... um... image and response... um... it's more erotic to me if I feel that I am the agent and I can articulate my own desire, and my own desire can shape and frame the object of my desire how I would like to see it. And... ...um... to me, things like FW don't do this... um... I think still a lot of female desire and erotic female sexuality is still suppressed, oppressed and still subterranean and it's still a big taboo area and I don't think women really do articulate their desire if they were discussing, I anticipate that maybe several of the questionnaires will appear like this, that people really still don't take it to the core... 'Oh I bought this y'know magazine... um... to really arouse myself...' um... I could be wrong, I don't know. Um... I think power is very sexy especially if it's you who's in power and in control and feeling empowered about something... um... and I think that something that is lacking from the kind of pornography for women that I've seen anyway. It's... it's... still very tame... it's still, in the sense that women are quite conservative about their sexual desire and women really haven't got a sexual appetite and ...um.... y'know, it's still almost rather shocking to imagine women being able to look at men and ...um... wanting to see erections and things, I don't know. It's... it's... it's... it's kind of openly discussed in very small quarters like... like among educated women who are doing women's studies or ... er... gender studies or... er... cultural studies or something like that... um... but I think in everyday life I don't think the changes have occurred for all women and so I think that even if you've got the perception to see outside of the parameters that we're currently living in, you go, y'know, you live your everyday life among the template of a very old-fashioned view of women and women's desires... um... so what's lacking for me is the fact that the ... that there is no sense that I am the agent in this

> negotiation when I look at these pictures… um… I feel as though it is second-hand and that it's mediated to me… er… through some other person's shaping of how they perceive female desire and female erotic experience… um… er… what they think the parameters of that… those experiences are.

Here again Laura expresses no hope of there being an 'authentic' representation of female sexuality because women are unable to be honest about their sexual desires. The imposition of a cultural ideal of women as non-desiring has ensured that women are unable to see or shape their own desire for themselves, of understanding their own experiences on their own terms. However, she does seem to be claiming that there is a space outside of these cultural taboos which women can occupy, that it is possible to move outside these perceptions but that *FW* and other popular culture forms are unable to offer a 'negotiation' that isn't second-hand or mediated. She believes that there is a particularly female take on sexuality but that this is so subject to cultural, social and political taboos that women can never fully articulate their sense of their sexual selves:

> I think it does strike me that in many respects women just don't feel safe in releasing their sexual feelings for discussion it's as though there is something prohibitive about having a sexual desire and there's something mutually exclusive about the categories really of erotic sensation and desire… um… of voyeurism and being a woman. It's as though, it's very hard to get over the idea that women are passive in terms of sexual… um… activity and desire… um… I think that a lot of women still keep their real sexual feelings extremely private because there is still a big taboo about women's sexual feelings… um… and so … I think there is, there is still a big lid on the intimate lives of women… um… and I really don't know who women talk to about it unless they have dialogues with themselves about it. Um… and I think there may also be a level of denial in operation concerning women's sexuality so that so that many women simply don't feel… um… I don't know it could be like a false consciousness syndrome… um… so that this is where we can get women speaking out against people like Claire Short trying to change the way we see pornography. Um… I think I would say there's a possibility there is a false consciousness syndrome and that women because we've been policed so strongly for such a long time, it's very difficult for many… many women to actually perceive that they can be very active and aggressive and still be feminine… er… and they can have sexual feelings and articulate them and sexual needs and want them fulfilling beyond simply a one to one responsive relationship to a man…. Sorry that sounds like I've taken a digression to the area of lesbianism… I meant the idea that women can be active sexually still has a lot of pejorative overtones, for example, the fastest thing that people do now is to think of you as a radical feminist as a kind of way of policing your outrageous ideas if you… you do venture towards discussing sexual desire, female sexual desire, female sexual appetite… um… So we kind of ghettoize the female sexual experience by that kind of label. And I think it is really difficult for different women of different generations to even realize they've got sexual desires, or sexual rights as it were, civil rights in a way… um… so I think that's a big factor in the kind of

data you're going to unearth in a project like this... um... that women's sex lives are still quite taboo, subject matters in a way. Or maybe they're still inchoate and being formulated and transformed and mutated into something different... um... I do think all women do have potential to be sexually active, to have sexual lives from very young age to a very old age, I've met some very sexy old women, older women who were in their seventies and eighties and still... er ... get turned on by men so... But actually getting people to talk about it in a very public sense or changing the... media's conception of that is a very big job and a very long way off I think... that's my feelings anyway.

The sheer length of this quotation and the ways in which Laura constantly 'did' the research for me rather than being a subject of it are very interesting and significant indications of the distance Laura places between herself and the magazine and the very politicized notions of her engagement with it. Laura does not want to deny women a sexual orientation which features men as their desirable object choice but at same time she does not conceive of it being easily available as a choice to all women at the present time. What strikes me as particularly difficult about this passage is just what would count as a valid expression of women's active sexuality focused on men? Her claim that women ought to be able to vocalize a desire to be the voyeur and actively sexual is precisely the kind of space which campaigns like Clare Short's attempted to close off as an authentic expression of female sexuality. And yet, Laura recognizes this problem too. In her anxiety about digressing into the area of lesbianism, Laura appears to be having trouble, as a feminist academic, in stating something which her feminist credentials almost require her to say: namely, what is the relation between her analysis and her personal feelings? She suddenly feels that the only position from which she recognizes she can 'speak' thus, is a lesbian position and that is not where she intended to stand. There is such a disjunction between her academic wish that there be this possibility of women speaking their desires and her personal reaction to *FW* that she is unable to cope with it.

Laura's movement in and out of her conceptual framework of 'we women' in this passage suggests she perceives herself as simultaneously separate from and part of a community of women. That community rests on a series of intellectual and aesthetic differences. For example, her earlier alignment with Clare Short's aims indicates that 'false consciousness' is not something that necessarily affects her now but that it may have done in the past. Her differentiated position is possible because education has been her route out:

Um... another issue I think is important is education I think... um... Um... oh... I don't know. I think that... that having gone through the process of education makes me feel more confident in articulating feelings about sexuality, it gives me a greater sense of independence as a person anyway in terms of economic things and in terms of ideas and independent thinking and... um... being outside of popular culture in a sense... um... and I think that's one factor why I find these things unsatisfying... um... another, another aspect on education is I have noticed

> in the course of my life anyway is that it's often less educated men who tend to give... who are more obsessed with pornography and the more educated a man is the more distant he becomes... he... he moves to a kind of position where he wants to disassociate from... that kind of male stereotype... er... I'm not saying that there are... there are several dimensions in which men may be the same across different stratification patterns... um... but I've noticed a distinct difference in university educated men and non-educated men as it were, non-university educated men... er... in terms of their attitude and their consumption of pornography... um...

Those last sentences neatly elide class and education – an important indication of Laura's orientation to the magazine. Throughout the tape Laura positions herself outside of popular culture and its influence. Education has enabled her to acquire a more knowledgeable and distanced position to items like *FW*. It gives her a 'superiority' over the products of popular culture and those who like them. It also enables her to assess them in terms of their articulation of an appropriately enlightened eroticism. Education also offers a means of changing men's attitudes towards pornography: less educated men are 'obsessed' by pornography and are embodiments of a male 'stereotype'. This summoning up of the picture of the uneducated and obsessed male, indicates another possible relationship to pornographic materials and also serves the purpose of further distancing Laura from the limited representations of popular culture. This 'male' reading position is evidently characterized by its lack of independence but through education Laura has been given the confidence to articulate her own relationship to sexual materials and is, therefore, not susceptible to the corrosive influence of porn. So she offers a picture of female sexuality circumscribed by cultural injunction but which it is possible to circumvent through the independence of thought made realizable by education. But, having stated her unwillingness to engage with materials that seem to exclude women, she still wants to retain an idea of the possibility of producing erotic materials. Having argued that heterosexuality has no such potential she turns to gay pornography as a possible medium:

> Another feeling... another point I wanted to make was like ... I do find the strongest images, the most powerful images have been in gay pornography... um... and ... er... it's just you can see men actively involved in sexual acts, you can see men actively aroused, it's very difficult to, it's very easy to fake a woman's arousal in terms of a photograph. But it's not very, it's not easy to fake a man's arousal, it's very obvious whether he's engaged or not um... Obviously there's, I presume there's a qualitative difference between having sex... um... just to have your photograph, having taken, having taken one having sex but... um... and sort of having sex in private just for the sake of having the sex. But nevertheless there's a very obvious feature in a man which gives you a sign that he is aroused and engaged and actively engaged in sex and I find that a lot more exciting and stimulating to think of a man being sexually aroused and seeing him being sexually aroused... um... than... er... seeing him not really as I said earlier on. Um... and I do think that the images of... er... Robert Mapplethorpe, I like those images of men as well.

In this section of the tape, Laura moves from generalized male and female sets of responses to her own interests. In turning to gay pornography she is able to measure the authenticity of the representations. Gay porn is capable of showing men actively having sex and enjoying it. A certain indefinable difference between sex for its own sake and sex for the camera is inevitable, yet there is a potential for representation in gay media which is not thoroughly mediated. Thus for Laura, gay porn is somehow more authentic and more nearly connected with her own capacity for sexual arousal than that offered in *FW*. Gay pornography 'allows' Laura to enjoy men enjoying sex because it is not tainted, for her, by associations with male power over her. Popular culture, heterosexual pornography and their 'definitions' of female sexuality are too tainted by the inequalities of male/female relationships to offer her the opportunity to be excited or stimulated by their representations of sexual activity. It would be possible to dismiss her reference to Mapplethorpe as merely the reintroduction of the hierarchical differences between the erotic potentials of art and mass media forms. Certainly, alongside her earlier comments about education it is clear that Laura approaches imagery from an 'educated vs mass' position and on that basis, Mapplethorpe's work is more arousing than the images in *FW*. However, she also draws on a notion of the 'authentic', the 'truth-telling' claims of gay male 'authorship'. Mapplethorpe's work is (despite her own appropriation of it!) of gay men, for gay men, by a gay man: the discriminatory effects of power are thus assumed to be diluted and gay porn can actually show this. It shows it by the erections of its models and the clear statement those give of pleasure and willingness to be there. Laura suspects that the female porn model's arousal is rarely genuine: it is too easily faked, thus hetero-porn cannot be regarded as authentic and confirms for her that male power = male sexuality = male power.

To conclude this section, Laura has a very fluent account of her sense of the impossibility of representing female desire: for her, *FW*'s failure to arouse her is indicative/symptomatic of its popular culture and heterosexist origins. Pornography is unable to escape the imperatives of the 'male gaze' and current male/female relations make impossible women's expression of sexual desire. For her, an 'ideal' reading experience would allow an articulation of *authentic* female desire untainted by male power. Laura's participation in an educated vs mass position alongside her equation of male sexuality with power, means a pornography that would work for her must be totally new: this is, I think, both an emotional and political response on Laura's part and consequently she can't 'let it put the bullet' – she *has* to be disappointed. However, although a utopian dream at present, its substance is at least partially glimpsed in the existence and form of gay pornography.

James

Laura draws on a number of the central themes of feminist anti-porn theorizing; indeed, many of my interviewees talked of pornographic representations as 'harmful' and 'damaging' to women. Often this was 'common-sense', but for others it required well-thought-out references to the anti-pornography critique of Dworkin et al. One respondent, James, one of two gay interviewees, talked at length about Dworkin and the ways in which her writing made sense to him. I knew beforehand that James had read and admired Dworkin's work and so I tried very hard not to interrupt his flow when we got around to discussing her role in his understandings of, and interests in, pornography. Again, I don't offer this interview as representative but James's narrative is illustrative of very interesting and complex array of knowledges, emotional engagements and cultural relationships between the use of sexually explicit materials and the critiques and discourses which circulate them.

> For a long, long time I had a lot of problems with porn. I felt very, very uncomfortable about it. Even when I was looking at it. Even, especially when I was looking at my dad's magazines [*Men Only* etc.] ... I felt really, really uncomfortable about it. And I mean even though I enjoyed looking at my mother's [*Playgirl*] magazines, even though I enjoyed looking at the male bodies, I felt there was something that wasn't quite right about it. And for a long time I really didn't want to see homo or hetero porn on video at all. And then I read, I actually read Andrea Dworkin's book on pornography which was such a ... a kind of liberating book to read in terms of how I felt about pornography. I think until then I felt that there was something very dirty about pornography and I think what... I felt guilty about that, I felt guilty about looking at it and I felt guilty about that. And I think the book, her book, did for me, was that no, you don't have to feel guilty about looking at porn – there are some aspects of pornography that are bad and those aspects are when you're using violence and you're using porn against children or you're using, mostly women, having sex with animals something like that. I mean personally for me I couldn't look at that.

In the first place, Dworkin's ideas are liberating for James because she allows him the language to express his instinctive youthful disgust with pornography. This does not mean having to employ discourses of morality or tastes instead James can understand what it was that upset him when he stumbled across his parents' collection of 'dirty books' as a politicised response which allows him to offset his 'guilt' at not finding heterosexual pornography arousing:

> So when I was reading her book, which was detailing so many bad aspects of pornography I felt 'oh thank god for that' I shouldn't feel guilty for seeing pornography as dirty, y'know? ... there are some aspects of pornography which are bad...'

Using her arguments he is able to separate various levels of pornographic representation and to assign them within a hierarchy running from violent, sexist, dirty to pleasurable. But it takes him some considerable time to achieve a notion of what is enjoyable and okay to view, because in fact, Dworkin doesn't liberate in the sense of allowing him to enjoy masturbating over gay representations. He has to read other writings about censorship and pornography in order to finally overcome his guilty feelings about his own private pleasures. Thus James undertakes a very complex dialogue with Dworkin, agreeing with much of the substance of her argument as it relates to women and taking certain elements and reinventing them or modifying them so that he can justify his own use of gay images. He does this by utilizing her conception of women as socially and economically unable to make choices about what they do sexually. The theme of pornography as violence against women underpins his argument: there are bad things in pornography, there's violence, but so long as the pornography he views does not include violence, it is by implication okay. This doesn't mean that James does not recognize his own strategic uses of Dworkin, the cutting and pasting of her theory in order to produce his own critique of pornography. For instance, he is aware there are many similarities between heterosexual and homosexual men's pornography:

> I have read for some men and I think on one level it doesn't really differ all that much from gay porn. It can be quite violent in its use of the word like fucking … I fucked her or I fucked him, its almost the same thing, like the word being used, I did this to that person can be quite violent and I think that seems to operate in both sexualities in these stories or whatever…'

This essential similarity is something Dworkin argues for, so how does James make his significant leap in regarding gay porn as markedly different from heterosexual porn? Here, the question of the authenticity of performance – a key feature of Dworkin's arguments about women in porn – is turned on its head. Applying Dworkin's claims about volition to his viewing of pornography James can believe the performers in gay porn appear in those materials out of free will and choice (as did Laura).

> But just going on from watching gay porn, I got to read other sort of stuff and after a while I realised that, well, really fundamentally I think watching gay porn is very different from watching heterosexual porn just because from the power relationship which operates between men and women in society. When I'm watching gay, well, they may not certainly be gay… when I'm watching two men having sex … I seem to think that in some way they have some choice about whether they make that video because socially men have more choices economically than women do, y'know? I know from reading and from my own knowledge that women choose to go into the pornography industry because they have to because they have no other way of earning money or they do it because they can make some money quick which can help them out in life or whatever… and it may not be a choice for them. And so that's why I find watching heterosexual porn quite problematic, because I'm not sure whether this woman is agreeing to what this man is doing to her… I really can't separate that. Maybe I'm still connecting it with what Andrea Dworkin is saying, I'm not sure, but I really do think that. Just I read somewhere that Linda Lovelace, years later gave an interview saying that she was kidnapped, blackmailed and forced almost with a gun to do everything that she did in *Deep Throat.* And ever since reading that, it's quite hard to separate women's experience of pornography from the violence used against them. Whereas I really do think for men, whether they're gay or straight, and I think in terms of how gay porn is in America, a lot of the men in gay porn are straight, but they know that they can make gay pornography and make a hell of a lot, a hell of a lot of money out of it. But I think that men going

> into the pornography industry do have some choice because men in our society can do other things. And obviously most of the men in pornography are young and attractive, and I think there are a lot more choices open to them in society as men. So for me, I don't have a problem watching these men, I feel that they are consenting. For me, I feel I can have some enjoyment over watching what they're consenting to.

Men consent to take part because there are other ways for them to make money (they are attractive and young). Women, on the other hand, are unable to make such choices (even if they are young and attractive). The fact that often these are heterosexual men performing gay sex is a further guarantee of the authenticity of the production: pornography featuring men engaged in sexual acts with each other is authenticated through the in-built assurance in Dworkin's work that the free will of heterosexual men is never in doubt. Again there is that element of the unrepresentability of female sexual desire that Laura explored in her tape, and this was indeed the reason for James bothering to look at *For Women*. He wanted to see what it would do, could it do anything to challenge the 'inherently' problematic relationship between women and sexual representations? His talk here and his brief foray into *For Women* illustrates a desire to take part in the debate that circled the magazine; his interests in Dworkin, his own use of gay porn and his uncomfortable responses to heterosexual men's porn bring him to *For Women* as something which ought to be looked at – a cultural form which needs to be assessed for its cultural significance.

One of the ways in which James felt *For Women* could be important lies in his invocation of gay sexuality as an oppressed sexuality and the similarities between this oppression and women's 'repressed' sexual lives. Via this emphasis on oppression, James manages to manufacture a space in which he can take pleasure in pornography as a necessary means of keeping in touch with one's homosexuality:

> I have used gay porn to find out things because in the gay porn they have, like, information and sort of, like, facts and figures and all sort of different things as well as the naked men so it can be kind of like finding things out as well. I do know that some gay men who are very closeted, even like married, it's their only access to a gay life, getting a magazine. There was one guy in particular who used to come round and see my partner on a regular basis and what he used to do was come round, get hold of a magazine and go off to his car and go for a drive and then about half an hour later he would come back. And he was married, with a really responsible job and children but he was actually a gay man and that was his only access to gay life. He couldn't possibly have or risk going cottaging or go to a gay club because the risk of being found out for him was just too huge. So his only access was through my partner... and his magazines.'

Gay pornography is then an act of validation of one's self rather than a mere exercise in gratification (though, of course, this ignores Dworkin's analysis of gay male porn as simply a reworking or feminization of men through the visual stylizations of female submission). Porn can act as a means of keeping in touch with one's secret desires, it can be a source of strength, a means of taking time out and being who you really are. Clearly James is talking about responses to pornography clustered around sexual feeling but not limited to immediate sexual release, they are collages of experiences, knowledges, challenges, fears and pleasures and Dworkin's arguments take their place in the cut-and-paste conditions and expectations through which he can assess the pleasures of sexually explicit materials. This is a key element that James looks for in *For Women,* not for himself but for heterosexual women – again, like Laura, he feels it must do something new, that it should offer some form of resource to women to imagine different forms of sexual pleasure and subjecthood. Hence his disappointment that 'its just *Cosmo* with men with no clothes on': the magazine's significance turns out to be only slight.

Michele, Laura and James draw on a range of criteria for judging the magazine and find it wanting; central to their consideration of the *For Women* is the validation of women's experiences of sex but within certain confines. One of the most firmly established of those is that they must approach *FW* as an object, it must be viewed from a 'distance' and *assessed* rather than enjoyed. As Bourdieu (1984) has argued, the context of viewing brings its own forms of perception. In coming to the magazine as an 'object', Michele and Laura focus on the form of the magazine, separating out the features, photos and stories as isolable entities and assessing their function in terms of their 'effects' on other women and society. And there are traces of the same orientation in James's account, as a gay man with interests in feminist politics, the magazine has to be assessed for its possibilities as a resource.

There is no one way of responding to *For Women*, but the orientations outlined here have consequences for a reader and their subsequent engagement with *FW*. To take the latter orientation, as Laura and Michele did, is to take a measuring and appraising approach to the magazine and that enables certain kinds of response. This response is less likely to result in enthusiastic participation because it sets out with a refusal to take part (although it is not necessarily the case that this refusal precludes a less distanced response). In a recent audience study of the film *Judge Dredd* and its audiences, Barker and Brooks develop these ideas much further than is possible for me here. They explore the presence of 'practical logics' (1999: 137) guiding cinema-going, these range from choosing modes of transport, particular cinemas to the choice of film and with whom to view it. They conclude:

> If an individual chooses to see a film on the presumption that it is of a certain kind, and may give certain kinds of pleasure, then many other things follow logically from that. If s/he chooses on another basis, quite other consequences

> have to be worked out. These patterns of choices, decisions and consequences are what we mean by 'practical logics'. (1999: 137)

The orientations discussed here indicate very different ways of approaching *For Women* having real consequences for the kinds of conclusions which these readers draw and that I can extrapolate from their interview transcripts. What each of them seem to share though is a sense that sexuality and sexual representations are not just to be looked at as isolated phenomena. Sexual representations are more than just written about or photographed bodies engaged in sex, rather they are symptomatic of wider possibilities. They are different in important respects, for example, Jane's investment in the magazine is a wider engagement with companionship and girlie-dom which can open up understanding of her own feelings and possibilities; for others, again the sexual representations are more than just sex but this is allied to, on the one hand, more political engagements with the macro-politics of sexual relations and, on the other, to a sense of explicit talk being a vehicle for education and the acquisition of self-knowledge. I'll return to those themes in the discussion of the more fantasy elements of the magazine in the following chapters.

Notes

1. Gemma Moss (1993) has criticized Barker's 'natural reader' as problematic on a number of levels, not least because it appears to play into those hands of critics who have claimed teenage girls are duped by their chosen media forms. She suggests that Barker's assertion that natural readers are to be defined in terms of their relationship to the contents of the magazine is flawed because it expects the analyst to be able to identify that relationship from the text. Moss questions whether we can in fact find 'natural readers': how would we know we have found them? If the researcher has already defined the nature of the contract before interviewing readers, 'it will lead to the dismissal of any data which doesn't fit the critic's existing assumptions about what the natural audience's relationship to the text in question should be.' (1993: 119) In another study, Barker has responded that this is inevitable but that 'the alternative does not avoid analysts' assumptions, it merely offers others in the same way.' (Barker and Brooks 1998: 15) But Moss also has one further criticism which is that Barker's formulation would 'divid[e] the audience for romance into "natural" readers whom we will study, and other kinds of readers whom we won't ... a pointless exercise which simply creates a mythical group wholly dominated by the romance's agenda, whom we would have great difficulty in actually tracking down.' (1993: 119)

   Although Moss's criticisms have some force, specifically that finding 'natural' readers might be difficult, they also tend towards the misreading of Barker's approach. The division of 'natural' and 'not' is not designed to identify those who are most at risk. Indeed, this surely runs counter to Barker's use of Volosinov and his analysis that readers are invited to respond to a historically and socially located text via their own similarly located positions. Identifying the fundamental principles of his approach, Barker writes

   > To study readers, we have to begin by identifying the characteristics of a form's 'natural audience'. This requires investigation of both the social characteristics of the audience,

> and the form of the cultural object, in order to determine the interaction between them engendered by the object's form, and its proposal to readers. We have to discover both who are likely to be willing and able to orient themselves to the dialogue proposed, and what transformations they are thereby involved in. (1989: 275)

2. Barker & Brooks, *Knowing Audiences: Judge Dredd: Its Friends, Fans and Foes*, 1998: 308 ff. Other researchers have looked beyond the standard questions of harm and influence to surprising findings, for example, Annette Hill *Shocking Entertainment*.

Raunchy Nude Photosets

From its launch, the magazine proclaimed its relationship to and difference from other women's magazines – that difference lay in its willingness to expose: 'What they don't show you in *Cosmo*'. The revelation of the male body was, and is, for the magazine, its detractors and its admirers, emblematic of *FW*'s difference from, and challenge to, mainstream women's magazines. This chapter examines *FW*'s male nudes via a discussion of the theoretical approaches which have tended to deny women's interest in nude males and then a proposal for seeing these images as playing a part in the processes of eroticizing the male body for women viewers. The first section gives a brief sketch of *FW*'s nudes and their 'history'; it is followed by an overview of the inability of much theoretical work to account for women's pleasures in viewing the naked male. I then introduce the responses of one enthusiastic viewer of male nudes whose descriptions of looking at photosets suggest an alternative model for understanding that viewing.

Each issue of *For Women* featured up to four individual photosets of between six and eight pages of as many as thirteen photos: usually arranged as one double-page spread and then a combination of single-page images and smaller insets. The photos were often organized to suggest a striptease with a fully or partially clothed 'framing' shot at the beginning and a centrefold-esque nude at the end. Approximately half the images of each photoset featured the model naked and, to use the jargon, full frontal, the only exceptions to this being those images of 'celebrity' models: a number of sports stars have stripped for the camera but have been too coy or shy to reveal all. Backgrounds varied: outdoor, studio and 'home' interiors all featured and props, especially those which might be labelled 'sporting' and/or 'artistic' often found a place in the photosets.

Each photoset includes a photographer credit with some names featuring regularly: a number are male and well known within 'glamour' photography: Jeff Kaine, Karl Grant, Colin Clarke and Dean Keefer. Some women's work is also featured: Nicky

Downey, Ruth Batten, Jeanette Jones and Mary Doyle; the styles and conventions of those photographs do not seem to be noticeably different from those produced by male photographers, there is certainly no clearly definable 'women's aesthetic'. Photographers were neither directly employed nor usually commissioned by *For Women*, although they were often commissioned by other publications within the Northern & Shell portfolio: photographs were sent speculatively to the magazine and certainly in the early issues were often the by-products of work for gay men's magazines.

The magazine offered a range of types of body and styles of photography, props etc., but there is no clear sequence from one type to another. At particular times, a certain kind of body or style seemed to be in favour, but Ruth Corbett suggested to me that this was more a matter of limitations in supply than a prioritizing by the magazine team. The emphasis on the worked-out body would seem to reflect the tendency in gay porn to celebrate gym culture, although in recognizing that I am not arguing the magazine caters to gay men either explicitly or covertly.[1] In interviews with me, the editors of the magazine were very clear that they had no intention of directly addressing a gay audience, although they would not expressly exclude them. One of the main criteria for judging images was that they were not 'too gay', a subjective judgement best outlined by Zak Jane Keir:

> Quite a few of the sets bought in in the early days had originally been shot for gay magazines and thus picture selection was a bit tricky. Basically, the male anus is not the number one focus of female sexual desire, but a lot of gay men like to see it. Therefore, we used to see a lot of shots that I called 'the ring of confidence', usually a model on all fours with buttocks raised and cock hanging down like a missile. Also, check shirts and Freddie Mercury moustaches, anything smacking of the "gay clone" we tried to get away from. (E-mail 10.10.2000)

Photosets of couples were used occasionally: originally a feature of sister publication *Women Only*, they were introduced to *FW* by Ruth Corbett who felt that they offered better opportunities for readers to write their own fantasies. Celebrity images were very sought after: early research had suggested that women would really like celebrity nudes, as Keir explained, 'What we did find women were prepared to admit to was wanting celeb nudes – not very gettable in those days, though we tried. I think we did all hold to the idea that women are not homogenous and therefore we should provide as much variety as possible' (ibid.) The magazine found these difficult to provide – their opportunities were limited to those men who already stripped for a living;[2] some sports stars, usually black,[3] and the occasional before-they-were-famous celebrity photos. The lack of willing models was explained by the production team as yet another inequality: men expect women to display themselves but are fearful of what such display of their own bodies might say about them – in particular that their willies might not measure up to the ideal.[4]

Between February 1995 and January 1996 the editorial team was forced to 'cover up' the models. The decision was made by the marketing and advertising departments who believed that genitals prevented the magazine achieving its full potential – advertisers were staying away because they were afraid of the possibility of their products being placed next to a penis and that the magazine was suffering from its banishment to the top shelf. The idea was that without full nudity, newsagents would move the magazine down to the middle shelf. Corbett was adamant that the idea would not work and readers' letters confirmed her suspicion that it would cost in circulation figures: if there weren't full frontals then what was *FW* offering that calendars and pop photography wasn't? She extracted the concession of a six-month trial and, as the hoped-for advertising and move from top shelf did not materialize, the magazine went back to full revelation in January 1996.

Refusing the Female Viewer

As chapter 3 showed, for many of the magazine's commentators, the novelty and futility of *FW* lay in offering the male body to women: there could be no erotic appeal to female viewers in male nudes presented for sexual purposes.[5] Similar themes can be found in academic responses to the erotic male body. In this section I want to address the ways in which the male nude for a female audience has been theorized, indeed, analysed almost out of existence. Although most commentators acknowledge the changing representations of men's bodies, these are often described as primarily aimed at men via advertising spaces, rather than an attempt to appeal directly to a female viewer (Nixon 1996; Mort 1996; Moore 1988; K. MacKinnon 1997).[6] Where a female viewer is considered, these images are described as symptomatic of women's increasing sexual freedom: the commercial presentation of eroticized male bodies for a 'female gaze' offering an indication of how far women have come (Leroy 1994: 300). For others, however, these images offer little scope for the transformation of patterns of female spectatorship: no matter how often men remove their clothes there is no *authentic* address to the female viewer (Galloway 1990).

In fact, there is little sustained analysis of popular images of naked men for women viewers: fragments are to be found within art histories, film studies, analyses of pop videos and exhibition catalogues.[7] Although discussion is spread over the three decades from the 1970s, most analyses start with the reiteration of the difficulties of representing the male body and the perceived necessity to maintain the fictions of male power. Hence Margaret Walters' observation that the 'male nude derives much of its power and meaning from the reverence accorded in patriarchy to the phallus' (1978: 8). This reverence means that the male body is only properly capable of representing heroism or power: any other symbolism will render the image 'shaky'. Furthermore, where images are presented for a female viewer, the image becomes so unstable that it fails to 'work' (Kent 1985). The notion of images of men 'working' derives from the insistence that the male body can, and has, only represented those ideals which humans would strive for. Images of the male body must engender the proper degree of awe in the viewer. The processes of looking are theorized as the desire to possess the person or thing represented, such desire being the attribute of the male psyche. With the act of looking constructed as inherently male, a female spectator can only be a peculiarity. This allows, for example, Sarah Kent to claim,

> Once a female observer is envisaged, her presence becomes a conscious element in the encoding of the image. The tensions, ambiguities and contradictions apparent in the male pin-up reflect a conflict of interests that is fundamental to this new interaction. The male model apparently puts himself at the disposal of the female viewer, while actually attempting to maintain a position of sexual dominance. And whereas the female pin-up and homo-erotic nude tend to be acquiescent or submissive – little more than a screen onto which men can project their fantasies – play-males try to assert their independence and to control the observer's responses. (1985: 87)

The 'conflict of interests' is based on psychoanalytic theory's exploration of the cinematic experience – the classic psychoanalytic account is Laura Mulvey's exposition of Hollywood cinema's inscription of the 'male gaze'. Briefly put, Mulvey (1975) describes three male looks in cinema – the voyeuristic look of the camera; the look of the men within the filmic narrative for whom the women of the narrative are the objects of their gaze and, third, the look of the male spectator which mimics the first two. Through the processes of voyeurism and fetishism, the male spectator takes pleasure in being able to eroticize and objectify the female on screen, thereby exerting a form of power over her. He looks and, through that action, takes possession of her. The look fetishizes the female body, removing the threat of castration through the reassuring signification of the woman as phallus.

This conception of viewing has, of course, been challenged (Prince 1996; Bordwell 1991; and, to a limited extent, by Mulvey (1981) herself), nevertheless, the idea of objectifying power as a central facet of viewing has continued to hold sway in the exploration of popular culture representations, even when not explicitly drawing on psychoanalytic accounts. For example, Mulvey's contention that women appear for their 'to-be-looked-at-ness' is a founding principle of theorizations of the female form in art, popular culture, film, TV, advertising etc. Indeed it is a central theme within Dworkin's account, outlined in chapter 1, which stressed that by representing women as 'objects' to be admired the male psyche receives a major fillip in terms of its ability to believe itself all-powerful. Looking is an act of possession, of being in control, of having the right to survey, to observe, to apprise oneself of all the details in the image. This feeling of powerfulness is, however, limited to the male spectator. In discussions of female spectators the issue of power is not so easily accommodated.

Theorizations of representational power have drawn on the structural inequalities of heterosexuality. Masculine domination of the feminine is a precondition of representation and absolutely central to the images constructed and presented for the male subject: the woman's body becomes an object to be fetishized and consumed. To theorize the female spectator a process of 'transvestitism' (Doane 1992) has been described wherein women view themselves and other women through the male perspective. By this means women can gaze fetishistically upon the woman in the image. This proposition makes theorizing other positions difficult as Conway observes in her account of lesbian spectatorship:

> One source of the limitations on theorising female spectatorship, noted by many critics, is the "theory-effect" of a totalising psychoanalytic film theory. Theory-effect, a sort of self-fulfilling epistemology, describes inquiry where theory becomes rigidified method and nearly supplants thought. The result is predictable investigation that produces only information that reproduces that theory. (1997: 109)

Such theorizations cannot account for what Williams' has termed the 'highly-contested, and much more diverse, sexual representations whose visibility is everywhere' (1994: 4).[8] Nevertheless in approaching images of men for women, the first question remains: does this image reverse the power dynamic and offer female viewers the power of objectification of the proposed erotic object? As the theory will not allow the objectification of the male except as a kind of 'stand-in' female, the question remains rhetorical and unable to account for the phenomenon it supposedly addresses.

The Subordinating Gaze

Discussions of pornography are often guilty of 'slippage': too often containing elisions of form, content and claims about viewers. Recognizing such slippage does not, however, address one of the most damning criticisms of pornography. Namely, its power to objectify and harm women through the cutting up and fetishization of parts of the female body in order to arouse male viewers. In an essay assessing the possibility of feminist erotica, Kathy Myers (1982: 14) observes:

> Many feminist critiques of the representation of women hinge on the assumption that it is the act of representation or objectification itself which degrades women, reducing them to the status of objects to be 'visually' or 'literally' consumed.

Myers goes on to separate the two theoretical traditions which give root to 'objectification'. Marxist analysis based on the idea of the commodity (the thing sold for profit) proposes women's gender and sexuality are represented in pornography as things to be purchased for male pleasure. Women become objects or articles for trade and experience this as alienation from 'female sexuality'. A second level of objectification is derived from Freud where parts of the body stand in for the whole. Thus, the repeated use of cropped images showing only the breast or the vagina, fetishize, fragment and reduce female sexuality to those parts.

The theoretical implications are clear: objectification is bad and, as Myers shows, is coupled with 'problem viewing', whether a result of the sexual disorder, 'fetishism', or the social disorder of 'dehumanising women as objects' (1982: 16). Conceiving objectification as synonymous with 'problem viewing' creates its own problems: as human beings we are guilty of objectification in order to 'conceptualise and give meaning to the object of our gaze.' (1982: 16) As Myers asserts

> It is ...important to create a working distinction between the process of fragmentation, which implies a breaking up or disabling of the physical form, and

> what could be termed 'a pleasure in the part' – the pleasure derived from looking at a picture which depicts the curve of an arm or the sweep of the neckline. Such images could be interpreted not as a butchering of the female form but as a celebration of its constituent elements, giving a sense of the scope and complexity of sensual pleasure which breaks with specific genital sexual associations and with the necessity of over-determining phallic substitution in the representation of the female form. (1982: 16)

Simply showing parts of the body cannot be seen as firstly objectifying and then, underpinned by dubious assertions about male sexuality, subordinating and harmful to women. Myers argues that essentializing objectification does not open up possibilities for imagining/imaging women in non-sexist ways. Myer's argument is directed to the possibility of constructing/evolving a 'feminist erotica', the creation of 'progressive' imagery. I agree with her concerns regarding the unthinking conflation of male viewing with objectification but the possibility of appraising images in terms of their progressiveness is once again a case of the analyst knowing what will count or which kinds of objectification are good. Myers analyses two images of women supposedly employing differentiated aesthetic appeals to gendered audiences: men like women to look sexual through vulnerability and accessibility; women like women to look sexual through power and inaccessibility: 'an ideal version of self' (1982: 16).

Although Myers stresses that contexts, address, modes of production and consumption are necessary elements of examination, her analysis turns on the idea that address to a male audience confirms objectification. Her proposal for the pursuit of a feminist erotica poses this question 'Does the risk of appropriation by men invalidate producing erotic imagery for women?' (1982: 19) Thus, we already know that male use of an erotic image *is* appropriating, rendering even the possibility of progressive images null and void. When considered alongside her questions and measurements of progressive/non-progressive imagery, Myer's challenge to theories of 'objectification' rings hollow. It seems the feminist critic/academic can do all the work of delineating an image as progressive or not: audiences are not necessary to answer the questions:

> How is the sexuality and subject position of the audience constructed – are they sexed as male or female? What kind of emotional responses does the image demand? Does it demand any kind of audience interaction to interpret the meaning of the image? To what extent does the image challenge assumptions already held? (1982: 19)

The irresistible demands of the image should challenge assumptions; it must do more than simply appeal to sexual feelings. I do not agree. Myers illustrates for me how little we understand the workings of images. As material that appeals to the body, pornography is subject to all the usual criticisms of low culture. Moreover in its record of the physical-ness of sexual activity and sexuality, it is deemed to anchor and fix the body it represents. We misunderstand the nature of the 'obviousness' of pornography. *Obvious* imagery and its supposedly easily acquired pleasures are precisely the materials we should be investigating and trying to understand.

Similarly art histories have tended to confirm the transhistorical nature of the continuing presence of 'woman' as the 'sign'. This use of women appears first in art and is continued in its offspring 'publicity', as Berger outlines in his *Ways of Seeing*:

> The continuity ... between oil painting and publicity goes far deeper than the 'quoting' of specific paintings. Publicity relies to a very large extent on the language of oil painting. It speaks in the same voice about the same things. Sometimes the visual correspondences are so close that it is possible to play a game of 'Snap'... It is not however on the level of exact pictorial correspondence that the correspondence is important: it is at the level of the sets of signs used. (1972: 135–8)

Berger shows how the cultural and economic practices of art have contributed to the framing of woman as object. Historical precedents give credence to the delineation of a regime of representation that is inviolate. And yet, Berger's account is also an acknowledgement of the historical and social specificity of the cultural 'signs' of gender: in tracing developments of perception linked to cultural and economic shifts the account of Art's engagement with the female body evidences modification and change as well as continuities. This specificity must be recognised in any attempt to account for women's enjoyment of male nudes if we are to move beyond the 'theory effect' that proscribes investigation. In the use of art history there is a tendency to reiterate the high/low distinctions whereby Art is capable of effecting change and commercial enterprises like magazines and advertising are not. For example, Walters is disparaging of 'news-stand' (avowedly sexual) nudes but claims:

> It has been possible, more recently, to find some nude picture books that do treat the male body gently, affectionately and imaginatively. Certain photographers and agencies – most notably, Jim French – have developed a market for genuinely evocative and stunningly photographed male nudes, that perhaps escape the limits of the mere pin-up. They are a protest, and an important and valid one, against the unthinking assumption that beauty belongs only to women... We need to be reminded for all our sakes, that men are beautiful too. (1978: 299)

Jim French's photographs are called 'Nude Studies' and have all the attributes of the classical male, eyes gazing into the distance, focused on a spiritual plane, well-toned bodies, powerful, contained musculature. Walters is not arguing for new types of representation of the male body at all, simply a return to an ancient one. These bodies may well be beautiful, but they do not escape the limits of cultural definitions of masculinity nor do they necessarily push at the boundaries of what might be considered appropriate ways of representing the naked male body as beautiful. Indeed Walters' pleas for treating the male nude with gentleness and affection offer a very traditional inflection of women's erotic nature. The tendency to view Art's intervention as the only meaningful approach to the erotic potentials of the male nude is a major theme in discussions of female artists' presentation of the male nude:

> The photographers in *What She Wants* have a common goal in representing gender otherwise. As such, this collection of artists is part of a new tradition which takes women's images of masculinity as a starting point. The images in this collection explore the varieties of fetishism with a light touch and humour, which is far from the 'one-dimensional', heavy, static, fixing characteristic of the fetishistic gaze. The good-natured curiosity and playfulness of the work counteracts the dreary sado-masochism of traditional fetishism. (Pajaczkowska 1994: 33)

The 'fetishistic gaze' is, of course, the commercial one but my challenge is not to the attempts by artists to explore the body but to the idea that there should only be 'good natured curiosity and playfulness'. It seems impossible to imagine that women might find an expressly sexual image interesting, pleasurable, fascinating, or sexually exciting precisely because it has 'dark depths' or fetishistic elements.

Can Women Look at Men?

Richard Dyer's exploration of the male pin-up and its instabilities is one of the most popular references in works on the male body. First published in 1982, his account stresses the contradictions apparent in images of men created for women. Dyer emphasizes the violence done to the established order of spectatorship, its dichotomies active/passive, male/female once a male body is presented to the female viewer. The submissive attitude of the 'sex object' is traditionally assigned to the female sex role (1992b: 99), emphasized in her eye contact which invites the viewer to feast his eyes and fantasize that her pleasure comes from being viewed by him. It is this effect that the male model must work to minimize, ensuring that eye contact with the viewer is refused, by either looking up out of the photograph or off beyond the viewer. Through his studious avoidance of eye contact, the male model retains power and refuses the female spectator active possession of the gaze. Any attempt to represent the male body as 'passive' is fractured by this refusal to give up the 'active' position. This forms the 'first instability of the male pin-up ... the contradiction between the fact of being looked at and the attempt of the model's look to deny it...' (1992b: 109).

Dyer also suggests that in posing the male erotic nude, power relationships are again at play: although the penis is often absent from the image, its symbolic power must be maintained so that the male body is presented in such a way that it becomes the all-conquering phallus. The emphasis on pumped up muscles and unyielding poses is, Dyer suggests, reminiscent of the absent erection/phallus. The erection/phallus is also signified in the activity of the model; these men cannot be represented in static and/or supine poses but must be seen to be 'active': that is, actually doing something more than merely being looked at. Dyer's ideas are persuasive and have been taken up by others (K. MacKinnon 1997; Mort 1996; Nixon 1996) in order to show the *difficulties* of representing the male body. However, his idea of *instability* has sometimes been taken to mean *impossibility*; for example, Alastair Foster (1988) asserts that the male portrayed in the pin-up or erotically charged advertisement is not simply refusing the gaze of the viewer – he is not even there for the viewer. This is narcissistic representation: a picture of man as he would like to be seen and as he likes to see himself.

Thus the male model works to refuse an engagement with the viewer on any level except that of envy: Foster harnesses his analysis to a critique of advertising and capitalist utilization of the body to sell products suggesting,

> These men are not objects of sexual desire, gay or straight. If they happen to be a turn-on for a particular individual that is a matter of coincidence, for they do not operate primarily within the domain of sexual fantasy – I will buy the product because I want him – but in the domain of envy – I will buy this product because I want to be like him. They are objects of an aspirant desire for material consumption. Their presence is intended to create an increasing desire for possessions, for status, for power, and to associate this with notions of masculinity. (1988: 61–2)

Images of men thus confirm rather than subvert the power dynamics which produce their contradictions and reinforce the powers of patriarchy and capitalism. Similar claims are made by Pollock (1992) in her brief explorations of the conventions of the male pin-up. Like Dyer and Foster, she stresses the lack of eye contact and the ways in which the spectator is inscribed within the image. In her example, the man appears in the distance leading a horse which she claims only allows the spectator the 'hypothetical position ... [of] some wood nymph catching a fleeting glimpse of this sylvan god through the blurred bushes of the foreground. What is absolutely lacking is any conceivable position of ownership or possession offered to the spectator.' (1992: 139). Pollock is primarily concerned with the use of women in advertising imagery and the ways in which the female figure has become the guarantor of the item for sale. Woman is the sign of the commodity, man is its purchaser, therefore, she suggests that male imagery is doomed to failure because the male figure is incapable of the symbolic work of the female: they cannot swap roles. This impossibility is supposedly corroborated by the ease with which patriarchy reappropriates radical imagery. Even feminist icons of the vagina have been appropriated by pornography confirming that women's sex can be stolen from them as well as offered as a commodity for sale. The radical image cannot retain its radicalism in the face of capitalist and patriarchal annexing of its vocabularies. This notion of reappropriation ensuring representational stasis confirms that the male body can never become the 'sex object'. In these claims, theories of the gaze and of objectification ossify viewing to the extreme that we cannot conceive of other possible and actual relationships to images. The fetishistic, scopophilic gaze of psychoanalytic theory is a construction of particular and at best hypothetical modes of use: proposing a very rigid set of responses to media forms. The evidence for this is extremely slim, relying on the reiteration of the mantras of psychoanalysis and ignoring all instances and evidence that would contradict its central claims.

Moreover, these claims are linked to the seeming agentless force that is the 'sexualization of culture'. Because theories of viewing cannot accept the idea of change and development in vocabularies of representation and therefore the relationships offered for viewers, sexualization is a kind of avalanche force which overwhelms culture rather than a development from within and through cultural change.

Although theory has been reluctant to admit it, we must recognize that women's erotic engagements are not a brand new phenomenon. Although there is a tendency to look on women's viewing of men as of recent genesis and, in some instances, as exciting and unique confirmation of women's increasing willingness to break taboos, women have looked for some considerable time. As Dutton has indicated with regard to bodybuilding,

> The first stirrings of a change in attitude can be traced back to Sandow, whose 'ladies only' posing sessions (significantly contemporaneous with the age of women's emancipation) first established the unclad male figure as an object of public female scrutiny. The double legitimation involved (for women, the legitimacy of looking; for men, the legitimacy of being looked at) meant a profound change in socio-sexual expectations, although not till more recent times has the shift in general social values given widespread currency to the newer understanding. (1995: 253)

From the early days of Hollywood cinema and the beginnings of the star system, images of men have been widely available to women. It is not possible to offer an exploration of the meanings of the star image here but research by Hansen (1991), Studlar (1996), Stacey (1993) and Fred and Judy Vermorel (1985) suggest women have had a fairly long engagement with representations of men for erotic and/or imaginative contemplation.[9] What is particularly disappointing is that although this evidence is available, it has yet to permeate theories of spectatorship or viewing as anything other than interesting eccentricities. The failure to engage with that tradition of fandom is a by-product of theories of spectatorship outlined above. Given the associations of spectatorship and the gaze with fixing, objectifying and castrating, why would women wish to label themselves 'spectators' or possessors of the gaze? But women *do* admit to being turned on by photographs of nude men: how might we begin to account for that? In order to propose an alternative reading of the nude male, I turn first to Julie to examine the ways in which she uses nude pin-ups and her strategies of viewing. I realize that one woman cannot be considered as representative of all women or even some women and their interest in the male body, but in examining her account of herself, her reading of *For Women* and her practices of pleasure in looking and masturbation, Julie offers an interesting case study opening up the possibilities of understanding an emergent pattern of involvement and pleasure in the displayed male body. In the succeeding section, I return to the standard accounts of viewing and their limitations in order to formulate an alternative approach to understanding male nudes.

Julie's Account

Julie was one of two women who replied to my letter in *FW* in January 1995. She initially completed a set of written answers to my questionnaire and then followed that up with a long and regular correspondence over three years. During that time she sent me more than fifty letters, most concerning the magazine and its contents, although she also wrote very candidly about her sex life. Often her comments about individual elements of the magazine appear very general: she writes that the story was 'good', 'interesting' and/or 'erotic' without explaining what she means by those labels. But at other times she moves from generalization to important statements (usually prefaced by my name) which indicate that her ideal viewing experience is dependent upon her being able to look at and use *FW* in certain ways:

> OK Clarissa, when I look at pictures of naked men I let my mind wander off into a world of fantasy. I have never yet found the perfect picture, so it may be his strong arms, his smooth chest, or his tight ass that attract me. But I will always include his penis, when I am interested in sex, this little bit is very important to me. While I fantasise I concentrate on his penis, how I make him erect, touching it, stroking it, sucking it. I imagine what it feels like, smells like and tastes like, where he will put it and how it feels. I have these thoughts about his mouth and testicles too, what his body feels like pressed against me, his weight and warmth etc etc.
>
> So it is all a form of sexual fantasy made possible by the pictures in *FW*. There are no set rules, I just pick his best bits and let my mind wander off.
>
> If the photos are of a couple I will sometimes substitute myself for the woman, or perhaps in my mind I will be 'accidentally' watching them having sex. Other times I will have them both make love to me. I also have fantasies about sex with other women. Please don't fall off your chair, couch or crash the car!! But this is true, in my own mind I can enjoy the best and most adventurous sex possible. However, this is getting away from your questions but perhaps it will help explain why I enjoy *FW*. I think you are less interested in the fantasy aspect of the magazine, and more in the reality of the reader.
>
> ... I don't have a problem with my fantasies, in fact I enjoy them, for daydreaming or masturbation. *FW* just gives me an idea to run with and develop in any way I want, it can suit me and how I feel at that time. So as you see I don't have a problem with pictures of naked women, I quite enjoy them sometimes. Particularly the pictures of Readers Wives I have seen in some men's magazines. They are not, by any stretch of the imagination, all beauties, but they are real people becoming aroused, feeling horny and fucking each other. That is (sex)life. I do also prefer the harder adult magazines showing erections, penetration and ejaculation, but these are very difficult to get. (Letter 3)

The above relation of her experience of the photosets as aids to masturbation details a *process* of becoming aroused. She lets her mind wander off, some part of the male body will trigger the response for her and that is what she is looking for in the image.

For her, viewing the photographs and finding the cue allows for mental activity that in turn enables the experience of bodily sensations and the use of all her senses. These felt sensations go as far as experiencing his weight and warmth. Thus the magazine enables her to feel more than might be possible on her own. She can have the most adventurous sex ever; these fantasies and consequent masturbation allow Julie to move beyond the ordinary, to explore her own responses and, in so doing, to learn more about herself:

> I think it [masturbation] is a very enjoyable and healthy activity, you can learn a lot about your body, its sexual responses, and your own likes and dislikes. (Letter 2)

Masturbation is a very important part of Julie's sexual repertoire and that quotation indicates a way of talking about self-pleasure as a form of knowledge which references the concerns of second wave feminism's masturbation projects. Central to that is the idea of a doubled pleasure – the sought for release of orgasm and the further, more appraising, pleasure of learning about oneself. The photosets are crucial to her reading of *For Women* and to her experiences of her own body. Shortly after our correspondence began Julie begins to criticize the magazine, not least because of the decision to remove the full frontal photographs:

> The lack of male members in recent issues of *FW* has been very disappointing and frustrating – I guess you could say they all have 'private dicks'!!! I do feel that *FW*'s greatest selling point is the nude male. I could never see men's magazines asking their models to cover up, or even to close their legs for that matter!! I was aware that it was just a trial but I think it does weaken the magazine, and also it shows poor management. I agree with your comment on recent models, they have been pretty poor all round, and rather silly photosets. (Letter 5)

Just as for Anne, the 'dick' is about more than seeing penises, exposure demonstrates the magazine's ability to 'hold its own', to remain true to its promulgation of 'equality'. But even when full frontals are a feature of the magazine, they are not uniformly successful. The failures are perhaps best categorized by their inability to tackle the 'real' nature of male arousal. In her very detailed relation of what she 'does' with the images, Julie mentions *Readers' Wives* making a claim for them being 'real', showing sex as it actually is – this seems much less about fantasy or her fantasies of same sex. I would link this to her earlier statement that she has yet to find the 'perfect picture' – what would constitute the 'perfect' image? This is an assertion of proprietorial viewing and suggests that 'a good image' can multiply the possible pleasures for Julie. This has less to do with the perfect physique or a value judgement of attractiveness (although these are important to her – as her derogatory comments on the real men features testify!), indeed in order to understand what Julie is looking for in *FW*, it is important to understand Julie's correspondence with me.

The reasons for Julie taking part in my research offer some insight into her orientation to *FW*:

> … first I was interested, because you were interested enough to ask, and the fact that you were adult enough to ask seemed reasonable to me. Let's be honest, it's not a subject everybody can speak about, but I felt you could.
>
> …. About making my contribution, well the magazine is just a way of passing out information on a huge scale. It is not personal or interactive in any way. It's just words scripted by writers…. We have gone one step further by exchanging views on a personal level, that's my contribution, and you have gone even further by documenting it. You (as a woman) have contacted other women (willing to share their opinions) analysed the information, and are making a statement, and that counts Clarissa. Perhaps at the moment only those directly involved are interested in what you are doing – I don't know, but some day it may be important to somebody and my opinion is as valid to me, as yours are to you, or to the next person. So rather than keep all my (brilliant!!!) ideas to myself I have shared them with you.
>
> …. Have you noticed, men have sex!! or should I say that sex is for men. Adult magazines, porn films, sex chat lines and much much more, they are all geared towards men. Fellas will ask each other, did he get a leg over, did he get a ride, did she give him a blow job, or perhaps how far did he get. I am sure you can think of many more examples where his pleasure is the main objective. This attitude has to change, women are there too!! and we have much the same entitlements. (Letter 6)

In 1995, when she began writing, the research offers Julie an opening, which she hopes will enable her to discuss and share intimate details with another woman without recrimination. Many of her letters talk of her wish to confide and share with others and as her agenda is a 'pen-friend' one, she wants to receive as well as give. In her early letters she states that she feels she knows me quite well and could discuss anything with me: her response to me is as another woman, one who has an interest in sex and channels that interest through *FW*. My status as a university researcher is only interesting to her in that it may spread the influence of our correspondence further but in other ways it limits what we can do in our letters, hence her dissatisfaction at my remaining 'neutral' on the topic of *For Women*.

In many of her letters she makes clear that she sees no need to be circumspect with me: she wants our correspondence to take the subject of sexuality further than is possible in face to face conversations and to include me in her meditations on sex. This going further involves more than just relating our complementary experiences as women, at times it was clear that Julie would have liked to have swapped sexual fantasies and experiences with their own potentials for sexual arousal. Hence her intensely descriptive telling of the story of her first sexual experience and her dissatisfaction, even anger, at my lack of response to that letter.

> I guess that's about it then? I thought at first your letter may have been delayed but at this time I guess you are not going to reply – that's OK if that's how you feel. I don't really see the point in apologising for what I wrote but I do apologise if what I wrote upset you. Perhaps I was OTT and I did not intend to offend you, although that appears to be what has happened. (Letter 9)[10]

In conducting a correspondence with me, Julie is able to construct a version of herself that she sees as different from her 'real' life, by that I do not mean that she constructs a fantasy of herself but that she is able to 'de-censor' herself. Letter writing enables her to construct a picture of me and this imagined person is someone she can 'talk' to as an equal and that this can enable certain further pleasures and involvements in her reading of the magazine. That she regards us as equals is evidenced by her refusal to regard me as a 'judge', although she wants to know my thoughts on certain topics, she is not interested in my judgement of her activities. In fact, she denies me any rights to judge by insisting on her rights to hold her own views about sexuality and *FW*. 'Do I worry about how my letters come across? The simple reply is "no not really". If you ask me a question you must accept my reply as my opinion' (letter 7). Central to Julie's engagement with me (and *FW*) is a sense of community between women, a sharing of secrets, experiences and desires. This is particularly interesting in that it stresses an awareness of 'women's issues' about sexuality. Julie assumes a shared knowledge and interest in women's rights to enjoy sexual activity as well as a shared enjoyment of *FW*.

> From your brief letter I think we share a lot of similar attitudes towards sex, I really don't have a problem speaking about sex, I think it is a very natural, beautiful and enjoyable union for adults to share, and if we are adults, we should be able to discuss it. (Letter 2)

Those shared attitudes were probably most explicitly acknowledged in letters we exchanged towards the end of our correspondence. I had written to Julie and told her of some problems I had not explained at the time but which had affected our correspondence. In reply she told me about her own bad experiences which illuminated, for me, both our correspondence and Julie's relationship to the magazine. The details are not for publication but her comments about her friends' responses are important,

> My basic theory on men is that they just want a leg-over so they can meet their mates down the pub and say what a great lay/lousy fuck they had. But women I find to be far more cruel and malicious. They labelled me a slut and a whore… I even got some hate mail from my 'friends' suggesting I find some people of my 'own type' to socialise with in future. For a while I actually considered suicide as an option, my life was hell, then I thought what right have they to judge my actions, but I did take their advice. I found people of my 'own type'. My friends now are honest, sincere and non-judgemental, our friendships are genuine and we never try to put each other down… While I am content to accept my past, I think I am

> still secretly afraid that some people might again try to hurt me or judge me because I don't fit into exactly what they want. (Letter 24)

Julie has a particular orientation to the magazine arising out of her particular circumstances and these lead her to her expectations of *FW*. The magazine needs to be as honest, sincere and non-judgemental as her new friends.[11] The magazine must offer Julie the possibility of not fitting in with a singular definition of 'womanhood' and allow her to explore female sexuality from a woman's viewpoint. That may seem contradictory but it is not. Honesty lies in acknowledging mistakes but recognizing their potential for growth and exploration, thus to judge others is to curtail their freedom for exploration and experimentation. For Julie an honest magazine does not airbrush 'reality': it embraces it. As she does, it can hold seemingly contradictory views on men and women: Julie often comments on the inequalities of men's sexual attitudes/behaviours but is still very desirous of sexual relationships with men. That does not mean, however, that Julie is a doormat. Her accommodation of male sexuality extends only if men have a capacity for self-recognition: men can change those aspects that are damaging but retain the sense of fun and possibilities. Julie wants and expects *FW* to manage the same levels of acknowledgement, acceptance and understanding alongside a desire for change.

Central to Julie's conception of a successful erotic experience is her sense of herself as a woman and her right to sexual fulfilment. From the beginning of our correspondence it was clear that Julie saw *FW* as symbolic of her sexual independence. Julie's first letter to me began with a statement of her right to read *For Women* and a signal of defiance:

> I have also received several moaning complaints about the amount of time I spend reading *FW*, especially as a lot of the time is spent ALONE! But I love it and I will not be stopped. (Letter 1)

For her, reading *FW* is a solitary occupation, one that attracts criticism but which she deflects through an assertion of women's sexual rights:

> This is the 90s, women no longer have to lie back and 'take it', we can enjoy sex too, as much as any man, I know I certainly do. (Letter 1)

Thus, her reading of *FW* is closely, even inextricably, tied to a discourse of sexual liberation for women. Such an assertion shows an awareness of feminist discourse around women's sexuality and sexual rights but Julie is also clearly aware of the connotations of what she says. She is therefore at some pains to ensure that she is not taken to be a feminist, a label she evidently feels is negative:

> For too long, women's sexual pleasure has depended on men, and what they want to, or are able to, give. But now, thanks to magazines like *For Women* you can decide during the day at work, that tonight you will be guaranteed an orgasm, and actually do it. I am not a crazy feminist, I just feel we are entitled to the exact

> same liberties as men. If this includes masturbation, and the availability of sexy magazines aimed at women, that's fine. (Letter 2)

Arranged within a rubric of the shared experiences of women, Julie's letters detail the move from repressed female sexuality through liberation to sexual equality and the right to orgasm. This right to orgasm is not organized within the discursive limitation of 'spontaneous' sexual activity, instead it is something one can plan for, timetable into one's life and not be reliant on anyone else for it. In so doing she evidently becomes aware of the inferences which could be drawn about her political motivations. She clearly states that her conception of rights is not based on feminist theorizations, in fact, feminists are 'crazy', whereas her formulation is made within the 'naturalness' of sex, its beauty, its share-ability and its maturity. Within this construction, feminism is incompatible with her idea of sex as a 'shared union', in a later letter she writes:

> I hate them [feminists] – they are too extreme, and always right, feminists will eventually kill love, romance and sex, if given the opportunity.

Sex is 'natural and beautiful', a fairly obvious reference to the ideological construction of heterosexuality as the approved mode of sexual activity (although Julie does not limit her fantasies to heterosexual activity). Her comments on one aspect of the magazine, which she particularly likes, illustrates her conceptualization of this naturalness:

> The photosets of couples ....are usually very good, and a huge turn on, they are usually better photographs, they make men seem more 'male' and women appear more 'female'. They show how the sexes complement each other in a very erotic and arousing way. Man and woman as they should be, naked, happy, together. (Letter 3)

Here naturalness means the complementary differences between the genders and the rightness of their union. Her judgement that photographs of this kind are 'better' is not necessarily dependent upon better production values. Rather it is their depiction of a man and woman in a state of arousal, their realistic representation that accords them this status.

Again naturalness is linked with her ideas of equality: in sexual union adult men and women have equal rights to pleasure and as adults they should be free to make the choice to take and speak of such pleasure. Julie makes distinctions between adult behaviour and that which she describes as 'childishness'. Such childish behaviour consists of an inability to discuss sexuality and sexual pleasure in an open and honest way. This is most plainly articulated in her recurrent comments on women and masturbation. The denial of women's solo sexual activities is of a piece with the denial of women's sexuality in general:

> An attitude I have encountered many times (not from you) is that people in 'Holy Catholic Ireland' do not have sex, I hate this childishness. I also have to be honest and say I have mostly experienced this attitude from English people, both men and women. It usually starts with a joke, but a lot of people feel it is true. As an Irish woman I enjoy sex, and sexual adventure, pleasure and orgasm. In Ireland we do have condoms, the pill, vibrators, sex shops and much more. But we also have the national attitude passed from generation to generation that somehow sex is dirty and wrong. This attitude is changing ... slowly! (Letter 7)

These passages suggest something more than just sexual liberation: her emphasis on changing sexual mores is reminiscent of 1960s liberation discourse, but it is also about understanding bodily needs and pleasures. Understanding the ways in which constraining forces – religion, men's backward notions of what constitutes sexual activity – conceptions of appropriate behaviour and correct 'feminine' attitudes towards sex are ideas that she wants to struggle against, risking censure in order to break through to her 'real' sexual self. 'Naturalness' and 'honesty' are thus terms that are linked by their relationship to getting to know what are your own boundaries, not those imposed by others. In this way the opportunities presented by my research enable her to vocalize her own desires. Enjoying sex means being able to talk of it in an 'adult' way:

> We all tend to speak about sex with a giggle – even with our friends, so sometimes the facts are unspoken or perhaps conveyed through innuendo, but I thought that by writing, the facts would be stated as facts. Perhaps I was using this as some kind of therapy for myself!!! Just to be able to say, I do ... I enjoy... or I dislike... and to at least feel that the other person is interested and open enough to hear what I have to say.
>
> Clarissa, I don't mean to take the 'fun' out of sex, whatever form it takes. Because I do feel that sex is great fun, sometimes just thinking about one person climbing on top of another, and puffing, panting and humping like their life depended on it, well the thought just cracks me up with laughter! But I don't mean to take away from love, closeness, sensuality, or attraction. But I feel that these should be discussed as subjects in their own right, and be able to be spoken about rationally and honestly. There is no problem for us to discuss our favourite clothes, or food or most enjoyable films. But if I try to explain to you the really great new way I found to masturbate, or you want to tell me about a brilliant kinky experience you had – well society has labelled these subjects as taboo. We cannot really speak openly about our good or perhaps very bad experiences. So really we cannot share information or learn from what other people may have or have not done.
>
> *FW* has opened the door, just slightly on women's sexuality – look at it this way, we would not be exchanging opinion if there was no *FW*? You think the magazine is very important to me and that I feel passionate about it, well this is not all true. I feel passionate about the 'subject', the magazine is just the first 'open platform'

> to discuss these subjects, and I think that is the real point. If a better magazine came on the market I would probably buy it instead of FW! (Letter 7)

For Julie, information and sharing confidences and opinions are a means of changing the status quo – until women realize or are prepared to discuss their sexuality openly in order to make a statement of their pleasure in sex then equality between the sexes is as far off as ever. Innuendo and giggling are the means by which individuals refuse to either accept the activities of others or deny the importance of those activities to themselves. The fun aspect of sexual activity is not denied by Julie, but her passion about the subject, sex, at times requires a more serious attitude in order to fulfil her personal project of learning from other women and their experiences. *FW* is clearly a substitute for this kind of conversation which is circumscribed by societal constraints, fear or disinterest. The importance of the magazine, for Julie, lies in its being the first of its kind (and the only one) to 'openly' discuss sexual matters. Within this particular framework, it is important to her that *FW* is aimed at a female audience:

> .. it deals with women's issues, and deals with sex from a woman's point of view. (Letter 2)

Thus central to her ideal is an awareness of herself as a woman who enjoys sex and what she wants from a sexually explicit magazine is recognition of her right as a woman to:

- find men attractive: 'I think that in 1995 an honest interesting magazine should show a few photos of hard cocks!'
- experience or share other's experience of sexual feeling of a female kind: 'I enjoy the photos and erotic stories, because they are both a turn-on. Also the letters and responses from other readers, they help to prove that I am normal!!!!'
- masturbate: 'I also feel that for far too long the subject of female masturbation has been kept under the covers (literally!) and this has caused a lot of women a lot of guilt... I think it is a very enjoyable and healthy activity, you can learn a lot about your body, its sexual responses and your own likes and dislikes.'
- experiment and discover for herself what is good or bad for her, stimulating and pleasurable or a turn off and unpleasant: 'Sex is always fun, even when it is bad, [when I have experimented] some things just did not do anything for me, others caused discomfort initially, but having tried them again I found them quite enjoyable.'
- want sexual activity and experience pleasure through that: 'Women do have an interest in sex, as much as men, and their attitudes are changing, they now realise that they are entitled to receive pleasure, and demand it if left unsatisfied.'

In fulfilling these criteria, the magazine has a dual role to play in Julie's life: it is a source of material that facilitates her sexual activities and is therefore an addition to her sex life. Secondly, it is a forum for discussing sexual activity and subjects related to women's sexuality. In this role, the magazine is a substitute, offering Julie a space to 'converse' on sexual matters denied her elsewhere. Within Julie's conception of the ideal reading experience, *FW* should allow her (and other women) to exercise choice over their preferred 'mode of pleasure'. When the magazine 'gets it right', it acts as a conduit to feeling, getting her ready to experience great sex:

> … thanks to magazines like *FW* you can decide during the day at work that tonight you will be guaranteed an orgasm, and actually do it. (Letter 2)

For Julie, an orgasm is something that can be planned and prepared for, facilitated by sexually explicit material:

> I often use *FW* as a turn on for masturbation or as a prelude for sex. Sometimes before going out for an evening I will look through some mags until I become excited, this can often leave me sexually aroused for several hours, and if my date does not go as planned, I still have my magazines when I get home! (Letter 3)

FW's status as a conduit to feeling is further emphasized in her description of what constitutes a good story:

> A good erotic story must have sex, reading it you should become aroused and be able to feel the exact same needs and sexual desires as the characters you are reading about. Their needs become your needs, and when they are satisfied, hopefully you enjoyed the story too!!! It must include the kind of realistic sex we have, a wet pussy, a hard cock, erect nipples and uncontrolled spurting come etc etc. I dislike a 'figure it out for yourself' story. (Letter 3)

For Julie there should be a directness, the story should include frank descriptions of sexual behaviour and pleasure in such a way that the reader can 'feel' the story as much as read it. The pleasures made available are not just cerebral but must be felt in the body too and in describing its realism she uses, what could be termed, the language of pornography: 'wet pussy… uncontrolled spurting come'. The story must be explicit but at the same time it should be 'true to life'. By dispensing with the veiled descriptions of male hardness and female softness so beloved of the romance genre, or the sophisticated language of the literary erotic text, the ideal *FW* fiction is unambiguous in its relation of the sex act. It is not creating a fantasy world of wonderful sexual couplings but a realistic portrayal of the physicality of sexual intercourse. Julie wants to read that the subjects of a story are aroused, that their bodies are responding and she wants this to be clear and indisputable: she 'dislike[s] a "figure it out for yourself" story'. The description should be straightforward enough that if the heroine's nipples are erect that is what she wants to understand quickly and directly.

Julie valued those elements of the magazine which allow her to expand her sexual horizons while at the same time maintaining links with her own experiences as a woman. So each feature is weighed and appraised for its continuance or enhancement of her access to discussions or understandings of sex. The gradual removal of various features of the magazine leads to it being less able to offer sharing. Sharing established Julie's place within a community of women who were sexually active and readers of *FW*; that community was most clearly articulated in her criticism of *FW*'s failure to deliver it:

> *FW* is a lot less interactive now, it's sort of just there, take it or leave it, there is no real sharing of information or ideas anymore, and there is no feedback from the readers. I did consider that the readers contributed as much (if not more) than the people who produced the magazine. It was easy in the past to have a feeling for, and about, the sort of people who read *FW* but now its much more difficult. It really does not serve the same purpose, it was like a bond between women via their sexuality and their sexual interests, now it seems to have lost all that. (Letter 27)

This quotation is an important statement of Julie's rights over the magazine – she has invested a lot of time in the magazine because it offered a bond between women. Sex and reading *FW* are important features of Julie's life and this leads us to the final requirement of her ideal: it must recognize that sexual activity is a constituent part of a woman's experience, that her sexuality is significant to, and inseparable from, her sense of self. Therein lies the transformative potential of the ideal.

That orientation to the magazine carries over into her reading of its nude imagery. Their models must not hold something back but often they don't show sexual feeling as her experience tells her it could be. On one level this is about equality:

> Men's magazines show women in every imaginable pose, including legs wide open and close up crotch shots, we should see men in these poses in *FW*, showing their pride and joy standing to attention, more bum shots too.
>
> The only place men and women are shown with the same degree of openness sexually, is in hard core magazines or videos. These are the only places I know of where 'total exposure' is given regardless of sex. Everything is revealed in its natural (ERECT!) state. (Answers to original questionnaire – letter 2)

But it also points to dissatisfaction with the superficial recreation of male arousal using men who are 'complete posers' (Letter 14). The idea of *FW* showing a *truth* is emphasized in her criticism of a set of photographs, *Fire & Ice* (Plate 9). Here she returns to her conception of 'naturalness' which again relates to a directness, the transparency of the image to represent sexual arousal:

> I really dislike whatever the photographer has done to give these photos the green and red colours. Also the use of light and shade, the human body is beautiful and does not need to be 'enhanced' in this way. This guy may have a very attractive body, I cannot tell from these photos. He does appear to have too much pubic hair, and a very small and unattractive penis, I've had bigger cocktail sausages!!! Photographed differently he could be very nice looking. (Letter 3)

Julie wants to see male bodies at the start of possible sexual arousal. The device of coloured filters gets in the way of seeing the 'real' body because he does not look as though he could be about to just naturally get aroused. At the same time she states that the 'facts' of his body are unattractive: his penis and pubic hair. This suggests that other kinds of enhancement would make him more attractive to her. That there is a contradiction here is evident and it appears to point to a dissatisfaction with the overt 'eroticization' of the male body using photographic devices, these serve to hide the 'reality' of sexual feeling and arousal.

Aesthetic judgement forms a part of her critique, for example, she says that she dislikes 'Black and white photos, poor quality photos, or photos where parts of the body are obscured' (Questionnaire). As she uses *FW* to 'develop ideas and fantasies' the use of clever or artistic techniques is a problem: 'I buy this magazine for sex, stimulation (and willies) and it did not provide any of these. In fact the men were almost all dressed in the photos, well at least they were not really naked.' (Letter 12) 'Dressing' the men in high-art references is problematic for Julie, the beauty of the male body is not so important as the 'naturalness' of what is represented. In order to imagine the model in *Fire & Ice* becoming aroused, to feel his weight and smell him as she described in the detailed account that opened this section, Julie would have to mediate these images, to look beyond the artistic conventions, strip those away and then begin to rebuild a narrative for herself. These images do not show 'natural' sexuality; they are of no interest to her.

Julie's principle of 'naturalness' applies to her viewing of the pictures, her reading of the stories, indeed her engagement with the magazine in toto and her relationship to me. That the principle crosses over into a variety of spaces indicates that 'naturalness' is not simply about 'fit' or suitability. Naturalness for Julie has nothing to do with 'Eden-like' naturalness; 'natural sex' for her does not mean one man/one woman, missionary position or only within marriage. It includes 'kinky sex', fantasy, masturbation, same-sex etc. Sexual desires have their own correct logic and requirements and provided an activity (any activity) leads to pleasure and positivity it does not need to be apologized for. 'Naturalness' is a key condition for Julie finding *FW*'s images exciting: it enables her to imagine the model becoming aroused and thereby provides the means of her own arousal. Julie's rules for viewing: that the picture must be explicit and detailed, must be pleasing but not arty, are indications of a socially generated viewing strategy. My 'reading' of *FW*'s nude images is based on the principles implicit in this enthusiastic reader's reponses and uses of those images.

Marvelling at the Male Body

Clearly the proposition that men's bodies cannot be sex objects or the subject of a female gaze is problematic to my argument here, but it is not wishful thinking on my part to argue that representations of the male body are available to women for sexual or other uses. As Julie's account shows, some women certainly have a sexual response to images of men. The difficulty lies in attempting to understand those responses within theoretical frameworks that dispute the existence of such responses or the possibility that mass-produced imagery invites them. Suzanne Moore's (1988) 'Here's Looking at You Kid!' offers some suggestive observations on the emergence of a set of visual characteristics presenting the male body to female viewers. Moore identifies the 'zooming in on male flesh' in the late 1980s and suggests that it is the rise of gay culture and a growing acceptance of homoerotic imagery that made a space for a female gaze possible. Unfortunately, Moore returns to the abstractions of psychoanalytic accounts of the male/female gaze in order to examine the links between individual cultural forms:

> What many of these new images of men do is to leave a gap for the female spectator to occupy, a position sometimes within the frame of the picture, sometimes outside it; sometimes active, sometimes passive. (1988: 56)

How these gaps are experienced, how the positions inside and outside of the frame are made possible and, perhaps more importantly, how individual women might discriminate between different objects of pleasure and desire is not explained. Although Moore poses more questions than she answers, her account draws attention to the opening up of various sites and sights within intersecting areas of popular culture, the development of a range of visual vocabularies centring on the male body which facilitate the idea of an erotic address to heterosexual women. A number of commentators, academic and professional, have located the emergence of that new visual vocabulary of the male in the Levis' advertising of the mid 1980s centred on the sexual possibilities of the male body (Mort 1988).

The new 'visual codings of masculinity'(Nixon 1996: 125) surfaced across a variety of media forms: from the popular range of posters, cards and calendars in the high-street chain Athena, to television advertisements and the rise of the men's magazine. Mort details the crossover of competing discourses, academic, radical and more populist, into visual representations which played with the idea of masculinity as a performance rather than a set of biological attributes. Cutting edge magazines like *The Face* showed the influence of gay culture and the possibilities of homoerotism[12] attempting a 'deliberate strategy of disruption' (Mort 1996: 73). Mort identifies a variety of interests cohering round the figure of the male which find their echoes in visual vocabularies and the development of 'communities of style'. In attempting to speak to a range of male consumers there was an explosion of imagery of the male – some of it drawing very explicitly on gay visual codings, some less so. Mort observes that

> …the cultures of sexual dissidence left their mark on more normalising images of men during the period … consumer culture involved an elaborate series of negotiations between homosocial and heterosocial accounts of the male self. (1996: 71)

Thus the commercial priorities of consumer markets are seen as key to understanding the visual explorations of the male body of the 1980s and early 90s. The once-burgeoning teenage market was perceived to be in decline and other key sectors had reached stalemate: the style press, although talking directly to a minority of men, appeared to offer ways of tapping into a highly volatile but lucrative market sector. Interestingly in these accounts of commercially driven exploration, women rarely feature – certainly not as the targets of these new images of men. Yet, at the same time, art exhibitions attempted to subvert the conventions of heterosexual masculine imagery: *What She Wants* (1994), *Women's Images of Men* (1985) and *Behold the Male* (1988) made their contributions to the development of visual vocabularies. These vocabularies also crossed over into television and film as well as entertainments based purely on the spectacle of the male body: witnessed by the advent of the male stripper and groups like *London Knights*, *Chippendales* and *Dreamboys*. These entertainments took the figure of the new man and added an overtly sexual appeal to women audiences. The sexy male body for women had arrived.

That consumer culture took a lead in the creation and circulation of 'sexy man' images has proved problematic to some observers. Kenneth MacKinnon's (1997) study of the erotic male sees the explosion of sexualized imagery for women as a reassertion of the dominant system precisely because of its articulation to capital. MacKinnon weighs the nature, formations and histories of the male erotic object drawing attention to the many and various sites of cultural representation where he is to be found. He concedes that these representations cannot refuse their erotic dimensions and that Mulvey's (1976) contention that 'the male figure cannot bear the burden of sexual objectification' needs qualification. However, as his title, *Uneasy Pleasures*, suggests, the presence of women's interactions with erotic media is not sufficient to allow MacKinnon to move beyond the reaffirmation of the power dynamics of representation. In other words, while his history moves across a very extensive range of popular culture formats, his analysis returns time and again to the phallus and the reiteration of the 'dominant system' whereby men look and women appear.

That system may not, in fact, be as resilient as MacKinnon asserts. In a much earlier exploration of the then very recent phenomenon of attractive men in advertisements, Carter cautions us against assuming fixity in gender relations, suggesting that

> to theorise commodity production as merely the replication of what is reinforces the tendency to formalise significant *change* into structural repetition (original italics) (1985: 107).

While acknowledging the capitalist origins of eroticized male imagery, Carter observes that 'what we are witnessing is still very much a tendency in process and it would be unwise to claim that we can already fully grasp it, or confidently predict its eventual destination' (1985: 111). Remaining alert to capitalism's role in the production of sexual images, should not mean the immediate measurements of commodification or the supposed repetitiveness and regressive effects of sexual imagery. Such enquiries ignore how and why people, in this case women, enjoy these performances, limiting these experiences to 'cheap thrills' in the service of bad influences. MacKinnon suggests that such representations have only made 'concessions' to a female spectator: 'they make voyeurism serve the interests of an improved sex life for a male-female couple or offer higher production values and better-looking male porn actors, or create an illusion of greater equality by having the woman sex partner on top!' (1997: 127). His emphasis on the structuring of the gaze concedes the presence of a female spectator because of the sheer number of images of men. It is only the commercial imperative to 'mask' male dominance which allows a voyeuristic space for women.

The Routine Spectacle of the Male Body

There are, however, other ways of conceptualizing viewing and here I want to draw on Paul McDonald's suggestion that representations of male bodies in music video have 'routinised the erotic spectacle of the male body' such that it is now 'one of the common signifiers of contemporary consumer culture' (1997: 280–1) Rather than see images of men for women as an aberration or an example of the commodified appropriation of female sexuality, they are participants in specific experiential communities – they offer particular ways of belonging to groups whose interests lie in music and video representations of that music. The point then is not to suggest that there are no disruptions of gendered conventions of looking, quite clearly there are and the pleasures of those disruptions may be amongst the possibilities explicitly offered to viewers by images of men. But the significance lies in the ways in which women experience and respond to those possibilities. Puzzled concern is a standard response to women's laughter at male strip shows (Chappell 1991; MacKinnon 1997) – as if there is no way of understanding those performances (whether on screen, stage or page) as engaging viewers, speaking to their desires, dreams and fantasies and how those make sense in women's wider experience. McDonald observes 'To concentrate on the body as an object presented in a structure of looking leads to a reading of the body as a static signifier. Reading the body as a performing body requires viewing the body as a source of action and movement' which allows us to see that the body produces 'meanings which are not contained in words but are specifically shown in physical terms' (1997: 281).

This suggestion moves beyond the conception of the body as a signifier of meanings to a more fluid notion of it offering imaginative experiences. Those experiences are cognitive in that viewers recognize the conventions and understand the performance of the body in terms of, for example, its music video-ness or its resemblance to, or difference from, other performances in video; those experiences are also affective, the performance invites emotional responses. In attempting to show how the male body in performance is not conforming to phallic power, McDonald explains 'the transformation of the body in its presentation and performance produces different ways of being male' (1997: 283). This framework avoids the reductionist account of the male body as phallus and allows for the understanding of female pleasure, the pleasure of the viewer, as arising from the presentation of a specifically *erotic* maleness. Where it has been shown that phallic power is not a part of the image, theorization has fallen back on the notion of the castrated or feminized male body. But as McDonald suggests, what is at stake is not the revelation of the male body

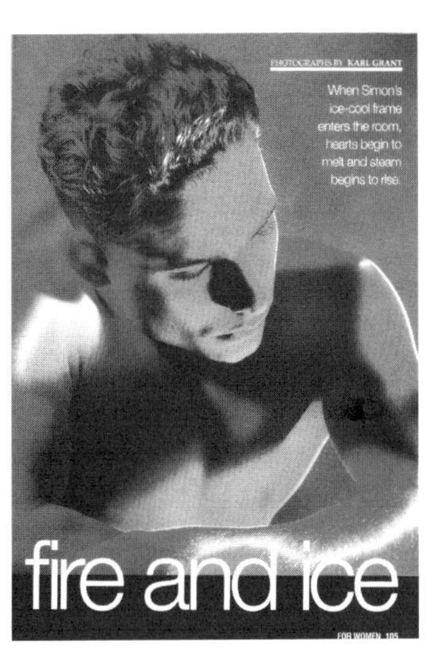
PHOTOGRAPHS BY KARL GRANT
When Simon's ice-cool frame enters the room, hearts begin to melt and steam begins to rise.
fire and ice
FOR WOMEN 105

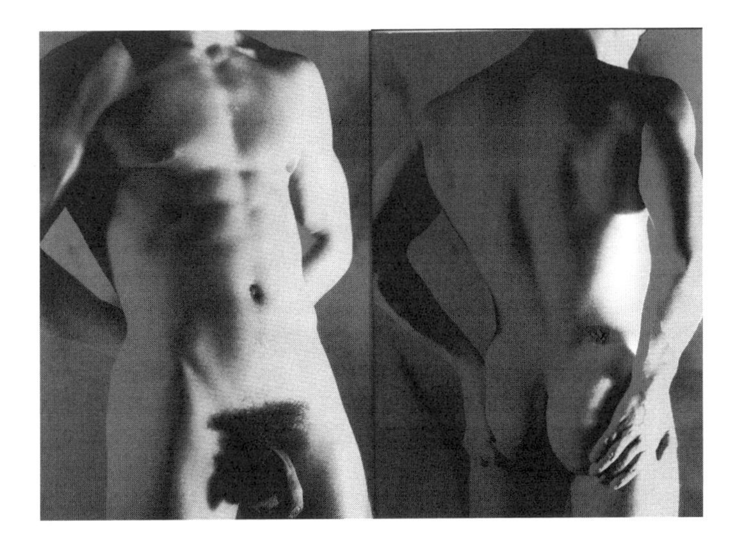

fire and ice
110 FOR WOMEN

Plate 9. *Fire & Ice* – the photoset Julie disliked.

Plate 10. 'Story-ed' Striptease.

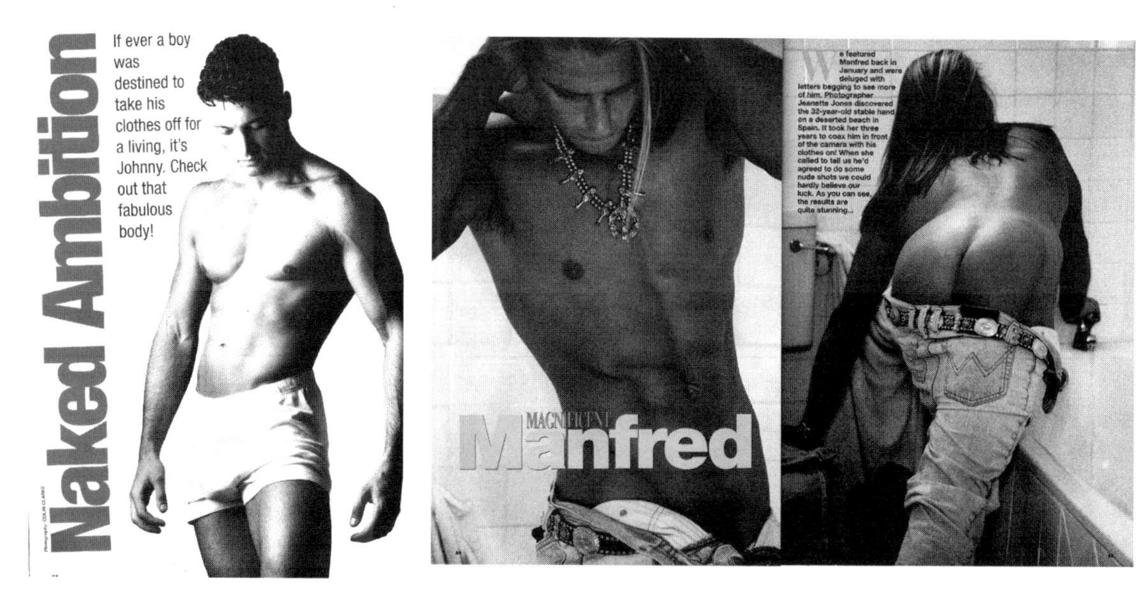

Plate 11. The pin up shots.

EXCLUSIVE PICTURES BY JEFF KAINE

Chris Lewis

Cricket hero Chris Lewis is the hot-shot of the England team, but he still found time to get his kit off for the girls. "I'm proud of my body," says 6'3" Chris, "especially my long, toned legs." He regularly bowls maidens over, but thinks that, at 25, he's too young to settle down. "I'm doing some fieldwork – finding out what I like in a woman," he says. In the meantime, these pics are enough to make a girl follow cricket. "I'm sure I've improved the image of cricketers. We're not all boring – we can be dead racy, too," laughs Chris.

Plate 12. The star strip – the *FW* team found it very difficult to persuade stars to pose.

Plate 13. 'Real Men' or Chubby Hubbies were much less inhibited.

100% real men

Don't know about a stairway to heaven, but DAVE, top, isn't a bit shy about exposing his todger.

The Lake District is heaving with tasty geezers - RICHARD, 24 is just one of them.

MAN WITH NO NAME - (left). Unfortunately, this lovely chap's name and address have gone astray, but he looks so cute we just had to include him.

Fit and fabulous, MICK show us what he's made of (right).

FOR WOMEN

63

Plate 14. Seizing the right to look ... Locker Room Lust.

LOCKER ROOM
LUST

There's something rather tantalising about a muscle-bound, finely-tuned male body stretching and pumping through an energetic workout, then relaxing afterwards under a long, hot shower. That's why we thought you'd enjoy these pics of sexy Simon Cotton.

PHOTOGRAPHS BY
COLIN CLARKE

You may have spotted Simon and the rest of his group, Climax, on the *James Whale* show a month ago. Climax, we think, was the operative word. How many television tubes popped that night? We're not telling...

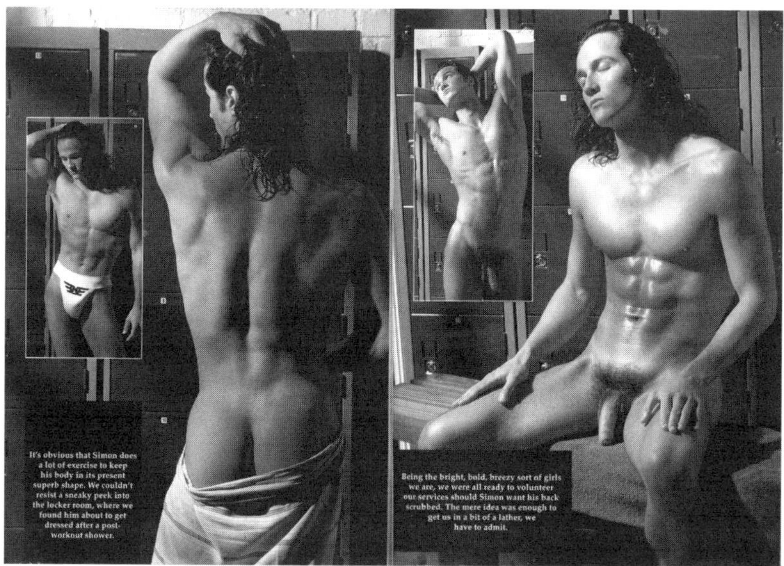
It's obvious that Simon does a lot of exercise to keep his body in its present superb shape. We couldn't resist a sneaky peek into the locker room, where we found him about to get dressed after a post-workout shower.
Being the bright, bold, breezy sort of girls we are, we were all ready to volunteer our services should Simon want his back scrubbed. The mere idea was enough to get us in a bit of a lather, we have to admit.

The necessity for exercise is the bane of many a girl's life, but we're all convinced that we'd be far more enthusiastic about our trips to the gym if we could only count on finding someone like Simon to do press-ups with. Don't you agree?

and its phallic or feminized signification but the body's performance of being 'male' in particular ways through dance and the performance of male desire and desirability. In pop videos spectacles of masculinity offer what McDonald calls the 'yearning mode': 'where the arching, stretching, praying and wistful looks of the boys [*Take That*], present and perform the romantic "problem" sung about in the lyrics. As the lyrics speak of emotional pain, the bodies of the boys are given and move in ways that show the body as suffering. The presentation and performance of the body in the yearning mode therefore signifies romantic loss as embodied sentiment.' (1997: 284)

This may not seem like a major step away from the suggestion that male bodies have been used throughout history to represent the human ideal,[13] however, the difference lies in the acknowledgement of the expressiveness and invitations to the viewer offered by such representations. So, in the analysis which follows, I draw from Julie's explanation of her 'process' of becoming aroused and incorporate MacDonald's conception of the performance and amplification of sexual emotion through the male body.

A key convention of *For Women*'s photographs is the fierce colour contrast between body and background: the body is lit or flashed in order to make the edges very sharp. In studio shots, the body is lit from the side with reflectors so that it has a more three-dimensional appearance. Key lighting enhances shadows and many of the images make use of chiaroscuro, light and shadow, in order to emphasize the planes and curves of the body. In other words, in most of the images, the body is absolutely prominent. As we have already seen, this was a particularly important feature for Jane's approval of an image. In outdoor and interior shots the use of low point of view and shallow depth of field work to blur the background or render it secondary. Borrowing from modernist photography's attempts to ensure the 'truthfulness' of the image, 'painterly' and 'artistic' flourishes and manipulation were avoided. Modernist conventions of fragmentation and repetition were also employed with alternations between torso shots and full body including the head and/or face. Some of the photosets mimic fashion shoots in their use of locations, accessories, poses and body styles including tanned and sculpted bodies. Settings and accessories often contribute to the possibility of storytelling referenced in the titles given to an individual photoset, for example, *Home Coming; Masterpiece; Overall Appeal* (Plates 10 and 11). Titles and captions sometimes indicate the narrative possibilities of the exotic via the ethnic/cultural origins of the model, for example, *Sittin' on the Dock of the Bay; Italian Job; Jungle Fever*.

Central to my argument here is the appearance of the images in *FW* as sets. In other descriptions of porn's photographic imagery there is a tendency to isolate individual images from the published groups. *FW* presents its readers with photosets structured to suggest at least a very loosely defined narrative rather than just a series of individual photographs: this is a trope of pornographic imagery, it is what distinguishes the photographic presentations of a porn magazine from the individualized pin-up. Analysis must acknowledge this. The only way to begin to understand the ways in which *FW*'s images work is to recognize the intratextuality of the photosets: the relationships of the individual image to the whole.[14] The grouping may facilitate a 'narrative' but this may not be so developed as to 'tell a story'. For example, the December 1993 issue features *Home Coming*, a series of ten photographs based around the theme of a GI returning home at Christmas – he is carrying presents – and removing his uniform. This 'story' is very obviously there; others may be less so with only a loose patterning recognizable as a striptease, as in January 1994's *Rough, Tough and Blue* with the model in blue jeans undressing in all but one of the images. The images are both intra- and inter-textual. Alongside their references to other images in popular culture, they are also intratextual – playing off each other. It is perfectly possible to find images in *FW* illustrating the representation of male sexuality as centred on power, sexual aggression, physical strength, masculine certainty etc. It would also be possible to uncover illustrations of passivity, masculine fragility and emotion. The relationship between individual shots in the photosets offers ways of viewing the same body from different perspectives: perhaps a celebration of muscular hardness but also an invitation to imagine the sensitivity and sensuousness of the body. Each photoset includes various views of the male and masculinity as active and passive, aggressive and calm, strong and fragile. Within their own six- or eight-page frames the photosets proffer a display of a male body in contrasting, embellishing and/or elaborating poses which are also complemented intertextually across the rest of the magazine.

Locker Room Lust

This 'playing off' of different images intended as a collection can be seen in the *Locker Room Lust* photoset reproduced here (Plate 14). This photoset appeared in the first issue of the magazine. It consists of six colour pages of ten photographs: three full page, one double page and six smaller insets. The scenario offers viewers the opportunity to sneak up on the unsuspecting Simon in the gym changing room:

> It's obvious that Simon does a lot of exercise to keep his body in its present superb shape. We couldn't resist a sneaky peak into the locker room, where we found him about to get dressed after a post-workout shower.

The caption offers a justification for looking: Simon is a perfect body to look at, he is irresistible. We learn that he performs with a group called *Climax* so he is used to an audience; in this scenario he is theoretically unaware of the camera so that his performance is a private one, just for *FW* readers. Simon's focus is on himself and his stretching and posing appears for his own pleasure. In keeping with the post-exercise *mise-en-scène*, this is not necessarily a narcissistic pleasure: his facial expressions suggest a serene satisfaction with the 'workings' of his body, a post-workout glow, suggestive of the spirituality of the perfect body in high-art traditions.

Many of the poses do reference classical art, especially sculptural forms: the emphasis on light and shade, the muscularity of the body, the introversion, the achievement of the perfect human form. And some of the poses are very 'feminized' with hands on hip and his hair swept up behind his head. The musculature of the stomach, huge shoulders, almost clenched fists and the ever-present backdrop of the male locker room counterbalance the feminine elements. The focus of the photographs changes from one to another: the muscularity of his chest, followed by a shot of the back, his pecs to the washboard stomach and his penis. The references to the exercise regime and superb shape amplify the vision before the viewer in that there is a constant reminder of the physique: as if to say 'Look at this body, it has been straining, stretching, exercising. Isn't it lovely?' His body is not an aggressively powerful one, moreover it is a body at rest – we're invited to imagine it engaging in exercise but that is not in front of us now: Simon is relaxing. Viewers are invited to look as long as they like and, as he is supposed not to know they are here, he will make no effort to cover up or prevent the show. Other body signs like the absence of body hair emphasize the smoothness, the musculature, and the sculptural form of the body. Subdued lighting and close range shots suggest an intimacy not available in more 'public' performances of male nudity. The final photograph of the set features a supine Simon, his muscles are relaxed, one shoulder is prominent and his head is thrown back slightly and towards this shoulder. The other arm rests on his bent knee and the body is half-turned to camera. Simon looks out at us. This look may or may not be challenging, the captions have told us that he performs striptease for women – it is inconceivable that he would challenge our viewing him now.

The first point to note is that there is a movement, a pacing of these images, large image followed by small image, by large and so on. These offer different views of the male body personalized through the use of captions and a bare-bones narrative. As with the pacing, the alternation of tensed muscle by relaxed pose is important to actually bringing the body alive: giving it a sense of movement. This is further enhanced by the use of light and shade which contributes to the invitation to enjoy the body in front of us. The tactile nature of the body is emphasized in these images, the bronzing effect of the lighting, the shine on the skin, the hairlessness of the chest, arms, legs and back add to the soft yet sculptural appearance of Simon's body. This idea of touching Simon's body is at odds with the images which all suggest his solitude, but it includes viewers in appreciation of his body and allows the idea of the body on display as there to be touched, as more than an image. This sets up the question, 'what would it be like to touch him? How would his skin feel?', addressing viewers' imaginations and their bodies.

The pin-ups in *FW* draw on 'equal opportunities', that women should have the right to look but it is clear that prior to the 'cover-up' in 1995 that the magazine thought this was a battle that was more than halfway won. For the magazine, women look and they want to see more. The sexual possibilities of male figures for women were almost taken for granted. The photosets are surrounded by articles and images in the magazine which contribute to the apparent 'reasonableness' of reading a sexually explicit magazine for women. Thus in *Locker Room Lust*, the captions, which introduce Simon as a member of *Climax* strip group, invite viewers to take a particular orientation to his image but offer no apologies for looking. How far viewers join in is not a matter of persuading them they *can* look: rather it is dependent upon how much investment they have in the 'female sexual culture' on offer. In offering Simon's body, *FW* is able to take us (viewers) where others fear to tread, the captions tell us the magazine has sneaked us into the locker room and invites us to enjoy Simon because

> Being the bright, bold, breezy sort of girls we are, we were all ready to volunteer our services should Simon want his back scrubbed. The mere idea was enough to get us in a bit of a lather, we have to admit.

The 'we' obviously refers to the 'girls' at the magazine and also introduces the idea of others who might not want to look at Simon. If it takes a 'bright, bold, breezy sort of girl' to appreciate his good looks and body, those who would rather not look are obviously not *FW* girls. When they 'admit' to getting in a bit of a lather, viewers are invited to empathize, not condemn. The last caption pulls the viewer in more explicitly by posing a question:

> The necessity for exercise is the bane of many a girl's life, but we're all convinced that we'd be far more enthusiastic about our trips to the gym if we could count on finding someone like Simon to do press-ups with. Don't you agree?

Again, an invitation to imagine being with Simon, and once again the gossipy tone is used along with a double entendre on press-ups to introduce the idea of a sexual interaction with Simon. The question highlights a number of assumptions: viewers are female (we girls), heterosexual and have an interest in men like Simon; more importantly, they are also comfortable with the idea of looking at men.

The text does two things with the issue of the display of the male body: by emphasizing Simon's role in *Climax* we are assured that it is normal for him to be seen naked and for us to look. It also suggests that we are being allowed to see something different, something unique about Simon. The display is at one and the same time public and private. Simon is employed as a male performer, a strip artist, so he is used to undressing for an audience but by the emphasis on sneaking into the locker room we have a sense of this being entirely different from his more usual stage performance. This is a private event: within the captioned narrative of the photographs, Simon is 'unaware' of us and therefore we are seeing more than his stage persona would allow. *FW* is able to show us the side of Simon which is not available publicly: the images offer the ordinary and the transgressive. In the images of *Locker Room Lust*, women's right to look hardly needs to be spoken: it is implied through the personalized captions. Viewers are addressed as an obvious and shared community, although not everyone is included: only bold and bright and breezy girls will see Simon's loveliness. But in asserting the naturalness of looking, these images seize and challenge the idea that women cannot look and in doing that they have an impact on other attempts to look. In taking up the invitation to view, women make these images theirs and make demands of them.

Conventional accounts of viewing would suggest that female viewers are incapable of this seizure. Dyer's idea of instability in the nude male image partly rests on the claim that eye contact is one of the main difficulties for the nude male and in the model's refusal to make eye contact is a refusal to acknowledge the viewer. Where women avert their eyes as a sign of modesty, men appear to have better things to look at. In so doing, the male model also fractures the idea that the image is an address to female sexuality: instead the image is merely an indication of the complexities of constructions of *male* sexuality. To refute this claim, it is not sufficient to simply draw attention to the frequency with which eye contact occurs within the magazine, instead, the *meaning* of eye contact needs examination.

As Dyer acknowledges, eye contact has no singular meaning, 'it is not a question of whether or not the model looks at his spectator(s) but how he does or does not' (1992: 104). Within gay culture, for example, looking has very particular significances (Mort 1996) understood as expressive of a range of emotions and sexual feelings, which are culturally and historically specific. As the male body has become more accessible to female viewers the understandings of the averted eyes have changed too. The models' full-on stare, the looking up and looking off are not necessarily, and always, disavowals of the fact of being looked at. As Dutton suggests, they give permission to view 'his body in more exclusively objective terms – literally as an *object* – without the suggestion of active sexual desire (and particularly sexual dominance) on his part' (1995: 341).

Dutton's suggestion relates specifically to bodybuilders' bodies and the possibilities of looking not predicated on overtly sexual feeling, his comments are a useful reminder that there may be a variety of expectations in looking at the body. The 'objective' look Dutton writes of has at least two components – to look at the built body as an object references its being interesting, of being the object of curiosity. It means that this particular body can be understood in terms of the work done to achieve it, what a built body looks like – its muscle formation, the veining etc. This body can also be looked on as a sexual body, sexed and/or sexy. It highlights the necessity for understanding 'objectification' as multi-faceted – that is, recognizing that the objects in images offer very different invitations to their viewers. This is not to simply reiterate that 'signs' are capable of different readings but to recognize that photographs and what they represent invite us to make sense of them in different ways. The status of the truth claim of photography is dependent upon the kind of photograph being looked at. Newspaper photographs offer very different 'truth claims' to fashion photography and as viewers we take up their invitations to 'believe' them differently. For some theorists, it is simply the presence of a woman that confirms the status of the photography, as Pollock commented regarding advertising. This truncates the making sense process to recognition of gender, we recognize an advertisement simply because a woman is present, how then do we assess an advert which features a man or just a cigarette packet? We recognize adverts by a variety of means, not least the positioning on the page, the place we find it or in the case of cigarette advertising, the presence of the government health warning.[15]

Dyer suggests that 'male pin-ups notoriously don't "work" for women' (1992: 109) because of their representations of heterosexist power differentials. Dyer's examples of the 'refusing male' are the *Playgirl* centrefold, a publicity shot of Paul Newman and a coverboy from *Oh Boy!* magazine. As he points out, each of these avoids eye contact in different ways: Newman, for example, looks beyond the camera benignly. What is missing from this account is the sense of distinct 'purposes', uses and contexts for these images. The denial of the fact of being looked at, here identified as a feature of most images of men, supposedly contributes to the continuing delineation of masculinity as powerful and denies women the right to look. The core issue is the claim that 'eye contact' eliminates the photographicness of the image. If there is eye contact it seems as if we are no longer looking at an image of Newman, we are looking at a totem of Newman, inscribed with power. This is perhaps a result of the conflation in psychoanalytic writing between the optical point of view in cinema and viewers' point of view, with, again, the notion that this produces a forced identification (as, for example, in Dworkinite claims of the objectification of women through the male viewer's supposed identification with the camera). But the Newman image (a black-and-white studio shot) was not produced in order to replicate 'masculinity' but presumably to send to fans of his films or to casting directors.[16] In other words, there is a historical and cultural specificity to this image lost in an account which privileges eye contact. But accounts of women viewing men are consistently ahistorical, seeking to confirm that female sexuality is not as body or nudity obsessed as male sexuality: for example, three decades ago, Mark Gabor made the following claim which continues to make its presence felt in discussions of women and girls' engagement with pop and film stars:

> Women tend to fantasise about them [movie stars] ... Yet, through nature or nurture, women generally are not inclined to isolate flesh – the nude male body – from the rest of their fantasies with men, as men do with their pin-up girls. It is likely that, for emotional excitation, women do not need to see the nude or semi-nude male pin-ups. Thus, most pin-ups of Hollywood film heroes are portraits or action shots of fully-dressed leading men rather than figure studies... (1972: 162)

Women's responses are supposedly based on the emotional appeal of the star, not his physical appearance, it is as if women never judged a book by its cover. To look at the display of the male body in a magazine like *For Women* is to engage with a set of proposals about the male body, of its ability to represent and perform sexual feeling, physical and emotional and to enable a sense of sexual presence and possibility. The problem with accounts which stress the assertion of masculine power in the image is that they look beyond what is in the image to the fact of 'male-ness' beneath – it is an image of a man therefore it cannot be anything other than an expression of innate manliness.

The description of Julie's responses to the images in *FW* suggests that eye contact is not *the* factor which determines the possibilities of sexual excitement in viewing the nude model. Indeed, eye contact is only important as a part of the conditions under which photographs can become a turn-on. I have used Julie as an exemplar of a viewing strategy that enables sexual response to the magazine. This viewing strategy is not uniformly positive in its response to images in *FW*; it is an appraising position that requires that certain conditions for enjoyment must be met if an image is to work. For example, Julie's response to a set of pictures entitled *Sun, Sea and Sand* from vol.1 issue 4, moves through his physical features and poses to an assessment of the 'naturalness' of the image.

> Clarissa I like his penis! I think it is a very interesting looking – er, instrument, particularly in the centre spread. His penis appears quite long and the pink glans is very attractive. I like his body its smooth with just the right amount of body hair, and not too much muscle. His face however is a let down, he looks quite sour. I dislike his pose on page 44 and 48/49, they don't look natural.

There are two linked conditions at work in Julie's account: firstly, the ideology of 'naturalness', a complex array of ideas centred around the exploration of sexual possibilities. *For Women* allows for that exploration when it maintains its distinctiveness from other women's magazines. The articles, stories and confessions are all a part of this, indeed they guarantee the distinction: the magazine presents a world of sex which references, reflects and comments upon significant issues for Julie's own perceptions of herself, sexual relations and interactions. 'Naturalness' demands that sexual desires have their own logic and requirements and that provided those lead to pleasure and positivity, there can be nothing wrong. Sexual desire is not an offshoot of, or subservient to, anything other than its own drives. It has its own story forms and thus a good photoset will have its own story form, making possible for Julie the second of her conditions. Photographs must be like the starts of narratives of sexual activity – he must look like he is about to get aroused, in that way she can bring together all of her senses to an imagining of a sexual interaction between them.

When women consume sexually explicit images they may of course be presented with hegemonic constructions of male sexuality as hard, thrusting, muscle-bound, but they also disrupt the idea that there is an order to viewing. The ambiguities of that order are highlighted in women's possession of images of men's bodies, at times very explicitly. The forms of social control which would keep the male body hidden are exposed as soon as the embargo on erections was invoked: publicizing the gender politics of sexual representations in the UK. As we've seen, readers exclaimed at the unfairness of the rules of representation as 'outdated' in their attempt to 'protect' women. They made explicit links to the politics of this regulation and to the ways in which this impacted on their own sense of being autonomous sexual subjects. In this sense, the pictures serve a subversive purpose for readers and as they lay claim to the right to see sexualized images, they also claim the prerogative of articulating their own desires and interests in those images. I've suggested the images in *FW* should be understood as offering viewers performances and amplifications of sexual feeling through the male body and that these are a part of a changing vocabulary of sexual representation whose significance is still being felt in the increasing address to female sexual consumers. That analysis arose out of attention to the responses of Julie, an enthusiastic reader, whose own account indicated the nature and form of her pleasures in *FW* as a pornographic text and the development of her own languages of appraisal and rights. The following chapter explores the magazine's fiction and continues the exploration of the conditions under which *FW* enabled women to pursue their interests in sexual communications.

Notes

1. As I suggested in chapter 3, the accusation of being 'really for gay men' was frequently offered as a challenge to the magazine's right to speak to and for women.
2. Page 7 fellas, members of the Chippendales, Climax and London Knights and models from 'sexy' videos have all made appearances.
3. Black stars were apparently much easier to persuade than their white counterparts. In a set of pictures taken at Hendon Football Club – only the black players on the team were willing to show their faces *and* penises in the same shot.
4. Barcan suggests this might be changing. Homie porn features male nudes as well as female and that the male amateur models get a lot of pleasure out of posing for pictures: 'The Home Blokes editor repeated how much men loved showing off their penis, often lamenting the censorship rules that prevent them from showing it in all its glory: "A lot of them ring up and complain. 'You oughta see it when it's *really* up!'" According to the editors, men rarely regret the experience, while women sometimes do.' (Barcan 2005: 266)
5. These comments conveniently ignored the proliferation of male strippers; nude pop stars in their music videos; the increasing visibility of the heroes' buttocks in Hollywood films and Page 7 fellas in daily newspapers.
6. The 1980s had seen a rise in advertising imagery focused on men's products and sold via images of men rather than women. Sean Nixon (1996: 125) describes a 'regime of "new man" imagery' as 'a specific set of visual codings of masculinity deployed in targeting new male consumers.' Mort (1996: 15) suggests the 'hybrid character' New Man probably reached the mainstream with the launch of the Launderette advertisement for Levi's in 1985.
7. Kenneth MacKinnon's *Uneasy Pleasures* is an exception being a book-length study – I address his work later in this chapter.
8. This is also true of much film theory which has tended to emphasize the 'spectator' over individual viewers. Recent research has begun to address specific audiences in order to investigate actual responses to films: for instance, Stacey (1993); Jacqueline Bobo (1995); Clover (1992); Hill (1997); and Barker and Brooks (1998) have complicated the assumption that gender is the only important factor in viewing.
9. For example, Miriam Hansen describes how women were afforded 'the forbidden sight of male bodies in semi-nudity, engaged in intimate and intense physical action' (1991: 2) by the film version of *The Corbett-Fitzsimmons Fight* in 1897. From as early as 1926, Hollywood had cottoned on to the appeal of male bodies, offering Valentino's naked torso for the delight of women viewers.
10. In fact, I didn't reply promptly to that letter because I had just given birth!
11. It should be clear that Julie also expected this level of honesty from me too.
12. The influence of art photographers Mapplethorpe, Weber and Ritts can be seen in style and fashion magazines.
13. Rozsika Parker talking about the *Images of Men* exhibition: 'Men's bodies have never stood simply for sex, rather they have represented a wide spectrum of emotion and experience, from defeat to victory, from suffering to strength. Take a look at Kenneth

Clark's book *The Nude* and you'll find naked men in chapters on "Energy", "Pathos" and "Apollo"...' (1985: 221)

14. Jobling (1999) argues for a similar approach to fashion spreads.
15. Trevor Pateman argues formal analysis should be accompanied by a general theory of communication in order to understand the processes of recognition. 'How is understanding an advert possible?' in H. Davis & P. Walton (eds) (1983) *Language, Image, Media*, London: Blackwell, pp.187–204.
16. The specificity of the star persona is discussed in Medhurst's short essay on the differences between American and British male film stars. Asking why can't chaps be pin-ups, Medhurst draws attention to the ways in which the standard representations of individual British leading men so epitomized 'englishness' that sex appeal is simply wiped out. ('Can Chaps be Pin-ups: The British Male Film Star of the 1950s', Ten-8, No.17).

7

Emotional Vibrations and Physical Sensations: *For Women*'s Fiction

Alongside its nude images and detailed discussions of sex, *For Women* presented readers with one or more explicitly erotic stories per issue. The inclusion of fiction is unsurprising, women's magazines have traditionally included fiction, and women's pleasures in reading have been well documented. Moreover, when sexually explicit materials are considered, women are supposed to prefer words to pictures – as Faust has asserted:

> Women are less interested in epidermal friction than in emotional vibrations which, in any case, lend themselves more to words than pictures... The great romantic favourites had nary a penis between them, yet they encouraged women to identify with the heroines and imagine a relationship with the hero. (1980: 97)

Of necessity, I touch on those analyses of pornography that have claimed that particular manifestations of sexually explicit materials are gendered. Within that theoretical tradition, the codes and conventions of pornography are traced and mapped on to the male psyche. As previously discussed, some writers go so far as to claim that pornography is *only* capable of addressing the needs of male readers and viewers: the gendered disposition of the genre is somehow inviolate, impervious to women's interventions or use. There is little point in a further rehearsal here of themes and claims similar to those outlined in chapter 1, but I offer Faust's observations of pornographic narratives as emblematic of that tendency to dismiss porn fictions as simply addressing male sexual needs.

> The social and psychological components of sexual conduct have no place in pornography: flirtation, courtship, refusal, seduction, and even mundane activities like undressing and sleeping are all left out. The men are always potent, the women always willing. That is, the women are presented as approaching sexual

> activity in exactly the same way as men do, living up to masculine fantasies of the sexually assertive, instantly aroused, uninhibited woman, who never has a headache, never asks for affection ... [and] climaxes as easily as she is aroused. She is, in fact, a man in disguise. (1980: 19–20)

Her observations seem less satisfactory at this time given that women's magazines, novels,[1] films etc. often feature explicit details of 'epidermal friction' and, in the case of explicitly erotic stories, the heroine often does not end up with the hero even after simultaneous orgasm.[2] Faust's description of masculinity in disguise is also rather unconvincing: why should having headaches make pornography more female, and therefore better? Pornographic fiction is expected to accommodate all the problems of 'real life' in order to rise above criticism. But this form of 'reality' is only required of fictional forms which are considered 'low' (ironically, the romance has been accused of being 'unrealistic' along with other popular formulaic fictions like the detective novel).[3] The problems are located in the absence of the 'real' features of life, like the headache: absence supposedly constituting an intention to deceive. Absence equals denial. But one further claim issues from these absences – absence equals evidence that the pornographic story is not *authentically* female.

As Skordarki's (1991) experiences working for soft-core titles showed, the social and psychological components which Faust would like to see are those very themes which are often excised from the text in order to satisfy censors rather than a naturally occurring trope of pornography and its writers. But Faust's criticism is not necessarily countered by that evidence, because the form of social and psychological components she would accept as 'realistically female' would actually prevent the heroine of a story *engaging in sexual activity*. What is the purpose of the headache in this supposed better story? The question of realism is addressed later in this chapter; at this point I draw attention to the fact that the range of features considered relevant and more appropriate to female sexuality and a rounded exploration of sexual conduct is limited to those approved by the theorist. That women are presented as sexually assertive and willing in pornography is seen as a damning indictment of the form, but as Barker has observed about criticisms of romance and their inclusion of love:

> If we were to say of detective novels that they 'unfailingly' contain some perspective on crime and its discovery; or of science fiction that it always presented some view of other times and places, would we feel we had learnt much? [Regarding romances and love] we feel the condemnation, and a sense of something dubious having been perpetrated. Why? There is no answer. (1985: 147)

A central claim contra pornography is that it offers limited representations of women, reduced to their constituent body parts and the either/or subjectivities of Madonna/Whore (Beneke 1990; Dworkin 1981; Hardy 1998; Itzin 1992; Moye 1985). The narrowness of characterization, plot and the exaggerations of sexual prowess and anatomy are supposedly a clear indication of pornography's 'harmfulness' and, at the same time, of its unimportance as a form of human expression. Usually these claims are just claims, but one author has attempted to show how pornographic narratives work to remove women's subjectivity: Simon Hardy's study *The Reader, The Author, His Woman and Her Lover*. Because Hardy gives some page references and volume numbers for the materials he analyses, I have been able to assess his methods and conclusions.[4]

Misunderstanding the Woman and her Lover

In his analysis of the UK publication *Men Only*, Hardy uses the insights of radical feminism, concurring with its claim that the unequal power structure that is patriarchy is reflected, embellished and eroticized in representations of heterosexual activity in soft-core magazines. 'Since the fundamental unit of patriarchy is found in the relation between two people, it is easy to imagine how it can be reproduced, as a concept, through the medium of discourse' (1998: 76). Hardy proposes a more sophisticated account than that of the anti-pornography feminists by engaging with readers' accounts of their use of pornography. Thus his investigation proceeds on two levels: the text and its reception. Unlike many accounts of pornography, which take photographs as their primary source material, Hardy limits his analysis to *Men Only*'s stories because he suggests these are much less open to conflicting interpretations. The audience research is divided into two sections. First, he encouraged readers to describe their history of porn use and found that a narrative pattern emerges running from the accidental discovery and non-sexual use of porn as a teenager through to recognition, as an adult, of the difficulties in reconciling pornography and relationships with 'real' women. The second section attempted to get at readers' 'point-by-point interpretation of several scenarios as they unfolded' (1998: 116). Hardy gives interviewees a story to 'decode' and then their responses are further 'pushed' so that they would 'elaborate on the ideas in the text, especially those concerning the subjective state of the women characters' (1998: 135).[5] Hardy's intention here was

> ...to force a crisis of interpretation. Since it was very difficult for any reader to avoid the connotations of power or female submission which saturated the text there were only two ways of responding to the questions: the readers could either elaborate these connotations himself, uncritically reproducing the text's discourse in its own self-justifying terms, or he could qualify his interpretation by identifying the text as sexist discourse, as merely pornographic representation or rather misrepresentation. In short the reader could become either a critic or an advocate of the discourse in the text. (1998: 135)

Hardy maintains that it is impossible to miss the text's saturation in gender power and that readers can be assessed for their acceptance or refusal of it. However, I believe his analysis of the text is seriously flawed, both in terms of its form and of its modes of use (although that latter element cannot be explored here). Beginning with a focus on the 'discursive' construction of the Woman and her relationship with her Lover (1998: 77), his analysis of stories divides them into scenarios defined as 'discrete sexual interaction between two or more people' (1998: 77). Most scenarios have two phases, 'initiation and interaction': the first offers the preconditions for interaction – the woman must be desirable and willing. Hardy found two categories of willingness: the resisting (at first) virgin and the initiating nympho. Although these two may seem to be different, in fact their place in the scenarios is to confirm that all women want sex, some just need a little more persuasion than others. Hardy also finds that this 'willingness to engage in the sexual scenario is contingent only on her being overpowered within it. In a word, for the Woman of pornography, to be aroused is to be powerless and to be powerless is to be aroused.' (1998: 85)

Moving on to the Woman's interaction with the Lover, Hardy found verbal and physical gestures of male power. The Lover orders the Woman to remove clothing, threatens her with orgasm, sexual taunts and, of course, his Big Cock. These threats take the stories to the limits of the permissible with the constant reminder of the woman's consent there as a sop to critics.[6] This is the relationship based on the inequalities of gendered power: the Woman usually adopts poses that stress her passivity and the 'dirtiness' of the act. Her submission to male desire is completed in her 'animalistic' and 'orgiastic' pleasure: a vital feature of the scenarios, 'the sexual conquest of the woman also represents the conquest of the social self by natural essence.' (1998: 95)

Although its status is not made absolutely clear, Hardy uses 'scenario of degradation...as the basic unit of analysis' (1998: 77). Sometimes 'scenario of degradation' draws on the Dworkinite analysis of heterosex as inherently degrading for women: a theoretical and methodological position which issues a command to Hardy that any instance of sexual activity must be seen as 'damaging' to women. At the same time, Hardy is not willing to completely discount the possibility of sexual interactions based upon mutual desire so his scenarios of degradation are not simply that women are having sex with men,[7] but *how* they have sex. There is an inconsistency here, the theorization cannot allow women to freely choose sex, because it is demanded of them by the various social and political imperatives that construct and constitute institutional heterosexuality. If pornography is a major constituent of heterosexism there can be no 'authentic' expression of female sexuality within its pages. In addition, the theory also claims that pornography eroticizes sexual activity as pleasurable because of its links to power and women's inability to freely choose. The pleasure comes from seeing women submit. This insists the analyst must search for signs of women's submission to male sexuality as the only relevant indicators confirming pornography's reflection of the real state of male/female relations. If male sexuality is conceived as dominating and bullying, and pornography 'tells the truth' about that sexuality, there is no point in looking for any other signs within the text. They are simply distractions or, for example, where women claim to want sex, the disguising of real politics. We are on the horns of a particularly circular argument, which Hardy compounds by drawing on symbolic interactionism.

The methodological tools of symbolic interactionists enable Hardy to conceive 'sex scenes' as replications in print of *actual social relations*. This methodology, again only briefly spelt out, requires that the researcher look for gestures: the verbal, the physical and the visual appearance of the characters. 'These three categories of symbolic communication therefore become the three corresponding locations at which evidence of a power dichotomy within the scenarios can be sought.' (1998: 87) The following conclusions are drawn: the woman's verbal gestures are usually pleading in the face of the man's threats; her physical responses are 'forced' out of her in that she can't help but orgasm; and her appearance is submissive to the Big Cock and the effects of being fucked. Hardy divides the textual elements of *Men Only* into important and unimportant features. Comic elements fall into the unimportant while the fiction is given attention because Hardy accords it a different truth status. Jokes are jokes – often puerile – but Hardy suggests we don't need to worry about them. The stories, on the other hand, are the means by which some very unpleasant lies are told about women, masquerading as fictional realities. This happens because, despite the appearance of these stories as fictions, 'a reader witnesses a fictional interaction in much the same way that an ethnographer or indeed any observer would witness a live interaction.' Readers also 'suspend … the fact that the scenarios are representations of interactions rather than actual interactions' (1998: 86). This is an uneven process: at times the narrative context must fall away completely leaving in place the most important messages of the text:

> … such gestures are open to be read in their own terms and in isolation from the narrative context. While the sequence of the stories always clearly establishes the consent of the woman, the ripping of clothing perfectly expresses the paradigm of rape in synchronic terms, out of time, so that its eroticism is not undermined by prior consent. In short, the violent gesture delivers connotations of power that the reader can enjoy, with the mitigating context edited out in the process of interpretation. (1998: 91)

These are the important elements for interpretation: the truths being offered to men, with a 'truth' status different from those pertaining to the woman's consent. The reader's belief in women's consent to sex is put into abeyance by the pleasures of removing that consent in a textual situation. His work operates with a skewed notion of modality arising out of his emphases on 'truth telling' and 'meaning making'. Hardy's claim, based on anti-porn theorizing, is that the subordination of women in the sex act is the only distinguishable and important 'fact' of the story for readers. Long before the reader is introduced, Hardy is making claims about readers' motives and the influence of the text.

> It seems plausible that men's reasons for wanting to see women submit, which they must do if they keep on buying this type of mainstream porn, are entirely sexual. That is to say, female sexual submission is an end in itself and does not serve some sinister politics. The submissive role of women in these scenarios and within heterosexual eroticism more generally may simply serve to affirm their sexual availability and perhaps to punish them symbolically for the sexual frustrations of men. In short, subordination of the Woman within pornography probably reflects the genre's preoccupation with the issue of sexual access, rather than any intrinsic male sadism.

> This is not to say that we can assume that the effect of pornography on its audiences, is, as its apologists like to put it, benign. In its relentless play on female subjugation pornography combines the pseudo-gratification of men's desire with a venting of rage against its object. (1998: 96–7)

Hardy's conclusions about the stories form the basis of his approach to reader's comments.[8] Interview transcripts are to be searched for evidence of agreement with the supposed basic principles of pornography – the sexual subordination of women. His conclusions about the stories are not sustainable. It is not simply that I disagree with Hardy's readings of the stories, he fundamentally misunderstands the nature of the materials he purports to examine: an *inevitable* result of his use of radical feminist theorizations of pornography. In my sample of his stories, I failed to find an instance of female submission: the women were not simply 'available' nor were they 'symbolically punished'. This failure on my part is not a case of being unable to recognize the messages of the text – that is, the eroticization of power dichotomies or the incitement of men's anger against women. His analysis of the stories is wrong: indeed he misrepresents the stories he claims to analyse – they are far more complex than his simplistic retellings suggest. Recognizing complexity means recognizing these are stories, not scenarios. A story has a narrative, propositions, form, conversations, motivations, and actions: above all, features which mark it as a story. Two of the stories I found, *Dangerous Spurts* and *Tess of the Dormobiles*, are not analysed in detail by Hardy but are used as examples of particular motifs/themes which, he claims, contribute to and are evidence of the overall practice of domination, subjugation and abuse of women. Like many theorists of popular culture forms, Hardy uses small snippets dislocated from the complete narrative as incontrovertible evidence of particular attitudes and effects.

The Willing Virgin in *Dangerous Spurts*

Hardy draws attention to this story's references to Laclos' *Dangerous Liaisons* and to it being 'played partly, although by no means entirely, for laughs' (1998: 82).[9] Despite this acknowledgement, Hardy categorizes this narrative as an example of the 'virgin variant' wherein a woman abnegates her subjecthood by the 'forced' recognition of her true (sexual) nature. Actually, contrary to Hardy's claims, this story does not require the 'heroine' to give up her subjecthood; it does the very opposite. A very shortened version of the story is as follows. For a bet, Rollo has to seduce Eve before midnight on New Year's Eve; her grandfather and fiancé (Biff) want to prevent the seduction. Rollo manages to gain access to the penthouse flat where Eve is hidden; she knows nothing of the bet but is rather fascinated by Rollo. Biff arrives; Eve flees with Rollo but during their escape he breaks his ankle. As Rollo and Eve contemplate their imminent capture, Biff tells her about the bet and demands she leave Rollo immediately. After some thought, Eve decides she will have sex with Rollo.

That outline gives no indication of the complexity of the narrative: drawing on farce and a picaresque structure, the story details a quite complex set of relationships; there are eight characters in all, although only two characters are central – Rollo and Eve.[10] The central issue for Hardy is the nature of Eve's consent. Hardy argues that these virgin variants (and *Dangerous Spurts* is apparently the best example he can find) contain suggestions of force and sadism undercut by female sexual compliance. Describing the scene where Rollo pins Eve to the sofa with his groin against her bottom, Hardy argues that

> such an assault does not become rape, for soon the inevitable first twitch of female arousal transforms it into sex: 'In spite of herself her stomach began to tingle'. *In spite of herself*, meaning in spite of her personhood and its inalienable autonomy, that part of her that is intrinsically female, her body, *tingles* in a situation of powerlessness. In short, physiological arousal endorses powerlessness as the normal condition given to women by their nature, irrespective of their socially acquired pretensions to equality. Conversely, powerlessness is celebrated as if it were a source of arousal in women rather than a political and problematic situation. (1998: 83) [Original emphasis]

The condemnation in Hardy's analysis should be clear but it is a misrepresentation of this scene in the story. For a start, there is no 'rape' but that obviously would not be sufficient to counter his claims about the removal of Eve's subjectivity. Eve fancies Rollo: readers have already been told that Eve has seen Rollo at a party and liked him (so much so that her fiancé saw it and was sufficiently jealous to drag her away and fuck her in a cloakroom – an episode in the story which is ignored by Hardy despite it being clear that this was neither wished for by Eve nor enjoyed by her[11]). Therefore, readers are aware that her reaction to Rollo is not the work of moments and that she trusts him. 'But her own body liked him, and she trusted him instinctively.' Trust implies judgement and thought, an acknowledgement of possible danger and then an assessment of likelihood. As her would-be seducer (a fact known by readers but not by Eve), that trust may seem misplaced except, of course, that as readers we have been introduced to other aspects of Rollo's character. He's fun-loving and spontaneous; he loves his grandfather, and he agreed to the seduction only to prevent the old man losing his home (individually none of these characteristics make Rollo trustworthy, but they are preferable to Biff's cruel disregard for Eve's feelings). In addition, Rollo is attractive in a particular way – he's a cross between Leslie Howard and Peter Rabbit (a strange combination but Eve likes it, he reminds her of a mug in her nursery). So, as a seducer, Rollo is associated with a very gentle and old-fashioned type of man. In his hesitation to take part in the bet, Rollo also indicated that *he* likes *her*: he saw her at the party too and they obviously 'connected'.

Their flirtation and kiss in the penthouse *is* a part of Rollo's attempt to win the bet. Eve enjoys it but at this point the seduction is driven by the grandfathers' bet and other external forces intervene to prevent it. Biff and his henchmen, the Ferrits, turn up and, as the door is being broken down, Eve makes her first choice: Rollo or Biff. The choice made can at least partly be understood as a response to Biff's earlier violation of Eve. As well as preferring the amusing and arousing company of Rollo, she now gets to enjoy the risk of a bit of wall scaling followed by hang-gliding.[12] When she finds out about the bet, Rollo is incapacitated by a broken ankle and cannot make Eve choose her course of action by physical means. Standing on the roof in possession of the knowledge of the bet, Rollo's reasons for attempting it and his apology and suggested better feelings, Eve reaches a decision. The bet offers an opportunity to get back at grandfather and everything he stands for, to reject Biff and to make up for the lonely years of her childhood. The New Year revellers below approve the choice and her own (sexual) pleasure in the escape justifies the choice she makes. She likes it and Rollo likes her, as they fuck he looks at her with adoring eyes and afterwards tells her she's magnificent. The end, of course, is access to a woman's body but is, I think, very different from Hardy's construction of the story.

The meaning of 'giving in' to sex here is not 'submission'. Two wagers begin the story and set up the narrative tension: plotting and revenge and, yes, the seduction of the innocent. As this is an erotic story in a soft-core magazine, readers *know* that sex will follow, but there are additional propositions to this story – *who will win the bet?; how will it be accomplished?; will Eve find out about the bet?* That last proposition and its fulfilment will fundamentally change the nature of the 'seduction'. The bet is the motivation for Rollo's actions and the challenge to Eve. It also indicates the nature of the men who are betting.[13] Eve does not submit to sex: her consent is motivated by various factors introduced throughout the story but especially the cold hand of obligation. Her relationship with her grandfather is a difficult one based entirely on money and duty (her's to him, he appears to acknowledge no responsibilities to her, encouraging Biff even though his actions mark him out as an insensitive lover: what kind of husband would he make?). Eve has thrown off restraint in the form of repressive family expectations. These are specific restraints: it is not merely throwing off repression of a generalized kind – the loneliness she has felt has been a result of the kind of family she has. Eve rejects her grandfather's power to dictate her life – he will condemn her to a marriage with Biff and more loneliness and duty. In one single act on the roof, Eve does not surrender to Rollo or signal her submission. She becomes a person with her own desires and a will of her own – she *chooses* to have sex with Rollo, publicly and to applause.

All this is lost in Hardy's account in its hunt for degradation or the subjugation of female will to bodily sensation. The story's themes are actually quite intricate, revolving around tradition, old enmities, ownership of women, familial relationships and finding the right person to let go and have sex with. That last is crucial to understanding this narrative. The theoretical tools Hardy employs reduce narratives to simply the presentation of 'power differences' understood only in terms of 'getting one over on women'. In doing this, other forms of understanding motivations, pleasures, intentions, feelings either within the text or for the reader are effectively removed. The basic unit of analysis, the scenario of degradation, suggests we experience the world in clumps: there's a scene of innocent pleasure, here's a violent encounter, and there's a bit of humour. Then, not only are they discrete forms which can be identified but there are no connections between them, other than those which the theorist identifies as contributing to 'unequal power relations'. Evidence of acceptance of unequal power relations can then form the backbone of the analytical approach to readers' responses: we only have to search for signs of acceptance or refusal of the inevitability or rightness of those power portrayals. During the course of his interviews it becomes clear that readers do in fact care about narrative and that they do not experience the stories solely in terms of 'scenarios'. Rather than revisit his textual analysis in the light of considerable evidence that *his* readings maybe flawed, Hardy constructs a case for understanding porn narratives in terms of their ability to draw in the reader via identification.

> The missing narrative event of first arousal, the intrusion of the captivating image of the female, occurs in the lived experience of the Reader before ever picking up the magazine. It is as if the producer of pornography assumes a state of disequilibrium in the consumer, before providing what is really the second half of the narrative, in which the reader's equilibrium is restored through the surrogate access provided by the Lover's conquest of the Woman in the text. The personal and the pornographic narratives are thus fused as part of the normal functioning of the genre. The Lover takes over the role of the reader as the text takes over from lived experience. From this point on, the Reader identifies intimately with the Lover. There is therefore a certain welding together of the reader's lived 'reality' with textual 'fantasy' inherent in the use of pornography. (1998: 123)

Identification is a key concept in film, literary and media analysis and here, the central claim of the merging of another's identity with the reader, is taken to the absolute limit. The reader and the lover become one and the same. Although theoretical stipulation of this kind is claimed to explain viewers' and readers' pleasures, it is a remarkably oversimplified explanation dependent upon the notion of audience's vulnerability to their chosen media forms. It is a conceptual conceit which Barker has argued 'benefits by remaining unclear' (2005: 354) and which has no real ability to grasp the complexities of the relationships viewers claim with their chosen media as Hill's examination of viewers' responses to scenes in violent movies found:

> Many participants did not consider the phrase 'identification' adequate to describe the variety of response they experienced when viewing this scene; terms such as 'sympathy', 'empathy', 'relate', 'feel for', 'understand', were used to qualify what 'identification' meant to individual participants. (1997: 40–1)

Moreover, 'sympathies' were extended to more than just one character. What proved to be most important were two paired areas of concern for viewers in responding to characters – 'context and biographical information' and 'realism and imagination' (1997: 41). The first was a significant component for viewers to understand the motivations of a character – armed with contextual knowledge viewers were confident about their assessment of individual characters. But Hill also finds that lack of this contextual knowledge does not prevent viewers building relationships with the characters on screen. The second pair, realism and imagination, are used by viewers to assess characters' actions by reflection on 'their own personal experience, preferences and imagination in order to choose which characters they wish to build a relationship with.' (1997: 44) Hill finds that this reflection is complex:

> [One] participant builds on his knowledge of the film, his knowledge of violence in the real world, his own understanding of the frustration Henry feels in order to create ties between the viewer and character, ties which could not be made without drawing on personal experience and the ability to create details, motives and emotions the character does not possess in the film itself. Once again, this participant does not wish to be Henry, but he interprets the character of Henry in a complex and personal way. (1997: 44)

My own research has shown that readers do indeed have very complex responses to their chosen media forms. Hardy's claims of identification with the hero of the porn story is based on the simple equation that men identify according to gender and that the male character is simply there to fuck in place of the reader. My suggestion is that these stories are processual, requiring of readers that they accrete elements of the story as they read and understand the characters, motivations and actions accordingly, building relationships with the characters as they go. Moreover, as they 'enter' the stories readers agree to engage with the 'rules' of the story. As Altman has suggested in relation to film:

> When we are in the world, we follow its rules. When we enter into the world of genres, we reveal tastes and make decisions of an entirely different nature, to the point where familiar norms directly conflict with another kind of satisfaction that looks nothing short of 'dirty' when seen from a cultural viewpoint. (1999: 147–8)

Thus fictions should be understood through their specific modes of inviting readers to suspend 'realities' in order that the 'rules' of the particular form can be followed. Again Barker's (1989) dialogic approach to stories, discussed in chapter four, is useful here emphasizing, as it does, the proposals of story forms: their invitations to imaginative progression through their particular forms of sequence, unfolding and resolution. Unlike Hardy, I do not view porn stories as documents of 'real' relationships, nor am I suggesting that they are simply fictional and therefore entirely removed from the 'real'. Indeed as Barker and Brooks have argued, 'if it were possible to insist, as the standard "scare" mode of argument does, that people respect and maintain a clear line between fantasy and reality, they would lose the power to imagine transformations' (1998: 288). The requirement to maintain a distinction between the 'real' from the 'fictional' is actually an attempt to ascribe value to particular kinds of texts. As Ang has described in relation to the soap opera *Dallas*, analytic conceptions of realism are unsatisfactory because they

> …are based on the assumption that a realistic text offers *knowledge* of the 'objective' social reality. According to the empiricist-realists a text is realistic (and therefore good) if it supplies 'adequate knowledge' of reality, while in the second conception a classic-realistic text is bad because it only creates an illusion of knowledge. But the realism experience of the *Dallas* fans … bears no relation to this cognitive level – it is situated at the emotional level: what is recognised as real is not knowledge of the world, but a subjective experience of the world: a 'structure of feeling' (1985: 45).

Ang further argues that the 'internal' realism of the world within the soap is combined with its 'external' unrealism (1985: 47) in order to allow viewers the possibility of playing with reality within the confines of a fictional world: 'A game that enables one to place the limits of the fictional and the real under discussion, to make them fluid' (1985: 49). Searching for 'messages' encoded in the text and their appropriate or otherwise 'decodings' by readers ignores the complexities of the interactions readers enjoy in all media forms, including pornography. Hardy notes that one of his respondents was particularly interested in 'the Woman's predicament in wanting to fulfil her kinky fantasies whilst being afraid of coming out with them – evidently finding a reflection of his own sexual issues in the figmental character' (1998: 137) but is unable to account for it except as a disguise of the 'masculine psyche' as 'authentic femininity' (1998: 138). Pleasure and 'bad' readings become coupled, as Hardy asserts, 'One does not have to make a preferred (i.e. uncritical) decoding in order to get pleasure from the text, but it certainly helps' (1998: 139). Readers' accounts are 'overwritten' by Hardy because of his own adherence to a strict split between fantasy and reality: to read and enjoy porn is to deny women their subjectivity; to accord women a subjectivity, porn's 'messages' must be rejected.

In turning to readers, Hardy imports a range of judgements and standards that readers must be measured against. The complaint about schoolboy humour is one such judgement; another lies in the very literal readings of the meaning of semen as an expression of male power over women.[13] This reaches its apotheosis in the readings of fellatio:

> In this scenario the resolution of the virgin's ambivalence into sexual surrender represents the victory of body over mind. This triumph of *basic instinct* over refined political sensibilities is symbolised by the insertion of male 'meat' into a female vegetarian's mouth. (1998: 84)

The above scenario comes from *Tess of the Dormobiles*; again, Hardy's account flattens out every nuance and motif in this story such that his reading of oral sex would suggest the narrative brutalization of the woman and the intention to brutalize 'real' women in 'real' life. I dispute his reading that fellatio, as an act, is inherently subordinating and degrading to women, a claim that is necessary in order that harm and consequences can be imputed to the carry over of those acts in to a reader's lived experience. However, the particular problem here lies in its being a misconception of fellatio within the individual story. *Tess of the Dormobiles* again revolves around questions of who to have sex with. Roland and Alison have been 'going out' but there is significant difference in their ages and interests. On holiday, which should have been their space for exploring a sexual dimension to their relationship, they become more and more aware of their incompatibility. Interestingly, this *prevents* them actually having sex – on Hardy's own premise this must seem strange. Roland is described as attractive and Alison thinks about having sex with him with some interest – if the stories are solely about *access to bodies,* as Hardy claims, why don't they fuck? They don't because these stories, humour and all, are about *recognizing the right partner to let go with.* In this story, Roland eventually appreciates the expansive and more mature charms of Tess, acknowledging along the way that her appetites are not evidence of nymphomania but of a zest for life. Alison chooses a jolly time with three students of her own age with whom she shares interests in hiking, vegetarianism and jokes. The insertion of meat into her mouth is a joke *she* makes in the context of an evening spent laughing at other outrageous jokes with her peers.

A theme of this book and of my critique of Hardy (although he is certainly not the worst offender) is that most accounts of pornography refuse to deal with their materials fairly. Generalization, misrepresentation, shoddy referencing, elision of difference, selection etc. are standard features of these accounts. There is a constant failure to take seriously the forms and characteristics of the materials under discussion in favour of searching for evidence of 'messages' already believed to be there. The 'messages' teach men to disregard women's 'natural' abhorrence/mistrust of sex and are successful in this teaching because men are vulnerable to the message since they want sex. The sexual messages of pornography are also so powerful that it might take years for men to realize that they are untrue and that sex in this form degrades women. In using 'scenarios of degradation' as the unit of analysis, Hardy privileges the sex act within the stories. My reading of *Dangerous Spurts* and of *Tess of the Dormobiles* would suggest that his privileging of sexual interactions is incorrect. It is not that the sex has no importance, these are pornographic stories and by their very nature must be explicit about sexual detail and action; my opposition to Hardy's analysis lies in the kind of significance he attaches to the sex acts described. Sexual intercourse always occurs in a porn narrative, that much is true, but it cannot be directly mapped onto or from sexual intercourse in 'patriarchy' or 'compulsory heterosexuality' because it is sexual intercourse within a pornographic story. In other words it is subject to the 'rules' of porn narratives not 'real' life. In a porn narrative, readers follow the 'rules' which allow for the imaginative exploration of recognizing desire, letting go and being seduced: the transformation of the ordinary into the sexually extraordinary. I cannot illustrate this claim further using Hardy's materials, but, before discussing its implications for the fiction in *For Women*, the next section explores women's erotic reading.

Pornography for Women is Different

Erotic fictions for women are not new: it is a commonplace of feminist literary studies that the formulaic fictions published by Mills & Boon in the UK and Europe and Harlequin in the USA have long provided a form of pornography for women. Women's sexuality is understood to be better addressed by Harlequin novels bearing their 'romance' label as a badge of respectability in order to arouse women's more labile and slow-burning sexuality. For example, in her history of Mills & Boon novels, Jay Dixon suggests that they 'follow a different [to men's fiction] "erotic dynamic", which is a female rhythm of small climaxes building to the final ecstatic orgasm' (1999: 148). Ann Barr Snitow draws on critic Peter Parisi's unpublished analysis of Harlequin romances as 'essentially pornography for people ashamed to read pornography ...offer[ing] release, ... specifically sexual release' (Snitow 1984b:

267). Both Parisi and Snitow see the 'pornographic' nature of the romantic text as the reason why the heroine, her life, locations and interests are essentially bland – there is no need for complexity or narrative intricacy where the unstoppable force of sexual feeling is the raison d'être. Thus '*every* contact in a Harlequin romance is sexualised' (original italics; Snitow 1984b: 267) allowing 'both heroine and reader to feel wanton again and again while maintaining their sense of themselves as not that sort of women' (1984b: 268).

Snitow is keen to emphasize the ways in which Harlequins articulate the heroine's need to 'tame' the hero and his sexuality: 'she is engaged on a social as well as a sexual odyssey' (1984b: 268). Taking care not to delineate Harlequin romances as 'erotica' opposed to 'pornography', Snitow is interested in the ways in which Harlequins and 'men's pornography' offer a return to 'furious' infantile 'gusto'. She observes that

> In pornography, the joys of passivity, of helpless abandon, of response without responsibility are all endlessly repeated, savoured, minutely described. Again, this is a fantasy often dismissed with the pejorative 'masochistic' as if passivity were in no way a pleasant or a natural condition. (1984b: 268–9)

In her essentially positive analysis, Snitow suggests that arguments about pornography's dehumanization of women misread the action of its stories: 'pornography is not about personality but about the explosion of the boundaries of the self. It is a fantasy of an extreme state in which all social constraints are overwhelmed by a flood of sexual energy' (1984b: 269). Thus she argues pornography is not just exploitative of gender difference but of *everything* and where social power is unequally felt and sexualities are pathologized those will find their way, often in exaggerated and excessive forms, into the narrative formations of sexually explicit materials.[15] The pornography we have is the pornography we deserve and is gendered simply as our social world is gendered. Although these novels may share abandon with male forms of pornography, Snitow suggests that the 'sexual atmosphere' is more difficult to convey to women and novels must meet certain preconditions. Hence the heroine's passivity, necessary because society insists she cannot seek the hero out; anxiety is also a feature of this passivity because she is constantly asking the question 'is this the one?' One-night stands are impossible for women readers to accept – good sex for women is only possible with emotional engagement, thus 'the romantic intensity of Harlequins – the waiting, fearing, speculating – are as much a part of their functioning as pornography for women as are the more overtly sexual scenes.'(1984b: 271) Asserting the physiological, social and emotional differences between men and women, Snitow's argument suggests that Harlequin's offer a masterly balance of 'romantic tension, domestic security and sexual excitement' (1984b: 272) wherein the heroine's passivity still achieves the education of the hero's passions. Four key structural elements to the successful sexual story are identified: the man must be hard, the woman likes his hardness, but she also recognizes that this is too hard and he must be tamed – his 'hardness must be at the service of the woman' (1984b: 273). Essentially, pornography for women must include romance and the justification of love *before* sexual activity.

Snitow's suggestions fit neatly with the historical accounts of the development of the romance genre and the increasing liberalization of sexual representations for women. For instance, Carole Thurston's (1987) book-length discussion of the romance novel maps the increasingly sexual content of novels to changing patterns of interest in readers, the take up of feminist ideas regarding the silencing of female sexuality[16] and the burgeoning market in sexology. Thus women readers' expectations 'about equality and autonomy' (1987: 142) are reflected in the romance heroine's sexual experience also centred on expectation and rights to orgasm. Thurston argues that this has led to the exploration of sexual activity as something the heroine *does* rather than simply being *done to* as was supposed to be the case previously. These claims suggest a linear development, of increasing liberalization of the stories and the sexual possibilities of the heroine, from no sexual activity to a more recent expression of full and happy sexual congress.[17] Although the precise details of when sex first enters the romance may be disputed (Dixon 1999) there is agreement that the stories are generally more explicit and 'active' now, while retaining continuities with the more sedate earlier stories, in order to indicate the sexual, as well as emotional, compatibility of heroine and hero. Thurston suggests that despite the increased number of sexual encounters between the hero and heroine before the declaration of love, the tension of the novel still revolves around the trials and tribulations on the way to the recognition of love. This continuity is a significant indication for Thurston that sex, while important to the story, is not a replacement for the main drama for readers.

> ... all the overtly sexual excerpts in the world cannot alone spell out the necessary and sufficient conditions that make a romance erotic, because they are lifted out of the stream of events and out of the context of the relationship in which they take place. Women romance readers seem to derive a sustained level of sexual awareness and pleasure from the tension built into the development of this loving relationship *over time*, and it is the process of conflict and resolution that takes place between two wills and bodies that creates the necessary tension to turn the entire story into a psychogenic stimulus. (Original italics; 1987: 154)

The recognition of the importance of the process of the romance and sexual relationship leads Thurston to conclude that women require time to develop a sense of sexual excitement. This is exploited in the stories by the 'twice-told tale' – the hero tells the heroine what he will do but does not do it until about 50 pages later, thereby indicating his restraint. The reader needs time 'to get herself into the pictures that form in her head, which in turn activate the pleasure switches in her brain' (1987: 154). This time element is linked to female biology and sexuality: the multi-orgasmic possibilities of a continuum of intensities of sexual excitement experienced by women.[18] Drawing on a variety of scientific and sociological studies, Thurston concludes that women are less likely to be turned on by visual stimuli preferring the written materials for their ability to stimulate imaginative elaboration without activating an 'internal censor'. This is why, she concludes, women don't like photographic images used for the front cover of stories; the specific identities of the hero and heroine should not be forced on the reader who wishes to 'identify' with the heroine or imagine a relationship with the hero. The parallels between this and Faust's implicit claim, which opens this chapter, that the inclusion of the penis might ruin the prospects of pleasure for a female reader, should be clear.

Ironically, given the heat of the pornography debates, claims about the pornographic nature of romance reading has become a means of valorizing/recuperating romance reading for women. Utilizing the pornography label, romance reading is rescued from the accusation that it is simply silly fantasy. If it is also about getting turned on, it serves a good purpose: the need for women to own and express their sexuality. As with many issues regarding women's media use, discussions of romance have tended to polarize around questions of 'is this a good image/message for women?'[19] The romance's central focus on the acquisition of a 'hero' is described as a limitation on readers who are thought to identify with the 'passivity' of the heroine who waits for sexual awakening (Greer 1971; McRobbie 1978). Where women readers are envisaged, explicit descriptions of sexual activity are seen as enabling a range of responses that are ultimately good for women in that they allow for an exploration of women's erstwhile repressed sexuality. At the same time there is significant effort to suggest that this is a better form of sexually explicit description than that which might pertain in pornography for men. For example, in Avis Lewallen's (1988) discussion of the 'bonk-busters' of the 1980s, the pros and cons of the representations of women within the novel *Lace* are weighed up. She finds that women are often the 'passive recipients of male desire' but they are also shown actively desiring sex. The difference between activity and passivity lies in who gets to 'occupy the dominant subject position': who leads the sexual action in a given scenario. These are to be discovered by a search for the symptoms of patriarchal structures within the text; once discovered, we can trace the attempt to impose reactionary definitions upon women readers against other more 'feminist' definitions.

> This is not to say that the women in the text are not objectified, but this objectification is for the female reader. It offers both glamorised images of powerful, sexy women, together with, at times, the more mundane reality assumed to lie behind the glamour. These women are not mere passive victims: even when abused and exploited, they fight back and their collective sisterhood provides them with an emotional and economic support network, which would seem to be an appropriation from feminism. The question is whether the context of this objectification alters the relationship female readers can have with it, or whether it merely colludes with conventional, sexist ways of seeing women. (1998: 97)

The evidence for an 'altered relationship for female readers' is left unarticulated; Lewallen is only able to gesture in the direction of possible masturbatory use of the novel and the suggestion that a discourse of bourgeois liberalism may impact upon women's sexual self-awareness. The suggestions are woolly but at least there is realism! In her conclusion, Lewallen argues that *Lace*'s 'realism' alongside the more politically suspect but exciting romance partially recuperates the novel for a female readership. In other words, it recuperates the novel for a positive academic assessment, the novel is seen to include elements which might be considered 'good' for women. The assessment of worth is not based upon what readers might consider to be valuable but what theorists are prepared to recognize as valuable. Radway's observations on the need to remain respectful of readers' reasons for reading and their pleasures seem apposite here.

> ...when analysis proceeds from within the belief system actually brought to bear upon a text by its readers, the analytical interpretation of the meaning of a character's behaviour is more likely to coincide with that meaning as it is constructed and understood by the readers themselves. Thus the account offered to explain the desire to experience this particular fantasy is also more likely to approximate the motives that actually initiate the readers' decisions to pick up a romance. While a romantic heroine may appear foolish, dependent and even pathetic to a woman who has already accepted as given the equality of male and female abilities, she appears courageous, and even valiant, to another still unsure that such equality is a fact or that she herself might want to assent to it. (1986: 78)

The arguments for women's pornography being different are part of a continuum of academic discussions delimiting appropriate access to sexually explicit materials for both men and women: the romance is validated as the closely guarded secret of women's domesticated fantasy life and evidence of women's transgressive sexuality. However, that picture is complicated by fictions specifically marketed as sexually explicit and for women. If women's pornography is the romance, what are women doing with openly sexual fictions?

Stories to Make Your Toes Curl!

A brief sketch of *For Women*'s fiction is necessary. Again, I focus on the period spring 1992 to December 1996. From my conversations with members of the editorial team, the fiction section seemed to have a fairly low priority until Liz Coldwell took over as editor in 1998. This was an effect of the prioritizing of the magazine's similarities to mainstream women's magazines – the focus on information – and its difference – the inclusion of male nudes. In its first issues the magazine's erotic section was limited to excerpts from published or to-be-published fiction: the 'saucy bits' were extracted from the novels of Julie Burchill, Anais Nin, Francesca Jones, Maria Caprio and Alina Reyes. By 1993 the magazine had moved to publishing original fiction but did not commission authors.[20] As a paid-for feature of the magazine, the stories also fell foul of cost-cutting experiments: disappearing for a six-month period during 1996. Again, readers' complaints ensured their return. The following guidelines are made available to prospective authors:

> We are allowed to be explicit in the language we use, but the erotic content should be sensual, rather than crude. We are not allowed to print stories which deal with

> anything illegal, including under-age sex, anal sex (unless those taking part are over 18 and in private i.e. no threesomes!), incest, bestiality, and anything which features extreme violence or appears to glorify rape or the use of force in a sexual encounter. Stories with a gay/lesbian theme, or those which deal with mild bondage/SM, are acceptable, as long as it is made clear that both partners are willing participants. Some attempt should be made to incorporate a plot. Detailed descriptions of sexual encounters are often very erotic, but our readers also like believable characters and an imaginative setting for the action. Try hard to avoid 'The Norm', wherein the narrator, who typically 'never used to believe those stories in magazines' suddenly and implausibly encounters their dream sexual partner at the door saying they have come to borrow a cup of sugar/mend the video/ask directions, and promptly bonks their lights out. As *For Women's* readership is overwhelmingly female, they are not interested in cartoon nymphomaniacs or men's magazine-style exaggerated descriptions of bodily parts. Use your imagination in terms of situation as well as sexual acrobatics. (http://www.mamohanraj.com/Writing/porn.html, accessed 30.1.2000)

Those guidelines make explicit the need to address a female 'sensibility' as well as staying within the law. Juffer's (1998) insights regarding the use of 'quality' criteria in order to designate women's aesthetics are apposite here: descriptions of the body and sexual situations and activities should be imaginative but not farfetched. Quality is tied up in the need to ensure that stories avoid the 'norm' but it is not simply about writing well or imaginatively. In an e-mail to me, Liz Coldwell wrote

> The quality of the fiction is very important – it has got to read like a proper story, with a beginning, middle and end and decent plot and characterisation, rather than a 'reader's letter' or confessional type piece. This is because we get genuine readers' letters and need to distinguish between fact and fiction.... We have strict distribution/legal guidelines, plus the magazine doesn't really exist to be arty or experimental in fiction terms – enough bad arty, experimental erotica is in print already. Criteria for judging the fiction: it has to be well written, have a situation and characters that the readers will be interested in and, sometimes, make a point as well as tell a story.

As with the photosets there are sets of criteria that the producers work with that are somewhat difficult to communicate: one of these is the meaning and form of 'quality'. I think this is an important indicator of the ways in which the production of the magazine runs right up against what may be a transitional moment in women's popular culture. Discussions of Mills & Boon and other popular female genres have tended to draw attention to the sublimation of sexual activity beneath romance and motifs of hardness and softness. The 1980s and 1990s saw a major move towards explicitness in women's media (*FW* was a part of this). As Sonnet (1999) has shown, the editors of the Black Lace imprint explicitly drew upon certain precepts of the feminist movement in order to justify their publications and their explicit descriptions of sexual activity. These precepts are also at work in interviews I conducted with the producers of *FW* and yet there is also another attribute to their justifications expressed in Coldwell's statements above about bad arty, experimental erotica. *FW* is not attempting to position itself behind a feminist message, nor is it attempting to challenge the ways in which mainstream porn stories are written: it holds no brief for the radical and/or feminist reworking of pornography. The magazine has a formula, Keir and Corbett knew it, understood it and worked within it (as Coldwell continues to do) but were unable to convey to me exactly what it was/is. They knew that for the readers who continued to buy the magazine (and to write to them with praise and complaints) *FW* 'worked', that they were able to join in and enjoy its elements, whether serious or playful, for possible sexual arousal. In producing each issue of the magazine the readers and their likes and dislikes act as a constraint on the work of the editorial team. I will go on to show that the issue of 'quality' is linked in complex ways to the magazine's contract of 'honesty' with its readers.

Regular authors included Lipstick Hart, Gillian Maclean, Helen Ward, Sally Bowles, D. Franklin and T. Wadlow. It is very likely that some of these names are aliases. Where initials are given these are often male authors, for example, Wadlow is Trevor Wadlow. Certain writers seem to utilize favourite motifs; for example, Lipstick Hart's stories (*Lauri's Stockings*, Jan 1995 and *Red Ribbons*, Feb 1995) often feature dressing up for sex in completely impractical outfits made of ribbons and tiny wisps of lace. Gillian Maclean's stories (*Havana*, May 1995 and *The Flesh is Weak*, July 1994) revolve around throwing off restraints imposed by one's social position. Stories are around 3,000 words, usually no more than three pages and there is often only one sex scene which offers the climax of the story, with a short 'what happens next' element to finish the narrative. Whether narrated in the first or third person, the stories' descriptions of feelings, emotions and actions are focused on the female protagonist, although some stories feature a switching between the hero and heroine. There are recurrent themes or situations that can be laid out as discrete forms for the benefit of analysis, although in so doing, there is an inevitable flattening of the individual stories. Each story will usually combine at least two or more of the following elements.

The Unhappy Heroine

The heroine often doesn't *know* that she's ready for excitement, it surprises her but she has felt unhappy/unsure/insecure/lonely for sometime and so, even if she does not recognize it, she has waited a long time and the time is right for her to take action, (*Scarlet Tulips*, June 1995). These stories end in positive feelings for her: she is reawakened by sex, although that awakening is not necessarily sexual. The *lasting* effects are not necessarily or primarily sexual, they can also be that she understands how buried she is in work (*Partners in Flight*, June 1995), a dire relationship, the mundanities of life or that she has buried herself and not allowed herself to feel and experience life properly (*Recovering*, May 1994). Often she's had heartbreaks, disappointments, but something shows her that perhaps the time is right to experience again. It doesn't matter that it won't last, indeed it is better if it doesn't last – a melodramatic emphasis on the ways in which true sexual feeling may be doomed or ephemeral (*Shades of Black*, Aug 1995; *Stargazer*, Dec 1995). But in the moment it is the most intense and fabulous feeling and its effects are not to be measured in long-term commitment or constancy to the individual man but in a heightened 'reality' for the woman. These stories often feature details such as colours becoming brighter and more vibrant. All the senses are invoked: sight, touch, smell, taste and hearing are given full reign and thereby lift the heroine out of the ordinary.

Sexual Feeling is Too Powerful to Resist

This is probably best illustrated by a quotation,

> They did not understand each other very broadly. But she knew, without knowing how or why she knew these things, firstly that he would not hurt her; and secondly that he needed shelter, anywhere, somewhere to hide. And he knew, on the same basis, that she found him, sexually, deeply attractive; and that this attraction would overrule, for the indefinite future, any other feelings or judgements that she might have or make against him. (*Gimme Shelter*, Sept 1994)

This theme is almost always tied to the unhappy heroine. A series of disappointments lead her to a meeting with a man who is so exactly right for her *now* that she must just go with the flow. At the same time as saying yes to sex, the woman is usually aware that she is learning something new about herself. The stories often centre on throwing social cautions to the wind, especially respectability. The man is usually unknown to others in the woman's ordinary life. He may even be a figment of her imagination as in *The Spirit Lives* (Sept 1995).

The Fantasy Scenario

In these stories the woman gets to act out a fantasy she has never had the courage to try before (author Trevor Wadlow is particularly fond of these). Sometimes the woman has planned the scene with her boyfriend (*Shopping*, Oct 1996) or she believes her boyfriend has planned it for her (*Happy Birthday*, Aug 1995). Often these end with a sting in the tale; for example, in *Happy Birthday* where Serena discovers that the sex party she attended was *not* a planned surprise from her boyfriend – she had gone to the wrong address.

Experienced Woman

These stories feature an older woman with a younger man who learns from her how to give and receive pleasure (*Recovering*, May 1994; *Deceptions*, vol.1, no.9; *The Chess Mistress*, Aug 1994; *Appropriate Punishment*, July 1995). These stories reference men's lack of respect for women: the 'boy' has to learn that women are not just receptacles for men's lust. For example, Chris is teased and tutored by the eponymous *Chess Mistress*:

> 'There is always a winner and a loser, but chess is not just about who wins or loses, it's also about how you play your game, the skill you use, that's more important. You can still lose despite playing well.' She placed each leg on the arm of the armchair opening up fully to him. 'You've always played the game to win, Chris. You have never worried about the skill involved have you? Winning was the

> most important thing to you. You cared little for your opponent.' It was true, he knew it. He showed no finesse or affection for his lovers.
>
> 'Now you've been shown another way to play the game, new skills, new ploys that have kept you besotted and mesmerised by your opponent.' (Aug 1994: 80–3)

Social codes regarding age differences and the supposedly dwindling attractiveness of older women are transgressed in these stories so that the 'worship' of the woman is made clear, especially in the motif of cunnilingus. This is a feature of almost all stories but in these in particular the hero performs with gusto. He doesn't mind getting covered in 'love juice' – that is a measure of the man and his ability/willingness to please. Fellatio also features as a motif in the story, showing the heroine's control of the passion: she takes over. In general, oral sex slows down the action of the story and offers the opportunity for full descriptions of male and female genitalia, their respective responsiveness both as givers and receivers of pleasure and, as Thurston has pointed out, the woman's capacity for orgasm.

Getting the Measure of Him

The men fall into two categories – relationship man and the lover. The 'relationship' is of some years' standing and no longer exciting, crucially, he has lost interest in her as a person as well as in sexual interactions: work, other women, laziness: all mean he no longer cares enough about her to bother about her sexual needs. The 'lover' is attractive but especially to *her*, so much so that on seeing him she can't help but start to imagine sex with him. Often younger than her, he is a stranger but appreciative of her in ways that she hasn't felt for some time. He's caring and considerate and able to recognize moods and emotions. His responsiveness to the world around him – food, art, colours, smells, perfume etc., indicates his being different from 'relationship man'. Thus, she knows that she is safe with him even as she thinks about danger, she knows *he's* okay – this *is* the one, at least for now.

Attempting Analysis

Such are the themes of the stories but to make any more substantial claims about the narratives I must turn to readers and their assessments of the stories and address those elements of the stories they see as important. Readers rarely expressed detailed opinions about individual *FW* stories, but I have looked at those fictions which elicited expressions of approval or disapproval. For example, Jane had a number of comments she wanted to make about the stories:

> The erotic stories in *FW*, they used to be really really good. Um... they were interesting and it was set from the female angle, I think. The last one I read which was in October 1996, it's called *Shopping* by T. Wadlow, oh, and I thought that was absolutely crap. I was going to read you an excerpt but... um... I'm not going to bother. Um... where are we now.

> Do you think they're different from men's magazines? Yes, I do, well they were. I think they're the same now, they're all about thrusting penises, swollen labias, um... all that type of stuff. Yeah, that's okay but there's nothing exciting about that, it's laid before you like a deck of cards, there's no mystery or magic. Um... I do like erotic stories, and I have liked them and I'll just tell you which ones. [Turns off tape]. Okay in May 1994... um... it's in fact a prize winners story, it's by Rachel Braverman on page 95 and it's a really good story, it's... I really enjoyed that one. I like it because it tells the story from a woman's point of view which is great, it's about disappointments, it's also about really hot sex which is great. As I say, it's written by or written from a woman's point of view. I didn't like *Reading Between the Lines* in June 1994... er... it was about a man and his wife, whatever. When she was in a drunken stupor in the morning, he inserted a tampax because she'd begun to bleed, well, there's nothing... nothing fun about that, is there? It's every woman's probably everybody's nightmare so no didn't enjoy that at all... [turns off tape] Um... in the same magazine on page 91... um... um... *Anomalies*, it's about Colin the Condom, it's a great story, full of humour and it tells it from the condom's point of view. Good read that one. Another one I enjoyed was *Blue Brass* .... in a Bookstall, um... bit of disappointing ending but basically just about a girl who's fantasizing or a man who's fantasizing and the girl comes back. A good story – that was in November 1994. ... Right there are more, but I'll take all night if I do that, that'll give you an idea. I like the stories that have a good story that are sometimes comical, that are well written, intelligently written, but I don't like stories that are... what's the point in writing about something that is just a nightmare and you would never want to happen, you can't relate to it then.

Although her comments are not very detailed I looked at her likes and dislikes in light of my conclusions about her reading of *FW* in toto enabling analysis of a set of principles guiding Jane's reading pleasures. Fortunately for me, Jane was not alone in singling out *Recovering*, four others had something positive to say about that story. My analysis of *FW*'s fiction begins with *Recovering*.

Recovering and the Healing Properties of Sex

Recovering, written by Rachel Braverman, was second prizewinner in the magazine's first readers' short story competition. Told in the first person, the story begins by explaining that the narrator, Claire, is recuperating in Greece following the break-up of her marriage. For a week she has insisted on being alone: bitter and angry, she is unable to respond to other people. Then, eight days into her stay, her sunbathing is interrupted by a young man who has climbed up from the beach. At first, she is irritated by his presence but then she begins to soften.

> Suddenly, I wanted to trace the smoothness of his face, the outline of his muscles. I could hardly resist putting my hand on his chest to feel it move as he recovered from the exercise. He breathed easily, obviously used to exercise. I found my own breath was keeping time with his.

> The power of this sudden want forced me to sit down. I hurriedly got myself under control. Think, woman, I told myself sternly. You are 33 years old, you've been put back on the shelf and fear you'll never get off it again. No wonder you start acting like a frenzied nymphomaniac the second anything remotely fanciable turns up. From a dirty little locked-up corner of my mind, I heard my ex-husband's favourite put down.
>
> '*Whatever happened to the girl I married? You're getting frigid in your old age!*' he'd say as I failed, yet again, to have an orgasm.

Annoyance turns to intense awareness of his physical presence: Claire wants to touch Jon but thinks this is a 'false' reaction caused by her emotional state and her problems. Two further themes emerge: her husband's disapproval of her lack of sexual response but also that she had once been different. Somehow it is easy to get along with Jon and they talk – to her surprise Claire finds herself cheered and interested:

> His world was so reassuring. It all fell into place. The eagerness, the enthusiasm, the frustration... He was on the brink, capable and prepared for the next stage.

She finds him attractive and he confesses that he is a virgin – would she teach him how to make love?

> The nerve of it.
> On the other hand, what a compliment.
> 'Is that why you climbed up here?' I asked.
> 'Only sort of.' He was so sweet when he was sheepish. 'I'm sorry. It was really stupid. I'll go.'
> 'No. You can stay.' I laid my hand on his arm, making him turn to look at me. 'It'll be fun.'
> Irresponsible? Possibly. Irresistable? Definitely. The thought of me – inhibited, rejected, cowed Claire – taking this boy by the hand and making a man of him thrilled me so I could hardly stand.

They make love; she leads and enjoys being in charge. She enjoys fellating him and so does he: he 'slid to my level, leaning back against the wall. "That was unbelievable," he said, and there were tears in his eyes.' He reciprocates, to her multi-orgasmic pleasure, and then they have penetrative sex:

> With Robert, it had always been the good old missionary position. I'd felt awkward and exposed, ridiculous even, at the thought of me wobbling about on top of him. But the longing in Jon's eyes made me feel like a goddess. I wanted him to see me, all of me.

Afterwards she starts to cry 'healing tears'.

> He wanted to see me again, but I said that wasn't a good idea. Part of me would have loved a toy boy, a dream lover to prove I wasn't just Robert's cast-off. Another part knew I had to get beyond that. It was as if my encounter with Jon had reminded me that I was capable of influencing my surroundings, and always had been. Of course, Robert had been a total pig and treated me very badly, but he had also been deeply unhappy. I'd forgotten how to reach out to him. Instead, I'd retreated into a passive shell, accepting his misery as my martyrdom. That night, I began to forgive us both.

The next day she packs up and is about to leave the island when Jon arrives at the quay (she didn't tell him she was leaving, but he turns up to wave her off). A brief goodbye from Jon as he gives her a small souvenir that she'll remember because it is 'ultra tacky'. The story ends, 'We watched each other while the boat pulled out. As it chugged clear of the harbour and out to sea, I saw Jon turn a cartwheel, wave and sprint back up the hill.'

In the space of the story, Claire has moved from bitterness through irritation, enthusiastic wonder to a reconciliation of her own emotions and a willingness to face the world again. The transformation seems to come in the shape of sex: certainly Claire feels rejuvenated by the sexual interaction with Jon and able to start to live again. But there was an earlier transformation that enabled the sex to take place and that was her acknowledgement and interest in his enthusiastic embracing of his future. Through that she sees that she could be something different from poor, cowed, rejected Claire and that the best way of achieving that, for now, is to be 'irresponsible'; to take a chance. In taking that chance she realizes that she is not just a victim and that she has to accept her past in order to get on with her life.[21] That also means that no matter how flattering or fun to have a toy-boy, Jon must be left behind. Although the sexual interaction is initiated by Jon's request, Claire's motivations are made very clear: almost from the start she cannot help but recognize his attractiveness. His enthusiasm also re-awakens her sense of herself as adventurous.

His desire to be with *her* is also important although its fullest expression is only possible at the end of the story. That he wants to see her again could be seen as simply evidence of his boyish/'typical male' selfishness but his turning up at the quay is emblematic of their connection – Claire was not wrong to take a chance. The tacky souvenir is a clear statement of the authenticity of his desire for Claire – it is a token (and it had to be tacky, in order to be innocent of 'payment') of a mutually felt, albeit brief affection. The story can end with infinite possibilities open to Claire (and Jon): she has learnt that she does not have to be shaped by other people's expectations nor does she have to be hampered by her own past emotions.

This element of the story was particularly appreciated by Julie:

> *Recovering* May 94 – I liked this one. This story starts with a woman feeling not very much loved, cared for, or wanted, she does not see her own beauty and

> worth. This is a phase a lot of women go through often. The sexual encounter renews her interest in life. I do believe even (especially?) when going through a bad patch, a good bonk does wonders to help put things in perspective. The sex act as detailed is very arousing, the honest description of their coupling is a real turn-on, plus the fact that he is a young virgin and she an experienced woman, it adds to the excitement.

The story is assessed for its 'recognizability' and for its 'realism' – it is something experienced by a lot of women and the sex, when it occurs, concurs with Julie's belief in the healing properties of sex. As Ang found, this notion of realism is not about being 'real' in terms of measurable knowledge but about being true to women's 'experiences', in this instance, emotional, physical and sexual. At the same time, the description of their sexual interaction is 'honest' enough to be a turn-on and the discrepancy in age/experience an intensifier of that arousal. Another reader suggested that the story was believable and, in the brevity of the liaison, utopian.

> I really liked this one – you could believe it. And…um… she's in charge but not in a …a domineering …so it kind of … you just get the sense of how good sex could be with two people when they… er… hardly know each other… They care…I mean … it's that time out thing… they *do* care for each other even if it can't last, d'y'know what I mean? (Mia)

How does this story differ from *Shopping* which Jane described as 'absolutely crap'? First, it is important to recognize that Jane wanted to show *how Shopping* was crap but was unable to find an excerpt of the story to read out as evidence. From that I would suggest that its failure for her was not to be measured in terms of its use of language or structure but that at a fundamental level the story disappointed her expectations. Written by regular author T. Wadlow, *Shopping* is a twist-in-the-tale story featuring the acting out of a woman's fantasies.

***Shopping*: Fantasy Really Can Come True**

> It had always been Helen's favourite fantasy to be seduced by a stranger in the changing cubicle of a department store and she had finally talked her boyfriend, Mark, round to the idea. Not that he was a stranger, of course, but if all went well according to plan – no speaking, lots of rough thrusting – her imagination would do the rest. (Oct 1996: 80–1)

Narrated in the third person, Helen is dissatisfied by her current relationship's stagnation. Arriving at the shopping centre – Mark goes off to the hardware store while Helen has a coffee before going to the dress department. Helen notes the admiring glances from men as she drinks her coffee. The café's counter assistant admires her and she mentally acknowledges his cute bottom. She moves off to the dress department, selects some dresses and enters the changing room. Stripping to her underwear, Helen begins to admire and caress her body.

> Helen had never masturbated before a mirror before. It was strangely arousing, like making love to yourself. And anyway, if it made her nice and wet for Mark, where was the harm?

As she approaches orgasm, a man enters the cubicle behind her and his hands replace hers on her body. 'In that moment, aroused as she was, it was easy to forget that they belonged to Mark.' Without speaking, they begin to fuck:

> Daring to take just a peek she opened her eyes slightly. The mirror reflected back the wanton self she had dreamed about. There were her swollen labia stretched around the shaft of a throbbing penis.
>
> As one hand delved impatiently at her crotch and another cupped her exposed breast Helen surrendered herself to the hard, rhythmic thrusting. No faces came to mind, no memories, no fantasies. It was exactly how she imagined it would be. Her body was simply a field of relentless pleasure enhanced by the imagined anonymity of her lover. The thought that she might just be within hearing distance of nearby shoppers only added to the excitement.

Alone again in the cubicle, Helen gets dressed – she can't find her knickers but it is only a 'minor loss' and she goes back to the café to meet Mark. He tells her he did not make it to the cubicle – the shop assistants were suspicious of him. Helen cannot believe it 'Maybe her imagination really had finally run away with itself? Yet it had seemed so real'. Still shocked and puzzled she goes to the counter to buy some coffees and finds her knickers on the tray. '"Have a nice day!" The counter assistant smiled as he took the money.'

The story is considerably shorter than most *FW* stories (approximately 1,500 words) but still manages to include the major themes I identified earlier – a vaguely unhappy heroine, sexual feeling that is too powerful to resist and a good time for both sexual partners. The difference in this story lies in the ending and in Helen's emotional state. Both the heroine and the reader must reassess the sexual interaction when the realization hits that it was not Mark but the counter assistant who entered the cubicle. This, coupled with the dreamlike state of Helen throughout the story, significantly impacts upon the kind of experiential realism that I believe readers enjoy in stories which work. Helen has to 'snap out of her reverie' to notice the café assistant; she has to suddenly remember her purpose in being in the shop. Once inside the cubicle, she 'wonders' about men's arousal; she masturbates and justifies that as getting 'wet for Mark' and then when she finds out that Mark didn't make it after all, she is 'distracted' and unsure of what just happened to her. The cheery 'Have a nice day!' lets her know. This heroine 'learns' that she's been had.

Wadlow uses the twist device in another story, *Shampoo and Conditioner* in which Elena arrives at her hairdressers just as Kevin is closing the shop – no problem; he'll do her hair. Again, Elena is a vaguely unhappy woman: her husband has left her for a younger woman and she's been adjusting to the loneliness and humiliation of a single life – helped by a vibrator. She has a good rapport with Kevin and she fancies him enough that he stars in some of her fantasies. After washing her hair and putting conditioner on, Kevin leaves her to relax. Elena leans back in her chair but then...

> She came to, aware of a gentle pressure on her knees. In the reflection on the ceiling she saw Kevin kneeling before her, trying to gently prise her legs apart. (April 1995: 90–2)

Kevin is very appreciative of her 'more mature charms' and one thing (cunnilingus) leads to another (penetrative sex). One multiple orgasm later

> Elena's eyes snapped open. The reflection on the ceiling showed her slumped in the chair with her legs spread revealing her stocking tops. She quickly closed them, her face flushing with embarrassment. 'Sorry, I must have dropped off.'
>
> Kevin was at the desk checking the till roll against the appointment book. 'You looked so peaceful there I though I'd leave you for a bit. You ready for your usual?'

Elena thinks it was all a dream and she's a little embarrassed by it although Kevin's easy banter and flattery 'you look fabulous' means she feels better and laughs as she leaves the salon. She gets outside and a sudden gust of wind tells her, her panties are missing. It wasn't a dream. Elena made no effort to bring this fantasy about but 'the sheer pleasure blew away any inhibitions she had'. Although both *Shopping* and *Shampoo* end with a revisioning of the sexual episode – the second story's heroine is less troubled by the revelation.

Although its premise is very close to that of *Shopping*, *Shampoo* evidently had not pleased or displeased Jane significantly enough to warrant a label, crap or otherwise. As Jane did not elaborate on her reasons for disliking *Shopping*, or why *Shampoo* should be 'okay', my conclusions can only be tentative, but I believe that *Shopping* is a problem for Jane because it fails to fulfil *FW*'s 'contract' to her – it fails to meet her expectations of the magazine. As we saw in the chapter 4, Jane has a great deal invested in her reading of *FW* – it enables her to revisit her sexual past and imagine her sexual future. The magazine and its fiction allows Jane to immerse herself in a world where women's desires are not indications of their deficiencies as wives and mothers or human beings; where women are desired because they are experienced and because they make demands for pleasure. The twist in the tale of *Shopping* indicates the danger of indulging in fantasy: the woman *thinks* she knows what she's doing but she is not in control. This lack of control/knowledge is also a feature of the *Reading Between the Lines* story that Jane hated. In this story a woman arrives home drunk and falls asleep. Her boyfriend, who evidently feels henpecked, sees she is menstruating and inserts a tampon in her vagina despite his, also evident, distaste for the warmth, smell and sliminess of menstrual blood. This episode is 'read' differently by the protagonists of the story: she thinks it is an emblem of his commitment, he is irritated by it and is pleased to receive a letter from his parents which means he can escape her. Jane thought this was a story about 'everybody's worst nightmare'.[22] For a woman looking for affirmation that female sexuality is whole, adult, pleasurable, and desirable and, above all, reasonable, this story, with its emphasis on a nagging, patronizing, bleeding and unknowing woman, really was her worst nightmare. Unlike Helen in *Shopping* and the unnamed woman in *Between the Lines*, Elena in *Shampoo* knowingly plays with fantasy/reality and allows herself to surrender to the moment. She knows the identity of the man fucking her and she desires him, the twist when it comes is about the event not the partner in it. In acknowledging that difference I do not want to make the claim that this story is better than *Shopping*: Jane's lack of enthusiasm for it – the 'stories in that [issue] were okay' – is certainly no endorsement of the tale's vision. However, I think we can make some comparison between her responses to these three stories and to *Recovering*. Wadlow's stories are quite conservative – where Claire (*Recovering*) learns to move on, to renew her energy and passion for life and sex confirms her optimism – these 'fantasies come true' are about stasis. Nothing is 'learnt' by the heroine other than a reminder that men will take women for a ride and fantasies, however well planned, can go wrong. Not all *FW*'s stories about acting out fantasy were so tinged with caution – where desire is great enough almost anything is permissible and pleasurable.

A Woman Called Sir: Enjoying the Possibilities of Sex

> Did you read the story this month? Fiction p.64, very, very, very, very, enjoyable… er… I mean good! (Julie, December 95)

In *A Woman Called Sir*, two readers found that exceeding the permissible was particularly pleasurable. The story can be summarized as follows: out with her boyfriend, Jen notices him looking at a man: she teases that Jeff would like to have sex with a man. She tells him that she'll show him how much he could like being fucked in the ass. They go back to the hotel where she gives Jeff a blow job and inserts a finger in his anus – he experiences the most fabulous orgasm. Encouraged by his excitement and his enthusiastic response to her whispered suggestions, Jen introduces a lilac vibrator, followed by a large strap-on dick, to their lovemaking. As she fucks him, anally and orally, to orgasm, Jen insists that Jeff call her sir! Throughout, Jen 'threatens' Jeff with further initiation: she'll introduce him to her gay friends who will really show him how to fuck. Jeff is turned on by her ideas and together they plan his further sexual education.

> One story was about… er… a woman… er … fucking her boyfriend … up the bum! I really liked that one! [Why?] I dunno… um… oh gosh it … was… different… It was just… well she's showing him… I mean he's so macho… so normal but she's … showing him he could be different… Some men are SO uptight! … It was just great!
>
> CS: Would you want to do that?

> Ha … would *I*? Mmmm… God… Well I think… I'd … love to…. Not the whole thing but I'd love to fuck my boyfriend… just once… or a few times [laughs] But I don't think… that's not why the story was good…. No… no… what's good, what's good is that … it's that thing of trust and that he says yes… Y'know… there's no … embarrassment… there's no …um… fear…Um… she keeps telling him… don't be macho… don't be … It just happens… um … it just happens and they … enjoy it… He tries something … he would never…he wouldn't know that he wanted… and he has a… great time! That's what's great! (Alison)

This story by Kate Jackson (Nov 1995: 64–8) is slightly longer than most *FW* stories, told in the first person by Jen, the initiator and the 'doer' throughout. Unlike other stories, Jen's emotional and sexual needs are not stressed and in no sense could Jen be labelled an unhappy heroine! Jen controls the sexual interaction of this story, dictating the pace and form of their sexual encounter, Jeff follows her lead as she 'educates' and pleasures him.

> I rolled over on top of him, smirking down at him. I had many more plans for him. He rubbed his nipples ruefully. 'I'm not sure if that qualifies as sex or not.'
>
> 'Did it feel like sex?'
>
> 'Yes.'
>
> 'Then it was sex. There's more to sex than the same old in and out.'
>
> He looked at me in wonder and maybe a little bit of fear. 'More?' he asked.
>
> 'Lot's more,' I replied. 'Wanna learn?'
>
> He nodded mutely.

For both Julie and Alison, this story is exciting because of the ways in which the man is required to put off his usual reserve and admit to feelings he has never had before. In so doing he has to admit that social conditioning is a brake on his feelings. He has to throw social expectations off in order to experience the kinds of pleasures he dreams of.

> 'All men are like that,' I said. 'Everybody has lots of nerves in their mouth, their nipples, their genitals and their anus. It doesn't matter whether you're straight or gay, you can enjoy all those body parts.'
>
> 'Yes, but I'm not supposed to.'
>
> 'You're not supposed to be having unmarried sex either, but that doesn't seem to bother you.'
>
> 'Well, everybody does it.'
>
> 'So? I'm not going to tell "everybody" I can make you come by sucking you off and fingering your ass. Besides, good lovers already know it. Believe me, you aren't the first man I've done that to, not by a long shot.'

This story is a very good example of the kind of play with fantasy that the magazine's fiction allows: the sexual interaction has its own logics. So long as the desire is great enough, inhibitions can and should be overcome, men and women can enjoy role swapping, playing sado-masochistic games, pretending to be gay lovers – these are spurs to exploration and satisfaction of desire within the story. In Julie's case we can trace a connection between this story and Julie's own experiences. In chapter 5, I intimated that Julie had come to *FW* as a result of distressing events which she experienced as constraints on her sexual and emotional life. Again, my conclusions must be tentative but I think that Julie's pleasure in this story lies in its articulation of constraints (appropriate behaviour, self-restraint and misunderstandings) and resolution of them ('trust me, try it, enjoy it, learn from it'). For Alison, too, this story had resonances with her experiences of being 'misunderstood' by men and of their refusing to let go. Alison had found that expressing her sexual fantasies and desires often resulted in accusations of being 'a kinky slut'. Thus, she liked the stories which explored the pleasures and possibilities of 'letting go'. This was not to be measured against her own experiences, she had not actually engaged in sexual activity of this kind for herself, but its descriptions and pleasures lay in its being able to allow her imaginative exploration of the possibilities of fucking her boyfriend and of their having the kind of relationship that would encompass this unashamed sharing.

The emotional climate of these stories and their emphasis on felt sensations and experiences are obviously important to readers. The woman's point of view was stressed by a number of readers but is not easily equated to 'identification' with the heroine.

> Mmm well, the people are … well I don't know if I'd say I like them but I think they're kinda real. Mm… do you mean … um… er… do I identify with them? I don't think I do, I mean I don't think I'm *her*. She's too old usually, not old but she's always older than me – at least I… er… and I don't think I'm like any of the ones I've read… I'm just not like them… I think they're kinda real but… but the men, they hardly get … they're definitely horny… but I don't think… I think about the people much. I mean I think that… er… er… one thing I like in the stories is the descriptions about the bits before the scene where they have sex. Like… it's usually about how hot… it's very evocative and I like that bit where it's just building up and building up… and really it's kind of the heat and the smell of the heat… D'you know what I mean? I mean it reminds me of times when *I've* just been carried away. I think that's what's going on… for me anyway, it's how… how evocative it is of times when I've really enjoyed sex and so… it makes you… I like ones where they do it from behind or where they talk about smells and things…. Um… er…
>
> CS: They work for you?
>
> [Laughs] Yes, yes, yes, they do. They work because they… they take you there… I mean to a place where you had hot sex yourself… And I think when they work

> that's what it is... I don't want to be her or even be with him... I want to be *me* doing *that*...! And if I can't... well... [laughs... a lot!] (Mia, interview)

For this reader the important 'identification' is with the mood, occasion, activity or sensations, not the protagonists as gendered individuals. This may explain why there is so much emphasis in the stories on what she wears, what he wears, how he smells, what perfumes they wear. It may also explain the locations – usually claustrophobic interiors shutting out the rest of the world – and the detailed descriptions of the mirrors, the colours and art on the walls, the flowers and the weather outside. Even in external locations, for example, the beach or public spaces like shops, the isolation of the space is emphasized – it is an inaccessible cove or the secret backroom. Thus, the location of the story emphasizes the spatial intimacy of the encounter: these two are alone with their sexual attraction.

> [He] carried her up the gold painted stairs to his apartment. Time had stopped dead. She found herself falling back into a pile of black velvet cushions heaped on his black velvet cushions heaped on his black satin counterpane. There was a stuffed toucan eyeing her from one side of the bed, and she could see that the room was a baroque mosaic of his fetishes. (*The Gift*, Dec 1994: 86)

The feel of the sheets, the sound of hands on stockings, the feel of denim jeans and leather jackets and the wiriness of pubic hair and the silkiness of skin are also described in detail; each of these contributing to the intimacy of the story, awaking senses in order to facilitate that imaginative development of felt sensations. I have argued that it is wrong to focus on sexual activity in sexual stories to the exclusion of other elements in the narrative; there is, of course, the danger that the sexual element is then ignored. Julie's comments make clear that the descriptions of sexual activity *are* important:

> The oral sex description was very well detailed and realistic up to a point, while I read I could almost 'feel' what Jan was enjoying (it made me wet!) but it was too short, 5 $^{1}/_{2}$. (Julie)

Mia also spoke of the need for the story to build up the right amount of 'heat' in order for them to work. Within the story, the motivations and scene-setting give permission for the heroine to experience, or give in to, sex (not the same thing as submitting to sex). For readers, those elements must also be in place in order that the explicit details of sexual activity are not simply, as Jane complained, 'all about thrusting penises, swollen labias, um... all that type of stuff. Yeah, that's okay but there's nothing exciting about that, its laid before you like a deck of cards, there's no mystery or magic.' Jane was not arguing for euphemisms or sublimation of sexual detail. The mystery or magic which is lacking in disappointing stories is emotional and/or experiential realism. This does not mean that women should have headaches or refuse sex in these stories (although they could do if that fitted the narrative), nor is direct experience of the activity required (neither Julie nor Alison had indulged in all the precise activities described in *A Woman Called Sir*). From my research, it is evident that readers require an acknowledgement that under specific circumstances a woman can forget her past, problems, inhibitions or social prohibitions and throw caution to the wind. If the conditions are right, a woman is 'free' to 'let go'. The narrative must have a naturalness, a logic to the awakening and then consummation of desire. Or, for another reader:

> What do I like? Um… er… oh er lots of fucking and yeah… oral sex really. Can't … oh what is it? If I was talking about a novel… well I would say that it was a good story well written all that stuff, but well… with erotic stories it doesn't really matter does it? … Yeah, I need to know some kind of characterization and a bit of kind of… well setting the scene is good. Like in those terrible blue movies you get – well a woman in a room and two guys come in and… she like says… [putting on a voice] 'oh let's fuck'…. no kind of story or anything… I need more than that. Not much I suppose but just enough to think these are real people… or you know… not aliens from the planet sex! And then… well… I suppose… a nice… long and fairly slow… fucking bit. (Mia)

Characters should not be 'aliens from the planet sex', they have to be believable, their motivations must be reasonable although that 'realism' is not about women showing a reluctance to have sex:

> *It's In His Kiss* is a work of fiction (unfortunately!) and it is quite funny in parts, and entertaining, but the story does not 'flow' like the ones I prefer to read. I prefer a story to build up, and I don't feel this one does, so it's just an OK story $4^1/_2$. I liked the sex, and the language used to describe it, I enjoyed the reference to Maddi using her fingers and a vibrator, neither of these developed in the story, and also the idea of Jan seducing her. But that didn't go anywhere either… There has been better and worse, I do feel it was too short, and the story did not develop very well – but it was entertaining and enjoyable. (Julie)

Julie's comments about 'flow' in this story are indications of the importance of narrative logic and of Julie's expectations that a good story will develop in particular ways. *It's In His Kiss* is narrated in the first person by Jan whose character is offered through her discussion of Maddi and her likes and dislikes in sex. Where Maddi is fairly wild, outspoken, attractive and sexy, Jan is a more quiet and unassuming individual. The discussion of Maddi's obsession with size and penetrative sex leads Jan to comment, 'I was sometimes tempted to try seducing her so she could experience something a little more tender, but I suspected that Maddi would probably demand that I strap a dildo to my crotch first.' For Julie the next step in the narrative *could* have been that seduction: it would have been logical within the story. The narrative proposals with Jan's first-person narration of her friend's obsession, and the unfolding of the story, through Maddi's various unsatisfactory sexual liaisons, suggest that Jan will have to teach Maddi to enjoy sex in other ways. Julie would have liked to have 'seen' that education. But it does not happen, instead the story takes another turn and Jan meets Dean. There is no narrative indication why Jan should have sex with Dean – she just gets lucky that he is so adept at cunnilingus.

Thus Maddi's 'education' – she has to learn that there are other dimensions to sex than a large penis – is not completed via a process of change and understanding differently through experiencing new sensations, she is just a 'witness' to Jan's experience of something better. The story is disappointing in only mentioning the possibility of Jan's seduction of Maddi. Thus, the story rates a $4^1/_2$ because it does not meet the expectations Julie has of it; expectations which are linked to sex as the bearer of self-knowledge and *FW*'s contractual obligation to expand boundaries.

As with *FW*'s photosets and its articles, readers require a level of 'honesty' in the fiction as a guarantor of quality. In the context of the fiction this means that individual stories are assessed for the following: how well does it handle the woman's reasons for wanting sex, how clearly does it show the motivations of the sexual interaction, how explicit is it – how evocative is it of sexual desire, can I feel what is happening to her – and what does she learn from the experience? For Jane, a particular problem lay in that third assessment; if the learning experience is not a positive one for the heroine then the story fails Jane's criteria. For Julie, the requirement is similar, she wants to see sexual activity leading to positivity and possible change, but she also requires the stories to follow their own sexual logics and that might mean that there is the possibility of learning from mistakes as well as pleasure. Thus, for Julie, *A Woman Called Sir* is an excellent story precisely because it takes its own direction: the characters reference prohibitions but they are not inhibited by them, sexual desire leads to out-of-the-ordinary (for the male character) sexual interaction and to pleasure. Reading stories allows Julie to balance risk and control – she wants and enjoys taking risks but only if she can 'control' it. The magazine gives a motive for taking risks and enables her to experience the pleasures of risk-taking without attendant dangers. When a story gets it right, readers are able to imagine sexual and emotional possibilities for themselves. The same story enabled Alison to imagine the possibility of fucking her boyfriend but more than that it allows her to imagine the possibilities of being sufficiently free of 'inhibition' to expand her own and her partner's horizons. Sexual detail is important to the stories but only in so far as it contributes to the imaginative possibilities for readers. Possibilities made imaginable precisely because headaches, sexual coercion and the fraught realities of women's sex lives are made peripheral. The discussion here has shown that arguments regarding pornography's singular intentions are severely limited in their understanding of readers' responses to sexually explicit stories. O'Toole's observations that 'A viewer may watch a fantasy scenario, be sexually aroused, and that will be the end of the experience' (1999: 43) are also limited. The readers I interviewed found pleasure in *FW*'s stories when they confirmed a recognizably female experience of sex and expressed a realistically mutual encounter. A suitably erotic story depends on balancing description, realism and fantasy sufficiently that the narrative opens up the possibilities of imaginative transformation for the heroine of the story and for readers.

Notes

1. At the same time as *FW*'s launch, Black Lace novels were launched in Britain to much media discussion of their erotic content combined with a quest for a traditional male hero. These novels were seen by some as sounding the death knell for category romances

while others thought that Mills & Boon and others could simply update their content. Much recent work on romantic fiction has tended to trace a developing and increasingly sexualized content in the category romance.

2. As I will go on to show, the heroine of *FW*'s stories often does not want a long-term sexual relationship. The notion that 'sexual pleasure cannot last' is a major theme in the stories and has an almost melodramatic aesthetic.
3. Of course, Faust's claim that romances are better because the penis is absent is only a mark of approval against pornography; it is not a generalized approval of romance *per se*.
4. The stories I have found are *Dangerous Spurts*, (vol. 56, issue 1, p. 53–4, 62, 94); *Tess of the Dormobiles* (issue 9, p. 53–4, 60, 94) and *Malcolm and Melanie go to Sweden* (issue 13, p. 53–4, 60, 94). The letter is *Bossed Around* (issue 13, p.68).
5. Hall's encoding/decoding model enters here with its insistence that texts are the conveyors of messages that can be accepted, negotiated or rejected.
6. As we have already seen, soft-core stories are highly regulated in the UK: rape and coercion are not permitted.
7. Although it is clear that Hardy regards some sexual activities as less likely to be chosen by women, for example, his comments regarding fellatio and sexual positions evidence a high level of distaste rather than analysis.
8. The same methodology is employed in Hardy's later work on *Black Lace* novels, 'More Black Lace: Women, Eroticism and Subjecthood', *Sexualities*, vol 4 (4), 2001.
9. As we've already seen, humour is of no significance in Hardy's analysis, so the punning names of the two initiators, Carless and Slocombe, are dismissed as rather tiresome and obvious despite their indicating the main 'quality' of each character. For Carless read callous and for Slocombe read an ability to please sexual partners by delaying his own gratification. Not surprisingly in a sexually explicit story, Slocombe is the more 'heroic' of the two.
10. I was, in fact, very surprised at the length of these stories from *Men Only*, they are twice those typically found in *For Women* and contrary to my own expectations featured comparatively little sexual action.
11. 'They had ended up in a darkened cloakroom, and Biff, who was very worked up, had abruptly pulled down her knickers and, before she realised it, pushed into her for the first time. Yet 10 minutes later they were downstairs again making polite small talk to the grown-ups. It had been so clinical – and so quick.'
12. Dangerous sports!
13. Slocombe appears slightly better than Carless as he is attempting to keep his home (no one wants to see pensioners on the streets!), but Eve is not overcome by compassion for *his* situation; indeed, that fact only really recuperates Rollo who is shown then as not simply up for any dangerous sport, he needs to prevent his grandfather's homelessness.
14. Dworkin expresses very similar disgust at semen and fellatio.
15. Her argument is largely in accord with Kipnis' claims of the transgressive possibilities of pornography.
16. She references Vance's (1984b) and Snitow's (1984b) suggestions that women's sexual experience were doubly hidden, first by androcentric culture which denied women their own pleasures and then by criticisms of that culture which refused to open up discussions of female sexuality to discuss what women like and do sexually. Vance argued this forcefully in her essay 'Pleasure and Danger', an impassioned plea for feminists not to be so cowed by the problems of sexual danger for women that they refuse to engage with issues of pleasure and positive experiences of sex.

17. The debate about the meanings and functions of Mills & Boon and other formulaic romances have oscillated between women seeking a return to the plenitude of infancy and maternal nurturance (for example, Modleski 1984) to the further objectification of the female, admittedly for female readers, but with the same result of ensuring female passivity.
18. These features of the romance prompt Thurston to ask if this might not be mischievous – establishing yet another standard women must attain (1987: 151).
19. This may seem to efface the importance of a study like Janice Radway's investigation of readers of romantic fiction, but I am troubled by the tendency in the employment of Radway's analysis which tends towards valorizing those aspects of women's reading which are predicated on acquiring knowledge. So, for example, there is discussion of the ways in which romance readers use the romantic settings as a means of learning about that location's culture and geography. If learning about geography is the reader's purpose, why not read an atlas or a travel book?
20. The magazine pays between £150–250 per story, according to the various erotic fiction writers websites including http: //www.mamohanraj.com/Writing/porn.html and http: //www.writing.co.nz/writing/erotic.htm, this is considered quite good. The terms erotica and pornography are used by writers to delineate both in terms of quality and payment: Mary Ann Mohanraj comments to would-be authors 'For market purposes, among other things, porn pays much better, and the writing quality is much worse. Go figure. On the other hand, you can put your own name on the erotica.' (http: //www.mamohanraj.com/ Writing/porn.html: 30.5.2001)
21. In his analysis of Jackie stories, Barker finds very similar themes are present, '...a theme of overcoming one's past emerges. The past is a trap; its experiences will block us. We must overcome the hold of their "tradition". I believe that this was the beginning of Jackie's response to the politics of the 1960s. Still expressed as personal re-examination, none the less, old experiences and past learning are no longer sources of morals.' (1989: 172)
22. *Reading Between the Lines* (June 1994: 62–4) was a readers' competition entry by Miranda Barrett, awarded a special prize, along with *Anomalies* by Carol Anne Davies, because they 'caught our [editorial] imagination with their quirky approach to the art of erotic writing' (June 1994: 62).

Conclusion

So you've come this far with me on the discussion of a group of women who at various periods of time identified themselves as readers of *For Women* magazine; that focus has been married to an investigation of the particularities of the magazine, its production and textual formation. Concluding a work of this kind is difficult: the investigations have ranged across areas of production, representation and consumption and have explored and debated many arguments and theorizations about pornography, popular culture, the representation of sexuality and women's use of media.

This book is a history, it has taken a snapshot of a particular publication at one point in its life and within the limits of the materials generated in literature searches, academic and commercial publications and audience research. It takes its place in a wider set of investigations into the meanings and contexts of sexually explicit materials – meanings and contexts which don't stop evolving. In particular, the theorizations and discussions of pornography continue and will continue to develop. Some elements of the discussion here remain true, in particular the problems with much of the accepted orthodoxies about pornography – a key claim I've made is that theorizations of pornography have too often offered blanket generalizations about harms and the objectification of women through representations which supposedly mirror the intricacies and inhumanity of the male sexual psyche. Where theorists have argued that pornography is more complex than the anti-pornography claims might suggest, this has tended to remain at the level of potentiality rather than derived from detailed exploration and analysis of sexually explicit representations and their consumption. I have argued that by moving away from generalization and paying attention to one instance of pornographic publishing, it is possible to understand firstly why that text takes the form it does and how individual readers are able to participate in it. I have argued that *For Women* emerges at a particular historical, social and commercial juncture. The magazine's existence and its popularity, albeit limited, cannot be analysed and understood without acknowledging those connections. Connections which made possible *For Women*'s representations of sex and their ability to 'speak' to women in ways which allowed individuals to take up and accommodate the imaginative worlds of sex offered by *For Women* through photographic imagery, 'serious' discussions and fictionalized fantasies to their own socially located circumstances.

Thus my account has attempted to refute the idea of pornography as a 'mono-logic' tool of ideological discourse. Using a theoretical framework derived from Barker (1989), Juffer (1998), Skordarki (1991) and Volosinov (1973) my analysis has charted the development and formulation of a 'pornography for women' within the portfolio of a mainstream soft-core publisher. Through factual, fictional and visual materials, this pornography for women attempted to articulate a recognizably feminine world of sexual feeling, which would make sense of women's contradictory experiences of sex sufficient that enough women (this being a commercial enterprise) would be persuaded to become regular readers of the magazine *For Women*. The commercial and institutional imperatives which created the product *For Women* were examined as constitutive of the textual formation of the magazine and a key claim I have made is that the status claimed by a publication is a crucial component of the ways in which it will be accessed and understood by its readers. Hence I stressed the ways in which *FW* articulated its own precarious existence and the difficulties of female sexual expression as linked phenomena. The magazine asserted its right to exist, in and through its expression of women's entitlement to sexual pleasure and experimentation. In so doing, the magazine spoke to socially located experiences of female sexuality, offering readers ways of making sense of their experiences of sex curtailed and frustrated by repression, inhibition, social injunction, fear and shame and their desires for more fun, arousing, positive and uninhibited possibilities. In balancing experience and possibilities, reality and fantasy, education and entertainment, the magazine offered its readers affirmation of their desires and suggested ways of understanding and using the magazine. Thus, I have attempted to reject the conception of response to pornography as based in purely physiological arousal, I have shown that responses to the magazine are social, emotional, and political as well as physical and sexual.

This has meant a focus on the intratextuality of the magazine, through the interplay of various elements – articles, readers letters and problem pages – the magazine asserted its 'honesty' and its ability to reflect a 'realistic' understanding of the dilemmas which face heterosexual women seeking sexual experiences. I found that this honesty and realism were important to readers in affirming their feelings, knowledges and dispositions thereby enabling them to use the less 'serious' elements of the magazine as spurs to fantasy, imaginative play, masturbation and sexual release. Thus realism and truthfulness were significant to the pleasures of the magazine because of their demarcation of the boundaries of possibilities, their acknowledgement and balance of risk and control. In the stories, 'honesty' and 'realism' act as guarantors of quality and establish the conditions under which the fictional woman is free to let go and enjoy sex however kinky or adventurous. A 'good' story will explain the woman's state of mind in ways that are recognizably 'true' to women's experiences and will detail a 'natural' sequence of arousal and fulfilment leading to better self-knowledge on the part of the heroine. In the photographs, the lack of erections was problematic to readers indicating a failure on the part of the magazine to be properly honest (although most recognized that this dishonesty was not necessarily the editorial team's fault), however, so long as the model looked *as if* he could be aroused then the potential for fantasy was present. Through discussion of one reader's enthusiastic enjoyment of the photosets, I have shown that sexual arousal required that the image fulfilled criteria of 'naturalness' and 'possibility'. The body should be as 'exposed' as possible to enable the assessment of its attributes, its feel, smell, weight etc. and to assess the likelihood of this man being aroused: in that way readers could begin to imagine their own sexual interactions.

In writing about women's sexual fantasies, arousal and release there is an unacknowledged problematic – that the enjoyment of a pornographic magazine requires the surrender of one's better judgement. Discussions of male readers of pornography have tended to focus on the addictiveness of pornography and the degenerative effects of such reading. Even where there is an attempt to discuss a more complex relationship between text and reader there is a tendency to stress the power of porn over its readers (Kipnis, 1996). This book has argued that these accounts are flawed, that indeed, pornography is only as influential as any other media form which seeks to convince readers of its ability to make sense of their experiences. For those readers for whom *For Women* 'worked' as a pornography for women, the magazine had achieved the right tone to enable them to look on the magazine as a friend, as a space in which they could indulge in sexual conversations, laughter and participation. This relationship placed expectations and obligations on the magazine, and I have tried to explore the ways in which readers were both pleased and disappointed by *FW*: such ambivalences indicated the nature of the relationship between the text and reader as a shared exploration of current sexual mores. However, my research has not been solely concerned with accounts of the success of the magazine. There were women amongst my interviewees for whom *FW* did not work; for example, Laura refuses to accept the magazine's proposition that it is possible to mediate an authentically female experience of heterosexual sex in the here and now. For Laura, heterosexuality is so tainted by men's power that she cannot allow herself to let go with a magazine like *FW*; as she said, 'I wouldn't let it put the bullet'. A dialogic account recognizes that Laura's response is as appropriate as Julie's and is an indication, as I showed, that different life experiences will affect the possible orientations and take up of individual discourses.

In the magazine simply being available to readers lies one of its transformative possibilities: the magazine enables readers' imaginative contemplations of sex without the risks and problems of male violence, coercion, physical, emotional and mental pressures. For others, the magazine also allows the sidestepping of social restrictions, of models of good behaviour, morality, dangers of sex, fear of disease and pregnancy. It enables moving outside of those injunctions that women don't do this, men can't let go, men will simply use you and throw you away. Readers used the magazine to assert their rights to pleasure, not only as a political statement of liberties but as a very personal reiteration of being deserving of pleasure. Of being entitled to think of themselves as beautiful, sexy, assertive, romantic, loving, worthy of loving, of the possibility of being politically motivated one minute and a sex kitten the next. In this articulation of the possibilities of women's heterosexual pleasures, the magazine opened up a dialogue on agency and sexual freedom: the right to stake a claim to experiences of pleasure and good and bad sexual practice. The dilemmas of being female, the problems of finding the voice to recognize one's own desire and needs are addressed in *For Women* and expressed in the take-up of its explorations by its readers.

Attwood has discussed the ways in which 'the [recent] making over of sex is not primarily or straightforwardly about the accommodation of male sexuality, but about the formulation of women's sexual pleasure as a kind of feminine auto-eroticism' (2005: 400). It's an important point, but she also goes on to discuss the power of commercialized sex to inhabit our fantasies, leading inevitably back to the problems of thinking about women's relationships with sexual materials:

- the problems of authenticity, can there be authentic representations of sex for women? Examination of texts for supposedly feminist elements or indeed for feminine elements effaces any possibilities of the authentic. In particular feminist anti-porn theorising has almost erased that possibility.
- popular culture tends to represent sex for women as 'sex for the sex-less' (Burchill, 2000) whereby it is dressed up as 'pampering' and 'treating oneself' rather than the bodily experiences of sex in its myriad forms: a form of self-care and therefore not really *sex*.
- conceives of power in particular ways, as a force which exhorts singular forms of response.

This brings me to one last argument, one which draws on the work of Michel Foucault. I've touched on elements of this claim throughout the preceding chapters but I want to end this book with a brief discussion of how and why my argument refuses the notion of power which underpins talk of women being exhorted to embrace their sexual objectification or to view themselves as sexual consumers in the service of capitalist industries. Foucault's fascinating histories of the medicalization and categorization of sexual 'types' have been immensely influential and turn on the notion of the productive force of discourses as nexi of power and knowledge. Contrary to historical earlier accounts which claimed that the Victorians (in particular) repressed sexuality, Foucault argues that an incitement to discourse in medical, educational and other institutional practices of categorization of sexual behaviours produced sexualities as we know them, and, importantly, also produced the voices of resistance to those categorizations.

> There is no question that the appearance in nineteenth-century psychiatry, jurisprudence, and literature of a whole series of discourses on the species and sub-species of homosexuality, inversion, pederasty, and 'psychic hermaphrodism'

> made possible a strong advance of social controls into this area of 'perversity'; but it also made possible the formation of a 'reverse' discourse: homosexuality began to speak in its own behalf, to demand that its legitimacy or 'naturality' be acknowledged, often in the same vocabulary, using the same categories by which it was medically disqualified. (1981: 101)

This powerful argument has been used to describe women's increasing use of sexually explicit materials and their employment of the language of getting in touch with hitherto repressed desires as a form of '"disciplining" fantasy in which the language of sexual freedom speaks instead as a colonising discourse: to the female reader who is the gendered subject of knowledge, power and pleasure.' (Sonnet, 2006: 33) I've argued somewhat differently here, the lengthy quotations from women readers illuminate the ways in which resistance to discursive constructions of female sexuality is lived and experienced, and that has shown that their resources for 'resistance' are wider than a 'reverse discourse'. The categorizations of pornography (examined in earlier chapters) assume purposes and meanings to pornography, uses and effects which are singular. But the arguments and evidence I've raised here have indicated that the *experiences* and *practices* of reading a sexually explicit magazine are considerably wider than the presumed masturbatory potential. Given the frequency with which respondents claimed not to use *For Women* as a spur to masturbation we must acknowledge that there is no necessary relation between pornography and sexual release, that in fact, the material can be read or viewed for other reasons. Of course, this explains how and why anti-porn feminists or academics can manage to restrain any sexual excitation in *their* reading of porn. In coming to a sexually explicit publication, readers bring expectations – pornography has social meaning before any instance of use of it – and they measure the material in front of them in light of those expectations. Those expectations need to be understood as orientations to pornography, in other words people don't *interpret* pornography, they respond to it and in and through those responses accord it a significance in their understanding of themselves, their pleasures, the sexual pleasures of others, the social, economic, medical and cultural place of sexuality, the imbrications of pornography in sexuality etc. There is no one meaning to pornography, no 'power' in pornography, there are no causal effects in pornography, there are, however, plenty of puzzles in porn and its relevance to its consumers and users. I hope this book has begun to open up some of those puzzles.

BIBLIOGRAPHY

Albury, K., 2005, Yes Means Yes: Getting Explicit about Heterosex, NSW: Allen & Unwin.

Albury, K., 1998, 'Spanking Stories: writing and reading bad female heterosex', Continuum: Journal of Media & Cultural Studies, vol.12, no.1, April: 55–68.

Alexander, F., 1998, 'Prisons, Traps and Escape Routes: Feminist Critiques of Romance', in Pearce & Wisker (eds), 1998a, Fatal Attractions: Rescripting Romance in Contemporary Literature and Film, London: Pluto.

Altman, R., 1999, Film/Genre, London: British Film Institute.

Anderson, D. & M. Mosbacher, 1997, 'Sex-mad, silly and selfish', Guardian, 24 November: G2: 24.

Andreae, S., 1994, 'Forbidden Fruit', Observer Magazine, March 20: 32–5.

Ang, I., 1996, Living Room Wars: Rethinking Media Audiences for a Postmodern World, London: Routledge.

Ang, I., 1991, Desperately Seeking the Audience, London: Routledge.

Ang, I., 1989 'Wanted: Audiences. On the Politics of Empirical Audience Studies', in: Ellen Seiter et al. (ed.), Remote Control: Audiences, Television and Cultural Power, London: Routledge.

Ang, I. and Hermes, J., 1988 'Gender and/in media consumption', in Curran & Gurevitch (eds), Mass Media and Society, London: Edward Arnold.

Ang, I., 1985, Watching Dallas: Soap Opera and the Melodramatic Imagination, London: Methuen.

Anthony, A., 1997, 'The Observer Interview, Ralph Gold: where there's muck, there's Gold', Observer, 18 May: Life: 6.

Appleyard, B., 1992, 'Way beyond the erogenous zone', Sunday Times, September 12: Review, 10–12.

Armstrong, S., 1995, 'More!'s Sexcess Story', Guardian, 20 November.

Arthurs, J., 2004, Television and Sexuality: Regulation and the Politics of Taste, Milton Keynes: Open University Press.

Arthurs, J. and Grimshaw, J. (eds), 1998, Women's Bodies: Discipline and Transgression, London: Cassell.

Assister, A. and Carol, A. (eds), 1993, Bad Girls and Dirty Pictures: The Challenge to Reclaim Feminism, London: Pluto.

Attwood, F., 2005, 'Fashion and Passion: Marketing Sex to Women', Sexualities, vol 8(4): 392–406.
Attwood, F., 2002, 'Reading Porn: The Paradigm Shift in Pornography Research', Sexualities, vol 5(1): 91–105.
Bakhtin, M. M. 1984, Rabelais and His World, Bloomington: Indiana University Press.
Bakhtin, M. M. 1986, Speech Genres and Other Late Essays, Austin: Univ of Texas Press.
Ballaster, R., Beetham, M., Frazer, E. and Hebron, S., 1991, Women's Worlds: Ideology, Femininity and the Women's Magazine, Basingstoke: MacMillan.
Barker, M. and Brooks, K., 1998, Knowing Audiences: Judge Dredd, its friends, fans and foes, Luton: University of Luton Press.
Barker, M., 1996, 'Review of John Tulloch & Henry Jenkins, Science Fiction Audiences', Media Culture & Society, vol.18, no.3: 364–7.
Barker, M. and Beezer, A., 1993a, Reading Into Cultural Studies, London: Routledge.
Barker, M., 1993b 'The Bill Clinton fan syndrome', a review article on Henry Jenkins, Textual Poachers, Media Culture & Society, vol.15, no.4: 669–74.
Barker, M., 1993c, 'Seeing how far you can see: on being a 'fan' of 2000AD' in Buckingham (ed.), 1993, Reading Audiences: Young People and the Media, Manchester: Manchester University Press.
Barker, M., 1989, Comics: Ideology, Power and the Critics, Manchester, Manchester University Press.
Barnard, B., 2005, *Flesh Trade: Tales from the UK Sexual Underground*, Manchester: Headpress/Critical Vision.
Barrett, M. & A. Phillips, 1992, Destabilising Theory: Contemporary Feminist Debates, Cambridge: Polity Press.
Bartky, S., 1990, 'Feminine Masochism and the Politics of personal Transformation', Hypatia No. 2 (special issue of Women's Studies International Forum, vol. 7, no. 5): 323–334.
Bayley, C., 1995, 'It's a dirty job. And everybody is doing it', Independent, June 13: II/6-7.
Beale, C., 1995, 'A sophisticate puts his talent to use at a new porn channel', Campaign, June 2: 15.
Bedell, G., 1995, 'Sex sells but have we sold out?' Good Housekeeping, January: 81-2.
Bedell, G., 1992, 'The language of lust', Guardian, April 22: 17.
Beetham, M., 1996, A Magazine of Her Own? Domesticity and Desire in the Woman's Magazine, 1800–1914, London: Routledge.
Bell, E., 1995, 'The new porn brokers' Observer, February 26: 2-3.
Bellos, A., 1994, 'Penthouse publishers repent over fake royal porn pictures', Guardian, October 8: 3.
Beneke, T., 1990, 'Intrusive Images and Subjectified Bodies: Notes on Visual Heterosexual Porn' in Kimmel (ed.), 1990, Men Confront Pornography, New York: Crown.
Bennet, J., 1996, 'Leaving Nothing to Imagination: Obscenity and Postmodern Sensitivity', in Paul Duro, (ed.), The Rhetoric of the Frame. Essays on the Boundaries of the Artwork, Cambridge University Press, Cambridge.
Bennett, T. (ed.), 1990, Popular Fiction: Technology, Ideology, Production, Reading, London: Routledge.
Bennett, T., Mercer, C. and Woollacott, J. (eds), 1986, Popular Culture and Social Relations, Buckingham: OU Press.
Bennett, C., 1994, 'A prophet and porn', Guardian Weekend, May 28: 20–27.
Berens, J., 1992, 'Porn Again, What Women Want From Erotica', Arena, September, reprinted in Jones, D. (ed.), 1996, Sex Power and Travel: Ten Years of Arena, London: Virgin: 196–9.
Berens, J., 1992, 'Wild women, safe sex and ice cream', Evening Standard, 28 April: 16.
Berger, J., 1972, Ways of Seeing, Harmondsworth: Penguin.
Billen, A., 1995, 'Dad, swag and bob-tails', Observer, Review, 5 November.

Bordo, S., 1999, The Male Body: A New Look at Men in Public and in Private, New York: Farrar, Straus & Giroux.
Bordwell, D. and Carroll, N. (eds), 1996, Post-Theory, Madison: University of Wisconsin Press.
Bordwell, D., 1989, Making Meaning: Inference and Rhetoric in the Interpretation of Cinema, Boston, Mass: Harvard University Press.
Botham, D., 1995, 'Soft Porn: Let's give the government a big hand', Guardian, January 25: 22.
Bourdieu, P., 1984, Distinction: A Social Critique of the Judgement of Taste, Cambridge: Polity Press.
Bower, M., 1986, 'Daring to speak its name: the relationship of women to pornography', Feminist Review, no.24, October.
Boyle, K., 2000, 'The Pornography Debates: Beyond Cause and Effect', Women's Studies International Forum, vol 23 no 2: 187–195.
Boyle, T., 1989, Black Swine in the Sewers of Hampstead, New York: Viking Press.
Braithwaite, B. and Barrell, J., 1988, The Business of Women's Magazines, 2nd Edition, London: Kogan Page.
Braithwaite, B., 1998, 'Magazines: The Bulging Bookstores' in Briggs & Cobley (eds) The Media: An Introduction, Harlow: Longman.
Braithwaite, B., 1995, Women's Magazines: The First 300 Years, London: Peter Owen.
Brewer, M., 1986, 'Daring to Speak its Name: The Relationship of Women to Pornography', Feminist Review, no.24, October.
Briggs, A. and Cobley, P. (eds), 1998, The Media: An Introduction, Harlow: Longman.
Bristow, J., 1997, Sexuality, London: Routledge.
Brockway, S. and Lazzeri, A., 1992, 'Are naughty pics of men's bits a turn-on?' Sun, 8 May: 26.
Brooks, A., 1999, Postfeminisms: Feminism, Cultural Theory and Cultural Forms, London: Routledge.
Brown, M., 1996, 'The Thick Blue Line', Guardian, 29 April.
Brown, M. E. (ed.), 1990, Television and Women's Culture: The Politics of the Popular, London: Sage.
Brownmiller, S., 1976, Against Our Will: Men, Women and Rape, London: Penguin.
Brule, T., 1994, 'The Gloss on the Pink Press', Guardian, 7 February.
Brunsdon, C., 2000, 'Post-feminism and shopping films', The Film Studies Reader, J. Hollows, P. Hutchings and M. Jancovich (eds), London: Arnold.
Buckingham, D., (ed.), 1993, Reading Audiences: Young People and the Media, Manchester: Manchester University Press.
Buckingham, D., 1991: 'What are words worth? Interpreting children's talk about television', Cultural Studies **5**: 228–45.
Burchill, J., 2000, 'The Word "Pampering" Means: "Have a Wash and Stop Being Such a Neurotic Cow". It is Sex for the Sex-less and Rest for the Rest-less' Weekend Guardian, 9th September: 3.
Burchill, J., 1996, 'Where's the Beef?' in Jones (ed.) Sex Power and Travel: Ten Years of Arena, London: Virgin.
Burgin, V. et al. (eds), 1985, Formations of Fantasy, London: Routledge.
Califia, P., 1986, 'The Obscene, Disgusting and Vile Meese Commission Report', http://eserver.org/cultronix/califia/meese/ accessed 30/8/00.
Carol, A., 1994, Nudes, Prudes and Attitudes: Pornography and Censorship, Cheltenham: New Clarendon Press.
Carol, A., 1993, 'Porn, Perversion and Sexual Ethics', in Harwood et al. (eds), Pleasure Principles: Politics, Sexuality and Ethics, London: Lawrence & Wishart.

Carse, A. L., 1999, 'Pornography's many meanings: a reply to C. M. Concepcion', Hypatia, winter: vol.14.1: 101–111.
Carter, A., 1978, The Sadien Woman and the Ideology of Pornography, New York: Pantheon.
Carter, M., 1995, 'Toughing it out on the top shelf', Guardian, April 3: G2T: 17.
Carter, M., 1994, 'Pleased? Actually, no, not really', Independent, March 30: II/ 25.
Carter, M., 1985, 'The Look of Love', Australian Journal of Cultural Studies, 3:1: 105–119.
Cawelti, J., 1976, Adventure, Mystery, and Romance: Formula Stories as Art and Popular Culture, Chicago: University of Chicago Press.
Chancer, L. S., 1998, Reconcilable Differences: Confronting Beauty, Pornography and the Future of Feminism, London/Los Angeles: University of California.
Chapman, R. and Rutherford, J., (eds), 1988a, Male Order: Unwrapping Masculinity, London: Lawrence & Wishart.
Chapman, R., 1988b, 'The Great Pretender: Variations on the New Man Theme' in Chapman and Rutherford (eds), Male Order: Unwrapping Masculinity, London: Lawrence & Wishart.
Chappell, H., 1991, 'Girls' night in: "Ooo-er! Gross! Amazing!"', Independent, 3 December.
Chaudhuri, A., 1995, 'It's my Party', Guardian, 7 November.
Chester, G. and Dickey, J. (eds), 1988, Feminism and Censorship: The Current Debate, Bridport: Prism Press.
Church Gibson, P., (ed.), 2005, More Dirty Looks: Women, Pornography, Power, London: BFI.
Church Gibson, P. and Gibson, R. (eds), 1993, Dirty Looks: Women, Pornography, Power, London: British Film Institute.
Clark, K., 1960, The Nude: A Study of Ideal Art, Harmondsworth: Pelican.
Ciclitira, K., 2004, 'Pornography, Women and Feminism: Between Pleasure and Politics', Sexualities, vol 7(3): 281–301.
Clover, C., 1992, Men, Women and Chainsaws: Gender in the Modern Horror Film, London: British Film Institute Publishing.
Cole, S. G., 1989, Pornography and the Sex Crisis, Toronto: Amanita.
Collins, C., 1996, 'To concede or to contest? Language and class struggle' in Barker & Kennedy (eds), To Make Another World: Studies in Protest and Collective Action: London, Avebury.
Collins, J. K., 1996, The Sex We Want: Straight Talking from 90s Women, London: Pandora.
Concepcion, C., 1999, 'On pornography, representation and sexual agency', Hypatia, winter: vol.14.1: 97–100.
Conway, M. T., 1997, 'Spectatorship in Lesbian Porn: The Woman's Woman's Film', Wide Angle, 19(3), July: 91–113.
Cook, S., 1992, 'Sweet sell of sexcess', Guardian, 27 June: 27.
Cooper, E. 1990, Fully Exposed: The Male Nude in Photography, London: Unwin Hyman.
Corner, J., 1991, 'Meaning, genre and context: the problematics of 'public knowledge' in the New Audience Studies' in Curran & Gurevitch (eds), Mass Media and Society, London: Edward Arnold.
Corner, J., 1998, 'Why study media form?' in Briggs & Cobley (eds), The Media: An Introduction, Harlow: Longman.
Cowie, E., 1981, 'Fantasia', M/F, 5/6.
Cranny Francis, A., 1994, 'Feminist Romance' in The Polity Reader in Cultural Theory, Cambridge: Polity.
Creed, B., 2003, Media Matrix: Sexing the New Reality, NSW: Allen & Unwin.
Curran, J., Morley, D. and Walkerdine, V. (eds), 1996, Cultural Studies and Communications, London: Arnold.
Coward, R., 1997, 'You got it, but do you have to flaunt it?' Guardian, 15 September: 17.
Coward, R., 1984, Female Desire: Women's Sexuality Today, London: Paladin.
Coward, R., 1982, 'Sexual Violence and Sexuality', Feminist Review, no.11, June.

Culf, A., 1995, 'X-Rated Channel Plays for Couples', Guardian, 20 October.
Culf, A., 1995, 'Women reject sex on middle shelf', Guardian, August 30: 3.
Cunningham, T., 1992, 'What turns you on?' Sun, 22 April: 7.
Currie, D. H., 1999, Girl Talk: Adolescent Magazines and their Readers, Toronto: Univ. of Toronto Press.
Darnton, N., 1995, 'For British women's magazines, sex is a recipe for success', New York Times, 13 February: 26.
Davidson, A., 1986, 'From mags to riches?' Marketing, 3 July: 22ff.
Davies, J., 1992, Daily Mail, 5th May.
Davies, N., 1994, 'Dirty business', Guardian Weekend, November 26: 12–17.
Davies, N., 1994, 'Under cover kings', Guardian, November 28: G2T: 2.
Davis, K., 1987, 'Romance', Out of Focus: Writings on Women & Media, London: Women's Press.
Davis, M., 1994, 'Personality versus Physique', Art Journal, 53.
Day, G. & C. Bloom (eds), 1988, Perspectives on Pornography, Sexuality in Film and Literature, London: Macmillan.
Diamond, I., 1980, 'Pornography and Repression: A Reconsideration', Journal of Women in Culture and Society, 5:4.
Dickinson, R., Harindranath, R. and Linne, O. (eds), 1998, Approaches to Audiences, London: Edward Arnold.
Dines, G., Jensen, R. and Russo, A., 1998, Pornography: The Production and Consumption of Inequality, London: Routledge.
Dixon, J., 1999, The Romance Fiction of Mills & Boon: 1909–1990s, London: UCL Press.
Doane, M. A., 1992, 'Film and the Masquerade: Theorising the Female Spectator', in M. Merck et al. (eds) The Sexual Subject: A Screen Reader in Sexuality, London: Routledge.
Doane, M. A., 1988, 'Masquerade Reconsidered: Further Thoughts', Discourse, 11, fall/winter.
Donnelly, M., 2005, *Sixties Britain*, Harlow: Pearson Education
Driver, S. and Gillespie, A., 1993, 'Structural Change in the cultural industries: British magazine publishing in the 1980s', Media Culture & Society, vol.15: 183–201.
Drotner, K., 1994, 'Ethnographic enigmas: the 'everyday' in recent media studies', Cultural Studies, vol.8, no.2: 341–57.
du Gay, P. (ed.), 1997, Production of Culture/Cultures of Production, Milton Keynes: The Open University.
During, S. (ed.), 1993, The Cultural Studies Reader, London: Routledge.
Dutton, K., 1995, The Perfectible Body; The Western Ideal of Physical Development, London: Cassell.
Dworkin A., and MacKinnon, C., 1988, Pornography and Civil Rights: A New Day for Women's Equality, Minneapolis: Organizing Against Pornography.
Dworkin, A., 1981, Pornography: Men Possessing Women, London: The Women's Press.
Dworkin, A., 1980, 'Why so called radical men love and need pornography' in Lederer (ed.), Take Back the Night, New York: William Morrow.
Dyer, R., 1993, The Matter of Images: Essays on Representations, London: Routledge.
Dyer, R., 1992a, Only Entertainment, London: Routledge.
Dyer, R., 1992b, 'Don't Look Now: The Male Pin-Up' in his Only Entertainment.
Dyer, R., 1991, 'Believing in Fairies: The Author and the Homosexual', in Fuss, D. (ed.), Inside/Out: Lesbian Theories, Gay Theories, London: Routledge.
Dyer, R., 1979, 'In Defence of Disco' in Frith &.Goodwin (eds), 1990, On Record, London: Routledge.
Easthope, A., 1992, What a Man's Gotta Do: The Masculine Myth in Popular Culture, London: Routledge.

Ehrenreich, B., Hess, E. and Jacobs, G., 1997, 'Beatlemania: A Sexually Defiant Consumer Culture?' in Gelder & Thornton (eds), The Subcultures Reader, London: Routledge.
Ehrenreich, B., 1983, The Hearts of Men: American Dreams and the Flight from Commitment, New York: Anchor.
Elleschild, L., 1994, 'Bad Girls and Excessive Women: The Social Construction of Promiscuity', Sexualities in Social Context, conference of the British Sociological Association, March.
Ellis, J., 1992, 'On Pornography', in Screen, The Sexual Subject: A Screen Reader in Sexuality, London: Routledge.
Ellis, K., Hunter, N. D., Jaker, B., O'Dair, B. and Tallmer, A. (eds), 1986, Caught Looking: Feminism, Pornography and Censorship, New York: Caught Looking.
Ellsworth-Jones, W., 1992, 'Virgin's guide to writing dirty books for women', Daily Telegraph, 16 June.
Engel, M., 1993, 'Strong, thick and glossy', Guardian, 20 December.
Epstein,D. and Steinberg, D.L., 1996, 'No Fixed Abode: Feminism in the 1990s', Parallax, no.3, September.
Faust, B., 1980, Women, Sex and Pornography, Harmondsworth: Penguin.
Featherstone, M., 1991 Consumer Culture and Postmodernism, London: Sage.
Ferguson, M. and Golding, P. (eds), 1997 Cultural Studies in Question, London: Routledge.
Ferguson, M., 1983, Forever Feminine: Women's Magazines and the Cult of Femininity, London: Heinemann.
Fiske, J., 1987, Television Culture, London: Methuen.
Fiske, J., 1986, 'Television: polysemy and popularity', Critical Studies in Mass Communication, 3(4): 391–408.
Forbes, J., 1994, 'Punishing sex: Disciplining Women in Contemporary Discourses of Sexuality', paper to Sexualities in Social Context, British Sociological Association Annual Conference, 28–31 March.
Formations, 1983, Formations of Pleasure, London: Routledge & Kegan Paul.
Forna, A., 1996, 'For women – or for men only?' Independent on Sunday, April 28: 3.
Foster, A., 1988, 'Heroes, Fools and Martyrs', Ten-8, no.28: 54–63.
Foucault, M., 1981, The History of Sexuality Vol 1: An Introduction, Harmondsworth: Penguin.
Fowler, B., 1997, Pierre Bourdieu and Cultural Theory: Critical Investigations, Newbury Park: Sage.
Franklin, S., Lury, C. and Stacey, J., (eds), 1991, Off-centre: Feminism and Cultural Studies, London: Harper Collins Academic.
Frazer, E., 1987, 'Teenage girls reading Jackie', Media Culture & Society, vol.9: 407–25.
Friedan, B., 1963, The Feminine Mystique, Harmondsworth: Penguin.
Frow, J., 1991, 'Michel de Certeau and the practice of representation', Cultural Studies, vol.5, no.1: 52–60.
Gabor, M., 1972, The Pin-Up: A Modest History, London: Pan Books.
Gallivan, J., 1992, 'So what do you use pornography for?' Independent, (Living Section), 28 October: 16.
Galloway, J., 1990, 'The phoney search for women's erotica', New Statesman & Society, 21 & 28 December: 26–28.
Gamman, L. and Marshment, M. (eds), 1988, The Female Gaze: Women as Viewers of Popular Culture, London: The Women's Press.
Gauntlett, D., and Hill, A., 1999, TV Living: Television, Culture and Everyday Life, London: Routledge.
Gelder, K. and Thornton, S. (eds), 1997, The Subcultures Reader, London: Routledge.
Geraghty, C., 1991, Women and Soap Opera: A Story of Prime Time Soaps, Cambridge: Polity Press.

Gerrard, N., 1994, 'Battlefield of the body politic', Observer, June 19: 6.
Gilbert, H. (ed.), 1993, The Sexual Imagination: From Acker to Zola, London: Random House.
di Giovanni, J., 1992, 'The pleasure principle', Sunday Times, August 30: 7/2-3.
di Giovanni, J., 1992, 'Crusading for candid sex', Sunday Times, 12 April: 4/4.
Glaister, D., 1996, 'Soft porn goes for wired uplift', Guardian, February 5: G2T: 12.
Gledhill, C. (ed.), 1991, Stardom: Industry of Desire, London: Routledge.
Gough-Yates, A., 2000a, ' Sweet sell of sexcess': the production of young women's magazines and readerships in the 1990s' in Berry (ed.), Ethics and Media Culture, Practices and Representations, Oxford: Focal Press.
Gough-Yates, A., 2000b, Seriously Glamourous? The production of women's magazines and readerships, Ph.D. thesis, University of Birmingham.
Gould, S., 1992, 'The production, marketing and consumption of sexually explicit materials', Journal of Public Policy and Marketing, no.11.
Grant, L., 1998, 'And men are still on top', Guardian, 28 April: 8.
Grant, L., 1997, 'Meanwhile, back in the real world', Guardian, 25 November: G2: 8.
Grant, L., 1996, 'Cut and thrust', Guardian, February 5: 2/6.
Gray, A. and McGuigan, J. (eds), 1993, Studying Culture: An Introductory Reader, London: Arnold.
Gray, A., 1992, Video Playtime: The Gendering of a Leisure Technology, London: Routledge.
Greenstreet, R., 1993, 'The questionnaire: Jacqueline Gold', Guardian, November 20: 86.
Greer, G., 1971, The Female Eunuch, London: MacGibbon and Kee.
Grey, A., 1993, 'Why Pornography should not be Censored', Political Notes, no.85, London: Libertarian Alliance.
Griffin, S., 1981, Pornography and Silence: Culture's Revenge Against Nature, London: The Women's Press.
Griffin, S., 1979, Rape: The Power of Consciousness, San Francisco: Harper & Row.
Griffin, S., 1978, Women and Nature, New York: Harper & Row.
Grimshaw, J., 1993, 'Ethics, Fantasy and Self-transformation', in Phillips Griffiths (ed.), Ethics, Cambridge: Cambridge University Press.
Gripsrud, J., 1995, The Dynasty Years: Hollywood Television and Critical Media Studies, London: Routledge.
Grossberg, L., Nelson, C., and Treichler, P. (eds), 1992, Cultural Studies, London: Routledge.
Gunther, A., 1995, 'Over-rating the X-rating', Journal of Communication, winter.
Hagerty, B., 1993, 'OK? we'll see!' Guardian (G2), 22 March: 14.
Hall, S. (ed.), 1997, Representation: Cultural Representations and Signifying Practices, Milton Keynes: The Open University.
Hall, S., 1987, 'Encoding and decoding in the television discourse' in CCCS, Culture, Media, Language, London: Hutchinson.
Hall, S., Critcher, C., Jefferson, T., Clarke, J. and Roberts, B., 1978, Policing the Crisis: Mugging, the State and Law and Order, London: MacMillan.
Hallam, J., and Moody, N. (eds), 2000, Consuming for Pleasure: Selected Essays on Popular Fiction, Liverpool: John Moores University & Association for Research in Popular Fictions.
Hallam, J., and Marshment, M., 1995, 'Questioning the "Ordinary" Woman: Oranges are Not the Only Fruit, text and viewer' in Skeggs (ed.), Feminist Cultural Theory, Manchester: Manchester University Press.
Hansen, M., 1991, Babel and Babylon: spectatorship in American silent film, Cambridge, MA: Harvard University Press.
Hardy, S., 1998, The Reader, The Author, His Woman and Her Lover: Soft Core Pornography and Heterosexual Men, London: Cassell.

Hartley, J., 1998, ''When your Child Grows up too Fast': juvenation and the boundaries of the social in the news media', Continuum: Journal of Media & Cultural Studies, vol.12, no.1, April: 9–30.
Harwood, V., Oswell, D., Parkinson, K., and Ward, A. (eds), 1993, Pleasure Principles: Politics, Sexuality and Ethics, London: Lawrence & Wishart.
Haste, C. 1992, Rules of Desire: Sex in Britain, World War I to the present, London: Pimlico/Random House.
Hattenstone, S., 1995, 'Selling Glamour', Guardian, 12 June: G2T: 17.
Hattenstone, S., 1995, 'Sex and the Single Men's Mag', Guardian, 10 April.
Hawkes, Gail, (1996), A Sociology of Sex and Sexuality, Buckingham, Open University Press.
Hawkins, G. & Zimring, F. E., 1988, Pornography in a Free Society, Cambridge: Cambridge University Press.
Heath, S., 1982, The Sexual Fix, London: Macmillan.
Hebditch, D. & N. Anning, 1988, Porn Gold: Inside the Pornography Business, London: Faber and Faber.
Heggli, G., 1993, 'Talking with readers: An alternative approach', Journal of Popular Culture, vol.26, no.4, spring.
Hellen, N., 'TV porn channel wins UK licence', Sunday Times, April 30: 1/9.
Hermes, J., 1995, Reading Women's Magazines, Cambridge: Polity Press.
Hill, A. & Thomson, K., 2000, 'Sex and the media: a shifting landscape' in R. Jowell, J. Curtice, A. Park, K. Thomson, L. Jarvis, C. Bromley & Stratford, N. (eds), 2000, British Social Attitudes: the 17th Report: Focusing on diversity, London: Sage.
Hill, A., 1997, Shocking Entertainment: Viewer Response to Violent Movies, Luton: University of Luton Press.
Hodge, R., 1990, Literature as Discourse, Baltimore: Johns Hopkins University Press.
Hodge, B. and Tripp, D., 1986, Children and Television, Cambridge: Polity Press.
Holbrook, D. (ed.), 1972, The Case Against Pornography, London: Tom Stacey.
Holland, P., 1983, 'The Page 3 Girl Speaks to Women Too', Screen, vol.24, no. 3.
Hollibaugh, A., 1984, 'Desire for the Future: Radical Hope in Passion and Pleasure' in Vance, 1984.
Horrocks, R., 1995, Male Myths and Icons: Masculinity in Popular Culture, London: MacMillan Press.
Howard, E., 1995, 'Fleshing out the market', Guardian, 3 April: G2T, 16.
Hunt, L., 1998, British Low Culture: From Safari Suits to Sexploitation, London: Routledge.
Hunt, L., (ed.), 1993a, The Invention of Pornography, New York: Zone Books.
Hunt, L., 1993b, 'Obscenity and the origins of modernity, 1500–1800', in Hunt (ed.), The Invention of Pornography, New York: Zone Books.
Hunt, M., 1990, 'The De-eroticisation of women's liberation', Feminist Review, no.34, spring.
Huntley, R., 1998, 'Slippery when Wet: the shifting boundaries of the pornographic (a class analysis)', Continuum: Journal of Media & Cultural Studies, vol.12, no.1, April: 69–82.
Iley, C., 1994, 'Why women are not pawns of porn', Sunday Times, August 7: 10/ 16.
Independent on Sunday, 1996, 'The shrug factor: pornography and the British: a special report: 1', 21 April: Real Life: 1–10.
Independent on Sunday, 1996, 'Pornography: a special report: 2', 28 April: Real Life: 3–5.
Independent on Sunday, 1992, 'Do women like looking at pictures of naked men? 26 April: 20.
Irigaray, L., 1985, This Sex Which is Not One, (trans. C.Porter with C.Burke), Ithaca: Cornell University Press.
I-Spy Productions, 1992, 'Pornography and Capitalism: The UK Pornography Industry' in Itzin (ed.), Pornography: Women, Violence and Civil Liberties, Oxford: Oxford University Press.

Itzin, C. (ed.), 1992, Pornography: Women, Violence and Civil Liberties, Oxford: Oxford University Press.
Jackson, A., 1994, 'What's a nice boy like you', The Times magazine, May 14.
Jackson, S., 1996, 'Ignorance is *Bliss*, when you're *Just Seventeen*', Trouble and Strife, no.33, summer.
Jackson, S., 2000, Heterosexuality in Question, London: Sage.
Jacobs, K., 2004, 'Pornography in Small Places and Other Spaces', *Cultural Studies*, 18:1.
Jacques, J., 1992, 'Nikki takes her pic of the hunks', Sun, 5 May.
Jarrett, L., 1997, Stripping in Time: A History of Erotic Dancing, London: Pandora.
Jeal, N. 1992, 'Today we have naming of parts', The Observer, 31 May: 52.
Jeffreys, S., 1990 Anticlimax: A Feminist Perspective on the Sexual Revolution, New York: New York University Press.
Jenkins, H., 1993, Textual Poachers, London: Routledge.
Jenkins, T., 1992, 'The joy of sex with slow motion replay' Independent (Living), 3 September: 12.
Jobling, P., 1999, Fashion Spreads: Word and Image in Fashion Photography Since 1980, Oxford: Berg.
Jones, D. (ed.), 1996, Sex Power and Travel: Ten Years of Arena, London: Virgin.
Jones, D., 1993, 'Murdoch, Mojo and Mr Blobby: Magazines', Guardian, December 27: 10.
Jong, E., 1995, 'The first foray of the fascist', Media Guardian, June 5: 16.
Juffer, J., 1998, At Home with Pornography, New York: New York University Press.
Kaite, B., 1995, Pornography and Difference, Bloomington and Indianapolis: Indiana University Press.
Kappeler, S., 1986, The Pornography of Representation, Cambridge: Polity Press.
Kaplan, E. A., 1984, 'Is the Gaze Male?' in Snitow et al. (eds).
Karacs, I., 1996, 'It's culture and it's sexy', Independent, March 8: 2/6.
Kehily, M. J., 1999, 'More sugar? Teenage magazines, gender displays and sexual learning' in European Journal of Cultural Studies, London: Sage, vol. 2(1): 65–89.
Kendrick, W., 1987, The Secret Museum: Pornography in Modern Culture, New York: Viking.
Kent, S. and Morreau, J. (eds), 1985a, Women's Images of Men, London: Writers & Readers.
Kent, S., 1985b, 'The Erotic Male Nude' in Kent & Morreau, Women's Images of Men, London: Writers & Readers.
Kennedy, H., 1994, 'How can she guess when yes means no', Observer, June 19: Review, 20.
Key Note Report, 1995, Men's Magazines, Hampton: Key Note Ltd.
Key Note Report, 1996, Women's Magazines, Hampton: Key Note Ltd.
Killick, M., 1994, The Sultan of Sleaze: The David O'Sullivan Story, London: Penguin.
Kipnis, L., 1996, Bound and Gagged: Pornography and the Politics of Fantasy in America, New York: Grove.
Kipnis, L., 1993, 'She male fantasies and the aesthetics of pornography', in Church Gibson and Gibson, 1993.
Kipnis, L., 1992, '(Female) Desire and (Female) Disgust: reading Hustler', in Grossberg, Nelson and Treichler, 1992.
Kleinhaus, C., 1996, 'Studying Sexual Images', Jump Cut, no.40, March.
Krizanovich, K., 1995, 'Talk dirty to me', Guardian, August 10: 2/12-13.
Kuhn, A., 1985, The Power of the Image: Essays on Representation and Sexuality, London: Routledge & Kegan Paul.
Lane, F. S., 2001, Obscene Profits: The Entrepreneurs of Pornography in the Cyber Age, London: Routledge.
Lawson, M., 1997, 'Lifting the net curtain on a hardcore world, Guardian, 15 February: 20.

Lawson, N., 1992, 'Full-frontal attacks', Evening Standard, 23 April: 11.

Lazzeri, A., 1992, 'Penthouse Petts', Sun, 6 May: 5.

Lederer, L. (ed.), 1980, Take Back the Night: Women on Pornography, New York: William Morrow.

Lee, J., 1988, 'Care to Join me in an Upwardly Mobile Tango? Postmodernism and the 'New Woman'', in Gamman & Marshment, The Female Gaze, London: The Women's Press.

Leroy, M., 1994, Pleasure: The Truth About Female Sexuality, London: Harper Collins.

Letherby, G. and Zdrodowski, D., 1995, '"Dear Researcher": The Use of Correspondence as a Method within Feminist Qualitative Research', Gender & Society, vol.9, no.5, October: 576–593.

Levy, A., 2005, Female Chauvinist Pigs: Women and the Rise of Raunch Culture, London, New York: Free Press.

Lewallen, A., 1988, 'Lace: Pornography for Women?' in Gamman & Marshment (eds) The Female Gaze, London: The Women's Press.

Lewis, J., 1997, 'What counts in cultural studies', Media, Culture & Society, London: Sage: vol. 19: 83–97.

Lewis, Paul, 1985, 'Men on Pedestals', Ten-8, no.17: 22–9.

Linz, D., and Malamuth, N., 1993, Pornography, Newbury Park: Sage.

Lumby, C., 1998, 'No Kidding: paedophilia and popular culture', Continuum: Journal of Media & Cultural Studies, vol.12, no.1, April: 47–54.

Lumby,C., 1997, Bad Girls: The Media, Sex and Feminism in the 90s, Sydney: Allen & Unwin.

Lury, C., 1996, Consumer Culture, Cambridge: Polity Press.

Lury, C., 1995, 'The rights and wrongs of culture: issues of theory and methodology', in B. Skeggs (ed.), Feminist Cultural Theory: Process and Production, Manchester: Manchester University Press.

Mackay, H., (ed.), 1997, Consumption and Everyday Life, Milton Keynes: Open University.

Marriott, D., 1996, 'Bordering On: The Black Penis', Textual Practice, vol.10: 1, spring.

Marcus, S., 1966, The Other Victorians: A Study of Sexuality and Pornography in Mid-Nineteenth Century England, London: Weidenfeld & Nicholson.

McCracken, E., 1993, Decoding Women's Magazines: From Mademoiselle to Ms, London: MacMillan.

McDonald, P., 1997, 'Feeling & Fun: Romance, Dance and the Performing Male Body in the Take That Videos' in Whiteley (ed.), Sexing the Groove: Popular Music & Gender, London: Routledge.

McDonald, M., 1995, Representing Women: Myths of Femininity in the Popular Media, London: Arnold.

McElroy, W., 1995, 'Pornography is Good', The Ethical Spectacle, November.

McKay, J., 2000, The Magazines Handbook, London: Routledge.

MacKinnon, C., 1994, Only Words, London: HarperCollins.

MacKinnon, C., 1982, 'Feminism, Marxism, Method, and the State', Signs, vol.7 no.3, spring.

MacKinnon, K., 1997, Uneasy Pleasures: the male as erotic object, London: Cygnus Arts.

McNair, B., 2002, Striptease Culture: Sex, Media and the Democratisation of Desire, London: Routledge.

McNair, B., 1996, Mediated Sex: Pornography and Postmodern Culture, London: Arnold.

McRobbie, A., 1997b, 'Pecs and penises: the meaning of girlie culture', Soundings: A Journal of Politics and Culture, no.5, spring.

McRobbie, A., 1996a, '*More!*: New Sexualities in Girls' and Womens' Magazines' in Curran, Morley and Walkerdine, Cultural Studies and Communications, London: Arnold.

McRobbie, A., 1996b, 'All the world's a stage, screen or magazine: when culture is the logic of late capitalism', Media, Culture and Society, vol.18, no.2: 335–42.

McRobbie, A., 1994, Postmodernism and Popular Culture, London: Routledge.
McRobbie, A., 1991, Feminism and Youth Culture: From *Jackie* to *Just Seventeen*, London: Macmillan.
McRobbie, A., 1978, 'Jackie: an ideology of adolescent femininity', Occasional Papers: Centre for Contemporary Cultural Studies, Birmingham: University of Birmingham.
Medhurst, A., 1998, 'Tracing desires: sexuality and media texts' in Briggs & Cobley (eds), The Media: An Introduction, Harlow: Longman.
Medhurst, A., 1985, 'Can Chaps be Pin-ups: The British Male Film Star of the 1950s', Ten-8, no.17: 3–8.
Media, 1995, 'The N & S portfolio', Guardian, April 3: G2T: 17.
Media Masses, 1993, 'Women's Porn', Guardian, (Weekend), 10 July: 61.
Mercer, K., 1992, 'Just Looking For Trouble', in Segal & McIntosh (eds), Sex Exposed: Sexuality and the Pornography Debate, London: Virago.
Merck, M., 1992, 'From Minneapolis to Westminster', in Segal & McIntosh (eds), Sex Exposed: Sexuality and the Pornography Debate, London: Virago.
Metcalf, A. & Humphries, M. (eds), 1985, The Sexuality of Men, London: Pluto Press.
Mills, E., 1995, 'Birthday suits without celebration', The Observer, 15 October.
Minsky, R., 1990, 'The trouble is it's ahistorical', Feminist Review, no.36, autumn.
Modleski, T., 1984, Loving with a Vengeance: Mass Produced Fantasies for Women, London: Methuen.
Moir, J., 1995, 'Two manicured fingers to the anti-Cosmo snobs', The Observer, Life, 23 July.
Moody, N., 1998, 'Mills and Boon's *Temptations*: Sex and the Single Couple in the 1990s' in Pearce & Wisker (eds), Fatal Attractions: Rescripting Romance in Contemporary Literature and Film, London: Pluto.
Moore, A., 1993, 'It's a man's man's man's man's world', Arena.
Moore, S., 1988, 'Here's Looking at You, Kid!' in Gamman & Marshment (eds), The Female Gaze, London: The Women's Press.
Moores, S., 1993, Interpreting Audiences: the Ethnography of Mass Consumption, London: Sage.
Moores, S., 1990, 'Texts, readers and contexts of reading', Media, Culture and Society, London: Sage, vol.12: 9.
Morgan, R., 1980, 'Theory and practice: pornography and rape' in Lederer (ed.), Take Back the Night: Women on Pornography, New York: Morrow.
Morley, D., 1986, Family Television: Cultural Power and Domestic Leisure, London: Comedia.
Morley, D., 1981, 'The *Nationwide* Audience: a critical postscript', Screen Education, no.39, autumn, pp. 3–14.
Morley, D., 1980, The *Nationwide* Audience: Structure and Decoding, London: Routledge.
Morrison, B., 1996, 'Big sister is watching us', Independent on Sunday, 28 January: 26-27.
Mort, F., 1996, Cultures of Consumption: Masculinities and Social Space in Late Twentieth Century Britain, London: Routledge.
Mort, F., 1988, 'Boy's Own? Masculinity, Style and Popular Culture' in Chapman and Rutherford (eds), Male Order: Unwrapping Masculinity, London: Lawrence & Wishart.
Moss, G., 1993, 'Girls tell the teen romance: four reading histories' in Buckingham (ed.), Reading Audiences: Young People and the Media, Manchester: Manchester University Press.
Moye, A., 1985, 'Pornography' in Metcalf & Humphries (eds), The Sexuality of Men, London: Pluto Press.
Mulvey, L., 1981, 'Afterthoughts on "Visual Pleasure and Narrative Cinema" inspired by *Duel in the Sun*', Framework, 6, summer.
Mulvey, L., 1975, 'Visual Pleasure and Narrative Cinema', Screen, 6.
Myers, K., 1982, 'Towards a Feminist Erotica' in Camerawork, 24.

Nead, L., 1993, 'Above the pulp-line: the cultural significance of erotic art' in Church Gibson & Gibson (eds), Dirty Looks: Women, Pornography, Power, London: British Film Institute.
Nead, L., 1992, The Female Nude: Art, Obscenity and Sexuality, London: Routledge.
Newman, J., 1991, 'Enterprising Women: Images of Success' in Franklin et al. (eds), Off-centre: Feminism and Cultural Studies, London: Harper Collins Academic.
Nixon, S., 1996, Hard Looks: Masculinities, Spectatorship and Contemporary Consumption, London: UCL Press.
Nixon, S., 1993a, 'Looking for the Holy Grail: Publishing and advertising strategies and contemporary men's magazines', Cultural Studies, vol.7 no.3: 466–92.
Nixon, S., 1993b, 'Distinguishing looks: masculinities, the visual and men's magazines', in Harwood et al., Pleasure Principles: Politics, Sexuality and Ethics, London: Lawrence & Wishart.
Norden, B., 1990, 'Campaign against pornography', Feminist Review, no.34, spring.
Observer, 1994, 'Shere Hite: A porn-again publicist', February 27: 21.
O'Kane, M., 1994, 'All in a night's work', Guardian, March 21: G2T, 2-3.
O'Rorke, I., 1997, 'Kind of Blue', Guardian, 28 July: G2: 22.
O'Shaughnessy, M., 1985, 'Models of masculinity' Ten-8, no.17: 9–15.
O'Sullivan, S., 1995, 'Magazines', The Guardian, 2 January.
O'Toole, L., 1998, Pornocopia: Porn, Sex, Technology and Desire, London: Serpents Tail.
Pajaczkowska, C., 1994, 'The penis and the phallus' in Salaman, What She Wants: Women Artists Look at Men, London: Verso.
Pajaczkowska, C., 1992, 'The heterosexual presumption' in Screen, The Sexual Subject: A Screen Reader in Sexuality, London: Routledge.
Pally, M., 1994, Sex and Sensibility: Reflections on Forbidden Mirrors and the Will to Censor, Metuchen, NJ: Ecco Press.
Parker, R., and Pollock, G., (eds), 1987, Framing Feminism: Art and the Women's Movement 1970–85 London: Routledge and Kegan Paul.
Parker, R., 1985, 'Images of men', in Kent & Morreau (eds), Women's Images of Men, London: Writers & Readers.
Parkin, M., 1992, 'In praise of naked men', The Mail on Sunday, 19 April: 49.
Partington, A., 1991, 'Melodrama's gendered audience' in Franklin et al. (eds), Off-centre: Feminism and Cultural Studies, London: Harper Collins Academic.
Patterson, K. J., 1994, 'Pornography law as censorship: linguistic control as (hetero)sexist harness', Feminist Issues, vol.14.
Paul, P., 2005, Pornified: How Pornography is Transforming, Our Lives, Our Relationships, And Our Families, New York: Times Books.
Pearce, L., & Wisker, G. (eds), 1998a, Fatal Attractions: Rescripting Romance in Contemporary Literature and Film, London: Pluto.
Pearce, L., & Wisker, G., 1998b, 'Rescripting romance: an introduction' in Pearce & Wisker (eds), Fatal Attractions: Rescripting Romance in Contemporary Literature and Film, London: Pluto.
Pearce, L., 1998c, 'Another Time, Another Place: the Chronotope of Romantic Love in Contemporary Feminist Fiction' in Pearce & Wisker (eds), Fatal Attractions: Rescripting Romance in Contemporary Literature and Film, London: Pluto.
Pearce, L. and Stacey, J., 1995, Romance Revisited, London: Lawrence & Wishart.
Peterson, D. and Dressel, P. L., 1982, 'Equal Time for Women: Social Notes on the Male Strip Show' Urban Life, 11: 185–208.
Petley, J., 2000, 'The Censor and the State, or Why Makin' Whoopee! Matters', http://www.melonfarmers.co.uk/brjp.htm (accessed 11.06.01).
Phillips, M., 2002, 'Why are we destroying childhood?' Daily Mail, January 12.
Phillips Griffiths, A. (ed.), 1993, Ethics, Cambridge: Cambridge University Press.

Picardie, J., 1993, 'Man on top', Independent Magazine, June 26: 20–4.
Picardie, R., 1995, 'Bunny business', Guardian, October 31: 8.
Picardie, R., 1994, 'The glossies' sensational appetite for sex is waning', Independent, March 30: II/ 25.
Pleasance, H. 1991, 'Open or Closed: popular magazines and dominant culture' in Franklin et al. (eds), Off-centre: Feminism and Cultural Studies, London: Harper Collins Academic.
Pollack, G., 1992, 'What's wrong with images of women?' in Screen, The Sexual Subject: A Screen Reader in Sexuality, London: Routledge.
Pollard, N., 1994, 'The modern pornography debates', Libertarian Alliance, London: A Joint Libertarian Alliance/British Association of Libertarian Feminists Publication: Pamphlet No. 22.
Potter, G., 1996, The Porn Merchants, Dubuque: Hunt Publications.
Prince, S., 1996, 'Psychoanalytic Film Theory and the Problem of the Missing Spectator', in Bordwell & Carroll (eds), Post-Theory, Madison: University of Wisconsin Press.
Radner, H., 1995, Shopping Around: Feminine Culture and the Pursuit of Pleasure, London: Routledge.
Radway, J., 1988 'Reception study: ethnography and the problem of dispersed audiences and nomadic subjects', Cultural Studies, vol.2, no.3: 358–76.
Radway, J., 1986, Reading the Romance: Women, Patriarchy and Popular Literature, London: Verso.
Radway, J., 1983, 'Women Read the Romance: The Interaction of Text and Context', in Feminist Studies, vol 9, no 1: 53–78.
Randall, J., 1994, 'Penthouse plans to go public', Sunday Times, October 16: 3/1.
Raven, C., 1994, 'What she wants', The Modern Review, August-September: 8.
Reay, D., 1996, 'Insider Perspectives or Stealing the Words out of Women's Mouths: Interpretation in the Research Process', Feminist Review, vol.53, summer: 57–73.
Rees, J., 1992, 'A load of new cobblers' Sunday Telegraph (Review), 19 April: vii.
Reinhold, S., 1994, 'Through the Parliamentary Looking Glass: 'Real' and 'Pretend' Families in Contemporary British Politics', Feminist Review, no.48, autumn: 61–79.
Rich, B. R., 1983, 'Anti-porn: Soft Issue, Hard World', Feminist Review, no.13, February.
Rich, A., 1980, 'Afterword', in Lederer (ed.), Take Back the Night: Women on Pornography, New York: William Morrow.
Rodgerson, G. and Wilson, E. (eds), 1991, Pornography and Censorship: The Case against Censorship by Feminists Against Censorship, London: Lawrence & Wishart.
Rodway, A., 1975, 'The Erotic Novel — A Critical View' in Webb (ed.), The Erotic Arts, London: Secker & Warburg.
Ross, A., 1989, No Respect: Intellectuals and Popular Culture. London: Routledge.
Royal Commission on the Press, 1977, Periodicals and the Alternative Press, London: HMSO.
Royalle, C., 1993, 'Porn in the U.S.A.' Social Text, 37: 23–32.
Rubin, G., 1993, 'Misguided, Dangerous and Wrong: An analysis of anti-pornography politics' in Assister & Carol (eds), Bad Girls and Dirty Pictures: The Challenge to Reclaim Feminism London: Pluto Press.
Rubin G., 1984, 'Thinking Sex' in Vance (ed.) Pleasure and Danger, London: Routledge and Kegan Paul.
Russell, D. E. H. (ed.), 1993a, Making Violence Sexy: Feminist Views on Pornography, Buckingham: Open University Press.
Russell, D. E. H., 1993b, Against Pornography: Evidence of Harm, Berkeley: Russell Publications.
Salaman, N. (ed.), 1994a, What She Wants: Women Artists Look at Men, London: Verso.

Salaman, N., 1994b, 'Regarding Male Objects' in Salaman (ed.), What She Wants: Women Artists Look at Men, London: Verso.
Salaman, N., 1993a, 'Women's Art Practice/Man's Sex ... and now for something completely different', in Harwood et al. (eds), Pleasure Principles: Politics, Sexuality and Ethics, London: Lawrence & Wishart.
Salaman, N., 1993b, 'Penis Envy' in Harwood et al. (eds), Pleasure Principles: Politics, Sexuality and Ethics, London: Lawrence & Wishart.
Schroder, K. C., 1994, 'Audience semiotics, interpretative communities and the 'ethnographic turn' in media research', Media Culture & Society, vol.16, no.2: 337–47.
Screen, 1992, The Sexual Subject: A Screen Reader in Sexuality, London: Routledge.
Segal, L., 1994, Straight Sex: the Politics of Pleasure, London: Virago.
Segal, L., 1993, 'Does pornography cause violence? The search for evidence', in Church Gibson and Gibson (eds), Dirty Looks: Women, Pornography, Power, London: British Film Institute.
Segal, L. and McIntosh, M. (eds), 1992, Sex Exposed: Sexuality and the Pornography Debate, London: Virago.
Segal, L. 1990, 'Pornography and violence: what the experts really say', Feminist Review, no. 36, autumn.
Seymour Monthly Monitor, 2001, Key Indicators on the UK Magazine Market, no 16, January.
Silverstone, R., 1994, Television and Everyday Life, London: Routledge.
Simpson, M., 1994, Male Impersonators, London: Cassell.
Simpson, R., 1987, 'Following a winning recipe', Marketing, 26 March.
Skeggs, B., 1995, Feminist Cultural Theory, Manchester: Manchester University Press.
Skeggs, B., 1991, 'A Spanking Good Time', MOCS, Bristol: Bristol Polytechnic, spring.
Skordarki, E., 1991, The Production of Men's Magazines: Three Case studies and a Sociological Analysis, Ph.D. thesis, London School of Economics.
Skynner, R., 1993, 'Home Front: Sex, highs and videotape', Guardian, Weekend, February 20: 14.
Slade, J. W., 1997, 'Pornography in the Late Nineties', Wide Angle, 19.3: 1–12.
Smith, C., 2005, 'A Perfectly British Business: Stagnation, Continuities and Change on the Top Shelf', in Sigel, L. Z. (ed.), *International Exposure: Perspectives on Modern European Pornography, 1800–2000'*, New York: Rutgers University Press.
Smith, C., 1998, 'Talking Dirty in For Women Magazine' in Arthurs & Grimshaw (eds), Women's Bodies, London: Cassell.
Snitow, A., Stansell, C. and Thompson, S. (eds), 1984a, Desire: The Politics of Sexuality, London: Virago.
Snitow, A., 1984b, 'Mass Market Romance: Pornography for Women is Different' in Snitow et al. (eds), Desire: The Politics of Sexuality, London: Virago.
Snitow, A., 1980, 'The Front Line: Notes on Sex in Novels', Journal of Women in Culture & Society, 5: 4.
Soble, A., 1986, Pornography: Marxism, Feminism and the Future of Sexuality, New Haven: Yale University Press.
Sonnet, E., 2005, '"Just a book", she said ...': Reconfiguring Ethnography for the Female Readers of Sexual Fiction', paper to *New Femininities Seminar Series*, March 23 (http://www.lse.ac.uk/collections/newFemininities/secondseminar.htm) accessed 23 April 2006.
Sonnet, E., 1999, ''Erotic Fiction by Women for Women': The pleasures of Post-Feminist Heterosexuality', Sexualities, London: Sage, vol.2 (2): 167–187.
Sontag, S., 1982, 'The Pornographic Imagination', Straus & Giroux, 1982, A Susan Sontag Reader, New York: Farrar.

Spillius, A., 1996, 'Who makes the profit?', Independent on Sunday, 21 April: 4.
Springett, P., 1993, 'Pop, porn and insurance offer riches', Guardian, August 2: 3.
Stacey, J., 1993, Star Gazing: Hollywood Cinema and Female Spectatorship, London: Routledge.
Stacey, J., 1988, 'Desperately seeking difference' in Gamman & Marshment (eds), The Female Gaze, London: The Women's Press.
Stam, R., 1989, Subversive Pleasures: Bakhtin, Cultural Criticism and Film, Baltimore: Johns Hopkins University Press.
Stein, M., 1990, The Ethnography of an Adult Bookstore: Private Scenes, Public Places, Lewiston, New York: Edwin Mellen Press.
Steinham, G., 1980, 'Erotica and Pornography: A Clear and Present Difference' in Lederer (ed.), Take Back the Night: Women on Pornography, New York: William Morrow.
Steinham, G., 1985, 'Erotica vs Pornography' in her Outrageous Acts and Everyday Rebellions, 2nd ed., New York: Henry Holt.
Stephens, J., 1992, 'Turning over a blue leaf', Today, 18 April.
Stoller, R., 1985, Observing the Erotic Imagination, Harvard: Yale University Press.
Strossen, N., 2000, Defending Pornography: Free Speech, Sex and the Fight for Women's Rights, New York: New York University Press.
Studlar, G., 1996, This Mad Masquerade: Stardom and Masculinity in the Jazz Age, Columbia: Columbia University Press.
Sullivan, C., 1994, 'The New Bottom Line', Guardian, 19 October.
Sullivan, C., 1992, 'More sex with your beefcake', Times, 15 April: 5.
Sweeting, A., 1995, 'The Search for Sound Profits', The Guardian, May 8.
Syedain, H., 1992, 'Female Touch Works in Recession', Marketing, February 27.
Tasker, Y., 1991, 'Having it all: feminimsm and the pleasures of the popular' in Franklin et al. (eds), Off-centre: Feminism and Cultural Studies, London: Harper Collins Academic.
Taylor, S., 1995, 'Men with attitude', The Observer, 2 April: Review, 5.
Teather, D., & Burkeman, O., 2000, The Guardian, November 23.
Thomson, R., 1994, 'Moral Rhetoric and Public Health Pragmatism: The Recent Politics of Sex Education', Feminist Review, no.48, autumn: 40–60.
Thompson, B. (1994) Soft Core: Campaigns against Pornography in Britain and America, London: Cassell.
Thompson, K., (ed.), 1997, Media and Cultural Regulation, Milton Keynes: Open University.
Thompson, L., 1997, 'Women: the naked lunch box', Guardian, 25 August: 4.
Thurston, C., 1987 The Romance Revolution: Erotic Novels for Women and the Quest for a New Sexual Identity, Chicago: University of Illinois Press.
Tincknell, E., 1991, 'Enterprise Fictions: Women of Substance' in Franklin et al. (eds), Off-centre: Feminism and Cultural Studies, London: Harper Collins Academic.
Tong, R., 1998, Feminist Thought: A More Comprehensive Introduction, 2nd, Oxford: Westview Press.
Treacher, A., 1988, 'What is life without my love? Desire and romantic fiction', in Radstone, S. (ed.), Sweet Dreams: Sexuality, gender and popular fiction, London: Lawrence & Wishart.
Tudor, A., 1976, 'Genre and Critical Methodology' in B. Nichols (ed.) Movies and Methods, Berkeley: University of California Press.
Udall, E., 1994, 'What? A nice girl like you?' Independent, January 13: 24.
Valverde, M., 1985, Sex, Power and Pleasure, London: The Women's Press.
Vance, C. S. (ed.), 1992a, Pleasure and Danger: Exploring Female Desire, 2nd edition, London: Routledge & Kegan Paul.
Vance, C. S., 1992b, 'More Danger, More Pleasure: A Decade after the Bernard Sexuality Conference' introduction to Pleasure and Danger: Exploring Female Desire, 2nd edition, London: Routledge & Kegan Paul.

Vance, C. S., 1992c, 'Pleasure and danger: Toward a Politics of Sexuality' in her Pleasure and Danger: Exploring Female Desire, 2nd edition, London: Routledge & Kegan Paul.
Vermorel, F. and Vermorel, J., 1985, Starlust: the Secret Life of Fans, London: W. H. Allen.
Viner, K., 1997, 'Now we are 25', Guardian, 6 February: G2: 4.
Volosinov, V., 1973, Marxism and the Philosophy of Language, New York: Seminar Press.
Walkerdine, V., 1997, Daddy's Girl: Young Girls and Popular Culture, London: Macmillan.
Walters, M., 1978, The Nude Male, London: Paddington Press.
Ward, V., 1994, 'Who's the sleaziest of them all?' The Independent, November 22: II/ 25.
Wark, M., 1998, 'Bad Girls do it in Public', Continuum: Journal of Media & Cultural Studies, vol.12, no.1, April: 83–90.
Wavell, S., 1993, 'Golden touch', Sunday Times, June 13: 4-5.
Weaver, T., 1992, 'Not so hard porn', Daily Mirror, 29 April: 9.
Webster, P., 1984, 'The forbidden: eroticism and taboo' in Vance (ed.), Pleasure and Danger: Exploring Female Desire, London: Routledge & Kegan Paul.
Weeks, J., 2000, Making Sexual History, Cambridge: Polity Press.
Weeks, J., 1993, 'An Unfinished Revolution: Sexuality in the 20th Century', in Harwood et al. (eds), Pleasure Principles: Politics, Sexuality and Ethics, London: Lawrence & Wishart.
Weeks, J., 1981, Sex, Politics and Society: The Regulation of Sexuality since 1800, London: Longman.
Weiermair, P., 1988, The Hidden Image: Photographs of the Male Nude in the Nineteenth and Twentieth Centuries, trans Nielander, C., Cambridge, Mass.: MIT Press.
Weiss, P., 1990, 'Forbidden Pleasures', in Kimmel (ed.), Men Confront Pornography, New York: Crown.
Wernick, A., 1987, 'From Voyeur to Narcissist: Imaging Men in Contemporary Advertising' in Kaufman, M. (ed.), Beyond Patriarchy: Essays by Men on Pleasure, Power and Change, Toronto: OUP.
Whitcroft, I., 1992, 'Photo Girl's Full Frontal Assault Rocks Magazine', Today, 11 June.
White, Celia, 1970, Women's Magazines 1693–1968, London: Michael Joseph.
Whitebloom, S., 1995, 'Soft porn firm takes hard line', Guardian, April 8: 36.
Whitehouse, M., 1977, Whatever Happened to Sex? London: Hodder & Stoughton.
Whitford, F., 1992, 'The shock of the nude', Sunday Times, December 20: 5/ 26-7.
Whittaker, N., 1997, Blue Period: Notes from a Life in the Titillation Trade, London: Gollancz.
Wicke, J., 1993, 'Through a gaze darkly: pornography's academic market', in Church Gibson and Gibson (eds), Dirty Looks: Women, Pornography, Power, London: British Film Institute.
Willemen, P., 1992, 'Letter to John', in Screen, The Sexual Subject: A Screen Reader in Sexuality, London: Routledge.
Williams, L., 1990, Hard Core: Power, Pleasure and the 'Frenzy of the Visible', London: Pandora.
Williams, L., 1994, 'Introduction: What Do I See, What Do I Want?' in Salaman (ed.), What She Wants: Women Artists Look at Men, London: Verso.
Williams, L. R., 1998, 'Sex and censoriousness: pornography and censorship in Britain' in Briggs & Cobley (eds), The Media: An Introduction, Harlow: Longman.
Williamson, J., 1978, Decoding Advertisements: Advertising, Ideology and Symbolic Expression, London: Marion Boyars.
Wilson, E., 1992, 'Feminist Fundamentalism: the Shifting Politics of Sex and Censorship' in Segal & McIntosh (eds), Sex Exposed: Sexuality and the Pornography Debate, London: Virago.
Wilson, E., 1989, 'Against feminist fundamentalism', New Statesman & Society, 30 June.

Willis, E., 1986, 'Feminism, Moralism and Pornography' in Ellis et al. (eds), Caught Looking: Feminism, Pornography and Censorship, New York: Caught Looking.
Winship, J., 1993, 'The Impossibility of Best: enterprise meets domesticity in the practical women's magazines of the 1980s', in Strinati et al. (eds), Come On Down, London: Routledge.
Winship, J., 1987, Inside Women's Magazines, London: Pandora.
Winship, J., 1985, ''A Girl Needs to Get Streetwise': Magazines for the 1980s', Feminist Review, no.21, winter: 24–46.
Winship, J., 1981, 'Woman becomes an individual: Femininity and Consumption in women's magazines, 1954–69', Stencilled Paper, Centre for Contemporary Cultural Studies, Birmingham: University of Birmingham.
Wolff, I., 1994, 'Blokes head for the Locker Room', The Observer, 13 November.
Wood, G., 1993, 'The Censor's Pleasure' in Harwood et al. (eds), Pleasure Principles: Politics, Sexuality and Ethics, London: Lawrence & Wishart.
Wortley, R., 1971, Pin-Ups Progress, London: Panther.
Young, L., 1994, 'Mapping Male Bodies: Thoughts on Gendered and Racialised Looking' in Salaman (ed.), What She Wants: Women Artists Look at Men, London: Verso.
Young, S., 1988, 'Feminism and the Politics of Power: Whose Gaze is it Anyway?' in Gamman & Marshment (eds), The Female Gaze, London: The Women's Press.

Appendix One: Researching Women Readers

Sexual pleasures and the use of erotic materials as part of those pleasures might well form the subject matter of discussion with a special or trusted set of friends. To discuss the subject with a stranger (other than in a therapeutic situation) is a fairly uncommon occurrence for most people. It is also a rather strange experience to ask women to take part in research of this kind. Reactions to my study ranged from frankly incredulous to scandalized. Initial response from readers was underwhelming; even more so than I had anticipated. Following a paragraph on my research in *For Women* in 1994, two letters arrived, one from two women at a northern university and one from an American woman living in London. I wrote back to them explaining the substance and purpose of the research but the students declined to be interviewed. The American woman agreed to an interview and I travelled to her home to meet her.

In December 1994, I tried again to elicit response through *For Women*. This time, rather than have the research mentioned in the editorial pages of the magazine, I sent a letter to the Mailshot (readers' letters) page. I cribbed my wording for the letter from Ang's (1985) successful missive and mentioned I was a regular reader of the magazine. Again I received two letters. My correspondence with these two women was to last more than three years and provided a rich source of material about the changing nature of their relationships with the magazine. Editorial staff at *For Women* were amazed at the lack of response: each month they received a full mailbag from readers expressing their likes and dislikes of the magazine. The reasons for this discrepancy can be tentative only but perhaps best explained by suggesting that the relationship between the reader and her magazine is very different to that offered to participants in a research project such as mine.[1] One further mention in *For Women* garnered three replies: two from women and one from a gay man. The women agreed to complete taped answers to the questionnaire, the man (who had given a PO box address) did not reply to my letter and questionnaire.

At the same time, through friends, my hairdresser and former colleagues, I was put in touch with a number of women and gay men who defined themselves as regular readers of pornography in general and occasional readers of *For Women* in particular. Two friends who had read pornography including *For Women* but who defined themselves as having no interest in pornography also agreed to be interviewed. I interviewed these women and men face-to-face in the autumn of 1994 and spring 1995. At a conference during summer 1995, I met a researcher who had read the magazine and agreed to tape-record her responses to my questionnaire. A letter to the *Guardian* Women's Page resulted in a one-line description of my research and elicited one response from a woman and her friend who read a lot of erotic fiction.[2] This resulted in one of two group interviews I managed to arrange.

My group of respondents is small, especially when compared with other recent audience studies (e.g., Ang 1985; Barker and Brooks 1998; Hermes 1995; Hill 1997; Radway 1986a), comprising fourteen women and two men. In common with many qualitative research projects, all the respondents were self-selecting. I'd expected to hear from a fairly equal number of positive and negative respondents but this was not the case. Although all the respondents expressed a number of criticisms of the magazine, in the main their overall reaction to it was fairly favourable, at least they thought the *idea* of a sexually explicit magazine for women was good whatever the resulting publication. This is a consequence of the implicitly positive agenda with which I set about gathering readers. Certainly the appearance of my letter in *For Women* on the readers' letters page, the wording which stressed my own reading of the magazine and desire to know from other women if they were like me in experiencing adverse responses to that reading from family and friends, probably put my research within the context of a 'search for community'. With hindsight, it seems inevitable that my letter would elicit responses from other *regular* readers. I probably 'frightened off' those women who had only picked up that one issue out of curiosity or who were disappointed or disgusted by it.

Why didn't more readers want to talk to me about *For Women*? Obviously there are the problems of discussing sex and sexual representations with a stranger. Worries about confidentiality will have put some women off. Moreover, *For Women* may not be a regular purchase for a sizeable proportion of its readers: perhaps it was too expensive and/or a novelty purchase soon forgotten. Thus it is likely that many readers just did not feel they had anything 'important' to say about the magazine. Letherby and Zdrodowski (1995: 584) comment '[when] the study group is self-selecting, it is likely that individuals who come forward will feel strongly about the issue and have something particular to say.' Those women who feel strongly opposed to pornographic material would be unlikely to read the magazine and therefore never saw my advertisement. Even those who had read it and were dissatisfied (like the students who contacted me but declined to be interviewed) may have felt they had little to say once they recovered from their initial anger, disgust or disappointment; they may also have been unwilling to have those reactions tested or questioned. Thus a certain level of investment in reading *For Women* characterizes the women who took part in this research but as my discussion of this interview material will make clear that does not necessarily mean a favourable response to the magazine.

Reflecting on Methodology: Collecting the Data and the Constructive Practice of Research

The various means of 'collecting' respondents meant it was not always possible to interview face-to-face. Thus I employed three different methods of response-gathering in this research:

- taped interviews, face-to-face with respondents in their own homes, or mine
- taped responses, questionnaires and cassettes sent to individuals who then recorded their own responses
- correspondence

All respondents effectively completed the same questionnaire of 49 questions (see appendix 2) divided into two sections. An open question format was used: the first section featured general questions about reading habits and responses to the magazine. The second section was intended to elicit responses about actual use of such materials and general feelings about sexual representations and its impact upon their reading of *For Women*. The need for self-reflexivity in reception research has been widely discussed (see especially Hermes 1995) recognizing that the results of an interview are the product of that situation and of the relationship between the interviewer and interviewed. It is an unfortunate by-product of this work that the interview begins to seem like a form of torture both for the researcher and the researched. To indicate eligibility to the title 'self-reflexive researcher' researchers stress the problems, practical and theoretical, in doing interviews. I certainly do not dismiss the importance of considerations of the conduct of interviews, the problems of expectations, of interviewer-agendas and the social relations (of power) between interviewer/ee. It is also appropriate to indicate the difficulties experienced in finding suitable venues and working tape recorders etc. But I should confess that apart from the tape recorder being obtrusive and irritatingly temperamental, the interviews I conducted were fun. The reason for this confession is not to suggest that I refuse the necessity of reflexivity but to argue for the interview as an achievement. Why do researchers want to conduct interviews if they are so problematic and, if they are as problematic as is constantly claimed, how will being sensitive to the problems change or cure the difficulties? There is no utopian interview situation where pure, unsullied, desocialized and evidential talk could be obtained. The interview is a situation in which we self-consciously use our relations with others to develop knowledge.

I hope I am an outgoing and friendly individual and I used that in the interviews and in my correspondences to get answers from readers. Because the subject matter was/is fairly sensitive, if not taboo, I thought it inappropriate to meet in a formal setting: I therefore used my own home or theirs. This worked well, setting the respondents at ease: it enabled wasting a little time making coffee or opening a bottle of wine and talking about the weather, or gossiping about the latest developments in a soap/celebrity's life/work. Where readers completed their taped responses on their own, this ice-breaking was not possible, but I sent a brief and chatty letter along with the questionnaire. To all respondents, I stressed my desire to get to the reasons why some women enjoyed *For Women*, in spite of the theory and the common-sense claim that women don't like or read sexually explicit materials. I also made clear that although I had some theoretical knowledge I had no better answers than theirs to explain why women might like pictures of naked men and explicit stories. I intended to indicate that I came to them with an open mind and a genuine interest in their *individual* engagement with sex and sexual representations. That ploy was successful because I *was* genuinely interested.

Of course, all that leaves me wide open to accusations of being non-reflexive but, in fact, what I'm emphasizing here is that there was something about *me* that made getting information so comparatively easy. I experienced difficulties in contacting interviewees but once I had they were extremely willing to talk. Diane Reay (1996: 57) suggests that as researchers we need to see how we are totally implicated in the research interpretation process – that we can experience real difficulties as a result of our own positioning and that in the end interpretation remains an imperfect and incomplete process. That is true and yet the opposite can also be argued, we can experience real advantages as a result of our own positioning. However imperfect and incomplete the process can be this should not cause despondency but spur further research and interest.

It is just as important to recognize how the supposed problems of researching people's talk might be productive and advantageous. As I suggested earlier, it is likely that those who select themselves to take part in an interview feel they have something important to contribute to the research. Thus their motives in coming need to be acknowledged too, they are not necessarily the 'victims' of the research interview. Indeed, in coming forward, I think it is fair to say, that most of my respondents were seeking to determine, control and manage the social context of the research interview in order to be able to say what mattered to them. A number of them viewed their contribution to the research as a conduit to getting their views out into the open. Indeed, it is also important to remember that talking, even talking about something as personal as sexual likes and dislikes, is a 'normal' activity. Under the right circumstances, people like to talk about those things that interest and involve them.

Some of my interviewees took the process of research very seriously, offering critical responses based on theoretical models made available through education, while others responded critically through more populist discourses about representations of women and children. Yet more discussed issues through a more subjective or empirical standpoint – 'I can only speak for myself and that's what I offer to you'. Of the women who did respond, their similarity begins and ends with their willingness to talk to me. They fall within an age range of 20–40 but how far this is indicative of the reader profile of the magazine is impossible to know, as I too fit that category it is not surprising that those people who came to me via friends should fall into that age range. Equally, class and educational status are probably also coincidentally linked to my social milieu; at least six respondents came from working-class backgrounds although they had subsequently 'shifted up' via education or employment. In addition to the narrow class focus of this study, the responses of women from different ethnic groupings are missing, only one of my respondents is black and, as she was interviewed with another white respondent, may have felt that race could not be raised as an issue. Even if race had surfaced there as a topic it would be impossible to offer any generalizations from the reactions of one individual.

Although the smallness of my group might be conceived as a problem, it has had its positive aspects. Because the number of women is small they cannot be regarded as a 'sample'; that is, I cannot claim to have achieved an appropriate socio-cultural mix in order to begin to ascribe generalized patterns of use representative of women's use of sexually explicit materials. 'Representativeness' is a concept belonging to quantitative research where knowledge is sought from a wide enough sample that out of a mass of data 'average' respondents will emerge. Although there may be a number of averages the intention is to describe and catalogue results as *standardized responses*. Because there were not enough women of particular social groupings, I could not be tempted into counting responses according to similarities in class, race or age.

Hallam and Marshment (1995: 176) also found it impossible to interview 'ordinary' women and that 'sociological trawling' would not have been helpful to their research into women viewing the television serialization of the lesbian romance *Oranges Are Not The Only Fruit*.[3] Attempting to impose sociological categories upon individual audience members is a tempting but ultimately fruitless exercise because

> ... these kinds of definitions would only have been interesting to us if they had correlated with readings of the text. And, in fact, we didn't find that there was, for instance, a lesbian reading of it, or a Black reading. People understood the text in the same way, they didn't think it was doing something different because they were Black or because they were lesbian. ... it's important to distinguish between how people understand something and how they evaluate it or respond to it emotionally. (183)

When respondents offer definitions of themselves, or self-representations it is not how accurate these are but what they allow speakers to accomplish (Buckingham 1993). Such an account does not see class or race as determining factors acting on individuals but as part of a process of socialisation. My intention in interviewing readers of *For Women* was to bring into focus their accounts of that reading in order to understand the ways in which the magazine can be said to speak to those women as sexual subjects. I should make clear that I claim no representative status for the readers here: I have studied how, in the lives of a number of individuals, a magazine operates in and through sets of requirements, expectations and possibilities such that the individual contains within herself the signs and symptoms of social processes. The 'social' is not a distributed phenomenon; it is fully present in every individual.

Analysing Respondents' Talk

In her study of *Dallas* viewers, Ang used letters to draw out the experience of watching *Dallas*, its pleasures and displeasures. In so doing, she cautions that this is not a 'direct and unproblematic reflection of the reasons why the writers love or hate Dallas.' (1985: 11) Buckingham (1993) has also criticized the superficial and partial attempt to validate the viewers' perspective – 'letting them speak for themselves' – without recognizing the ways in which such speech is situated within specific social contexts. Speech is seen, not as simply reflecting meanings, but actively constructing meaning.[4] In order to get at women's reasons for reading *For Women*, I examined each interview transcript for that woman's expectations of the magazine: what was their ideal reading situation; what was an ideal image; how would an ideal story unfold; what would an ideal magazine offer. I found these expectations would govern their response to the magazine. I looked for coherence in each woman's talk, attempting to uncover their own 'philosophies' rather than impose rules or rhetorics around sexuality and sexual representations and then fit them into it. To do this I looked for inconsistencies and incoherencies in what they said, not to discredit their accounts of themselves, their reading or their expectations of that reading, but in order to see how those inconsistencies actually do fit together. I assumed that the magazine needed to provide the familiar and the distinctive in order to be pleasurable to readers. Thus, I also tried to discern how well formulated their expectations of a sexually explicit magazine for women were and how those were connected to an individual's knowledge/experience of her/himself and the sexual world. I did not intend to 'test' whether the women/men were right or wrong in their assessments/judgements about individual images or stories but to uncover what exactly it meant when they said 'this image was good or this one was bad'. What 'compromises' were necessary between their ideal and their routine experiences?

Without exception, my respondents were very open and answered the questions at some length, occasionally pausing to gather their thoughts and to qualify some of their statements. I was made aware of the importance that they attached to undertaking the questionnaire by their very measured and serious responses. Although sex is often a subject for ribald conversations all of my respondents took the questions very seriously and were at some pains to answer me with thoughtful responses. That does not mean, however, that the interviews, tapes and letters were not at times very humorous; in fact, many of the taped interviews were very difficult to transcribe because of the frequency of laughter and general hilarity. Certainly when it came to discussing the images of nude males and sexual practices, laughter was the overriding characteristic of these passages. Obviously the act of recording one's views on sexuality and sexual materials requires a throwing off of reserve and I am immensely grateful to all of these people for their time, effort and candour, my thanks cannot be repeated often enough, and I hope that I have been as generous in my analysis as they were with their responses.

The research on which this book is based was originally conceived as an analysis of production, text and reception, and I was very aware of the need to ensure that the textual analysis offered did not re-write the responses of my readers. Feminist interventions into women's magazine use have tended to stress the ideological construction of a 'cult of femininity' (Ferguson, 1983). The same principles of investigation which characterize the theorizations of pornography with the imputing of a series of claims about 'effects' on men are used on women's magazines. The presumptions about the 'object' (its unity, the 'documentary' nature of its representations, its consumption and direction of users) are all present in accounts of the textual formations of women's magazines. Joke Hermes (1995) has rejected the conception of audiences as either all-powerful in, or oppressed by, their relationship with the text. Repudiating the right of academics to seek to unravel the text Hermes argues textual analysis merely allows academics to impose meaning upon a text which is not necessarily available to its readers. 'Text analysis assumes that texts offer a limited range of meanings that cannot but be taken up by readers' (1995: 10). She also cautions that academics are in 'the business of meaning production and interpretation, while the majority of media users are not: much media use is routine and insignificant, it has no distinct, generalisable meaning' (1995: 16). Drawing on interviews with eighty men and women, Hermes found that the context of reading was more important than the magazine text. I dispute her wholesale dismissal of textual analysis but Hermes' cautions are important reminders that the principles of textual investigation should not be at the expense of readers. In chapters 3, 4, 6 and 7, I offer my alternative formulations for the textual investigation of *For Women*

Notes

1. In chapter 3 I describe and analyse a number of letters to the readers' letters page, many of these suggest that readers who write in wish to take some part, however small, in the production process of the magazine. For example, a number of readers write requests to see particular individuals featured in the photosets, others will request more fiction or a greater focus on sexual problems. What characterizes these letters is a desire for influence over editorial decisions and the future direction of *For Women*. In taking part in research such as mine, the opportunities for influence over a favoured media form is much less apparent to, or immediate for, participants.
2. This gives a pretty neat illustration of the hit-and-miss nature of acquiring respondents – Catherine had been on a long journey and had stopped at a service station where she was given a voucher for a free copy of the *Guardian*; this was the one and only time she had bought the newspaper and had discovered my one line at the bottom of the Sidelines feature.
3. The most interesting thing, for me, about this research is that by happy accident they were unable to carry out a perfect research project. Hallam and Marshment did not have the money or time to carry out a large-scale project; they found interviewees via very informal/haphazard routes; they conversed rather than interviewed in their own homes; they did not obtain personal information prior to the viewing sessions and were unaware of what turned out to be very salient factors in their respondents' personal histories. This rather accidental methodology contributes to some of their most surprising and interesting discoveries.

4. Audience studies constitute an increasingly large field within cultural and media studies. I am unable to offer a detailed survey of that material here, but interested readers could try out Moores 1993, Barker & Brooks 1998, Barker, Arthurs & Harindranath 2001, *Particip@tions – The Online Journal Of Audience And Reception Studies* at http://www.participations.org.

Appendix Two: Questionnaire – *For Women* Magazine

Many thanks for your interest in this project. Please answer as many or few of the questions as you feel comfortable with – take as long as you like over any individual question. If there are any areas where you feel I have not asked a relevant question, please feel free to add it.

1. Age:

2. Status:

3. Children:

4. Education:

5. Employment:

6. Do you read other women's magazines apart from *For Women*?

7. Had you ever read or seen sexually explicit material before *For Women*?

8. If yes, did you like or dislike it? What did you like/dislike?

9. Was it made for women to read or for men?

10. Do you think sexually explicit magazines generally available are made for women?

11. When did you first buy *For Women*, what made you buy it? Do you buy it regularly?

12. What were your first impressions of *For Women*?

13. Do you think *For Women* is specifically for women?

14. What do you think makes it different from material aimed at men?

15. What kind of people do you think read *For Women*?

16. What do you think of those people?

17. What do you think they get out of these magazines?

18. Do you think you are like those people?

19. In what ways are you like them, or how are you different?

Part I
Reading *For Women* magazine

20. Do you like looking at pictures of naked men?

21. What do you particularly like?

22. What if anything do you particularly dislike?

23. Does looking at naked men ever make you feel uncomfortable?

24. How do you feel about pictures of naked women (in either *For Women* or men's magazines)?

25. Does looking at naked women ever make you feel uncomfortable?

26. How do you feel about the erotic stories in *For Women*?

27. Do you think they are different from those in men's magazines?

28. Do you like erotic stories? What do you like/dislike about them?

29. What do you think of the problem page?

30. What do you think of the articles? Which ones do you like best? Why?

31. What part of the magazine do you most enjoy? Why?

32. Is there anything you feel strongly about in *For Women*: is there anything which makes you angry/depressed/revolted or that you particularly like/find amusing?

33. Is there anything else you would like to say about *For Women*?

Part II

This section takes the form of more personal questions and I would like to draw your attention again to the fact that participation is entirely voluntary. Only answer those questions you feel happy with. It would also be useful if you could indicate where you feel questions are problematic and why.

34. When you read *For Women* do you do it alone or with someone else?

35. How do other people (family, friends, partner) feel about you reading it?

36. Do they ever read or watch sexually explicit material?

37. Do you ever read/watch it together?

38. In what ways do you use *For Women* (or any other sexually explicit material): for ideas/a laugh/as a turn-on?

39. Have you ever tried something you saw or read about in *For Women* or any other magazine?

40. If you have tried something, did you enjoy it?

41. Have you ever not enjoyed experimenting in this way?

42. How do you feel in general about sexually explicit material?

43. What kinds of material would you call pornographic? Would you call *For Women* pornographic?

44. Is there anything you think should be banned? If yes, what is it and why? If not, why?

45. Have you ever been upset by seeing sexually explicit magazines or videos? What upset you?

46. Is there anything you feel you have said here that you would want to change?

47. In general, do you like to talk about sex? Do you get much chance to talk about sex? Who would you usually talk to about it?

48. How do you feel after answering all these questions?

49. Is there anything you feel should have been asked or would like to add?

INDEX